UNCOMMON LAW

*Being sixty-six Misleading Cases revised
and collected in one volume, including
ten cases not published before*

by

A. P. HERBERT, M.P.

*With an Introduction
by*

LORD ATKIN

THIRD EDITION

METHUEN & CO. LTD. LONDON
36 Essex Street W.C.

First Published . . November 14th 1935
Second Edition . . March   1936
Third Edition   . .   1937

PRINTED IN GREAT BRITAIN

ACKNOWLEDGMENT

MOST of these cases were originally reported in the pages of *Punch*, to the Proprietors of which paper I render thanks for their courtesy in permitting me to reprint them.

I wish to thank also Mr. E. S. P. Haynes, Mr. H. G. Strauss, Mr. George Bull, and other legal friends who have generously assisted me with advice and information on the rare points of law with which I was not familiar.

A. P. H.

INTRODUCTION

By Lord Atkin

I cannot imagine why my friend A. P. H. did me the honour of inviting me to write an introduction to this volume. He has evidently a low opinion of the House of Lords as a tribunal, and the names he has given to his Law Lords are contumelious. Could any one respect the opinions of a Lord Lick, Lord Arrowroot, Lord Mildew, Lord Flake, Lord Sheep, or Lord Bottle? When he does seek to reform the House by introducing a Lady Chancellor he makes her, sorry as I am as a colleague to say it, a spoilt minx, who complains about the Woolsack. Her male predecessors have found it comfortable enough—indeed are said to have left it reluctantly. But overcoming any natural prejudices so induced, I cordially welcome the collection in one volume of the cases which have delighted so many lawyers and laymen. I have no intention of cataloguing them. As the world now knows, they are chiefly concerned with the legal experiences of Mr. Albert Haddock, who seems to have suffered as many tribulations as St. Paul and to whom the resemblance of the author as a stern moralist is at once apparent. The author has stated that these 'frolics in jurisprudence' are 'shyly intended not only to amuse but to amend'. 'Shyly' is a gem. To many lawyers it will seem that it is all to the good that legal principles and procedure should be discussed in public in any guise, and still better that attention should be riveted on them by the wit and humour of A. P. H. The general impression of law is too often that it is the product

vii

of a black art administered as a mystery which none but
initiates need hope to understand. I do not, however,
think that I should put this book in the hands of a layman
as a compendium of English law. And I am glad that
the title is altered to 'Uncommon Law': for many of
the shafts of the satirist are levelled at statutes and regulations for which the Legislature and Whitehall are solely
responsible, and the withers of the Common Law are
unwrung. But criticism in the interests of amendment is
always valuable—and could it come in more attractive
form? The author says that the reports are composed in
'assiduous imitation' of the Bench. There are several
judgments the diction and close reasoning of which many
judges would be glad to imitate. One may also notice that
the Bar share with the Bench the same powers of expression. Indeed the rapid interchange between Bench and
Bar may be compared to the activities of Mr. Disney's
Hare, whose speed is such that he plays a game of tennis
with himself as both server and striker. There are times
when the motley is exchanged for the mantle of the prophet or the gown of the teacher. But great satirists have
always had a serious purpose. Whether all the reforms
which Mr. Haddock or the author favours would be
beneficial may be disputed elsewhere. A. P. H. will have
the last word, as in the House of Commons case. No
opponent will wield his weapons with the dexterity of
the author, or even have the opportunity of encountering him in the same field. Let us be grateful to our
famous social reformer 'Mr. Punch' to whom in the first
instance we are indebted for the privilege of enjoying
these fine products of a witty and learned lawyer: and
let us avail ourselves of the present opportunity of giving
them a paramount place among our valued books.

                                                    ATKIN

INTRODUCTION

To 'Misleading Cases', by Lord Hewart, the Lord Chief Justice of England

IF (and it is more than possible) I were tempted to ask why in the world the bold and brilliant writer of this book invited me to add an introduction to it, at least two answers might be offered. When Catullus wondered how he should dedicate his *lepidum novum libellum*, fresh from the bookseller's, he chose his friend Cornelius Nepos—

> 'namque tu solebas
> Meas esse aliquid putare nugas.'

And, again, Mr. Herbert may have decided that it is more agreeable on the whole to suffer an introduction than to be committed for contempt of Court. But of course nobody ever was in less need of introduction than this particular discerner of the thoughts and intents of the heart. These 'Misleading Cases in the Common Law' speak for themselves. *'Res ipsa loquitur'*, as the man in the street said when a sack of flour, in the best manner of the attic declension, fell upon him from an upper room. Our humorists, if we may dare to call them ours, are truly said to have realized that you must be unforced and spontaneous, if you have to lie awake at night for it. And, although aversion to law and courts of law is naturally strong in the human mind, there are no doubt many thousands of distinctly respectable persons who will chuckle, and chuckle again and again, over the neatness, the deftness, and the

dexterity—the sense, the satire, and the scholarship—
of these criticisms wrapped in the pleasant disguise of
parody. Occasionally grave but usually gay, the unauthorized reporter will show you in 'A Swan Song'
(though the Common Law rarely invades the sacred
precincts of probate and divorce) how a leading counsel
on the eve of retirement might open for the petitioner;
he will explain to you in 'The Reasonable Man' that,
although what that hypothetical person would do in a
given case affords the test of what amounts to actionable negligence, the law has never recognized the
possibility of the existence of a reasonable woman,
whose existence must therefore be regarded as impossible; and he will divert you in 'The Fish Royal'
with the strange case of the dead whale washed up on
the coast of Dorset, and the attempts of the inhabitants
to persuade or provoke the authorities—first the Home
Secretary and then the Ministry of Agriculture and
Fisheries—to remove this property of the Crown and
so abate the nuisance. (The tail of the animal, by the
way, seems to appertain to the Queen Consort in order
that Her Majesty may be furnished with the necessary
whalebone for her Royal purposes.) But enough of
statistics; and, after all, this is not a Digest. When the
indignant taxpayer, if the epithet be not tautologous,
has pondered 'Can a Worm Turn?' when the thirsty
golfer, subject to the same condition, has considered
'Is a Golfer a Gentleman?' and when the crossword
fiend has mastered the problem of defamation in 'The
Cross Action', they may reflect, jointly and severally,
that it is the capacity for laughter which above all
distinguishes mankind from the brute creation. And
if perchance the book should come to the hands of
a lawyer—like the attorney in *Pendennis*, 'by profession

a serious man'—he may recall the words of that Master
of Balliol who said that there is no road to moral or
intellectual improvement like the knowledge of our
own defects. Nay, perceiving as he must the inde-
finable quality of genius, he will assuredly predict that
these 'Misleading Cases' will be read and quoted when
Bullen and Leake and the Law Reports are obsolete
and the name of Smith is utterly forgotten.

HEWART

DEDICATION

Of 'Still More Misleading Cases'

To the Right Honourable Viscount Buckmaster, P.C.

My Lord,

The humble author still delights to have the blessing of a great man printed at the beginning of his book; but he no longer returns thanks publicly by advertising the great man's virtues. By this respectful epistle I hope to restore an old and gracious custom.

You, my Lord, are a great lawyer, a great Liberal, public servant and reformer, a man of courage and chivalry, principle and wit. Like my poor self, you would not, I think, be ashamed to have it said that you had bees in your bonnet; for it is better to have bees in the bonnet than flies on the brain. Although a lawyer and a lord, you are not afraid to attack the trenches of tradition; and you are never too tired to pursue a forlorn hope, whether it be the reform of the marriage laws or the protection of wild birds and pedestrians. I should be proud indeed if you would bless this little book with your name and a kind word; but I only dare to ask it because these frolics in jurisprudence are sometimes essays in reform as well, and are shyly intended not only to amuse but to amend.

Not to amend His Majesty's judges—you at least will understand from my assiduous imitation how great is my respect for the Bench—but some of the queer laws which it is their lot to administer. The more we honour the former, the more the latter must enrage us —as when we see the British lion compelled to perform humiliating and senseless tricks.

To you, my Lord, with admiration and respect, I dedicate this work.

A. P. HERBERT

INTRODUCTION

To '*Still More Misleading Cases*', *by Viscount Buckmaster, G.C.V.O., LL.D., P.C., formerly Lord Chancellor*

Law and legal procedure have always been a mystery
to the uninitiated, a snare to the unwary, and a red
rag to the unhappy man possessed by reforming zeal.
'A sty for fattening lawyers in on the bones of honest
men' was the comment of Thackeray on a Court now
mercifully extinct. How law could exist without procedure or we without law need not be considered, but
one thing at least is certain—its loss would deprive us
of much amusement.

Bardell v. *Pickwick* will be read when the trial of the
six Carpenters or the seven Bishops is neglected, and
Mr. Herbert's misleading cases turned to with relief by
many who find Smith's leading cases a little dull. But
Mr. Herbert does more than jest: through the mask of
legal form he challenges some of our most venerated
institutions. Why, he asks, is a man prevented from
seeking intoxication after certain hours in our clubs
and inns when if he chose, *et voluntas absit*, he could do
so in the Houses of Parliament, and why, when the
hour has struck, must he cease to pour down his throat
libations to the British Empire at a public dinner while
he might still be drinking to its confusion at Westminster. Why, again, when you embark on litigation
must it be like setting foot on a moving staircase on
which rest is only to be found at the top where the
taxing master *vice* the ticket collector may relieve you
of all your spare cash. Further, why must coroners sit

when the only result of their verdict is to decide in what plot of ground a dead man's bones may rest, and even this decision be only reached by dissecting in public secrets a man may have died to conceal or attacking a witness who has no chance of defence.

So, also, why is it a corrupt practice to offer a man a glass of beer that he may entertain friendly feelings for you at the poll, but not corrupt to promise him and his fellows employment which will provide beer diurnally.

These and many other questions are tried out in the following pages with excellent humour, but in every case the jest is barbed with truth.

The citizen, distracted by the horns and groans of motor-cars, or in peril of his life from their wheels; the author who, searching for an unusual name, accidentally stumbles on a real one and is made to pay damages for libel; the reluctant payer of taxes on men-servants; the man run over by the negligent driving of a Post Office van who finds his misfortunes aggravated by the fact that the van was not one of Messrs. Carter Paterson's; even the judges themselves may find in the following pages some solace for their afflictions.

The case upon divorce sounds a deeper note. The covering of humour cannot there conceal the fierce and just indignation against a law which reason alone has never been able to vindicate. The facts as they are stated may not be literally true, but they only illustrate what is almost a daily occurrence. A man or woman can obtain divorce on the ground of adultery because it denies one of the essential obligations of the contract and unties the knot; but let each party make the denial and nothing but death can unloose the bond. In other words, our laws regard divorce as a prize for good behaviour and not as a social remedy for the admitted evil of ill-adjusted lives. I wish that some one without the aid of divine revelation would try to answer this case.

I do not know if Mr. Herbert has forsaken the road that leads to the Bench, but there is still open the one that leads to Parliament and its privileges, and I wish he would tread it. Meanwhile, may he long continue to give us amusement and instruction.

BUCKMASTER

TABLE OF CASES

(1) FARDELL v. POTTS

THE REASONABLE MAN

THE Court of Appeal to-day delivered judgment in this important case.

The Master of the Rolls: In this case the appellant was a Mrs. Fardell, a woman, who, while navigating a motor-launch on the River Thames, collided with the respondent, who was navigating a punt, as a result of which the respondent was immersed and caught cold. The respondent brought an action for damages, in which it was alleged that the collision and subsequent immersion were caused by the negligent navigation of the appellant. In the Court below the learned judge decided that there was evidence on which the jury might find that the defendant had not taken reasonable care, and, being of that opinion, very properly left to the jury the question whether in fact she had failed to use reasonable care or not. The jury found for the plaintiff and awarded him two hundred and fifty pounds damages. This verdict we are asked to set aside on the ground of misdirection by the learned judge, the contention being that the case should never have been allowed to go to the jury; and this contention is supported by a somewhat novel proposition, which has been ably, though tediously, argued by Sir Ethelred Rutt.

The Common Law of England has been laboriously built about a mythical figure—the figure of 'The Reasonable Man'. In the field of jurisprudence this legendary individual occupies the place which in

another science is held by the Economic Man, and in
social and political discussions by the Average or Plain
Man. He is an ideal, a standard, the embodiment of
all those qualities which we demand of the good citizen.
No matter what may be the particular department of
human life which falls to be considered in these Courts,
sooner or later we have to face the question: Was this
or was it not the conduct of a reasonable man? Did
the defendant take such care to avoid shooting the
plaintiff in the stomach as might reasonably be expected
of a reasonable man? (*Moocat* v. *Radley* (1883) 2 Q.B.)
Did the plaintiff take such precautions to inform himself of the circumstances as any reasonable man would
expect of an ordinary person having the ordinary
knowledge of an ordinary person of the habits of wild
bulls when goaded with garden-forks and the persistent
agitation of red flags? (*Williams* v. *Dogbody* (1841)
2 A.C.)

I need not multiply examples. It is impossible to
travel anywhere or to travel for long in that confusing
forest of learned judgments which constitutes the
Common Law of England without encountering the
Reasonable Man. He is at every turn, an ever-present
help in time of trouble, and his apparitions mark the
road to equity and right. There has never been a
problem, however difficult, which His Majesty's judges
have not in the end been able to resolve by asking
themselves the simple question, 'Was this or was it not
the conduct of a reasonable man?' and leaving that
question to be answered by the jury.

This noble creature stands in singular contrast to his
kinsman the Economic Man, whose every action is
prompted by the single spur of selfish advantage and
directed to the single end of monetary gain. The

Reasonable Man is always thinking of others; prudence is his guide, and 'Safety First', if I may borrow a contemporary catchword, is his rule of life. All solid virtues are his, save only that peculiar quality by which the affection of other men is won. For it will not be pretended that socially he is much less objectionable than the Economic Man. Though any given example of his behaviour must command our admiration, when taken in the mass his acts create a very different set of impressions. He is one who invariably looks where he is going, and is careful to examine the immediate foreground before he executes a leap or bound; who neither star-gazes nor is lost in meditation when approaching trap-doors or the margin of a dock; who records in every case upon the counterfoils of cheques such ample details as are desirable, scrupulously substitutes the word 'Order' for the word 'Bearer', crosses the instrument 'a/c Payee only', and registers the package in which it is despatched; who never mounts a moving omnibus, and does not alight from any car while the train is in motion; who investigates exhaustively the *bona fides* of every mendicant before distributing alms, and will inform himself of the history and habits of a dog before administering a caress; who believes no gossip, nor repeats it, without firm basis for believing it to be true; who never drives his ball till those in front of him have definitely vacated the putting-green which is his own objective; who never from one year's end to another makes an excessive demand upon his wife, his neighbours, his servants, his ox, or his ass; who in the way of business looks only for that narrow margin of profit which twelve men such as himself would reckon to be 'fair', and contemplates his fellow-merchants, their agents, and their goods, with that degree of suspicion and distrust which the law deems admirable; who never swears, gambles, or loses his temper; who uses nothing except in moderation, and even while he flogs his child is meditating only on the golden mean. Devoid, in short, of any human weakness, with not one single saving vice, *sans* prejudice, procrastination, ill-nature, avarice, and absence of mind, as careful for his own safety as he is for that of others, this excellent but odious character stands like a monument in our Courts of Justice, vainly appealing to his fellow-citizens to order their lives after his own example.

I have called him a myth; and, in so far as there are few, if any, of his mind and temperament to be found in the ranks of living men, the title is well chosen. But it is a myth which rests upon solid and even, it may be, upon permanent foundations. The Reasonable Man is fed and kept alive by the most valued and enduring of our juridical institutions—the common jury. Hateful as he must necessarily be to any ordinary citizen who privately considers him, it is a curious paradox that where two or three are gathered together in one place they will with one accord pretend an admiration for him; and, when they are gathered together in the formidable surroundings of a British jury, they are easily persuaded that they themselves are, each and generally, reasonable men. Without stopping to consider how strange a chance it must have been that has picked fortuitously from a whole people no fewer than twelve examples of a species so rare, they immediately invest themselves with the attributes of the Reasonable Man, and are therefore at one with the Courts in their anxiety to support the tradition that such a being in fact exists. Thus it is that while the Economic Man has under the stress of modern conditions almost wholly disappeared from view his Reasonable cousin has gained in power with every case in which he has figured.

To return, however, as every judge must ultimately return, to the case which is before us—it has been urged for the appellant, and my own researches incline me to agree, that in all that mass of authorities which bears upon this branch of the law *there is no single mention of a reasonable woman*. It was ably insisted before us that such an omission, extending over a century and more of judicial pronouncements, must be something more than a coincidence; that among the innumerable tributes to the reasonable man there might be expected at least some passing reference to a reasonable person of the opposite sex; that no such reference is found, for the simple reason that no such being is contemplated by the law; that legally at least there *is* no reasonable woman, and that therefore in this case the learned judge should have directed the jury that, while there was evidence on which they might find that the defendant had not come up to the standard required of a reasonable man, her conduct was only what was to be expected of a woman, as such.

It must be conceded at once that there is merit in this contention, however unpalatable it may at first appear. The appellant relies largely on *Baxter's Case*, 1639 (2 Bole, at page 100), in which it was held that for the purposes of *estover* the wife of a tenant by the mesne was at law in the same position as an ox or other *cattle demenant* (to which a modern parallel may perhaps be found in the statutory regulations of many railway companies, whereby, for the purposes of freight, a typewriter is counted as a musical instrument). It is probably no mere chance that in our legal text-books the problems relating to married women are usually

considered immediately after the pages devoted to
idiots and lunatics. Indeed, there is respectable
authority for saying that at Common Law this was
the status of a woman. Recent legislation has whittled
away a great part of this venerable conception, but so
far as concerns the law of negligence, which is our
present consideration, I am persuaded that it remains
intact. It is no bad thing that the law of the land should
here and there conform with the known facts of everyday experience. The view that there exists a class of
beings, illogical, impulsive, careless, irresponsible,
extravagant, prejudiced, and vain, free for the most
part from those worthy and repellent excellences which
distinguish the Reasonable Man, and devoted to the
irrational arts of pleasure and attraction, is one which
should be as welcome and as well accepted in our Courts
as it is in our drawing-rooms—and even in Parliament. The odd stipulation is often heard there that
some new Committee or Council shall consist of so
many persons 'one of which must be a woman': the
assumption being that upon scientific principles of
selection no woman would be added to a body
having serious deliberative functions. That assumption, which is at once accepted and resented by those
who maintain the complete equality of the sexes, is not
founded, as they suppose, in some prejudice of Man
but in the considered judgments of Nature. I find that
at Common Law a reasonable woman does not exist.
The contention of the respondent fails and the appeal
must be allowed. Costs to be costs in the action, above
and below, but not costs in the case.

Bungay, L. J., and *Blow, L. J.*, concurred.

(2) TINRIB, RUMBLE, AND OTHERS *v.* THE KING AND QUEEN

Fish Royal

(Before Mr. Justice Wool)

In this unusual action, the hearing of which was begun to-day, an interesting point is raised concerning the rights and duties of the Crown in connexion with a dead whale.

Sir Ethelred Rutt, K.C. (for the plaintiffs): May it please your Lordship, this action is brought by Mr. Tinrib, Mr. Rumble, and the other plaintiffs on behalf of the inhabitants of Pudding Magna, situated, milord, in the county of Dorset——

The Court: Where is Dorset?

Sir Ethelred: Milord, I have a map here. Dorset, milord, if your Lordship will glance at the bottom left-hand corner—— Dorset, milord, is, milord, Dorset——

The Court: Quite—quite. Get on, please, Sir Ethelred.

Sir Ethelred: I am greatly obliged to your Lordship. Pudding Magna, milord, is situated in the north-east corner of Pudding Bay, or the Devil's Entry. The inhabitants are mainly fisher-folk of lowly origin and modest means, and, so far as can be ascertained, the place is not referred to in any of the works of Mr. Thomas Hardy, Mr. William Wordsworth, or any other writer——

The Court: O si sic omnes!

Sir Ethelred: Ha! Milord, in the night of June 21st

7

last a dead whale was washed up on the shore of Pudding Bay, at a point south-west by south from the township of Pudding Magna. Now, the whale, milord, together with the sturgeon and the swan, is Fish Royal, and belongs to the King; or, to be precise, the head of the whale belongs to His Majesty the King and the tail to Her Majesty the Queen. Your Lordship will recall the case of *Rex* v. *Monday* (1841) 3 A.C., which decided the latter point.

The Court: I recall nothing of the kind.

Sir Ethelred: Your Lordship is very good. The loyal inhabitants of Pudding Magna, milord, made haste to extract from the carcass of the whale the whalebone, the blubber, and other valuable and perishable portions, with the intention, I am instructed, of holding them in trust for the Crown. And I may say at once that any other construction of their motives will be most strenuously resisted, if necessary, by sworn evidence. Three days later, milord, the wind, which had been northerly, shifted to the prevailing quarter, which is south-east——

Sir Wilfred Knocknee, K.C.: You mean south-west.

Sir Ethelred: I am very greatly obliged to me learned friend. Me learned friend is perfectly right, milord; the prevailing wind is south-west, milord; and, milord, on the fifth day the presence of the whale began to be offensive to the inhabitants of Pudding Magna. They therefore looked with confidence to the Crown to remove to a more convenient place the remnant of the Crown's property——

Sir Wilfred (aside): For which they had no use.

Sir Ethelred: Really, milord, me learned friend must not whisper insinuations of that kind under his breath; really, milord, I am entitled to resent, milord——

The Court: Go on, Sir Ethelred.

Sir Ethelred: Your Lordship is extraordinarily handsome and good. Accordingly, milord, the Mayor of Pudding Magna addressed a humble petition to the Home Secretary, milord, begging him to acquaint His Majesty with the arrival of his property and praying for its instant removal. And by a happy afterthought, milord, a copy of this petition was sent to the Minister of Agriculture and Fisheries.

Happy, milord, for this reason, that the original communication appears to have escaped the notice of the Home Secretary entirely. At the Ministry of Agriculture and Fisheries, however, the Mayor's letter was handed to a public servant named Sleep, a newcomer to the Service, and one, it seems, who combined with a fertile imagination an unusual incapacity for the conduct of practical affairs. This gentleman has now left the public service, milord, and will be called.

It appears, milord, that, when the Mayor's letter had been lying unconsidered on Mr. Sleep's desk for several days, the following telegram was handed to him:

'*To the King London whale referred to in previous communications now in advanced stages decomposition humbly petition prompt action*

Tinrib'

Mr. Sleep, milord, according to his own account, turning the matter over in his sagacious mind, at once hit upon a solution which would be likely to satisfy the requirements of His Majesty's Treasury with regard to public economy. Two days later, therefore, a letter was addressed to the Director of the Natural History Museum informing him that an unusually fine specimen of *Balaena Biscayensis* was now lying in Pudding Bay and that the Minister was authorized by His Majesty to offer the whale to the Museum in trust for the nation, the Museum to bear the charges of collection and transport.

On July 3rd, milord, the Secretary to the Natural History Museum replied that he was desired by the Director to express his regret that, owing to lack of space, the Museum was unable to accept His Majesty's gracious offer. He was to add that the Museum was already in possession of three fine specimens of *Balaena Biscayensis*.

Milord, for some days, it appears, Mr. Sleep took no further action. Meanwhile, milord, the whale had passed from the advanced to the penultimate stages of decomposition, and had begun to poison the sea at high water, thereby gravely impairing the fishermen's livelihood. Mr. Tinrib, milord, was in constant, but one-sided, correspondence with Mr. Sleep; and on the 12th of July, milord, Mr. Sleep lunched with a friend and colleague at the Admiralty, Mr. Sloe. While they were engaged, milord, upon the discussion of fish, the topic of whales naturally arose, and Mr. Sleep, milord, unofficially, milord, expressed to Mr. Sloe the opinion that the Ministry of Agriculture and Fisheries would be willing to grant to the Admiralty the use of the whale for the purpose of target-practice; and he suggested that one of His Majesty's ships should be immediately detailed to tow His Majesty's whale out to sea. He also pointed out the peculiar advantages of such a target for the exercise of such vessels as were called upon to fire at submarines. Mr. Sloe, milord, undertook to explore the opinion of the Admiralty on the proposal, and the conference broke up.

That was on the 12th. On the 17th, milord, Mr. Sloe unofficially, milord, at a further lunch, intimated

to Mr. Sleep that he could find no support among their
Lordships of the Admiralty for the proposal of the
Ministry of Agriculture and Fisheries; for, while excellent practice was to be had from a disappearing
target, their Lordships could not sanction the expenditure of ammunition on a target which must, at most
ranges, be quite invisible. Further, it was their opinion
that by the date of the autumn firing-practices the
whale would have suffered dissolution by the ordinary
processes of nature.

The inhabitants of Pudding Magna, milord, did not
share this view. On the 20th, milord, Mr. Tinrib and
a deputation waited upon Mr. Sleep. They pointed
out to Mr. Sleep that all fishing was suspended in
Pudding Bay; that Pudding Magna was now scarcely
habitable except on the rare occasions of a northerly
wind; that the majority of the citizens had fled to the
hills and were living in huts and caves. They further
inquired, milord, whether it would be lawful for the
fishermen themselves to destroy the whale, so far as that
could be done, with explosives, and, if so, whether the
Crown would refund the cost of the explosives, which
might be considerable. As to this, milord, Mr. Sleep
was unable to accept the responsibility of expressing
an opinion; but the whale was undoubtedly Crown
property, and he questioned gravely whether the
Treasury would sanction the expenditure of public
money on the destruction of Crown property by
private citizens. He also pointed out that the Treasury,
if approached, would be likely to require a strict account
of any whalebone, blubber, and other material extracted from the whale's carcass. Mention of explosives
however, had suggested to his mind that possibly the
War Office might be interested in the whale, and he

3

undertook to inquire. The deputation agreed, milord, that this perhaps would be the better course, and withdrew.

On the 24th, milord, a letter was dispatched to the War Office pointing out that the whale now lying in Pudding Bay offered excellent opportunities for the training of engineers in the removal of obstacles, and could well be made the centre of any amphibious operations, landing-parties, invasions, etc., which might form part of the forthcoming manœuvres. The War Office would doubtless take note of the convenient proximity of the whale to the Tank Corps Depot at Lulworth.

On the 31st, milord, the War Office replied that the destruction of whales by tanks was no longer considered a practicable operation of war, and that no part of the forthcoming manœuvres would be amphibious.

From this date, milord, Mr. Sleep seems to have abandoned his efforts. At any rate, on the 4th of August, Mr. Tinrib received the following evasive and disgraceful communication:

'WHALE, CARCASS OF

'*Dear Sir,*

'*I am desired by the Minister of Agriculture and Fisheries to observe that your representations to this Department appear to have been made under a misapprehension. It should hardly be necessary to state that the whale is not a fish but a mammal. I am therefore to express regret that the Ministry of Agriculture and Fisheries can accept no responsibility in the matter.*'

In these circumstances, milord, the inhabitants, or I should say the *late* inhabitants, of Pudding Magna have been compelled to institute these proceedings, and humbly pray——

The case was adjourned.

(3) REX *v.* GARVIN, RIDDELL, JOHNSTON, THOMAS, ROBINSON, BEETLE, PULBOROUGH, AND OTHERS

THE SABBATH-BREAKERS

THE hearing of this case was concluded to-day in the Court of Criminal Appeal.

The Lord Chief Justice (delivering judgment): In this painful case the defendants are the proprietors and editors of certain Sunday newspapers. They were charged at the Old Bailey, upon an information laid by the Sunday Society, with certain offences under the Sunday Observance Act, 1677—an Act of the reign of Charles II, which has never been repealed. All the defendants were found guilty, and they were sentenced to fines ranging from five hundred thousand to two million pounds, or in the alternative to imprisonment. for a very long time; and they have now appealed on the ground that these sentences are excessive.

That the offences were committed is not seriously disputed. By the Act it is laid down that

'*No tradesmen, artificers, workmen, labourers, or other person whatsoever shall do or exercise any worldly labour, business, or work of their ordinary callings upon the Lord's Day, or any part thereof.*'

It was proved to the satisfaction of the judge and jury that the accused persons have for many years distributed, sold, and in some cases printed their newspapers upon the Lord's Day, or some part thereof; and it is only necessary for this Court to consider the facts of the case so far as they may affect the measure of punishment.

It was urged in evidence by the very able Secretary of the informing Society, Mr. Haddock, that the dissemination of what is called 'news' is always an anti-social and disturbing act; that 'news' consists, as to ninety per cent, of the records of human misfortune, unhappiness, and wrongdoing, as to nine per cent of personal advertisement, and as to one per cent of instructive and improving matter; that the study of the newspapers is harmful to the citizen because (a) by their insistence upon railway accidents, floods, divorces, murders, fires, successful robberies, the rates of taxation and other evils, and (b) by the prominence which they give to exceptionally good fortune, the winners of large sweepstakes, the salaries and faces of beautiful actresses, and the occasional success of what are known, it appears, as 'outsiders', he is led to the conclusion that industry, thrift and virtue are not worth pursuing in a world so much governed by incalculable chances; and, in general, that the conditions of mind most fostered by the news of the day are curiosity, cupidity, envy, indignation, horror, and fear.

Now, whatever may be desirable or permitted upon a week-day, it is argued by Mr. Haddock that to influence great numbers of the citizens in this way for pecuniary gain on the morning of the Sabbath is clearly contrary to the intention of the Act. But evidence was called to show that there are large masses of the population who because of the existence of the defendants' journals ignore the news of the world throughout the week, and only begin to consider it at about that time on Sunday morning when the bells are summoning them to matins, from which hour until the midday meal they remain, as one witness put it, 'embedded' in the news. And numerous divines swore that they expect their largest congregations upon Christmas Day, which is one of the only two holy days in the year on which no newspapers appear to seduce their flock with the activities of racehorses or the contents of trunks.[1]

These are grave charges. And it is necessary to consider the particular character of the various journals in question. The defendant Garvin, who appears to possess an unusual command of language, maintained that his paper, *The Observer*, was in a class by itself and was deliberately designed for the special needs of the Sabbath reader; but this defence was put forward by several others, though on different grounds. He was asked to say whether in his opinion a man of average powers could in the same morning give proper attention to bodily cleanliness, to divine service, and to one of his leading articles. The witness replied that his leading articles were half-way between a cold bath and a religious exercise, and that this was the place which they occupied, very fitly, in the life of the nation. I have here four or five columns extracted from one of these articles (Exhibit A). It is headed 'THE CATACLYSM —SANITY OR SURRENDER?—DISRAELI, THE DIE-HARD AND THE DELUGE'. It begins:

'*This week the chiaroscuro of human affairs is coloured full-blooded in the tones of madness. After Mesopotamia —Manchester. After Clynes—Catastrophe. After Baldwin—what? In this journal we have never concealed our opinion, etc.*'

It was argued by Mr. Haddock, I think with some force, that on Sunday morning at eleven o'clock no

[1] Presumably a reference to the cloak-room school of murder.

Christian Englishman should be thinking about Mesopotamia or chiaroscuro. Yet this writer has at least the intention of elevating, however depressing his messages in fact may be. But what is to be said of the witnesses Ervine and Agate, who have admitted in evidence that every Sunday morning, in two columns or more, they direct the attention of their numerous followers to the performance of stage-plays, the personal appearance of actresses, the material rewards of playwrights and managers, the problems of sex, and other matters which are without doubt 'worldly' within the meaning of the Act?

And these unfortunately are not the worst. There are other papers represented in that dock which devote a considerable space to accounts of crime and criminal proceedings, the past conduct of pugilists, and the future behaviour of horses; and it was argued for the prosecution that the same law which forbids the subject to witness a play by the poet Shakespeare on Sunday evening should, *a fortiori*, protect him in the morning from the more sensational dramas of the underworld. There are papers published on Sunday morning, it appears, which many Britons are compelled to conceal from their wives; while in other households two copies are purchased in order that the reading of neither spouse may be interrupted. In these papers an importance is attached to the crimes of passion which neither their number nor their moral teaching would seem to justify; and no governess is unwillingly caressed but some representative will be at hand to report the proceedings. I am satisfied that the purveying of these reports for money has not the educational or religious purpose which might excuse it, and that it is a 'worldly business' within the meaning of the Act.

I see no reason why any of the sentences should be reduced. These papers are not poor papers. On the contrary, they make no secret of their large circulation and extensive influence; and many of them go so far as to publish statistical records of their sales, glorying in the fact that every Sabbath they distract greater numbers of His Majesty's subjects from holy thoughts than this or that other paper. It is in the power of this Court to vary sentences either in a downward or an upward direction, and the sentences of certain of the defendants will be increased to penal servitude for terms of years calculated *pro rata* according to circulation. The defendant claiming the largest circulation will be boiled alive, and an order will be made to that effect.

These papers must not be printed again. It has been urged that this order will deprive many citizens of their weekly entertainment; but I am satisfied that the needs of the people are amply supplied by certain papers which are published during the week, and especially on Wednesdays. The appeal must be dismissed.

Frog, J., and *Batter, J.*, concurred.

NOTE—Those who object to Sunday swimming, swings, or cinemas read Monday morning's *Times* without a qualm of conscience, and would be resentful if they were told that they were 'admitting the thin end of the wedge of the Continental Sunday'. While the Sunday Cinemas Bill was being bitterly opposed in Parliament by the Thin-End-of-the-Wedgers I made preparations to prosecute one of *The Times* Sabbath workers. It was not a simple thing to do. The prosecution must be authorized by two magistrates, and in this case they had to be Aldermen of the City of London. *The Times* office had to be watched for three successive Sundays, and this was done. I believe that in the end we even had the Aldermen ready, but the thing fell through—I forget why. EDITOR

(4) REX *v.* HADDOCK

Is a Golfer a Gentleman?

This case, which raised an interesting point of law upon the meaning of the word 'gentleman', was concluded at the Truro Assizes to-day.

Mr. Justice Trout (giving judgment): In this case the defendant, Mr. Albert Haddock, is charged under the Profane Oaths Act, 1745, with swearing and cursing on a Cornish golf-course. The penalty under the Act is a fine of one shilling for every day-labourer, soldier, or seaman, two shillings for every other person under the degree of gentleman, and five shillings for every person of or above the degree of gentleman—a remarkable but not unique example of a statute which lays down one law for the rich and another (more lenient) for the poor. The fine, it is clear, is leviable not upon the string or succession of oaths, but upon each individual malediction (see *Reg.* v. *Scott* (1863) 33 L.J.M. 15). The curses charged, and admitted, in this case, are over four hundred in number, and we are asked by the prosecution to inflict a fine of one hundred pounds, assessed on the highest or gentleman's rate at five shillings a swear. The defendant admits the offences, but contends that the fine is excessive and wrongly calculated, on the curious ground that he is not a gentleman when he is playing golf.

He has reminded us in a brilliant argument that the law takes notice, in many cases, of such exceptional circumstances as will break down the normal restraints of a civilized citizen and so powerfully inflame his

18

passions that it would be unjust and idle to apply to his conduct the ordinary standards of the law; as, for example, where without warning or preparation he discovers another man in the act of molesting his wife or family. Under such provocation the law recognizes that a reasonable man ceases for the time being to be a reasonable man; and the defendant maintains that in the special circumstances of his offence a gentleman ceases to be a gentleman and should not be judged or punished as such.

Now, what were these circumstances? Broadly speaking, they were the 12th hole on the Mullion golf-course, with which most of us in this Court are familiar. At that hole the player drives (or does not drive) over an inlet of the sea which is enclosed by cliffs some sixty feet high. The defendant has told us that he never drives over, but always into, this inlet, or Chasm, as it is locally named. A steady but not sensational player on other sections of the course, he says that before this obstacle his normal powers invariably desert him. This has preyed upon his mind; he has registered, it appears, a kind of vow, and year after year, at Easter and in August, he returns to this county determined ultimately to overcome the Chasm.

Meanwhile, unfortunately, his tenacity has become notorious. The normal procedure, it appears, if a ball is struck into the Chasm, is to strike a second, and, if that should have no better fate, to abandon the hole. The defendant tells us that in the past he has struck no fewer than six or seven balls in this way, some rolling gently over the cliff and some flying far and high out to sea. But recently, grown fatalistic, he has not thought it worth while to make even a second attempt, but has immediately followed his first ball into the Chasm, and

there, among the rocks, small stones, and shingle, has
hacked at his ball with the appropriate instrument
until some lucky blow has lofted it on to the turf above,
or, in the alternative, until he has broken his instruments or suffered some injury from flying fragments of
rock. On one or two occasions a crowd of holiday-
makers and local residents have gathered on the cliff
and foreshore to watch the defendant's indomitable
struggles and to hear the verbal observations which
have accompanied them. On the date of the alleged
offences a crowd of unprecedented dimensions collected,
but so intense was the defendant's concentration that
he did not, he tells us, observe their presence. His
ball had more nearly traversed the gulf than ever before;
it struck the opposing cliff but a few feet from the sum-
mit; and nothing but an adverse gale of exceptional
ferocity prevented success. The defendant therefore,
as he conducted his customary excavations among the
boulders of the Chasm, was possessed, he tells us, by a
more than customary fury. Oblivious of his surroundings, conscious only of the will to win, for fifteen or
twenty minutes he lashed his battered ball against the
stubborn cliffs, until at last it triumphantly escaped.
And before, during, and after every stroke he uttered a
number of imprecations of a complex character which
were carefully recorded by an assiduous caddie and by
one or two of the spectators. The defendant says that
he recalls with shame a few of the expressions which he
used, that he has never used them before, and that it
was a shock to him to hear them issuing from his own
lips; and he says quite frankly that no gentleman
would use such language.

Now, this ingenious defence, whatever may be its
legal value, has at least some support in the facts

of human experience. I am a golf-player myself—
(*laughter*)—but, apart from that, evidence has been
called to show the subversive effect of this exercise upon
the ethical and moral systems of the mildest of mankind.
Elderly gentlemen, gentle in all respects, kind to animals, beloved by children, and fond of music, are
found in lonely corners of the downs, hacking at sand-
pits or tussocks of grass, and muttering in a blind,
ungovernable fury elaborate maledictions which could
not be extracted from them by robbery or murder.
Men who would face torture without a word become
blasphemous at the short fourteenth. It is clear that
the game of golf may well be included in that category
of intolerable provocations which may legally excuse
or mitigate behaviour not otherwise excusable, and
that under that provocation the reasonable or gentle
man may reasonably act like a lunatic or lout respectively, and should legally be judged as such.

But then I have to ask myself, What does the Act
intend by the words 'of or above the degree of gentleman'? Does it intend a fixed social rank or a general
habit of behaviour? In other words, is a gentleman
legally always a gentleman, as a duke or solicitor
remains unalterably a duke or solicitor? For if this
is the case the defendant's argument must fail. The
prosecution says that the word 'degree' is used in
the sense of 'rank'. Mr. Haddock argues that it is
used in the sense of a university examination, and
that, like the examiners, the Legislature divides the
human race, for the purposes of swearing, into three
vague intellectual or moral categories, of which they
give certain rough but not infallible examples. Many
a first-class man has 'taken a third', and many a day-
labourer, according to Mr. Haddock, is of so high a

character that under the Act he should rightly be included in the first 'degree'. There is certainly abundant
judicial and literary authority for the view that by
'gentleman' we mean a personal quality and not a
social status. We have all heard of 'Nature's gentlemen'. 'Clothes do not make the gentleman,' said
Lord Mildew in *Cook* v. *The Mersey Docks and Harbour
Board* (1896) 2 A.C., meaning that a true gentleman
might be clad in the foul rags of an author. In the old
maxim 'Manners makyth man' (see *Charles* v. *The
Great Western Railway*) there is no doubt that by 'man'
is meant 'gentleman', and that 'manners' is contrasted
with wealth or station. Mr. Thomas, for the prosecution, has quoted against these authorities an observation
of the poet Shakespeare that

'The Prince of Darkness is a gentleman',

but quotations from Shakespeare (in Court) are generally meaningless and always unsound. This one, in
my judgment, is both. I am more impressed by the
saying of another author (whose name I forget) that
the King can make a nobleman, but he cannot make
a gentleman.

I am satisfied therefore that the argument of the
defendant has substance. Just as the reasonable man
who discovers his consort in the embraces of the supplanter becomes for the moment a raving maniac, so
the habitually gentle man may become in a bunker a
violent, unmannerly oaf. In each case the ordinary
sanctions of the law are suspended; and while it is
right that a normally gentle person should in normal
circumstances suffer a heavier penalty for needless
imprecations than a common seaman or cattle-driver,
for whom they are part of the tools of his trade, he must

not be judged by the standards of the gentle in such special circumstances as provoked the defendant.

That provocation was so exceptional that I cannot think that it was contemplated by the framers of the Act; and had golf at that date been a popular exercise I have no doubt that it would have been dealt with under a special section. I find therefore that this case is not governed by the Act. I find that the defendant at the time was not in law responsible for his actions or his speech and I am unable to punish him in any way. For his conduct in the Chasm he will be formally convicted of Attempted Suicide while Temporarily Insane, but he leaves the court without a stain upon his character. (*Applause*)

(5) REX *v.* HADDOCK

Is It a Free Country?

THE Court of Criminal Appeal considered to-day an important case involving the rights and liberties of the subject, if any.

Lord Light, L.C.J.: This is in substance an appeal by an appellant appealing *in statu quo* against a decision of the West London Half-Sessions, confirming a conviction by the magistrates of South Hammersmith sitting in Petty Court some four or five years ago. The ancillary proceedings have included two hearings *in sessu* and an appeal rampant on the case, as a result of which the record was ordered to be torn up and the evidence reprinted backwards *ad legem*. With these transactions, however, the Court need not concern itself, except to observe that, as for our learned brother Mumble, whose judgments we have read with diligence and something approaching to nausea, it were better that a millstone should be hanged round his neck and he be cast into the uttermost depths of the sea.

The present issue is one of comparative simplicity. That is to say, the facts of the case are intelligible to the least-instructed layman, and the only persons utterly at sea are those connected with the law. But *factum clarum, jus nebulosum*, or, 'the clearer the facts the more dubious the law'. What the appellant did in fact is simple and manifest, but what offence, if any, he has committed in law is a question of the gravest difficulty.

What he did in fact was to jump off Hammersmith

24

Bridge in the afternoon of August 18th, 1922, during the Hammersmith Regatta. The motive of the act is less clear. A bystander named Snooker, who, like himself, was watching the regatta from the bridge, has sworn in evidence that he addressed the appellant in the following terms: 'Betcher a pound you won't jump over, mate,' that the appellant, who had had a beer or (as he frankly admitted) two, replied in these words: 'Bet you I will, then,' after which pronouncement he removed his coat, handed it to the man Snooker, climbed on to the rail, and jumped into the water below, which, as was sworn by Professor Rugg of the Royal Geographical Society, forms part of the River Thames. The appellant is a strong swimmer, and, on rising to the surface, he swam in a leisurely fashion towards the Middlesex bank. When still a few yards from the shore, however, he was overtaken by a river police boat, the officers in which had observed his entrance into the water and considered it their duty to rescue the swimmer. They therefore took him, unwilling, it appears, into their boat, and landed him. He was then arrested by an officer of the Metropolitan Police engaged in controlling the crowds who had gathered to watch the regatta, was taken to the police station and subsequently charged before the magistrates, when he was ordered to pay a fine of two pounds.

The charges were various, and it is difficult to say upon which of them the conviction was ultimately based. The appellant was accused of:

(*a*) Causing an obstruction
(*b*) Being drunk and disorderly
(*c*) Attempting to commit suicide
(*d*) Conducting the business of a street bookmaker

(e) (Under the Navigation Acts) endangering the
    lives of mariners

(f) (Under the Port of London Authority By-laws)
    interfering with an authorized regatta.

It may be said at once that in any case no blame
whatever attaches to the persons responsible for the
framing of these charges, who were placed in a most
difficult position by the appellant's unfortunate act. It
is a principle of English law that a person who appears
in a police court has done something undesirable, and
citizens who take it upon themselves to do unusual
actions which attract the attention of the police should
be careful to bring these actions into one of the recognized categories of crimes and offences, for it is intolerable that the police should be put to the pains of
inventing reasons for finding them undesirable.

The appellant's answer to the charges severally were
these. He said that he had not caused an obstruction
by doing an act which gathered a crowd together, for
a crowd had already gathered to watch the regatta,
both on the bridge and on the banks. He said that
although he had had one beer, or even two, he was
neither drunk nor disorderly. Snooker and others
about him swore that he showed no signs of either condition when on the bridge, and it was powerfully
argued that the fact of a man jumping from a high
place into water was not *prima facie* evidence of intoxication. Witnesses were called to show that a man at
Bournemouth had constantly jumped from the pier in
flames without any such suggestion, and indeed with
the connivance of the police and in the presence of the
Mayor and Council. In the alternative, the appellant
said that, assuming that he was intoxicated before his

immersion, which he denied, he must obviously have been, and in fact was, sober when arrested, which is admitted; while the river police in cross-examination were unable to say that he was swimming in a disorderly manner, or with any unseemly splashes or loud cries such as might have supported an accusation of riotous behaviour.

In answer to the charge of attempted suicide the appellant said (a) that only the most unconventional suicide would select for his attempt an occasion on which there were numerous police boats and other craft within view, (b) that it is not the natural action of a suicide to remove his coat before the fatal plunge, and (c) that his first act on rising to the surface was in fact to swim methodically to a place of safety.

As to the betting charge, the appellant said that he had never made a bet in his life; no other person but Snooker heard or saw anything of the transaction; and since Snooker, who on his own showing had lost the wager, confessed in cross-examination that he had not in fact passed any money to the appellant, but, on the contrary, had walked off quietly with the appellant's coat, the credit of this witness was a little shaken, and this charge may be said to have fallen to the ground. The appellant himself said that he did what he did (to use his own curious phrase) 'for fun'.

Finally, as to the Navigation and Port of London Authority Acts, the appellant called overwhelming evidence to prove that, at the time of his immersion, no race was actually in progress and no craft or vessel was within fifty yards from the bridge.

But in addition to these particular answers, all of which in my judgment have substance, the appellant made the general answer that this was a free country and a man can do what he likes if he does nobody any harm. And with that observation the appellant's case takes on at once an entirely new aspect. If I may use an expression which I have used many times before in this Court, it is like the thirteenth stroke of a crazy clock, which not only is itself discredited but casts a shade of doubt over all previous assertions. For it would be idle to deny that a man capable of that remark would be capable of the grossest forms of licence and disorder. It cannot be too clearly understood that this is *not* a free country, and it will be an evil day for the legal profession when it is. The citizens of London must realize that there is almost nothing they are allowed to do. *Prima facie* all actions are illegal, if not by Act of Parliament, by Order in Council; and if not by Order in Council, by Departmental or Police Regulations, or By-laws. They may not eat where they like, drink where they like, walk where they like, drive where they like, sing where they like, or sleep where they like. And least of all may they do unusual actions 'for fun'. People must not do things for fun. We are not here for fun. There is no reference to fun in any Act of Parliament. If anything is said in this Court to encourage a belief that Englishmen are entitled to jump off bridges for their own amusement the next thing to go will be the Constitution. For these reasons, therefore, I have come to the conclusion that this appeal must fail. It is not for me to say what offence the appellant has committed, but I am satisfied that he has committed *some* offence, for which he has been most properly punished.

Mudd, J., said that in his opinion the appellant had polluted a water-course under the Public Health Act, 1875.

Adder, *J.*, concurred. He thought that the appellant had attempted to pull down a bridge, under the Malicious Damage Act, 1861.

The appeal was dismissed.

NOTE—See also *H.M. Customs and Excise* v. *Bathbourne Literary Society* (page 408) for the law relating to fun and laughter.

(6) REX *v.* THE LICENSING JUSTICES OF MUDDLETOWN

'THE RED COW'

(*Before Mr. Justice Wool*)

STARTLING charges were made in this case to-day at the Muddletown Assizes by Sir Ethelred Rutt, K.C., in his opening speech for the prosecution. The arrest and trial of the Licensing Justices were brought about by the untiring efforts of Mr. Albert Haddock and have aroused great popular enthusiasm; cheering crowds surrounded the court, and the judges have received five thousand anonymous letters, couched about equally in the language of menace and congratulation.

Sir Ethelred Rutt: Milord, in this case the defendants are seventeen Justices of the Peace who are charged under the Public Health Acts with exposing the public to an unhealthy and insanitary condition of affairs in the public bar of 'The Red Cow' inn, or, in the alternative, with conduct amounting to a public nuisance.

The facts are these. Until recent years there were two licensed houses in Sunset Street, 'The Red Cow' at the western end and 'The Blue Swan' at the eastern. Each house had its own regular and sufficient clientèle, but neither was overcrowded. The guests took their refreshment seated comfortably on benches and watched with interest, in the case of 'The Red Cow', the game called 'darts'. 'The Red Cow' was famous for darts, and 'The Blue Swan' for skittles.

The Judge: What are skittles?

Sir Ethelred: Milord, I am instructed that skittles are a sort of ninepin.

The Judge: I thought it was a beverage.

Sir Ethelred: Perhaps your Lordship is thinking of the expression 'Beer and skittles'? (*Laughter*)

The Judge: Is not that the same as whisky-and-soda?

Sir Ethelred: No, milord, it is a game.

The Judge: Very well. Don't waste time, Sir Ethelred.

Sir Ethelred: Your Lordship is very good. Well, milord, 'The Blue Swan' was famous for skittles, and on several occasions had won the challenge shield of the Amateur Skittles Association, for which twenty-seven public-houses in the district annually compete. Now, at the Licensing Sessions it was represented to the justices by certain virtuous persons that two public-houses in one street was an excessive number, and out of proportion to the needs of the population—that one of them, in short, was 'redundant'. Their arguments were supported by counsel of the most learned and expensive kind; the justices, all of whom were teeto-tallers, accepted them, the licence of 'The Blue Swan' was, in the strange jargon of the day, 'referred for redundancy', and, in the end, was extinguished.

Now, milord, these well-meaning persons appear to be governed by two main assumptions, both, in my submission, milord, fallacious: One, that the sole function and purpose of a public-house is the sale and consumption of alcohol; and two, that where there are two public-houses there will be sold and consumed a greater quantity of alcohol than where there is only one.

The Judge: Two and two make four, Sir Ethelred.

Sir Ethelred: Milord, I am prepared to argue that. (*Laughter*)

The Judge: Are you relying on *Stagger* v. *Root*?

Sir Ethelred: No, milord; that was a *nisi prius* action.

The Judge: What has Mr. Wriggle to say to that?

Mr. Wriggle, K.C.: Milord, I ask for a ruling.

The Judge: You must not ask me for a ruling before lunch.

Sir Ethelred (continuing): Now, milord, neither the Licensing Justices nor the persons who appeared before them to oppose the renewal of the licence of 'The Blue Swan' had ever entered 'The Blue Swan'.

The Judge: I never went to 'The Blue Swan'.

Sir Ethelred: But possibly you were called to the bar, milord? (*Laughter*)

The Judge: Many are called but few chosen. (*Laughter*)

Sir Ethelred: And therefore, milord, they were wholly unacquainted with the character of 'The Blue Swan'. Both 'The Blue Swan' and 'The Red Cow' were social centres corresponding, milord, in their different ways to the Athenaeum or the Bath Club. The Bottle and Jug Department——

The Judge: What is that?

Sir Ethelred: Milord, I am instructed it is a special counter at which patrons attend with their own jugs or other vessels to purchase liquor for removal and consumption off the premises.

The Judge: Is there a Bottle and Jug Department at the Athenaeum?

Sir Ethelred: No, milord; the Athenaeum is registered as a club.

The Judge: Then what has it got to do with this case?

Sir Ethelred: Milord, if elderly bishops were seen leaving the Athenaeum with jugs of stout in their hands the casual observer would form an impression of the character of that institution which would be largely unjust. And that is what has happened in the case of these two houses. The residents of Sunset Street gathered at these places, milord, for the exchange of ideas and to discuss the news of the day, for the relation of their misfortunes, for mutual comfort, encouragement, and advice, and, in short, for the legitimate purposes of social intercourse. On those premises, milord, many a tired man and disappointed woman have received from the society of their fellows the spiritual contentment which arms them for the trials of the morrow and tends to develop in the mind a political outlook of a conservative rather than a revolutionary nature. 'An Englishman's home,' said Lord Mildew in *Fox* v. *The Amalgamated Society of Woodworkers*, 'is his castle'; but the public-house is a fortress of the Constitution, in which the germs of Bolshevism, milord, are imprisoned and sterilized by the loyal forces of good-fellowship and beer. And it would ill become His Majesty's judges, milord, to countenance without good cause the diminution of these strongholds and so to encourage the growth of opinions which are hostile to existing institutions.

The Judge: What has this to do with sanitation?

Sir Ethelred: I am very grateful for your Lordship's interruption. Milord, what happened, in fact, was this. After the closing of 'The Blue Swan', milord, the clients of 'The Blue Swan' did not, as was expected, abandon the pursuit of good-fellowship and beer, but they transferred their custom to 'The Red Cow' instead. The only practice which they were forced to abandon was the innocent practice of skittles, for 'The Red Cow' has no skittle-alley. It is not possible, milord, to drink beer and play skittles at the same time, so that the effect of the new conditions upon the former clients of 'The Blue Swan' was that they drank not less beer but more.

Milord, 'The Red Cow', catering for the clients of two houses instead of one, has become extremely over-crowded, so much so that at the busy hours of the day it is no longer possible to play darts with safety and satisfaction. Milord, a man cannot throw a dart at a small target and drink beer at the same time, so that the effect of the new conditions upon the old clients of 'The Red Cow' has been that they drink not less beer but more.

The interference, therefore, of the well-meaning persons already referred to in matters of which they had no practical understanding has resulted in a measurable increase in the consumption of beer. More-over, it is now consumed under unhealthy and degrad-ing conditions. Most of the clients of 'The Red Cow' must now take their refreshment standing instead of sitting; men and women are crushed together in circumstances conducive to familiarity and vulgar talk, or stand pressed against the bar, where the propinquity of the bottles is a constant provocation to further indulgence. The atmosphere becomes hot, smoky, malodorous, and foul, and in place of the quiet con-versation of former years there is a deafening hubbub. Women complain that when they go out into the night air they take cold, and that they suffer headaches, not from the beer, but from the noise and the atmosphere. Moreover, the noise makes it necessary to raise the voice, the atmosphere affects the throat, and both these conditions stimulate the thirst, so that again not less alcohol is consumed, but more. The tone of 'The Red Cow' is lower, and this has attracted a rougher element. Under cover of the noise a vulgarity in conversation is possible which was never present before; vulgar talk leads to loose conduct, and the moral standards of Sunset Street have declined.

Milord, it is the prosecution's case that for all these evils the Licensing Justices are responsible. If well-meaning persons were to concentrate in the Athenaeum the members of several other clubs, it is probable that the Athenaeum would suffer a similar decline in social amenities, in culture, and in moral tone; but the haunts of the rich are left alone. Milord, the defendants have turned 'The Red Cow' into a squalid, unwholesome, and unhealthy resort; they must be taken to have foreseen the natural and necessary consequences of their unfortunate act, and, in my submission, they must pay the penalty.

Three cheers were given at the conclusion of Sir Ethelred's speech.

The Court adjourned.

(7) PRATT, G. E., *v.* PRATT, P., AND MUGG

A Swan Song

(*Before Mr. Justice Foot*)

MUCH comment was caused in legal circles to-day by an unconventional speech of Sir Oliver Slick, K.C., M.P., opening a case in the Probate and Divorce Division. Sir Oliver is retiring from practice in a few days' time, and it is thought that he may be suffering from overstrain.

Sir Oliver: May it please your Lordship, my dear old fellow, in this case I appear for the petitioner, Mrs. Gladys Eleanor Pratt, who is praying for a dissolution of marriage on account of—well, I mean, she wants to get rid of the man and that's all about it, milord. Milord, this is probably the last case in which I shall ever appear, so, to tell you the truth, I take a pretty detached view of the whole proceedings. Well, I mean, look at old Twopenny here (*Mr. Albert Twopenny, of the firm of Twopenny and Truelove, solicitors for the petitioner*)—he'll never give me a brief again after this, *but I don't care!* And that's what makes the whole thing so terribly *funny*!

(Sir Oliver here laughed heartily.)

The Judge: Sir Oliver, if this is your swan song, I am sure that you would wish it to be in tune with the traditions of the Bar and with your own fine record.

Sir Oliver: Certainly, milord; you're a good sort, milord, and I don't want to offend you, though you've given me a packet of trouble from time to time. Well, milord, the facts are these. The parties were married only a year ago at Westminster, and lived happily together for about three weeks, milord. Temperamentally, perhaps, they were unsuited; the husband was fond of golf and the woman of lawn tennis. However, the wife remained and is to this day devoted to her husband; but last year, milord, on July 20th—no, 21st—Mrs. Pratt noticed that Mr. Pratt's affections were cooling, and on the 24th, milord, she found him telephoning to a strange woman, a Miss Elizabeth Mugg, milord, who has been cited in this case as a—what-d'you-call-it?——

The Judge: Sir Oliver, I'm not sure that I follow you.

Sir Oliver: 'Woman Named', milord, that's the expression I wanted. (*Sir Oliver then lowered his voice and continued in tones suggestive of profound moral indignation.*) Milord, there seems to be no doubt that this woman, by a protracted course of duplicity and cunning, has deliberately stolen away this husband from his wife. It is difficult, milord, to frame language strong enough to describe a woman who, without any provocation, it appears, from her unfortunate partner in guilt, has wormed her way into the affections of an English husband, and invaded, corrupted, and finally broken up an English home. Picture, milord, the state of mind of my unfortunate client as, day by day and bit by bit, she sees that devotion which is her right transferred to the supplanter. On the 26th, milord, this poor woman had a nervous breakdown; on the 29th she had fits. Milord, do you think I've done enough of this?

The Judge: I beg your pardon, Sir Oliver?

Sir Oliver: I mean, need I give the Court any more

of this gup? Because, of course, you know the whole case is a put-up job——

The Judge: Sir Oliver, I think you are not very well. Perhaps it would be fairer to your client to adjourn.

Sir Oliver: Never was better, old boy. Fit as yourself, and fitter. Well, I wasn't playing bridge half the night, milord, as I happen to know you were!

(Sir Oliver here laughed again in a genial manner.)

The Judge: If you are in good health, Sir Oliver, we will continue the hearing, but you will please confine yourself to the facts of the case.

Sir Oliver: Well, milord, the facts are very simple. This is just one of the ordinary trumped-up upper-class divorce cases, you know, which nowadays, as a rule, we don't bother to open at all. The lady's just bored with him, that's all. Well, I mean, in these days, living with the same husband, week after week, for a whole year—Society girls can't *stand* it. There's nothing unpleasant in the case, nobody's done anything wrong, but my client wants to marry a chap in the Guards—Jack Filter—*you* know, milord, fellow with the eyeglass you met at the club the other day, so we've pitched this yarn about Pratt and Elizabeth Mugg—— Don't interrupt, Twopenny!

(Mr. Twopenny spoke earnestly to Sir Oliver at this point, and subsequently on several occasions, but Sir Oliver did not appear to hear what was said.)

Sir Oliver (continuing): I'm sorry for Pratt in a way—that's the respondent, milord—he's a very good fellow and adores Mrs. Pratt. But it's his own fault, really. The trouble was, you see, milord, that he married the girl for her money and then fell in love with her. I can tell you, between ourselves, my dear old Lordship, we had a job to get him to agree to this divorce at all.

Didn't like it, not a bit. But in the end we got him over the money. You see, he's terribly in debt, milord, and she's going to pay him a decent maintenance. Of course, technically, I know, milord, we shall ask the man to pay Mrs. Pratt maintenance, and a fat maintenance, too; but that's all eyewash. Besides, we made things easy for him over Elizabeth Mugg, and that helped to turn the scale, because he thought he had to go to Brighton with her, and he hates Brighton. But when he found he needn't even see Elizabeth Mugg he didn't mind being divorced because of her so much. In point of fact he never has seen Elizabeth Mugg. I mention that because I don't want any one here to take too seriously what I said about Elizabeth Mugg just now, because Elizabeth Mugg is really a very nice woman and knows her job thoroughly. Elizabeth has been in eighty-nine divorce cases, she tells me, under various names, and has never met one of the parties yet. In this case, of course, she went down to Brighton and stayed a night at the 'Cosmopole'. Pratt's valet stayed there the same night, and put a pair of Pratt's boots outside Elizabeth's room. During the night her boots met Pratt's, and the next day the valet met one of the chambermaids and identified the boots, and there you are. You'll have all the evidence, of course, Pratt's bill, and the cloak-room ticket and the menu and everything, but that's all there is to the case.

The Judge: Sir Oliver, I never like to interrupt counsel when opening a case, but are you materially assisting your client?

Sir Oliver: I should be sorry if you thought I wasn't, milord, because Mrs. Pratt is really quite a decent little woman. In fact, everybody in the case is thoroughly decent, including your Lordship, if I may say so, and it seems to me a great pity that all these decent people should be put to all this trouble and expense and publicity when the whole thing might easily be done in two minutes at a registry office or through one of the big stores. On the other hand, of course, I have to live, and you have to live, milord, and Elizabeth Mugg has to live, so we mustn't complain. Speaking for myself, I'm doing very well out of this case, because my client is not only decent but rich, and old Twopenny here knows how to make 'em cough up—well, I mean he's marked me a pretty fat fee on the brief—well, I mean for a potty little bogus divorce. I mention these points, milord, because it is so nice to get a touch of reality in a case like this. How you can sit up there, milord, day after day, swallowing all the stuff served up to you by members of the Bar like me, who ought to know better——

The Judge: Sir Oliver, this is an occasion without precedent in all my long experience, and I find a difficulty in dealing with it. But if you are unable to conduct yourself in accordance with the traditions of your profession and the interests of your client I shall be compelled to ask you to withdraw from this Court.

Sir Oliver (bowing): Milord, I bow to your ruling. Milord, I have little to add at this stage of the case. My client will now go into that box and tell the tragic story of her married life. She will tell you of affection blighted, of a home made desolate, and a heart destroyed. She will tell you that even at this late hour she is ready to hold out the hand of forgiveness and clasp to her bosom the rightful partner of her life, if he will but tear himself from the embraces of the supplanter, Mugg, a woman, milord, who, as you will shortly hear, has from first to last—from first to last, milord—played a part in the lives of these two people which is without precedent, milord, in my experience for treachery, deceit, ingratitude, and cunning. Call Gladys Pratt.

The Judge: At two o'clock?

The Court adjourned.

(8) TROTT *v.* TULIP

Is 'Highbrow' Libellous?

(Before Mr. Justice Wool)

This action for defamation was to-day brought a stage nearer to its conclusion with the closing speeches of counsel and his Lordship's summing-up to the jury. This was the twenty-seventh day of the hearing.

His Lordship (addressing the jury): In the whole course of my professional career, which has included, necessarily, many warmly contested claims for defamation of character in many different fields of society, I do not remember one which with such an appearance of simplicity has revealed upon examination such sharp and complicated differences, supported, may I say, by such stubborn animosities.

The facts are simple enough. The parties both belong to what is called the literary world, and in that world are sufficiently well known, Miss Clelia Trott as a writer and Mrs. Tulip as a critic of original works of fiction. You were invited by the plaintiff's counsel to consider upon a somewhat higher plane the activities of Miss Trott, which are admittedly creative, than those of Mrs. Tulip, as being chiefly occupied in tearing to pieces the things which other men have made. But this distinction, however attractive to the lay mind, I must ask you to dismiss from your own. In many ponderous and ill-drafted enactments our ancestors have been careful to secure to the most repellent of the King's subjects the common rights of free expression so long as

42

it takes the harmless form of venomous and enraging
words. How far this is just to those of our fellows who
are unhappily unable to express their indignation except
by blows it is not for us to inquire. And how far that
condition of suppressed fury which follows a verbal but
unactionable assault is socially more desirable than the
healthy breach of the peace which follows a blow is also
not within the scope of this inquiry. I mention these
matters only to confuse you and to display the superior
alertness of my intelligence. It is enough for you that
before the law, at any rate, a literary or dramatic critic
is as good and useful a citizen as an original author, and
is entitled to the same measure of justice, if he can get it.

The facts of this case are simple enough. The defendant, Mrs. Tulip, in reviewing a recent work of Miss
Clelia Trott's, a book called *Midnight*, employed the
following words: 'It is no good, Miss Trott. All your
murders and detectives, your vamps and mysteries, do
not deceive us, charming though they are. The truth
is, Miss Trott, *you are a bit of a highbrow.*'

Miss Clelia Trott, so far from being disarmed by
the sprightly and almost complimentary manner of the
review, has brought an action for defamation, complaining particularly of the word 'highbrow', which is
said to have prejudiced her professionally as a writer of
disturbing narratives for railway reading or, as they
are sometimes called, it appears, 'best-sellers'.

The law of libel is exceedingly complicated and
wholly unintelligible. . . .

(His Lordship here gave a brief explanation of the
law of libel, beginning with the Star Chamber.)

His Lordship (continuing): The question of malice is
a question of fact for the jury to determine, and the
jury alone. The evidence which we have heard and

5

the demeanour of the defendant in the box leave no doubt in my own mind that the word complained of was prompted in fact by legal malice and spleen; but it will be for you to say. Far more difficult, in my opinion, is the question, 'Is the word "highbrow" defamatory or not?' and this question also, I am glad to say, it will be for you to answer, though you will be paid one guinea for the twenty-seven days of this trial, and I am paid five thousand pounds a year.

We have had in this case the advantage of the expert testimony of nineteen well-known writers and authors, fourteen literary critics, seven editors, and two philologists. And the one thing that emerges from this mass of informed opinion is that the expression complained of must be the most remarkable word in common use to-day. For though each of these authorities came prepared with a full and impressive theory of the origin and significance of the word, no two of these explanations were in any respect the same. Moreover, at the first hint of opposition or disagreement these ladies and gentlemen, almost without exception, betrayed a degree of passion and obstinacy remarkable in persons devoted to the contemplative way of life, and so excessive as to make the extraction of useful information by process of cross-examination impossible.

If, therefore, we were to place any reliance upon the expert evidence (which, fortunately, it is not the habit of these Courts to do) we should be forced to the conclusion that the word 'highbrow', having a different meaning in the mouth of every authority, has in fact no meaning whatever, and you might well find that to employ such a term in connexion with another person could not be defamatory; as one man might say to another, 'You are a Bimbo', or 'You look like a Togg', without offence; for these expressions, though presumably hostile in intention, have no known significance, discourteous or otherwise.

But you, members of the jury, may not so easily escape from your responsibilities. Somehow or other you are to answer the questions which will be put to you in the affirmative or in the negative as the case may be. And for this purpose you will do well to ignore for the most part the nebulous testimony of the literary gentlemen who have stood in that box before you.

Now, it is urged by the defence that the word 'highbrow' was invented by an American journalist (who has not been called by either side) to express his natural surprise on his observing that there were persons about him more richly gifted than himself; that it means no more than one who is superior in intelligence to the average of his (or her) fellows, and is therefore, so far from being libellous, a complimentary expression, as against the opposite term 'lowbrow', which is said to signify a person having a low or shallow forehead and comparable in aspect and in mental development to an anthropoid ape. According to this theory the human race is roughly divided into two main species, the highbrow and the low-, and no person whose profession it is to provide printed reading for his fellow-men can complain with reason of being included in the former category. On the contrary (according to the defence), to say of an author that she is a highbrow is as much as to say that 'she has more brains than a monkey, and indeed than many men', and is therefore, at any rate, a statement pleasantly intended.

For the plaintiff, on the other hand, it is urged that though this may well have been the origin of the term it has acquired by popular usage a definite, or, at any rate, a definitely offensive, significance. The witnesses who supported this view (so far as any witness may be said to have supported anything in particular) seemed to suggest that highbrow means not merely a person of superior intelligence but one who is offensively conscious or indeed boastful of his (or her) superiority. And they employed, with a warmth which I was not always able to restrain, various expressions of an ethical or moral significance, such as 'prig' and 'Pharisee'. One witness indeed went so far as to describe a highbrow as an 'intellectual Pharisee', and you will remember, no doubt, the disorderly scene which followed.

According to this theory the divisions of the human race are not two, but three—the lowbrow, the high-lowbrow, or broad-brow (or those of an intelligence and tolerance superior to the average), and the highbrow, who, though not necessarily more gifted than the second class, has in an intellectual sense the defects of character or outlook sufficiently suggested by the expressions 'prig', 'Pharisee', and 'smug'. The existence of such a class, it is contended, is a matter of popular tradition, however small it may actually be; and the mere suspicion of the highbrow taint is enough to alienate from public favour a writer with the peculiar appeal of the author of *Midnight* and *Two in Pyjamas*. One witness, Mr. Snood, who controls, I understand, a number of railway bookstalls, told us that he is in the habit of selecting the books to be displayed upon his stalls by a scrupulous examination of the 'dust-covers' or paper wrappers. And he went so far as to say that he can tell at a glance from the picture on the dust-cover whether the book which it conceals is healthy and suitable for the general public, or highbrow and not so.

We have, therefore, these two opposing interpretations of the disputed word 'highbrow'—first, that it is laudatory and signifies intelligence; and second, that it is insulting and signifies intelligence plus arrogance (and, according to the witness Frankau, *plus* long hair as well; or, if we adopt the words of the witness Vines, *plus* long hair, anaemia, and moral flabbiness).

Now, if there is any substance in the former contention, we should expect to find among the members of the literary craft an eagerness, or at least a readiness, to be named by this name, for, though few writers lay claim to moral excellence, they have all, I take it, a certain confidence in their own intelligences. On the contrary, however, though every author who gave evidence was able without hesitation to name at least one among his contemporaries as a highbrow, I observed a curious reluctance, even in those writers who professedly cater for the educated orders of society, to be themselves considered highbrows. In fact, we may here again detect a parallel in the field of morals, for all men are proud of their purity, but few will accept without demur the title of a Puritan.

It may be well to remind you of certain passages in the evidence which bear upon this part of the case. Take, for example, the witness Frankau:

Counsel: What do you mean by a 'successful' novelist, Mr. Frankau?

Witness: I mean twenty thousand.

Counsel: Twenty thousand novelists, Mr. Frankau?

Witness: A sale of twenty thousand.

Counsel: In your opinion is it possible for a highbrow to be successful in that sense?

Witness (decidedly): Quite impossible. He may be

a successful highbrow, but a successful novelist—
never.

Counsel: Why not?

Witness: There is no red blood in him. The
people want red blood. Red corpuscles. He-men.
You never saw a highbrow sitting a horse.

Counsel: Is that a fair test of literary merit?

Witness: It is the test of a Man.

Counsel: You are a person of high intelligence,
Mr. Frankau?

Witness: One of the best.

Counsel: Then you are not a highbrow?

Witness: God forbid!

Counsel: Can you name any highbrows?

Witness: (rapidly): Mr. Shaw, Mr. Belloc, Mr.
Squire, Mr. Murry, Mr. Galsworthy, Mr. Drink-
water, Mr. Lawrence, Mr. Noyes, Mr. Huxley,
Mr. Joad, Mr.——

Counsel: That will do for the present. Is Mr.
H. G. Wells a highbrow?

Witness: No. I can see Wells sitting a horse.

Counsel: Can you not see Mr. Shaw sitting a
horse?

Witness (laughing): Absurd!

Counsel: In your opinion was William Shakespeare a highbrow?

Witness: No; he made good.

This witness, therefore, makes two distinctions: (*a*)
between the highbrow and the successful, and (*b*)
between the highbrow and the author who can without
merriment be imagined astride of a horse. How far
this is helpful will be a question for the jury. He was
followed by the witness Shaw, an extremely skittish old

gentleman, who seemed to have no idea of the procedure, purpose, or indeed the dignity, of a court of law.

Counsel: In your opinion, Mr. Shaw, what is the nature of a highbrow?

Witness: Everybody is a highbrow. The question is nonsense. Only a civilization which spends more on vaccination than it spends on the theatre, and is more excited by a battleship than by an elementary school, could have given birth to such a word. The filthiest peasant in Russia and the stupidest statesman in Whitehall are both highbrows, because each of them knows another man who is more foolish than himself, and that man knows it. The only person alive who is not a highbrow is the stupidest man in the world, and you will find him in Harley Street, Downing Street, or——

Counsel: Stop a moment, Mr. Shaw.

Witness: Why should I stop a moment? You brought me here, presumably, to advertise myself, and advertise myself I will. There is only one division of the human race—the civilized, who appreciate my plays, and the barbarians, who don't.

With these words the witness left the Court, and only his obvious inability to furnish useful information on any subject whatever prevented me from having him forcibly brought back.

We then had the assistance of a Mr. Haddock, who told us that he was a humorous writer, but produced no evidence to support the statement. He was asked: In your opinion is 'highbrow' an offensive word?

Witness: Undoubtedly.

Counsel: Have you been called a highbrow, Mr. Haddock?

Witness: Once.

Counsel: And you resented it?

Witness: Bitterly.

Counsel: Can you give us any idea of what you mean by a highbrow?

Witness: A highbrow is the kind of person who looks at a sausage and thinks of Picasso. She thinks life is nothing but a frame for art. You cannot talk to her about the weather. She has no soul for detective stories. She cannot swim. She reads in the bath. She——

Counsel: One moment, Mr. Haddock——

Witness: She quotes French writers at breakfast. She has just read a book which you have not. She says so. She cannot understand the attraction of chorus girls. She would rather her daughters were brainy than beautiful. She has no sense of humour.

Counsel: But, Mr. Haddock——?

Witness: Wit, sometimes, Sir Ethelred, but no humour. She knows too much. She talks too much. She takes no exercise. She does not care if it snows. She drinks too much coffee. She does not care for the Colonies. Her soul is in Florence. She cannot cook. She would be at a loss in a conversation with a bookmaker. She——

Counsel: But is the jury to understand, Mr. Haddock, that in your opinion the highbrow is necessarily of the feminine gender?

Witness: Of course. It is one of the special diseases of women.

Counsel: But are there no highbrows among men?

Witness: There are, of course. There are many feminine men, Sir Ethelred.

At this point I directed the witness to leave the box. It is fortunate, perhaps, that the plaintiff in this case is a woman, for this makes it unnecessary for us to find an answer to the difficult sex question which was raised by Mr. Haddock.

The various obsessions of these authors, young and old, modern or out of date, however interesting in a medical sense, are singularly sterile for the purposes of this Court. But from this and other passages with which I will not weary you we may safely conclude, I think, that the word highbrow, though devoid of any exact scientific significance, has even in literary circles the general force of an abusive term; and it may not inaptly be compared with a boomerang flung by a savage, of which the direction is often uncertain, but the intention behind the throw is seldom in doubt; moreover, in the end it is as likely as not to do as much injury to the thrower as to the target.

This opinion is fortified by the evidence which we have had from lay or non-literary quarters. The witness Vines, for example, a major, was crystal clear. The genus highbrow, in his view, has many species, but all are vile. Moreover (which is unusual), he has seen these monsters in the flesh. They are banded together, he assured us, in secret or semi-secret societies, which have no other purpose than the performance of indecent plays on the evening of the Lord's Day; they are distinguished in the males by long hair, Malacca canes, and curls, and in the females by tortoiseshell glasses, Spanish shawls, and shapeless Oriental garments; they have no contact with the life of the people, are incapable of cricket, unacquainted with golf, are wholly without patriotism or decent feeling, and openly praise the so-called artistic works of unknown French and

Italian painters whose moral character, it is to be feared, is too often as dubious as their own. This witness gave his evidence in a manly and straightforward way, and to my mind it is convincing. The picture which he drew of the observances of these creatures is so revolting that no lady or gentleman of right feeling could well submit to be named by their name without some effort to secure such protection as the law affords. And I am satisfied that on this point at least the plaintiff has made good her case.

The learned judge had not concluded his address when the Court adjourned.

NOTE—The jury found for the plaintiff, but awarded damages of $\frac{1}{4}d$. only. This case was heard in 1927, and it may be that a jury would find a different verdict to-day. Mr. Aldous Huxley, for example, is known to glory in the appellation 'highbrow', and states a reasoned case in favour of being one.

(9) REX v. HADDOCK

Is Magna Carta Law?

THE hearing of this appeal, which raised a novel point of law, was concluded in the High Court to-day.

Mr. Justice Lugg (delivering judgment): In this case the defendant, one Haddock, is appealing on a case stated from a conviction by a Court of Summary Jurisdiction under the Transport and Irritation of Motorists Act, 1920. The defendant was summoned before the Gerrard Street magistrates on a charge of causing an obstruction in a public thoroughfare by leaving his motor-car unattended for two hours and ten minutes on the night of December 31st, 1925.

The case for the defence was that the motor-car had not in fact caused an obstruction, and it was sworn in evidence that the road was not in fact a thoroughfare at all in the ordinary sense of the term, but a short blind alley terminating in a blank wall, against which wall the motor-car was left with the lights burning, according to law; and the police-officer who made the charge was unable to say that during the period in question he had seen any other vehicle, or indeed any other human being, enter the thoroughfare which the defendant's vehicle was obstructing. The magistrates, however, very properly, as I think, brushed aside this somewhat frivolous defence and ordered Mr. Haddock to pay a fine of two pounds and the costs of the prosecution, with additional costs of one pound for conducting his defence in rhymed couplets.

Mr. Haddock has now appealed on a point of law,

which I confess is novel to me, under the fourteenth chapter of Magna Carta. The fourteenth chapter of Magna Carta is directed against excessive fines, and provides that:

'*A freeman shall not be amerced* [*that is, fined*] *for a small fault, but after the manner of the fault, and for a great fault after the greatness thereof. . . .*'

And it has been powerfully argued by Sir Rowland Wash that since there is nothing in the Irritation of Motorists Act or in any other statute repealing or suspending this particular chapter, the Irritation of Motorists Act must be read in conjunction with that chapter; that the fine of two pounds is excessive and not 'after the manner of the fault', which is a small one, and that it ought to be reduced.

Now, in private, and even more in public, life there is no doubt that persons are accustomed to speak loosely of Magna Carta as the enduring foundation of what are known as the liberties of the subject, and to assume that that Charter is as potent a measure to-day as at the time of its origin. But, if we examine the Great Charter, as I did for the first time in bed this morning, we are led towards the conclusion that, if this is the foundation of the liberties of the subject, then these liberties are not so numerous as is commonly supposed; for out of the thirty-seven chapters of Magna Carta at least twenty-three have become obsolete, or have been abolished by later legislation, while among the fourteen which are not definitely extinguished there are at least as many for the benefit of the Crown as for the benefit of the subject, and the remainder have only a precarious existence, if any. In Chapter 8, for example, and Chapter 18, which begins:

'*If any that holdeth of us lay-fee do die, and our sheriff or bailiff do show our letters-patent of our summons for debt, which the dead man did owe to us, it shall be lawful to our sheriff or bailiff to attach and inroll all the goods and chattels of the dead. . . .*'

it is laid down very clearly that debts owing to Government Departments take precedence of all other debts; but it would be difficult to found upon these chapters any extravagant description of Magna Carta as the fountain of individual freedom. Again, the ordinary citizen will extract no particular satisfaction from the assurance of Chapter 23, that:

'*All weirs from henceforth shall be utterly pulled down in the Thames and Medway, and through all England, but only by the sea-coasts.*'

Macaulay said that the blood of the uttermost settler in the northern deserts of Australia flowed more freely in his veins as he lay beneath the Southern Cross and studied by its light the unforgettable conclusion of Chapter 29:

'*To no man will we sell, to no man deny, to no man delay, justice or right.*'

But we in this Court are well aware that these undertakings have very little relation to the harsh facts of experience. All that can be said is that much justice is sold at quite reasonable prices, and that there are still many citizens who can afford to buy the more expensive brands. If a man has no money at all he can get justice for nothing: but if he has any money he will have to buy justice, and even then may have to go without right (for the two expressions are not always synonymous). Indeed, there is something to be said for selling, denying, and delaying some sorts of justice. The thoughtful observer will distinguish between litigation which is a genuine pursuit of justice, such as a prosecution for embezzlement or murder, and the litigation which is a mere luxury, hobby, disease, profession, or species of blackmail, such as are many libel actions and nearly all suits for breach of promise of marriage. The proper business of the Courts could not be conducted if every citizen who conceived himself insulted could immediately bring an action for defamation without cost to himself. Fish-porters and charwomen pass through life exchanging frank opinions about each other's characters, but never, so far as is known, feel the itch to bring an action for defamation. They could not if they wished: so it might be said that justice is denied them. But they do not wish: and no great hardship is suffered. As for the delay, there can be no dignity without what appears to the thoughtless to be delay. But, beyond that, there will always be a certain delay in the Courts so long as the Crown and Parliament decline to equip them with an adequate supply of judges and shorthand-writers. At all events, the statutory pledges of the Crown set out above mean very little to-day.

Again, in Chapter 30, it is laid down that:

> '*All merchants shall have their safe and sure conduct to depart out of England, to come into England, to tarry in and go through England as well by land as by water, to buy and sell, without any manner of evil tolls (i.e. extortions) by the old and rightful customs.*'

But he would be a bold advocate who contended that this was an accurate statement of the law, or, at any rate, the practice of the land to-day. No man, merchant or no, can depart out of England, come into England, tarry in England, or buy or sell without all manner of tolls, extortions, and hindrances by the Crown, which is very right and proper but is not Magna Carta.

Again, it was argued before me that at least that portion of Chapter 29 still has effect which reads:

'Nor will we proceed against a freeman, nor condemn him, but by lawful judgment of his peers or by the law of the land.'

But it was proved in evidence that in fact this method of condemning the freeman is the exception rather than the rule, and it was suggested that this portion of Magna Carta must be interpreted in the light of recent statutes, so that it reads:

'Nor will we proceed against a freeman, nor condemn him, but by lawful judgment of his peers or by the law of the land, or Government Departments, or Marketing Boards, or Impregnable Monopolies, or Trade Unions, or fussy Societies, or Licensing Magistrates, or officious policemen, or foolish regulations by a Clerk in the Home Office made and provided.'

And in fact in the present case the defendant was not proceeded against by the law of the land, but by regulation; nor was he condemned by his peers, but by a policeman who expected half a crown, and by a magistrate antipathetical to the motorist.

Now, Lord Mildew said in *Klaxon* v. *Great Western Railway* (1871) 2 Q.B.: 'The whole is greater than the part', and this is undoubtedly the law. So if, on a detailed examination of a statute, as of a bicycle, it is found that nearly every part is obsolete or has been destroyed, there is a strong presumption that the whole has for practical purposes ceased to exist. And in this case I am satisfied that so little of Magna Carta is left that nothing of Magna Carta is left, and therefore that chapter on which the appellant relies must be taken to have perished with the others.

The appellant has done his country an ill service in raising this point, for but for his rash act generations of English orators might have continued in the fond belief that Magna Carta was still the abiding bulwark of our liberties, and for that act I shall order him to pay a further fine of five pounds.[1] But it is no part of my duty to conceal the truth, and I am compelled to declare with some reluctance that Magna Carta is no longer law.

The appeal was dismissed.

---

[1] He recalled how, in the chancel of Tewkesbury Abbey, he once came across a stone to one of the barons of Magna Carta on which were the words '*Magna Carta est lex. Deinde caveat rex*' ('Magna Carta is the law, and let the king look out'). (Mr. Stanley Baldwin in Westminster Hall, July 4, 1935)

IN RE MACALISTER—RUNCIMAN *v.* PRIM,
RUSSELL *v.* PRIM, SIMON *v.* PRIM, LLOYD
GEORGE *v.* PRIM, PHILLIPS *v.* PRIM,
WALTER *v.* PRIM, STEPHENSON *v.* PRIM,
KENSINGTON *v.* PRIM, STANLEY *v.* PRIM,
KENWORTHY *v.* PRIM, MACLEAN *v.* PRIM,
BENN *v.* PRIM, HADDOCK *v.* PRIM

WHICH IS THE LIBERAL PARTY?

THE hearing was continued to-day[1] of an action in the
Probate Division arising out of the will of the late Miss
Mary Macalister, of Peebles, who left a legacy of one
million pounds 'to the Liberal Party'.

Mr. Justice Tooth (*in his judgment*)*:* Lord Mildew said
in *Fox* v. *The Mayor of Swindon*, 'Dead men tell no tales';
and it were better sometimes if they made no wills. In
the painful case which is now approaching its conclusion, the defendant, Mr. Prim, is the executor of a Miss
Macalister, and the several plaintiffs are thirteen persons, each of whom asks for a declaration that he is or
represents 'the Liberal Party' and is therefore the proper
recipient of a legacy of one million pounds. The testatrix, an unmarried woman of great age, was active in
politics, it appears, at the time of Mr. Gladstone's first
Home Rule Bill, and after the death of Sir Henry
Campbell-Bannerman lived the life of a recluse in a
mountain cottage. It is therefore not surprising that,
out of touch with modern conditions, she did not describe
the object of her bounty in terms of greater precision,

[1] This was early in 1927.

6

but it is unfortunate; and testators would do well to provide some indication of the particular Liberal Party which they have in mind, such as a telephone number or a Christian name.

It has been proved in evidence before me that there are five main Liberal Parties, and the relations between them are such that no one of these parties will willingly share a taxi with any other, while each of them has at least one offshoot which is accustomed to foam at the mouth when the parent body is mentioned. This being so, the efforts which I made to bring about a compromise between the parties were naturally unsuccessful, and any proposal for a division of the spoils resulted only in a further division of the Israelites. Indeed, it says much for the sincerity with which these colleagues detest each other that, rather than share a common bank-balance, they would cheerfully continue with thirteen independent overdrafts.

I was asked by Mr. Carruthers, who represents the fourth Parliamentary Liberal Party from the left, to base my decision on considerations of principle, and to say that that Liberal Party is *the* Liberal Party which preserves intact and untarnished on the field the holy banner of the true Liberal faith. But when I followed this line of inquiry I was disappointed to find that each of the plaintiffs was the one authentic repository, torch, trumpet, and organ-voice of Liberal principle; and, though few of them were so far in agreement as to be able to construct a common catalogue of these principles, they all were agreed that the other parties had consistently ignored them. Further, though many of them were insistent that principles were everything and persons nothing, the discussion of principles in this Court has invariably led to the most distressing exchange of 'personalities', for those who attached the most importance to principles were loudest in their denunciation of persons.

Again, I have found it difficult to arrive at any clear definition of political principle. The evidence on the whole goes to show that a man who has made up his mind on a given subject twenty-five years ago and continues to hold his political opinions after he has been proved to be wrong is a man of principle; while he who from time to time adapts his opinions to the changing circumstances of life is an opportunist.[1] One of the plaintiffs, a Mr. Lloyd George, in his evidence bitterly described a man of principle as 'one who religiously keeps to the left in a one-way street', while the witness Simon, who followed, described the witness George as one who drives on both sides of the road everywhere. The witness George said that he had little use for principles which wore side-whiskers and crinolines, and the witness Simon replied that these, at any rate, were preferable to principles which were naked and unashamed. I asked the witness Asquith[2] if the widespread assertion that gentlemen prefer blondes was the kind of generalization which he had in mind when he spoke of principle. He replied that, if a man of principle had for thirty years of Parliamentary life endured without flinching the honest obloquy of the multitude and the insidious calumny of cabals in the conviction that men of gentle birth are, for the most part, more powerfully attracted by women of fair complexion and light colouring, then it would need more than the

[1] And may be bitterly described as one who 'trims his sails', 'tacks to and fro', or 'changes course', though these are not merely innocent but necessary incidents of skilful navigation. (See Strauss on *Sea-Terms and Sea-Ways*.)

[2] Afterwards Lord Oxford and Asquith.

occasional spectacle of a public-school man in the embraces of a dark woman to extract from him a recantation of his faith. He added that, though he envied a man (such as the witness George) who was able to change his mind every ten minutes, for his own part he was unable to achieve any material alteration of opinion in less than ten years. He also said that the chameleon was endowed with the power of changing its colour for the purpose of concealing itself from view, but there were some chameleons who changed so rapidly and often that the only effect was to attract the attention of their enemies.

These observations, however entertaining, have advanced me very little towards a just disposition of the dead woman's property. The plaintiff George and others invited me to ignore the question of principle and direct my mind to the realities of the situation. They said that the other plaintiffs consisted for the most part of collections of fossils of great age, embedded in the rocks of principle, and having none of the attributes of life except a miraculous power of polysyllabic speech; and they argued that it could not have been the intention of the testatrix to leave so much money to a number of talking fossils while there was any Liberal Party which could be said to be actually alive and possessed the substance of popular approval if not the trappings of principle. And this appeared to be a promising line of inquiry until it was sworn in evidence by the witness Runciman that the Liberal Parties referred to were supported entirely by Conservatives.

I have therefore turned my attention in another direction, which was suggested by one of the plaintiffs, a Mr. Haddock, of Hammersmith, who confesses frankly that the Liberal Party which he represents is a

party of one, but insists nevertheless that it is the only
Liberal Party. It has struck me as odd that no one of
the distinguished Liberals concerned in this case has
used the word Liberty, and had it not been for the
obscure Mr. Haddock the subject might never have
entered my head. But Mr. Haddock has argued with
some force that there must at one time have been some
shadowy connexion between the Liberal Party and
the idea of Liberty. What is more important, he has
called evidence to show that the testatrix, Miss Macalister, was herself an earnest lover and apostle of
liberty, resented strenuously all that large body of
human actions which may be roughly classed as
'interferences', and attached herself to the Liberal
Party on the assumption that it stood for freedom,
not only in Ireland, but in England. Now, in
cross-examination, the witnesses Asquith, George,
Grey, Simon, Runciman, and indeed nearly all the
plaintiffs, have confessed that they have been guilty
from time to time of legislation, or proposals for legislation, of which the main purpose was to make
people do something which they did not wish to do, or
prevent people from doing something which they did
wish to do. Few of them could point to an item in
their legislative programmes which had any other purpose, and, with the single exception of Mr. Haddock,
they have no legislation to suggest of which the purpose
is to allow people to do something which they cannot
do already. On the contrary, it appears, they are as
anxious as any other party in Parliament to make rules
and regulations for the eating, drinking, sleeping, and
breathing of the British citizen. On these grounds,
therefore, Mr. Haddock has argued that these plaintiffs
have not the idea of liberty in the forefront of their

political equipment, and do not therefore deserve the name of Liberal as the testatrix understood it; and in my judgment that argument is well founded. Mr. Haddock's own programme is simple: (a) to propose no legislation unless its purpose is to allow people to do what they like, and (b) to support no legislation whose purpose is to stop people from doing what they like.

Here and there, he admitted, good cause being shown, he is prepared to compromise; but that, *prima facie*, is his foundation and beginning. For example, the first measures which he intends to introduce are a Bill to repeal the Marriage Act of 1886, by which a wedding may not take place after three o'clock in the afternoon,[1] a Bill to allow the sale of Bodily Refreshments at any Hour at which Any One is Willing to Sell Them, a Bill for the Institution of the Death Penalty for Police Officers who Enter Respectable Clubs Disguised in Evening Dress, Bills to amend the laws relating to Divorce, Lotteries and Gaming, Sunday Toil and Entertainment, and other beneficent measures whose purpose is neither to improve, uplift, enrich, nor reform the British subject, but to increase, by however little, his liberty and contentment. I have decided therefore that Mr. Haddock alone of these plaintiffs has made good his claim to be that Liberal Party which the testatrix had in mind, and an order will be made accordingly. The plaintiffs George and Asquith to pay Mr. Haddock's costs.

NOTE—'Indignant persons sometimes reply to such comments that the blessings of the Shop Hours Act must not be sacrificed to the mere "convenience" of the consumer and pleasure-seeker. But this is to put

[1] This has been done (1934).

the cart before the horse. In purely pleasure-trades, such as entertainment and refreshment, the convenience of the customer should be considered first, and the convenience of those engaged in the trade second—provided always that they are assured decent conditions of life and labour. That is, if the public want to eat, drink, buy chocolate, or go to the cinema at certain times, that need must be the first consideration. If this means long, or late, hours there must, by law, be maximum hours of labour, two shifts, etc. (which would increase employment); and if it means Sunday work those working on Sunday must be secured their free day during the week. But no man is compelled to be a publican, tobacconist, waiter, or cinema-attendant, and if he chooses those professions, he must (subject always to the humane safeguards already mentioned) accept the conditions of his trade, as the author, journalist, and actor have to do. If it is said that in practice it is impossible to enforce such safeguards the answer is that it has never been really tried; and if the same zeal and energy were put into the attempt as are successfully devoted to shutting the pubs by clockwork, and prosecuting the small trader under the Shop Hours Act, it should not prove difficult. At all events, these are the correct principles.' (Albert Haddock Valerian Lecture on 'Home Affairs')

(11) SUET *v.* HADDOCK

Status of Authors

With his Lordship's address to the jury this case approached its conclusion to-day. He said:

Gentlemen, in this case the plaintiff is a manufacturer, and the defendant, Mr. Haddock, is, among other things, an author, which fact should alone dispose you in the plaintiff's favour; for, while the life-blood of our country is its trade and commerce, we do not, fortunately, depend upon our literature for anything that matters.

The defendant Haddock does not appear to have been uniformly successful in any of the regular departments of writing; at any rate he has not grown rich, which, as I ruled at an earlier stage of the case, is *prima facie* evidence of incapacity. Recently, however, he has devised and practised a style of writing which is quite new to this country, and, like other novelties, has proved most profitable. Calling himself a 'Commercial Critic', he writes each week, in a paper called *Veritas*, a reasoned article appraising the latest products of British or foreign manufacturers. He uses the style and manner of the fashionable literary or dramatic critic, and, as you have heard, he contends that the public need for expert and impartial guidance is at least as strong in the commercial as in the literary field.

Some of his earlier notices were extremely flattering, so much so that extracts from them were widely circulated by the manufacturers in their advertisements of the goods concerned, and there was soon shown an eagerness among the other manufacturers to have their products reviewed in Mr. Haddock's column.

Mr. Haddock, however, following in everything, as he says, the model of the literary or dramatic critic, who will not 'notice' a book or play if he has to pay for it, declined to write about any article of which he had not received a free sample for review. And such is the prestige of Mr. Haddock's column that a large number of important firms have complied with this curious condition. The Rolls-Royce Company sent him for review a copy of their 1928 model, and you will remember the patronizing manner in which he wrote about it:

'The work shows promise. This young Company, whose name is new to me, have evidently the root of the matter in them, and, if they will try again, may well produce something which is really worth while.'

The sometimes grudging character of his praise, however, did not prevent other firms, confident in the excellence of their wares, from pressing them upon him. Mr. Haddock has now a small fleet of motor-cars for review, he lives in a review house, his clothes and his furniture are free samples, he has more free pianos, gramophones, billiard-tables, and wireless-sets than he is able to enjoy with comfort, and the evidence is that he subsists almost entirely on goods and services provided free of charge by traders and manufacturers desirous of his impartial but favourable opinion.

Whether or not he has been impartial it will be for you to say. There is abundant evidence that he has not been afraid to cause annoyance, though against that you must weigh the suggestion of the plaintiff that many of the goods commended by Mr. Haddock have been accompanied by large sums of money. His habit of comparing unfavourably the British manufactures of to-day with the products of past centuries and foreign countries has given especial pain. Tradesmen have complained that, if only a commodity is Russian, American, or French, it is certain of his applause. His constant references to Chippendale and Sheraton have admittedly irritated the modern furniture trade. And his comment on a British piano, 'Not a bad piano, but how much better they do these things in Germany!' was not considered helpful.

His answer to these complaints is that in this, as in everything, he is only following the traditional lines of British criticism.[1] In the present case, as you know, he has gone too far for the satisfaction of the plaintiff. The plaintiff manufactures, among other things, a patent medicine called 'Sinko', which is widely advertised as having the power to remove or remedy 'That Sinking Feeling'. Now what the defendant wrote about 'Sinko' was brief and blunt:

> '"*Sinko*" *does* not *remove That Sinking Feeling, for I have tried it.*'

The plaintiff says that these words are defamatory, and claims damages. The defendant says that the words are true, or in the alternative that they are in the nature of fair comment upon a matter of public interest.

You have heard the evidence. Several witnesses have sworn that, like the defendant, they took a dose of 'Sinko', and that, so far from being relieved, their condition was worse than before.

Witnesses for the plaintiff, on the other hand,

[1] See *The Theatre Vivant* and *One Night in Moscow*, by Mr. Perivale Commode.

martyrs in every case to the discomforts of sinking, have sworn that no sooner was the cork removed from the bottle than they experienced a sensation of buoyancy, well-being, and general beatitude. The expert medical testimony for the plaintiff is that 'Sinko' is made of *hydrogenalin*, a new and secret chemical compound. The expert medical testimony for the defence is that 'Sinko' is made from wood-shavings, lubricating oil, and bits of straw. All this evidence you will carefully sift, and I shall put to you the following questions:

(1) Was the defendant sinking?
(2) Did 'Sinko' relieve his 'sinking feeling'?
(3) If not, would it have relieved the sinking of a reasonable man?
(4) Damages?

Now, if the defendant has *not* established to your satisfaction that the words complained of are true in substance and in fact—and, in order to muddle you, I should explain that they may be true in fact but not in substance, as they may be correct in substance but erroneous in fact—then there remains the defence of fair comment. The defendant says that, as a critic, he has the right to make a critical statement, which, though not necessarily supported by the general experience, is a fair expression of his own individual opinion, such as any reasonable man with the same experience might make. He has quoted, I think irrelevantly, certain adverse criticisms on his own work, upon which, without success, he has taken legal proceedings. In *Haddock* v. *Thwaites* the defendant said of Mr. Haddock's book, *Daffodils*, 'Tosh! . . . drivel . . . vulgar and insincere . . .' and, although several other papers had printed more favourable opinions, it was held that these expressions were fair comment on a matter of public interest. And the defendant now claims the same freedom of comment upon other men's wares as is permitted to the critic of his own.

This is a large and, I think, an untenable claim. It assumes that literature is as important as trade, and that the author has the same rights as the business man. But this has never been the law. It must be clearly understood that an author, as such, has no rights. At Common Law he ranked with women and *cattle demenant*, and any man, in the absence of malice, violence, or fraud, is entitled to take away his livelihood by hostile utterances however ill founded. But it is quite another thing for an author to take away the livelihood of an honest trader by ill-considered judgments on the quality of his goods, for this is to assail the whole fabric of our Commonwealth. I shall therefore direct you that there is no evidence on which you may find that the defendant's words were in the nature of fair comment, and unless he has satisfied you that he was in fact sinking, that the prescribed dose of 'Sinko' did not relieve his sinking, and, further, that it would not have relieved the sinking of a reasonably sinking man, understanding by that a reasonable man sinking within the recognized limits of everyday experience, you will find for the plaintiff; and in that case you will award him damages of, I suggest, about ten thousand pounds.

The jury retired.

(12) CHICKEN *v.* HAM

The Lawyers' Dream

The House of Lords to-day delivered judgment in the notorious Gramophone Libel case.

The Lord Chancellor: My Lords, this case may well go down to history as 'The Lawyers' Dream'. From first to last it has occupied the attention of the Courts for more than four years. Two juries have disagreed about it and one was imprisoned; there have been two trials of the action in the King's Bench and two appeals to the Court of Appeal, while for the past fourteen days it has monopolized the attention of your Lordships' House. Twenty-five King's Counsel have been concerned in the case, each accompanied by a member of the Junior Bar, which juniors have received by custom a remuneration equal to two-thirds of their leaders' fees. These fees have with few exceptions been a thousand guineas marked on each brief, plus a daily payment by way of stimulus of one hundred guineas or more; and there are present at the moment no fewer than eight learned counsel who will receive between them a sum of about six hundred and fifty pounds for sitting quietly in their places to-day and listening as attentively as they are able to your Lordships' learned judgments. These judgments are five in number, and each of these, therefore, lasting an hour or less, will cost somebody about one hundred and fifty pounds, a figure for which it is possible to engage the most expensive variety artist for a week.

It is not therefore astonishing that the costs of this

case are estimated already at a figure between two and
three hundred thousand pounds. But it would be very
wrong to suppose that this sum has not been expended
for the benefit of the community. The point which
your Lordships are required to decide has never been
decided before, and, if your Lordships are able to
decide it now, it need never be decided again, nor can
it be decided otherwise. It is never likely to arise
again, but that is another matter. Your Lordships'
House is almost the only authority in this mortal world
whose word on any subject is the last word for ever.
Your pronouncements have the unalterable force of a
law of nature; and if we are able by taking pains to
add a single grain of certitude to the shifting sands
of human affairs is there any one who is prepared
pedantically to count the cost? 'It is something,' as
Lord Mildew said in *Rex* v. *Badger*, 'to dot an "i" in
perpetuity.'

This is an appeal by one Ham against a decision of
the Court of Appeal sitting *in ludo*, reversing a judgment
by the Divisional Court (Adder, J., and Mudd, J.),
reversing a decision by Judge Brewer in the Shepherd's
Bush County Court. The facts are these. The man
Ham made a gramophone record, which consisted of
a number of uncomplimentary statements, composed
and uttered by himself, concerning the private life
and personal appearance of Mr. Ebenezer Chicken, the
head and father of the well-known multiple stores.
This record he sent as a Christmas present to Mr.
Chicken, who, at a gathering of his friends and relations, put the record on his own gramophone, when
there issued from the instrument, to the astonishment, horror, and satisfaction of the company, a
series of defamatory and abusive expressions directed

unmistakably against the head of the household. Mr.
Chicken, therefore, brought a suit for defamation
against Mr. Ham.

Now, my Lords, you are aware that by the mysteri-
ous provisions of the English law a defamatory statement may be either a slander or a libel, a slander being,
shortly, a defamation by word of mouth, and a libel
by the written or printed word; and the legal consequences are in the two cases very different. A layman,
with the narrow outlook of a layman on these affairs,
might rashly suppose that it is equally injurious to say
at a public meeting, 'Mr. Chicken is a toad', and to
write upon a postcard, 'Mr. Chicken is a toad'. But
the unselfish labours of generations of British jurists
have discovered between the two some profound and
curious distinctions. For example, in order to succeed
in an action for slander the injured party must prove
that he has suffered some actual and special damage,
whereas the victim of a written defamation need not;
so that we have this curious result, that in practice it is
safer to insult a man at a public meeting than to insult
him on a postcard, and that which is written in the
corner of a letter is in law more deadly than that which
is shouted from the house-tops. My Lords, it is not for
us to boggle at the wisdom of our ancestors, and this is
only one of a great body of juridical refinements handed
down to us by them, without which few of our profession would be able to keep body and soul together.
Jus varium, judex opulentus.

Now, in this case it was held by the County Court
judge that Mr. Ham's utterance through the gramophone was a verbal slander, and that therefore the
plaintiff must prove that he had suffered some special
and material damage. This he was unable to do, for,

on the contrary, his friends have visited him with even greater persistency, and as a result of the publicity which the case received the business of Chicken's stores was actually augmented. Mr. Chicken, therefore, appealed to the Divisional Court, which held that the utterance complained of was libel and not slander. The Court of Appeal by a majority reversed this decision and held that it was slander and not libel; but, for reasons which I am wholly unable to follow, a new trial was ordered; and Mr. Chicken added a new wing to his stores.

With the proceedings of the next few years we need not concern ourselves in detail; they culminated in a second hearing by the Court of Appeal, which held on this occasion that Mr. Ham's action was libel and not slander. Mr. Ham appealed. Mr. Chicken added another wing to his stores, and a large new issue of capital was made.

Now, my Lords, we are called upon to decide whether the words complained of, which are without doubt defamatory, and have so been found, are in the nature of a libel or a slander. I have myself no doubt as to the answer. The law is that the spoken word, if defamatory, is a slander, and I do not follow the Master of the Rolls when he says that by 'spoken' we are to understand 'spoken' in the sense in which the word was understood at the date when 'spoken' became the essential element in the definition of slander, that is, spoken by the vocal organs of the human frame without the intervention or assistance of a machine.[1] It is clear that these words were spoken by Mr. Ham through this instrument, and the absurdity of any suggestion that they were not is apparent if we accept the only

[1] But see page 154

other alternative and say they were *written* through the gramophone. The law is clear. The appeal must be allowed.

Lord Lick: I do not agree. This is a libel and not a slander. The law is clear. *Potts* v. *The Metropolitan Water Board* shows that the distinction in law is not between the spoken and the written insult, but between that which is uttered once, and once only, and that which is uttered in such a form that it is capable of indefinite repetition or publication at the will of others than the original utterer. A statue is not a slander, neither is it written (*Fish* v. *Mulligan*). There is nothing absurd in speaking of writing on a gramophone. Indeed, the first half of the word is derived from a Greek word meaning 'I write'. In *Silvertop* v. *The Stepney Guardians* a man trained a parrot to say three times after meals, 'Councillor Wart has not washed to-day'. It was held that this was a libel. The appeal must be dismissed.

Lord Arrowroot: I do not agree. The law is clear. The appeal must be allowed.

Lord Sheep: I do not agree. In my judgment this case has been from the first a brilliant and elaborate advertising manœuvre for the advancement of Mr. Chicken's stores, which this year, I notice, declared a dividend of fifty-six per cent. It is clear to me that the man Ham is in this case the tool and servant of the man Chicken; that the defamatory utterances of Ham were made at Chicken's own instigation and in a manner ingeniously calculated to provoke prolonged discussion and disagreement among His Majesty's judges; that, this object having been attained, to the great notoriety and advantage of Mr. Chicken's business, Mr. Chicken in any event will cheerfully pay the costs of the entire proceedings; and that your Lordships' House has for the first time been employed as an advertising agent for a multiple store. But as to the point ostensibly at issue I concur with my learned brother Lord Lick. The law is clear. This is a libel and the appeal must be dismissed.

Lord Goat: The law is clear——

(At this point, however, his Lordship suffered a heart-attack, perished, and was removed.)

The Lord Chancellor: Our learned brother's unexpected demise is particularly unfortunate at the present time, two of your Lordships having held for the appellant and two for the respondent. Opinion therefore is equally divided, this House is unable to say whether the words complained of are a libel or a slander, and the judgment of the Court of Appeal must stand.

The House then rose.

NOTE—But *quaere*—in view of the fact that the two decisions of the Court of Appeal are contradictory it is doubtful whether it can be taken that the point is definitely settled.

(13) REX *v.* THE COMMISSIONER OF METRO-POLITAN POLICE, CHIEF INSPECTOR CHARLES, INSPECTOR SMART, SER-GEANT OLIPHANT, AND CONSTABLE BOOT

Exploits of Boot

AT the Old Bailey the hearing of this case approached its conclusion to-day when Mr. Justice Swallow began his address to the jury. He said:

Gentlemen of the jury, the facts of this distressing and important case have already been put before you some four or five times, twice by prosecuting counsel, twice by counsel for the defence, and once at least by each of the various witnesses who have been heard; but so low is my opinion of your understanding that I think it necessary, in the simplest language, to tell you the facts again.

The prisoners are officers in the London Police Force, and, at the instigation of a public-minded citizen, Mr. Albert Haddock, they are accused of conspiring to do certain unlawful acts. Now, it is my duty to inform you that, although a given offence by a single individual may be negligible, a conspiracy by a number of persons to commit that offence in concert may be a much more serious affair; and in view of the stupidity which I see carved upon your faces I will explain that by an illustration which should be intelligible to the most bovine member of the jury, and may even pene-trate to the slumbering consciousness of the fourth gentleman from the left in the back row. For any

77

member of a quartet to sing out of tune is undesirable; but if by arrangement they *all* sing out of tune, the act is many more than four times more deplorable.

Some of the offences alleged in this case appear trifling in themselves. By the wise ordinances of our land it is unlawful to buy or sell chocolates after the hour of half-past nine o'clock in the evening or to buy cigarettes, cigars, or matches after the hour of eight. It is not for the subject to question or comment on these provisions. It is about the hour of half-past nine that the thought of chocolate first enters the minds of large numbers of the citizens, and it is right and proper that at that precise hour the supply of chocolate should be sternly cut off by a maternal Government. As for the cigarettes, these regulations are in line with the ancient tradition of this island, which has always been to discourage and irritate the foreign visitor by every form of inconvenience and restriction, and so dispose him to return to his own country.

Now, the evidence for the prosecution is that at eight-five p.m. on April 14th the defendant Boot, being in plain clothes, entered the bar of the Folliseum Theatre and asked the barmaid for a packet of Anodyne cigarettes. Miss Perceval, as she has told you, replied that the magic hour was past; but Boot pleaded with her, and, no one else being present except the vigilant Haddock, who happened, it appears, to be preparing his mind for the performance, Miss Perceval at last relented. As you have seen, Boot has a pleasant countenance and manly figure, and Miss Perceval liked the look of him. Her evidence is that he put her in mind of a Mr. Thomas Mix, a gentleman who has not been called in evidence and is not known to the police. At nine-thirty-five the defendant Boot again entered the bar and asked for a box of chocolates. Miss Perce-val, who had just refused a number of similar requests, was moved by the spectacle of this strong man pleading for sweetmeats, and as a personal favour made him a surreptitious sale at the end of the interval, when every one had left the bar except, as it happened, Mr. Haddock. That gentleman was refreshing his mind for the second act, and had been intensely irritated by Miss Perceval's refusal to sell him chocolates, of which, as he told you, he is passionately fond.

Boot then took Miss Perceval's name and address and informed her that a charge would be made. The management was prosecuted and fined, and the tender-hearted Miss Perceval was dismissed from their employ-ment. There is no doubt upon the evidence that Boot deliberately broke or procured a breach of the law, and he has told you that what he did he did by the general or specific instructions of his co-defendants.

Now, this is only one of a number of similar episodes. In recent years, it appears, there has entered for the first time, systematically and unashamed, into the administration of British justice the repellent figure of the *agent provocateur*, which is a French expression signifying an official spy who causes an offence to secure a conviction; and I use that phrase partly to impress upon you your own profound ignorance and partly because there is no other. There is no other phrase, and for a very good reason; the idea is so repugnant to British notions of fair play and decency that it has never found expression in our language. I have seen no comment, judicial or other, upon the importation of this loathsome practice; it has stolen in, unblessed and almost unobserved, and has taken a firm place in the national life. It is not employed for the suppression of the major crimes, where official dishonour might be forgiven in a noble cause; no constable causes himself to be murdered or robbed for the protection of the public by the apprehension of a dangerous person. But it is the constant support of small prosecutions for small offences wisely invented by righteous people for the hindrance or prevention of public enjoyment.

The defendant Boot has been prominent in many of these. In one of his exploits, as you have heard, a humble tobacconist had a cigarette-machine in his shop; Boot invited him to place a sixpence in the slot for him, and, on the man obligingly doing so, he was gloriously prosecuted for an offence against the Shop Acts. Boot, it is said, has more automatic-machine prosecutions to his credit and has deprived more barmaids of their livelihood than any officer in the Force. Boot is always in disguise. With the defendants Charles and Smart, as you have heard, he lurks in theatres and in public-houses, in sweet-shops and night-clubs, in borrowed overalls or chartered evening dress as the occasion demands; he endears himself to women, is affable to men, and at last, by a shameless exploitation of his personality, demands and is granted, at the public expense, tobacco, chocolates, matches, beer, snuff, champagne, and barley-sugar, or whatever other commodity it may be unlawful at that time and place to purchase. The ordinary citizen, however rich, contents himself with an occasional lapse, but Boot is constantly breaking the law. And this is the more shocking from the honest aspect of the man. If the evidence is to be believed, seldom in the history of wrongdoing can a countenance so open and engaging have been associated with so much duplicity.

It is urged for the defence that these officers have broken the law for the law's good; but this is as much as to say that the police may break a man's head if he complains of headache. This, however, is a matter to be considered in mitigation of sentence, if any; though I may say at once that I shall not consider it. It cannot be too clearly understood that the police are not entitled to break the law, and so long as I am on this Bench I shall do what I can to discourage the hateful practices of the *agent provocateur*. If the public cannot be prevented from enjoying themselves in an honest and straightforward manner they had better be allowed to enjoy themselves. And if you find, as you had better find, that these officers, high and low, have been guilty of conspiring together to do things which the good Mr. Haddock is not allowed to do, then you will return a verdict of 'Guilty'. If, on the other hand, you find that, on the weight of the evidence, adding one thing to another and taking this away from that, looking upwards and downwards and sideways and all round, they have not been guilty of the acts alleged, then you will return a verdict of 'Not Guilty'; and I shall ignore your verdict. Now, gentlemen, I have done my duty. Do yours.

The jury retired.

NOTE—See the judgment of the Lord Chief Justice in *Rex* v. *Bitter* for an authoritative discussion of the principles which should limit the use of the *agent provocateur* (page 393).

And see *Fairway, K.,* v. *Fairway, T. M., and Baxter* (*King's Proctor showing cause*) (1929). In this case the successful petitioner for a decree *nisi* had obstinately retained her virtue for five of the six statutory months, which, for greater security, she passed in a monastical institution. Constable Boot, however, disguised as a St. Bernard dog, obtained admission to the nunnery and ultimately to her affections.

(14) THE BISHOP OF BOWL, EARL RUBBLE, EVADNE LADY SMAIL, JOHN LICK-SPITTLE, GENERAL GLUE, AND OTHERS *v.* HADDOCK

A Cross Action

(Before Mr. Justice Snubb)

THIS action, which raises a novel point in the law of libel, drew a large house yesterday.

Sir Antony Dewlap, K.C. (in opening the case for the plaintiffs): This action for defamation is brought by a number of distinguished citizens suing in conjunction in respect of an ingenious series of malicious libels composed, written, and published by the defendant, Mr. Albert Haddock, an author and journalist of loathsome antecedents and inconsiderable income. The action is unusual, milord, not by reason of the expressions complained of, which are no more than the ordinary envious outpourings of an unsuccessful man, but by reason of the channel which the defendant has selected for his abuse. Milord, that channel is no other than the innocent and familiar 'Crossword'——

Mr. Justice Snubb: What is that?

Sir Antony Dewlap: Forgive me, milord. Milord, with great respect, milord, a crossword puzzle is a form of puzzle, milord, in which a number of numbered squares in a chequered arrangement of—er—squares, milord, have to be filled in with letters, milord, these letters forming words, milord, which words are read both horizontally and vertically, milord—that is, both across

82

and down, if your Lordship follows me—and which words may be deduced from certain descriptions or clues which are provided with the puzzle, milord, these descriptions having numbers, milord, and these numbers referring to the squares having the corresponding numbers, milord, which are to be filled in with the correct letters and words according to the descriptions which have the corresponding numbers, milord, whether horizontally or vertically, as the case may be. Does your Lordship follow me?

Mr. Justice Snubb: No.

Sir Antony Dewlap: Milord, I have here an easy example which will perhaps assist your Lordship; and, if I may amplify that in this way, milord—milord, if I were to ask you to give me the name of a learned and sagacious High Court judge in five letters, beginning with 'S', I think your Lordship would readily arrive at a solution? (*Laughter*)

Mr. Justice Snubb (*benevolently*): I should give you the name of my learned brother Swift. (*Laughter*)

Sir Antony: Your Lordship is too modest. (*Laughter*) That, however, milord, is the principle of these puzzles. Now as a rule, milord, the descriptions or clues provided are brief and the correct solutions are the names of mythical animals and Biblical characters, prepositions, foreign towns, classical writers, obscure musical instruments, vegetables, little-known adjectives, and so forth. In the puzzle, however, or series of puzzles, which the defendant has written and published in *The Crossword Times*, most of the clues are wordy and long, and all of them refer or are alleged to refer, in terms which whether directly or by implication are grossly offensive, to living persons, and as a rule to living persons of position and distinction. The first puzzle, milord, to take a few examples, included the following descriptions:

Across

2. Bibulous bishop.
4. Titled lady, banting at Nice.
5. Peer. Powders his face.
6. The favourite indulgence of No. 2 (above).
7. No. 4's next husband—if he's not careful.

Down

4. Political. A time-server. Or so they say.
5. An English humorist. Or so he says.
7. That clever young dramatic critic with the toupee.

Now, at first sight, milord (and this, I believe, is the case for the defence), these 'descriptions', though deplorable in tone, are innocent enough so far as any individual is concerned. No. 2 (across) for example, says simply, 'Bibulous bishop'; no particular bishop is indicated, and, *prima facie*, milord, we might take it to refer to any of the bishops. In the same way, milord, with regard to No. 4 (across), it might be said that there were at any moment any number of titled ladies staying on the south coast of France for the benefit of their health. And, to turn to the 'Down' clues, there are hundreds of public men and women of whom a malicious person might with equal plausibility employ the words 'Political. A time-server. Or so they say.'

But, milord, we have to consider this puzzle as a *whole*; we have to consider each of the words to which the clues direct us not in isolation but in relation to some other word, whether vertical or horizontal; and we have to remember that each of these words is exactly limited in length, and must have neither more nor fewer letters than there are squares provided for it. And, if your Lordship has followed me so far, you will see that these limitations divest the clues of much of their innocent vagueness and impersonality.

Milord, to take a distasteful example, there are very few bishops in four letters. Milord, in fact there are only three, if we except, as surely in this connexion we must except, the venerable Bishop of Bung. There are the aged Bishop of Bowl, the Bishop of Moat, and Bishop Loon of Huddersfield. Here again the suggestion, nay, the accusation, is so preposterous and vile in every case that, as the defence maintains, no reasonable man will immediately attach it to any one of the three. Say to me, milord, 'A bibulous bishop in four letters', and I do not think particularly of the Bishop of Moat, the aged Bishop of Bowl, or even of Bishop Loon. Each of these names will enter my mind, only of course to be indignantly expelled. So much is true.

But take the thing a stage farther, milord. Take the 'Down' clues. Take No. 7. The clever young dramatic critic, milord, is in eleven letters, and it is unhappily a fact, milord, that we have only one well-known and comparatively youthful dramatic critic in eleven letters —namely, milord, Mr. Lickspittle.

Now take another and a most disquieting step. The first letter of the dramatic critic, milord, must, if the puzzle be correctly conceived, be the last letter of the intemperate divine. And if, as seems clear, Mr. Lickspittle is the only solution to No. 7 (down) we are driven reluctantly to the hypothesis that by No. 2 (across) may be intended the aged Bishop of Bowl. And when we find that No. 5 (down)—'An English humorist. Or so he says'—is in seven letters, and, if in seven letters, must almost certainly begin with 'W', for the well-known Mr. Wagwise, we are inclined to invest that hypothesis with the certainty of a scientific proof. After this, the fact that a plausible solution for No. 6 (across) is

P O R T

is of small consequence, for the majority of bishops take port wine for their health, though it is true that the aged Bishop of Bowl is, perhaps, more delicate than the others. More serious is the fact that the name of Evadne Lady S M A I L may be fitted with sinister exactitude into the space provided for No. 4 (across), and that 'No. 4's next husband—if he is not careful', in three letters, has suggested to many competitors the name of Major B A T.

But, milord, I will not weary you with the detailed working out of the puzzle. It is enough to say that a number of citizens *have* assiduously worked it out on these lines, and have been forced, however reluctantly, to fill these scandalous squares with such honoured names as Bowl, Smail, Lickspittle, Lord Tiptree, Sir Thomas Tick, the Right Honourable Mr. James Rusk, Father Mahony, and many others.

Nor was the defendant content, milord, with defaming these ladies and gentlemen in a single puzzle. Nearly all have appeared, milord, in each of the six puzzles of the series, though with different but equally objectionable 'clues' attached to them. The Bishop of Bowl, milord, invariably appears—as 'a prosy humbug', as 'an intolerably hearty and overpaid clergyman', 'the world's worst golfer', 'canting Tommy', 'the sniffing parson', and other vile expressions of the kind. Indeed, milord, I am informed that to those who followed the whole series the name of Bowl quickly became a regular starting-point or foundation from which they would proceed to build up the whole structure. In the last two puzzles, milord, this unhappy victim of the defendant's spite had not even the satisfaction of a principal (and horizontal) place in the puzzle, but was degraded to the position of a word in four letters, reading downward, an indignity intolerable, milord, to a man of his years and sensibility.

It will be suggested by the defence, milord—impudently suggested, milord—that in all this the various plaintiffs have nothing to complain of but a coincidence or series of coincidences; that the defendant has made no use of their names directly or indirectly; that all he has done is to construct a series of puzzles entirely concerned with imaginary or historical figures; and, as evidence of his innocent intentions, he will produce what purport to be the correct solutions of his puzzles.

These, milord, consist of colourless or invented names, such as Otho, Freg, Xerxes, Smith, Thompson, Brown, and so forth, and need not, I submit, milord, be taken very seriously. In any case, milord, it is well settled that the intention in this class of case is immaterial, that he who publishes a defamatory statement concerning another person is liable, milord, though he had no intention of referring to that other and no knowledge that his statement would be supposed to refer to that other. To this, however, the defendant will reply that he has not in fact published any statement whatever; that the words he has written, '2. Bibulous bishop', are not, by him at least, connected with the aged Bishop of Bowl, and that if any persons have chosen to write down in a space so labelled the word 'Bowl' those persons and not he are the publishers of the libel, if any, and it is against them that this action should have been brought.

This will show you, milord, the kind of man we have to deal with. I will now call, milord, the unfortunate Bishop of Bowl.

The Judge: We will now have lunch.

NOTE—At the next hearing it was announced by Sir Antony that a settlement had been reached, the plaintiffs accepting the defendant's explanation of his conduct and the defendant undertaking not to do it again. The legal question, then, remains in doubt, and any enterprising paper may be sure of a circulation until it is decided. EDITOR

(15) ENGHEIM, MUCKOVITCH, KETTEL-BURG, WEINBAUM, AND OSKI v. THE KING

Free Speech—Why?

This was a petition to the Crown by certain British subjects, made under the Bill of Rights, and referred by the Crown to the Privy Council.

The Lord Chancellor: This is a petition to the Crown by certain members of a political party who were convicted of holding a public meeting in Trafalgar Square contrary to the orders of the Home Secretary and police. The petitioners are keenly interested in the 'Hands Off Russia' movement, and, although there is no evidence that any person in this country proposes to lay hands on Russia, they have been in the habit for some weeks past of gathering at Lord Nelson's monument on Sunday afternoons and imploring the few citizens present to keep their hands off that country. At these meetings banners are held aloft which invite compassion for persons in a state of bondage, and songs are sung expressive of a determination to improve the material condition of the human race. These at first sight unobjectionable aims have unfortunately inflamed the passions of another body of citizens, who interpret them as an unwarrantable interference with the affairs of their own country, and have therefore banded themselves into a rival movement whose battle-cry is 'Hands Off England'. This party, though their banners and their songs are different, express the same general ideals as the petitioners, namely, the maintenance of

liberty and the material advancement of the poor and
needy. Their principal song has a refrain to the effect
that their countrymen will never consent to a condition
of slavery; while the songs of the petitioners assert that
many of their countrymen are in that condition
already, and resent it. So that at first sight it might
be thought that these two bodies, having so much in
common, might appropriately and peacefully meet
together under the effigy of that hero who did so much
to ward off from these shores the hateful spectres of
tyranny and oppression. When, however, it was
announced that the two movements did in fact propose
to hold meetings at the same time and place, the police
were so apprehensive of a disturbance of the peace that
both gatherings were by order prohibited. For it
appears that the spectacle of the national flag of these
islands is infuriating to the petitioners, while the simple
scarlet banner of the petitioners is equally a cause of
offence to the other movement, though that same
colour is the distinctive ornament of many institutions
which they revere, such as His Majesty's Post Office
and His Majesty's Army.

These, however, are political matters which fortunately it is not necessary for this Court to attempt to
understand, though we may observe that an age in
which it is possible to fly across the Atlantic in thirty
hours might be expected to hit upon some more
scientific method of deciding by what persons a given
country shall be governed. The 'Hands Off England'
movement obeyed the order of the Home Secretary,
but the petitioners did not; their meeting was begun,
and was dispersed by the police. They were prosecuted and fined, and they now ask for a gracious
declaration from the Throne that these proceedings

were in violation of the liberties of the subject as secured by the Bill of Rights, and in particular of the rights, or alleged rights, of Public Meeting and Free Speech.

Now, I have had occasion to refer before to the curious delusion that the British subject has a number of rights and liberties which entitle him to behave as he likes so long as he does no specific injury or harm. There are few, if any, such rights, and in a public street there are none; for there is no conduct in a public thoroughfare which cannot easily be brought into some unlawful category, however vague. If the subject remains motionless he is loitering or causing an obstruction; if he moves rapidly he is doing something which is likely to cause a crowd or a breach of the peace; if his glance is affectionate he is annoying, if it is hard he may be threatening, and in both cases he is insulting; if he keeps himself to himself he is a suspicious character, and if he goes about with two others or more he may be part of (a) a conspiracy or (b) an obstruction or (c) an unlawful assembly; if he begs without singing he is a vagrant, and if he sings without begging he is a nuisance. But nothing is more obnoxious to the law of the street than a crowd, for whatever purpose collected, which is shown by the fact that a crowd in law consists of three persons or more; and if those three persons or more have an unlawful purpose, such as the discussion of untrue and defamatory gossip, they are an unlawful assembly; while if their proceedings are calculated to arouse fears or jealousies among the subjects of the realm they are a riot. It will easily be seen, therefore, that a political meeting in a public place must almost always be illegal, and there is certainly no right of public meeting

8

such as is postulated by the petitioners. It was held so long ago as 1887 by Mr. Justice Charles that the only right of the subject in a public street is to pass at an even pace from one end of it to another, breathing unobtrusively through the nose and attracting no attention.

There are, in fact, few things, and those rapidly diminishing, which it is lawful to do in a public place, or anywhere else. But if he is not allowed to do what he likes, how much less likely is it that the subject will be permitted to say what he likes! For it is generally agreed that speech is by many degrees inferior to action, and therefore, we should suppose, must be more rigidly discouraged. Our language is full of sayings to that effect. 'Speech is silver', we say, and 'Silence is golden'; 'Deeds—not words'; 'Least said—soonest mended'; 'Keep well thy tongue and keep thy friend' (Chaucer); 'For words divide and rend,' said Swinburne, 'but silence is most noble till the end'; ' "Say well" is good, but "Do well" is better'; and so on. The strong, silent man is the admiration of us all, and not because of his strength but because of his silence. The talker is universally despised, and even in Parliament, which was designed for talking, those men are commonly the most respected who talk the least. There never can have been a nation which had so wholesome a contempt for the arts of speech; and it is curious to find so deeply rooted in the same nation this theoretical ideal of free and unfettered utterance, coupled with a vague belief that this ideal is somewhere embodied in the laws of our country.

No charge was made in this case of seditious, blasphemous, or defamatory language, and in the absence of those the petitioners claim some divine inherent

right to pour forth unchecked in speech the swollen
contents of their minds. A Briton, they would say, is
entitled to speak as freely as he breathes. I can find no
authority or precedent for this opinion. There is no
reference to Free Speech in Magna Carta or the Bill of
Rights. Our ancestors knew better. As a juridical
notion it has no more existence than Free Love, and,
in my opinion, it is as undesirable. The less the subject loves the better; and the less everybody says the
better. Nothing is more difficult to do than to make
a verbal observation which will give no offence and
bring about more good than harm; and many great
men die in old age without ever having done it. The
strange thing is that those who demand the freest
exercise of this difficult art are those who have the
smallest experience and qualifications for it. It may
well be argued that if all public men could be persuaded to remain silent for six months the nation would
enter upon an era of prosperity such as it would be
difficult even for their subsequent utterances to damage.
Every public speaker is a public peril, no matter what
his opinions. And so far from believing in an indis-
criminate liberty of expression, I think myself that
public speech should be classed among those dangerous
instruments, such as motor-cars and fire-arms, which
no man may employ without a special licence from
the State. These licences would be renewable at
six-monthly periods, and would be endorsed with the
particulars of indiscretions or excesses; while 'speaking
to the public danger' would in time be regarded with
as much disgust as inconsiderate or reckless driving.

What is in my mind is well illustrated by this case;
for the evidence is that the one manifest result of the
'Hands Off Russia' movement has been to implant

in many minds a new and unreasoning antipathy to Russia; while the cry of 'Hands Off England' has aroused in others a strong desire to do some injury to their native land. We find therefore that there is no right of Free Speech recognized by the Constitution; and a good thing too.

NOTE—See also *Rex* v. *Cochran* (page 243), where the supposed Freedom of the Press is considered.

(16) MARROWFAT v. MARROWFAT

Is Marriage Lawful?

The President of the Probate, Divorce, and Admiralty Division gave judgment in this action to-day. He said:

The petitioner, Mr. Andrew Marrowfat, is praying for a restitution of conjugal rights, his wife Gladys having deserted, or rather left, him (for it is a subtle distinction of the English that, while a husband who departs abruptly 'deserts' his wife, a wife in similar circumstances 'leaves' him). The facts are clear, but Sir Humphrey Codd, for the respondent, has advanced and indefatigably argued a novel point of law. A cynical writer has somewhere remarked that human marriage is in the nature of a lottery, and Sir Humphrey now suggests that this observation has some significance in law. The transactions governed by the Gaming and Lotteries Acts are of various kinds. They may be wholly unlawful, such as lotteries, dicing, or snakes-and-ladders (played for money); or they may be not illegal (such as wagers on horse-races arranged with credit bookmakers over His Majesty's telephones), but so little loved by the law that the law will not assist the parties to adjust any difficulty or disagreement which may arise.

This department of the law is a labyrinth of which Parliament and the Courts may well be proud; and in the days when it was still my duty to know and study the law it gave me as much trouble as the law of libel and slander. It is now, however, the duty of counsel to ascertain and inform me of the condition of the law.

And Sir Humphrey tells me that the common characteristic of every class of gaming transaction is this—
that a person makes a sacrifice in the hope of receiving
a benefit, but the reception of this benefit depends upon
the operation of chance and not upon the exercise of
his own skill and judgment. Sir Humphrey says that
this was exactly the character of the contract of
marriage entered into by the petitioner, and that the
Court should no more assist him to enforce that contract than it will assist a person who bets on horse-races
to recover his losses, or even his winnings.

Now, in what circumstances was the contract made?
The evidence is that in 1925 the petitioner was travelling as passenger in an ocean-going steamship, the
Orchid, between Australia and Colombo; that he met
the respondent (then Gladys Willows) for the first time
on the evening of the First-class Fancy Dress Ball, when
he drew her (by lot, it appears) as his partner for dinner.
The respondent was dressed as a Columbine and the
petitioner as an Oriental prince. After dinner they
danced, and after dancing they proceeded on to the
upper or boat deck to seek some relief from the tropical
heat of the evening. On the boat deck the unexpected
spectacle of the Southern Cross and other constella-
tions excited in the petitioner a warm affection for the
respondent, and he was moved to such protestations
and, it appears, caresses as are commonly the preliminaries of a matrimonial entanglement. In fact an
offer of marriage was made and accepted, a few days
later, in a four-wheeled cab at Colombo.

Now, Sir Humphrey says that the petitioner throughout was governed by chance and not by judgment or
selective skill. Chance embarked the two parties in the
same steamship, chance threw them together at the

fancy-dress dinner, and chance directed that at that meeting the respondent should be dressed in the fascinating costume of a Columbine, which she never wore before or after. It is common ground that she is not a good wife; but never, says Sir Humphrey, between that first meeting and the making of the contract did the petitioner have an opportunity to estimate by reason and discretion whether she was likely to be a good wife or not, for those attributes which are most in evidence and most agreeable in ocean-going steamships are not the same as the attributes of a good wife in the home. The petitioner therefore sacrificed or staked his liberty and his fortune without knowing and without the means of knowing what return, if any, he would receive. He selected his wife as many citizens select a racehorse, with no stronger reason for believing it to be the fastest runner than that it has an attractive name or elegant tail. Such is Sir Humphrey's argument, and in my judgment it is well founded. I am satisfied that this contract was in the nature of a gaming or gambling transaction, and therefore the petitioner is not entitled to the assistance of this Court, and his suit is dismissed.

So much for this case. But in the public interest I am bound to ask myself whether this decision has not a wider ambit than the particular affairs of Mr. and Mrs. Marrowfat. Can it be said that any matrimonial arrangement is different, in essence, from theirs? I spoke just now of racehorses, which are a common subject of wagers. But if one may accept the evidence of numerous newspaper placards and headlines, there are men who are able with almost infallible accuracy to predict the future behaviour of racehorses in given circumstances. Indeed, so confident and successful are many of these prophets that the element of chance seems to be wholly removed, and it becomes matter for argument whether the transactions of those who act upon their information ought properly to be classed as wagers or as lawful investments depending upon skill; and I hope that at some future date I may be called upon to determine some delicate dispute of that kind.

But can the same be said of him who selects from the very numerous women in these islands some particular female to be the partner of his life? The prophet of the racecourse has in nearly every case definite material on which to found his predictions: such-and-such a foal has run faster than such-and-such a filly over such-and-such a distance, in wet weather or in dry weather, with a cough, with glanders, with enthusiasm, and so forth; and therefore it may be expected to do this, that, or the other thing in the same or in some other circumstances. But the case of the prospective husband is *ex hypothesi* completely opposite. He is backing a horse which has never run before, or, if his fancy be a widow, has never run over the same course in the same company. The form of a racehorse is public property, but the form of a bride is of necessity concealed. (*Laughter*) Have I been indelicate?

Sir Humphrey: No, my Lord.

The President: Lord Mildew said in *Simpson* v. *Archdeacon Dunn* (1873) 2 Q.B., at page 514: 'The critical period in matrimony is breakfast-time.' But for too many couples the first breakfast which they take together is the wedding-breakfast. And how many husbands ascertain before marriage the opinions of the beloved on reading in bed, on early rising or late retiring? It was argued in the case just decided that a man of average judgment should be able to make satisfactory deductions from general conduct, but how is a man to deduce from the conduct of an unmarried woman at lunch-time the behaviour of the same woman, married, at the morning meal? It is a commonplace of literature that no one can predict the conduct of a woman. Women complain, in moments of dissatisfaction, that all men are alike, but men complain with equal indignation that no two women are the same, and that no woman is the same for many days or even minutes together. It follows that no experience, however extensive, is a certain guide, and no man's judgment, however profound, is in this department valuable. In all matrimonial transactions, therefore, the element of skill is negligible and the element of chance predominates. This brings all marriages into the category of gaming (see *Wagg* v. *The Chief Constable of Ely*), and therefore I hold that the Court cannot according to law assist or relieve the victims of these arrangements, whether by way of restitution, separation, or divorce. Therefore it will be idle for married parties to bring their grievances before us, and, in short, this Court will never sit again.

It is not without a pang that I thus pronounce the death-sentence of Divorce, which has meant so much to so many in this Court. To those learned counsel who have made a good thing out of it I offer my sincere condolences, and particularly to Sir Humphrey Codd, who by his own argument has destroyed his own livelihood. We shall all have to do the best we can with the limited and tedious litigation which arises from Probate and Admiralty; but any persons who want a divorce will be compelled in future to divorce themselves.

The Court adjourned, for good.

(17) CARROT & CO. *v.* THE GUANO ASSOCIATION

THE EXPERT WITNESS

(*Before Mr. Justice Wool*)

THERE was a dramatic climax to-day to Sir Ethelred Rutt's cross-examination of Mr. Stanley in the Canary Guano case. Sir Ethelred, in his opening speech, described Mr. Stanley as 'the vilest thug in Christendom'. Troops lined the approaches to the Court, and there were some sharp exchanges between Sir Ethelred Rutt and Sir Humphrey Codd, in which both the famous advocates constantly thumped on the desk, raised their eyebrows, and blew their noses. Sir Ethelred's brief is marked four thousand pounds, with 'refreshers' of two hundred pounds a day, and it is the general opinion in legal circles that the case will never finish. Had the defendant company been unable to secure his services, it is calculated that the case would have been clearly intelligible from the beginning, and in all probability would have been concluded in a day.

Sir Humphrey Codd (concluding his examination-in-chief): And, in fact, Mr. Stanley, the gist of your evidence is that there are, in fact, *no* vitamins in canary guano?

Mr. Stanley: That is so.

(Sir Ethelred Rutt then rose to cross-examine. Three well-dressed women fainted and were thrown out.)

Sir Ethelred: You are Mr. Stanley?

Witness: That is my name.

Sir Ethelred: But of course, Mr. Stanley, your name is *not* Stanley at all—but Moss?

Witness: Yes.

Sir Ethelred: Would it be fair to suggest that before the Great War your name was Moses?

Witness: Yes.

Sir Ethelred: And before the South African war was your name Finkelstein?

Witness: Yes.

Sir Ethelred: What was your name before the Crimean war?

Witness: I forget.

Sir Ethelred: You forget? *Very* well. And you appear as an expert witness for the plaintiff?

Witness: Yes.

Sir Ethelred: Exactly. Now, Mr. Finkelstein, in your opinion, suppose a ton of canary guano is shipped at Hamburg f.o.b. Cardiff, adding two pounds of the best beef suet, and making the necessary adjustments for the Swiss Exchange, what would be the effect on a young girl? Just tell the jury that, will you?

Witness: That would depend on the voltage.

The Judge (*who took long-hand notes throughout the proceedings*): That—would—depend —on—the — voltage. Go on.

Sir Ethelred: And that was on the 22nd, I think?

The Judge: My *note* says 'Bees-wax'.

Sir Ethelred: Milord, with great submission—that was the *last* case, I think.

The Judge: Oh! But what about the charter-party?

Sir Ethelred: I beg your pardon, milord. I am very much obliged to you, milord—— So that, *in fact*, Mr. Stanley, in the case of a widow, and counting thirteen to the dozen, the price of canary guano would vary with the weather in the ratio of 2 to 1, or 1 to 2 in the northern hemisphere?

Witness: That is so. Except, of course, at high water.

Sir Ethelred: Except at high water. Quite, quite. I understand that. Milord, I don't know whether the jury follow that.

The Judge (to the jury): You hear what the witness says? There are thirteen to a dozen in the case of a widow, except at high water in the northern hemisphere.

Sir Ethelred: Milord, with great respect, that is not quite——

The Judge (sternly): Sir Ethelred, you go too far!

Sir Ethelred: I beg your pardon, milord. I am very much obliged to you, milord. (*To the witness*) Have you got varicose veins, Mr. Stanley?

Witness (warmly): No!

Sir Ethelred: I put it to you, Mr. Stanley, that you *have* got varicose veins?

Witness: Must I answer that, your honour?

Sir Humphrey: Milord, I object. Me learned friend——

Sir Ethelred: Milord, I do submit—I have a reason for asking, milord.

Sir Humphrey }
Sir Ethelred } Milord!

(The two famous advocates here engaged in a violent altercation in undertones.)

The Judge: Without anticipating anything I may have to say at a later stage, and subject to anything which may be disclosed in evidence next year, and bearing in mind the relations of the parties, and without prejudice to the issue of forgery, and *prima facie* and *statu quo*, and not forgetting the Boat Race, I think it right to say that so far as I understand the law (and, of course, I am a mere child in Sir Ethelred's hands) I shall at a suitable moment be prepared to say that the question is relevant and should be answered, subject to the consideration that this sentence has now continued so long that it may be arguable that the law has altered in the meantime.

Sir Ethelred: I am very much obliged, milord.

The Judge: But I don't see where it is leading us. (*To the witness*) *Have* you got varicose veins?

Witness: Well, milord, it's like this——

The Judge (*impatiently*): Come, come, my man, don't beat about the bush! Either you have varicose veins or you have not.

Witness: Yes, milord, I have.

The Judge: Very well, then. (*Writing*) 'Do—you—suffer—from—varicose—veins?' *Answer:* 'I—do.' Now then, Sir Ethelred, do let us get *on!*

Sir Ethelred (*to the witness*): Now take your mind back to the 22nd of May, 1884. On the 22nd of May, 1884, Mr. Stanley—milord, I have rather a delicate question to put to the witness. Perhaps your Lordship would prefer me to commit it to writing?

The Judge: By 'delicate', Sir Ethelred, I take it that you mean 'indelicate'? (*Laughter*)

Sir Ethelred: Yes, milord.

The Judge: Then I am afraid we must have the question.

Sir Ethelred: Milord, there is a woman on the jury, and in view of the delicate character of the question, I propose, with your permission, to write it down in invisible ink and hand it to the witness in a sealed box.

The Judge: Very well, Sir Ethelred. This is great fun.

(Sir Ethelred then wrote rapidly on a piece of paper

and handed it to the witness, who was unable to conceal his emotion. The question and the answer were then examined by counsel, tied up with string, and carefully disinfected, after which his Lordship carried them to the jury-box, where the foreman unpacked them and fainted. Meanwhile, to Sir Ethelred's obvious annoyance, public interest in the case was steadily mounting; there was a baton charge in the corridor outside the court, and in the streets the troops were compelled to fire a volley over the heads of the crowd.)

Sir Ethelred: So on the 22nd May, 1884, Mr. Stanley, did your wife bear you a male child?

Witness: She did.

Sir Ethelred: Was that your *fourth* wife?

Witness: No.

Sir Ethelred: Ah! Would it be fair to say that you have committed alimony?

Witness: Never!

Sir Ethelred: I put it to you that the suggestion I have put to you is consistent with the hypothesis that the answers you have given are easily distinguishable from the true facts? Yes or No?

Witness: It is a lie.

Sir Ethelred: Do you smoke in the bath?

Sir Humphrey: I object.

Sir Ethelred: I put it to you that you do smoke in the bath.

Witness: No.

Sir Ethelred: I suggest that you are a bully and a blackguard.

Witness: Nothing of the sort. Don't browbeat me, sir!

The Judge: Now then, Mr. Stanley, you mustn't get into an altercation. Answer the question.

Witness: He didn't ask me a question. He made a statement.

The Judge (sternly): Mr. Stanley, this is not far removed from contempt of Court. It is my duty to protect learned counsel. Now answer the learned counsel's question.

Witness: I am sorry, milord.

Sir Ethelred: I put it to you that you are a bully and a blackguard.

Witness: No.

Sir Ethelred: Very well. Did you stay at the Grand Hotel, Palermo, in September 1911 with a woman purporting to be your wife?

Witness: Yes.

Sir Ethelred: Was she your wife?

Witness: Yes.

Sir Ethelred: On the evening of the 11th of September were you in your private room with a woman?

Witness: Very likely.

Sir Ethelred: Be careful, Mr. Stanley—the house was being watched, you know. At nine p.m. did you draw the blinds in your private room?

Witness: Very likely.

Sir Ethelred: Ah! So you drew the blinds? Will you tell the Court and jury why you drew the blinds?

Witness: To annoy the watchers.

The Judge: If you are not careful, Mr. Stanley, you will be placed in the Tower.

Sir Ethelred: Would it surprise you to learn that this letter which you wrote on the 30th May is in your own handwriting? Yes or No?

Witness: No.

Sir Ethelred: Did you know a Mr. Trout who died of indigestion?

Witness: Yes.

Sir Ethelred: Then do you still say that you do not smoke in the bath?

Witness: Yes.

Sir Ethelred: I suggest that you do smoke in the bath.

Witness: No.

Sir Ethelred: I put it to you that you smoked in the bath last April.

Witness: Very well. Have it your own way, Sir Ethelred.

Sir Ethelred: And you have committed alimony?

Witness: No.

Sir Ethelred: Why not?

Witness: I resent the innuendo.

Sir Ethelred: Is that your mentality, Mr. Moss?

Witness: Leave my mentality alone.

Sir Ethelred (sternly): Answer the question!

Sir Humphrey: Really, milord, I must object.

The Judge: I don't think the mentality of the witness is admissible, Sir Ethelred.

Sir Ethelred: Very well, milord. At Palermo, in September, there would be good sea-bathing?

Witness: Yes.

Sir Ethelred: Would it be fair to say that you bathed at Palermo?

Witness: Yes.

Sir Ethelred: In company with this woman who accompanied you?

Witness: Yes.

Sir Ethelred: Mixed bathing?

Witness: Certainly. My wife is a woman.

Sir Ethelred: Of course, Mr. Moss, I don't suggest that there is anything wrong in mixed bathing.

Witness: Then why did you refer to it?

Sir Ethelred: Milord, I claim the protection of the Court.

The Judge: Mr. Moss, I am here to protect learned counsel, and I will not have them insulted. It is little I am allowed to do in these proceedings, but at least I can do that. Sir Ethelred is paid a great deal of money for cross-examining you, and the longer he cross-examines you the longer will the case continue and the more will Sir Ethelred be paid. It is therefore very selfish of you to take the bread out of his mouth by objecting to his little excursions into fancy. Moreover, he has the mind of a child, and has not the least idea how people really behave. He gets his ideas from French plays and detective stories, and you must admit that he is most entertaining. Moreover, he is very sensitive, so please answer his questions kindly, and don't upset him.

Sir Ethelred: I am very much obliged to your Lordship. Is three litres of acilysalic acid, Mr. Stanley, a greater or a less proportion than the same quantity of gin?

Witness: It is not.

Sir Ethelred: I put it to you that it is.

Witness: It is a lie.

Sir Ethelred: What was your name before it was Finkelstein?

Witness: Rutt.

The Judge: Did you say 'Pratt'?

Witness: 'Rutt', milord—Rutt.

The Judge: Oh—Wright.

(Sir Ethelred at this point seemed overcome, and for a moment he was unable to proceed. The Judge ordered the windows to be opened.)

Sir Ethelred: Now tell the jury this. What were you doing on the night of the 30th June, 1891?

9

Witness: I was in bed.

Sir Ethelred: Did you, on the 30th June, 1891, deposit your infant child on the doorstep of the Foundling Hospital?

Sir Humphrey: Really, milord, I must object. Me learned friend is not entitled——

Sir Ethelred: Milord, my instructions are, milord——

Sir Humphrey: Milord, me learned friend——

Sir Ethelred: Me learned friend, milord——

(Both counsel here talked at the same time, exchanging angry glances, thumping on the desk, and scratching each other.)

The Judge: I think I must allow the question. (*To the witness*) Did you, in fact, dispose of your child in the manner suggested?

Witness: I did, milord.

Sir Ethelred: I see. Would it be true to say, Mr. Moss, that at that date your son had a piece of red flannel tied round his middle?

Witness: It would.

Sir Ethelred: Exactly. Now take your time, Mr. Stanley, and be very careful how you answer. Had the child, or had he not, *in fact*, a little mole on the left elbow?

Sir Humphrey: Really, milord, with great respect, milord, me learned friend has no right, milord——

The Judge: That seems to me a perfectly proper question, Sir Humphrey.

Sir Ethelred: Well, Mr. Stanley?

Witness (*with emotion*)*:* God forgive me, he had. My little boy!

Sir Ethelred: Then you, Mr. Stanley, are my father.

Witness: My son! My son!

(Sir Ethelred here vaulted over the bar and embraced

the witness, who seemed much affected by this dramatic reunion.)

The Judge: Is there any precedent for this proceeding, Sir Ethelred?

Sir Ethelred: No, milord.

The Judge: Then do not do it again.[1]

The hearing was adjourned.

NOTE—It is 'contempt of Court' to make faces at a cross-examining K.C. (*In re Fitzmaurice*) but not (*Martin's Case*) at a solicitor's clerk. A member of the jury may powder her nose in the box, but not use lipstick or (*Rex* v. *Salmon*) eat oranges. And see *Marrable* v. *Rowntree*, where the jury, on being discharged, sang 'For he's a jolly good fellow', and were committed for contempt. EDITOR

[1] But see Lord Mildew in *Doggett* v. *Port of London Authority*: 'There is no precedent for anything until it is done for the first time.'

(18) HADDOCK v. THE KING; HADDOCK v. CONSTABLE BOOT; HADDOCK v. THE SOUTHERN RAILWAY

The Let and Hindrance

A DECISION of the highest constitutional importance was given in this case by the House of Lords to-day.

The Lord Chancellor: These three appeals have, by leave of your Lordships, been treated as one appeal. The facts are quickly stated. The appellant, Mr. Albert Haddock, presented himself at Victoria Station with a railway and boat ticket for the French port of Calais, issued to him by the Southern Railway. The official at the barrier of the platform inspected the ticket and requested Mr. Haddock to exhibit his passport. Mr. Haddock replied, in direct but courteous terms, that the Southern Railway had contracted to carry him to Calais, that it was not a term of that contract that he should exhibit or even carry a passport, and that he declined to exhibit his passport to a subordinate official of the Southern Railway, who would be better employed in making his journey comfortable than in barring his passage and thus unnecessarily augmenting the nervous strain incidental to a journey. There was some debate, but at length the official, either impressed by Mr. Haddock's personality and command of language or preferring to leave the responsibility of a decision to his colleagues at Dover, permitted him to pass on to the train.

At Dover, when Mr. Haddock approached the steam-packet, the same request was made and was again refused. But here the official was not to be persuaded, and, although satisfied that Mr. Haddock's ticket was in order, would not allow him to approach the vessel, but even offered him physical resistance, amounting technically to an assault. Mr. Haddock insisted; the attention of Constable Boot was attracted; the constable and the official conferred together; it was decided between them that Mr. Haddock's refusal or inability to exhibit his passport was a suspicious circumstance suggesting that he was a criminal fleeing from justice, and Mr. Haddock was detained—or, to use the proper term, arrested—for inquiries. Mr. Haddock immediately presented his banker's letter of credit and various documents and photographs which established his identity and respectability; but these were not considered sufficient and the vessel proceeded to France without him.

The Southern Railway have attempted to justify their conduct by pleading that they acted as they did under the orders of His Majesty's Secretary of State for Foreign Affairs; and Mr. Haddock was ill-advised enough to bring in the first place an action against the Crown for inducing a breach of his contract with the Southern Railway. Here, as the Courts below have successively decided, and as he himself must be very well aware, he has no tittle of a case. 'The King can do no wrong',[1] and therefore he cannot induce a breach of contract or be liable for any other tortious act. This may seem strange to those students of history who supposed that the despotic privileges of the Crown

---

[1] '*Rex non potest peccare*'; but *vide* Strauss's *Life and Times of King John*. A foreign ruling prince cannot be cited as a co-respondent in a divorce-suit in England: *Statham* v. *Statham and the Gaekwar of Baroda* (1912) (page 92). The correct form of the maxim, therefore, would seem to be '*Nullus rex potest peccare*'.

were surrendered or destroyed in the seventeenth century, but that is the law. In this case, therefore, Mr. Haddock's appeal must be dismissed.

But the quaint old rule that the King can do no wrong does not mean that he is entitled to command his subjects to do wrong, or to save them harmless if they obey him. It would not, for example, be a good defence to a charge of murder that the King, through the Foreign Secretary, had expressed a dislike for the murdered man; though the King in his clemency might graciously pardon the murderer *after he had been convicted*. This distinction is important—indeed it is fundamental.

The appellant (who cannot, we think, be quite so guileless as he appears to be) then brought actions against Constable Boot for false imprisonment, and against the Southern Railway for assault (by their servant) and breach of contract. It was urged upon us that the appellant has a bee in his bonnet; but, as Lord Mildew observed in the case of *Merivale* v. *Prout*: 'John Hampden had a bee in his bonnet'; and the presence of a bee in that locality is at least a guarantee against cerebral inertia.[1]

It is admitted by the Crown that the Foreign Office did, and does, issue instructions to the Southern Railway that they are to carry no person to France except such as exhibit a passport satisfactory to the Foreign Office. But the Foreign Office is not entitled to issue an instruction to any subject unless that instruction is authorized by an Act of Parliament or by some still surviving, and indubitably surviving, remnant of the prerogative of the Crown.

In this case there is no such Act of Parliament,

[1] And see Bracton: '*Melior est conditio bombinantis quam moribundi.*'

and the Crown's advisers have not even pretended to discover one. The Foreign Office issues a somewhat peremptory pamphlet entitled, 'Passport Regulations', in which it is stated that every British subject who leaves these shores 'must' do this or that in relation to passports. But it is nowhere stated on what authority that 'must' is founded. And unless it can be shown that these commands and regulations are made by virtue of the Royal prerogative they have no better juridical sanction than the rules of grammar or the canons of metrical composition.

Is there any such prerogative? Has the Crown, as such, without the authority of Parliament and in times of peace, a power to forbid the subject to leave the kingdom unless he has the consent of the Foreign Secretary? We find that it has not.

On the contrary, our researches have led us to the singular conclusion that such a power or custom did once exist but has been expressly taken away. In Magna Carta it is clearly provided and promised by the Crown—'for us and for our heirs for ever'—that:

> '*All merchants shall have their safe and sure conduct to depart out of England, to tarry in and go through England, as well by land as by water, to buy and sell, without any manner of evil tolls, by the old and rightful customs, except in time of war.*'

The power which was wrested from King John by the barons (who also suffered, no doubt, from the presence of bees in their bonnets) has not been restored to the Crown by any subsequent enactment or decision; and in this old-fashioned House we hold that Magna Carta, except where it has been expressly superseded,

is still the law.[1] It would be strange if it were otherwise. The King's Dominions and possessions beyond
the seas have been conquered, held, and maintained in
prosperity through the readiness of his subjects to leave
these shores and venture abroad. And that readiness
has been in a large measure the fruit of liberty. In
times of peace, for many centuries, it has been the un-
wavering policy of the King and Parliament to extend
to the subject who is willing to travel in foreign parts
not merely consent but encouragement and even inducements. And one of these inducements has been
the personal passport.

What is the passport? It is a document signed by
His Majesty's Secretary of State for Foreign Affairs
*requesting and requiring in the name of his Majesty all those
whom it may concern to allow the bearer to pass freely without
let or hindrance, and to afford him every assistance and protection
of which he may stand in need*.

Evidence has been given in this case which shows
that, even where the subject is in possession of what is
called a 'valid' passport and obsequiously exhibits it to
all who desire to inspect it, the document is in fact
productive of more 'lets and hindrances' than any
other circumstance of a journey abroad. But in essence
the possession of a passport remains a privilege. For
the British subject it may even be a right; but it can
never be a duty. The distinction of its origin, the use
of His Majesty's name, and the generous enthusiasm of
its language, may suggest, and are without doubt intended to suggest, that the bearer is a person especially
dear to the Crown and therefore of high moral character. But no man is entitled to argue the converse.

[1] But see *Rex* v. *Haddock* (page 53) in which it was *held* (Lugg, J.) that
Magna Carta was obsolete.

Nevertheless, by the arrogance of the Crown's servants and the weak compliance of the subjects, the character of the passport has been in fact transformed. *What was a privilege has become a duty; what was a talisman has become an instrument of torture; what was intended to acilitate free movement has become an engine of obstruction.*[1] In time of war the Crown has an undoubted prerogative to restrict and regulate the movements of the subject. But, my Lords, we are not at war. We are at peace; and it is desirable that the subject should go about the world as readily and as freely as before. It is said that in recent times the readiness of our citizens to venture abroad has diminished, and we are told that the Dominions Office is making special efforts to induce a greater number to leave this country and seek their fortunes over the seas. These efforts are not wholly successful, and, now that we have heard of the obstacles to travel which have been placed by the Foreign Office in Mr. Haddock's path, that does not surprise us. Drake himself, confronted with the same discouragements, might well have degenerated into a stay-at-home.

We were told that these Passport Regulations (so-called) are of assistance in preventing the undesirable alien from entering this country; but this is a somewhat fantastic reason for preventing the respectable Briton from leaving it. We were told that they are of use to the police in the apprehension of escaping criminals. But this has nothing to do with us, with Mr. Haddock,

[1] See *Pétain* v. *Bullock* (1927) 2 A.C. 142, where a Channel swimmer, arriving at Dover, was not permitted to land, having no passport, and was compelled to swim back to France. It was *held* that she could not recover from the landing-officer for medical expenses resulting from the fatigues of the return journey. But Monckton points out (*Key Cases in Private International Law*) that plaintiff in that case was an alien and was wearing no clothes. *Quaere*—would this decision cover the case of a British subject, properly dressed?

or indeed with the Foreign Office. The police must devise some method of apprehending the guilty traveller without obstructing and persecuting the innocent.

We were told, again, that the regulations are made for the convenience of the traveller. We do not believe it. They were made for the preservation, in peace-time, of an autocratic power justified only by a state of war, and for the benefit of the passport officers in this and other countries. But whether or not these defences have been erected in sincerity they have no foundation in law. If it is necessary for the good of the realm that such restrictions exist, then Parliament must say so in clear and unmistakable terms. Parliament has not said so, and Mr. Haddock is entitled to proceed to France without exhibiting his passport to any man in these islands. If the French authorities refuse to admit him without a passport that is his own affair. He had in fact a valid passport on his person, which he judged, and rightly judged, was only of interest to the foreign persons to whom it was addressed. Constable Boot and the Southern Railway have injured the appellant; and they may not shelter behind the instructions of the Foreign Office, for those instructions were *ultra vires*, unconstitutional, against public policy, and an 'evil toll' such as is expressly forbidden by Magna Carta. They must pay the consequences. The damages claimed are not extensive, and I recommend that in addition Mr. Haddock receive a grant of five thousand pounds from the Crown in recognition of his public services. There is something to be said for the view that the Pass-port Office might be indicted as an unlawful conspiracy; but that question we are not called upon to determine.

Lord Lick, *Lord Arrowroot*, *Lord Sweet*, and *Lord Sheep* concurred.

(19) LAVENDER *v.* LADLE

(Before Mr. Justice Wool and a Special Jury)

THIS case, which has attracted much public interest, was a libel action arising out of the recent marriage of Miss May Fairy, the well-known musical-comedy star, to Lord Lavender, a subaltern in the Hotwater Guards. It is well known, explained Sir Humphrey Codd, K.C., for the plaintiff, that there exists a tradition in the Brigade of Guards that an officer who marries an actress must resign his commission. Lord Lavender, however, appears to have had the intention of ignoring precedent, for up to the day before his marriage his resignation had not been received. The defendant, Captain Ladle, who is adjutant to the Second Battalion, then wrote to Lord Lavender drawing his attention to the custom and intimating that it was the expectation of his Commanding Officer that Lord Lavender would comply with it. As a result of that letter Lord Lavender resigned, and Miss Fairy (now Lady Lavender) brought an action for defamation against Captain Ladle, the innuendo complained of being that, as an actress, she was a woman of low moral character and not a fit and proper person to be the wife of an officer in His Majesty's armed forces.

Lady Lavender, in the box, said that she had been first attracted to Lord Lavender by his manly and martial aspect in dress uniform. This uniform included a very high helmet, with chin-strap, which lent an air of

dignity and strength to an otherwise weak and undistin-
guished countenance. Out of uniform he was a different
man, and many of her actor friends thought that she
had brought discredit on her profession by marrying so
insignificant a person.

The Judge: Did any one suggest that you ought to
resign from your profession? (*Laughter*)

Lady Lavender: No, milord. *My* services could not
be spared so easily. (*Laughter*)

Continuing, witness said that it had been her ambition
to marry a soldier and be a mother to her husband's
troops; she considered she had been cheated. Her
character was unimpeccable——

Sir Humphrey Codd: You mean unimpeachable, perhaps?

Witness: I mean what I say.

She belonged, she added, to the hardest-working
profession in the world. She loved her art. An
actress who wished to be successful had no time
to be wicked. What with rehearsing, resting, the
care of the skin, and eight performances a week, a
musical-comedy star had no time for so much as
a naughty thought. Often she worked for fourteen
hours in the day; she thought that this was more than
they did in the Guards. (*Laughter*) She had received
passionate notes from the stalls, but had never replied
to them. She had accepted flowers from strangers, but
gifts of jewellery or fruit were politely returned. She
had always made it a rule to go straight home from the
theatre. She had first met Lord Lavender at a Charity
Bazaar. She lived with her mother; very often her
mother sat in the wings; her mother was much upset
by the insinuations of defendant. (*Witness here was
overcome.*)

The Judge: Let her have a good cry.

(A juryman protested against the brutal questioning of Sir Ethelred Rutt, K.C.)

Witness, re-examined, said she had announced her intention of giving up the stage. Technically, therefore, at the date of her marriage she was an actress no longer.

Sir Nigel Playfair said that, like other actors, he had been knighted by His Majesty the King.

Sir Humphrey: Does that suggest to you that in the opinion of His Majesty the actor's profession is a not wholly ignoble one?

The Judge: You cannot expect him to tell us what is in the mind of His Majesty.

Sir Ethelred (cross-examining): You are not a musical-comedy actress, Sir Nigel? (*Laughter*)

Witness: Alas, no!

Sir Ethelred: Would you admit that there is a distinction between an actor such as yourself and an actress like the plaintiff, who is accustomed to kick her legs in the air?

Witness: I have often kicked my legs in the air. (*Laughter*) There is a distinction, certainly. (*Laughter*) She does it better. (*Loud laughter*)

Sir Ethelred: Would you say that an actress of those antecedents would be a suitable wife for the Commanding Officer of a battalion of Guards?

Witness: I should have thought that was a question for the officer concerned.

(*Re-examined*): In his experience the character of the acting profession was almost monastic. He could not name a more virtuous profession. Actresses painted their faces, but so did every other woman. He had seen Miss Fairy in an 'undressing' scene, but at the end of it she was wearing far more clothes than most of the ladies in the stalls.

Captain Ladle said that the rule in question was not a rule but a tradition. Every officer was aware of it on joining, and no hardship was involved.

Sir Humphrey: Not to the officer perhaps; but how about my unhappy client, stigmatized before the world as a person of a lower caste?

(A person in the gallery said "Shame!" and was removed.)

Sir Humphrey: Is there any rule against marrying authoresses, composers, or female painters in water-colours?

Witness: No.

Sir Humphrey: If an officer had become engaged to Miss Sybil Thorndike or Madame Sarah Bernhardt would he be expected to resign?

Witness: If they are actresses, certainly.

(At this point the jury intimated that they would like to stop the case.)

The Judge: You find for the defendant?

The Foreman: No, milord, for the plaintiff.

The Judge: Ah! You find that the plaintiff is possessed of such singular beauty and charm that there can be no possible defence for the foul wrong of which she complains?

The Foreman: Yes, milord.

The Judge: I quite agree.

Sir Ethelred: But, milord, the case for the defence is not completed!

The Judge: The procedure is unusual, I admit, Sir Ethelred, but in this case justified, I think.

Sir Ethelred: Milord, I plead that this was a privileged occasion.

The Judge: Stuff and nonsense, Sir Ethelred! The radiant plaintiff is not to be deprived of her rights by legal quibbles of that kind. I find, and the jury find, that the defendant has rashly committed to paper the suggestion that the plaintiff is in some way an inferior being to himself, Lord Lavender, and his brother-officers. We have only to look round this Court to appreciate the fantastic nature of such a charge. Physically, plaintiff is without doubt the most nearly perfect specimen of humanity within these walls; mentally, she has shown herself at least as alert and well-informed as the officers named; and, morally, the worst that can be said against her is that she has worked her way to a high place in the difficult profession of public entertainment and has given pleasure to many thousands of her fellow-citizens.

The Brigade of Guards is an ancient, honourable, and illustrious unit of His Majesty's Army. They retain, as few other units do, the pomp and pageantry, the brightly coloured uniforms, the resplendent bands, the ceremonial trappings and evolutions of the past. They have, in fact, a closer kinship, in spirit and procedure, with the colour and glitter and music of the theatre than any other unit in His Majesty's forces; and it is surprising, therefore, to find in this unit alone a superstitious taboo, for matrimonial purposes, of the personnel of the theatre.

I have spoken of the historic attachment of the Guards to music. During his cross-examination of the witness Playfair, counsel for the defence made the strange suggestion that, while to act in a non-musical drama might, even in the fastidious air of an infantry barracks, be considered respectable, to act in a musical comedy was not so. It is not clear to me why the addition of music and laughter should make what is otherwise desirable dangerous. And I am the more perplexed when I learn that a female who painted, made jokes, composed music, or wrote verse would not be considered unfit to marry into the Guards, even, it appears, if she practised those arts for the sole purpose of theatrical performances. Nor has any evidence been called to show that the officers of this unit, on their rare evenings of pleasure, are careful to visit only the more serious dramatic pieces and shun those which are embellished with laughter, singing, and dancing; I am therefore led to the conclusion that we have here a traditional taboo which, whatever its historic origin, cannot be defended in the light of reason and the facts of the present day.

In times past, when the acting profession was less well established and the military more important, some special measures may have been desirable to protect the younger members of His Majesty's bodyguard from entangling alliances with strolling players. But to-day, as Lord Mildew said in *Fox* v. *The Amalgamated Society of Wood-workers*, 'The boot, if I may say so, is on the other leg'. We live in an age of peace; and if we have any logic or faith the arts of peace must now be preferred to the arts of war. His Majesty's Foot Guards are trained to handle explosives and move from place to place with good order and despatch; they are prepared to repel the King's enemies and put down rebellion by means of fire-arms and pointed weapons; and, until such an emergency arises, they are a pleasing ornament to our city, and serve a useful purpose in keeping the streets clear on the occasion of public processions and ceremonies. But it is impossible, in the scale of social values, to weigh their services or gifts against those of the plaintiff, who, although admittedly unable to discharge a fire-arm in a given direction, is accustomed night after night to increase the happiness of thousands by the refining arts of music and dancing, by graceful poses or the recitation of English poetry.

The plaintiff's retirement will cause a loss to her profession and to her countrymen. I do not apprehend that Lord Lavender's resignation will leave a dangerous gap in the defences of the land. Indeed, the plaintiff has told us that she has lost some credit among her colleagues by allying herself to one who, whatever his knowledge of musketry, is not remarkable for intellectual attainment or the habit of serious study. I find, in general, that the actor's profession is, in law and in fact, as good and worthy as any other. I find, in particular, that this delicious lady—don't keep bubbling at me, Sir Ethelred—I say, this delicious lady has been defamed by the defendant, and she will have any damages she likes to ask for. Hip, hip, hooray!

(20) HADDOCK v. THWALE

WHAT IS A MOTOR-CAR?

THE Court of Appeal to-day gave judgment in this case, which raises an interesting point concerning the rights of the pedestrian and the legal nature of a motor-car.

The Master of the Rolls: This is an appeal from a judgment of the Lord Chief Justice dismissing an action for damages brought by Mr. Albert Haddock against Mr. Frank Thwale. Mr. Haddock, while crossing a public thoroughfare in London, was knocked down by Mr. Thwale's motor-car and received bodily injury. Such events are now so familiar a part of the life of our streets that few citizens any longer resent or even remark upon them. But Mr. Haddock saw fit to make an accusation of negligence against Mr. Thwale and to demand compensation.

Mr. Thwale replied that Mr. Haddock himself had been guilty of negligence in passing across the road in front of his advancing motor-car, which was approaching the crossroads at a reasonable speed of thirty-five miles an hour; that Mr. Haddock was in fact what is contemptuously known as a 'jay-walker', that is to say, a pedestrian who may in the near future be expected to have wings. (*Laughter*) Mr. Haddock replied that seven minutes before the accident he had been a prudent and reasonable man, patiently waiting for the motor-cars to go by in order that he might cross the road and keep an appointment, which in his judgment was as important as any of the affairs of the various motorists whose vehicles blocked his passage; that he stood for several minutes under a board marked 'PLEASE CROSS HERE'; that he made five separate attempts to cross at that point, but in each case was driven back in fear to the pavement; that the constable on duty took no steps to arrest the stream of motor-cars; that the said stream continued, and threatened to continue, without interruption; that he was reluctant to spend the remainder of the day on the wrong side of the road; and that at last, growing desperate, he did, in fact, scuttle across the road to a refuge eight yards away in the usual manner of the pedestrian—that is to say, as it were a criminal in flight, a soldier pursued by a sniper, or a common hen; that he underestimated the speed and ferocity of Mr. Thwale; that Mr. Thwale, though some distance away when the crossing began, was travelling too fast to avoid him, and that, if he is a jay-walker, Mr. Thwale may fairly be described as a jackal-driver.

The Lord Chief Justice directed the jury that it was the duty of both parties to take reasonable care and to avoid as much as possible the consequences of the negligence of the other, and to recollect that what happened might have been due to the simultaneous negligence of both. The jury found that there had in fact been contributory negligence on the part of Mr. Haddock, and returned a verdict for Mr. Thwale. Mr. Haddock appealed on the ground of misdirection of the jury.

The appellant has conducted his own case with singular ability and charm, and he has advanced a novel proposition. He asks this Court to say that the Lord Chief Justice was wrong in law in placing upon all fours the negligence of a motorist and the negligence of a pedestrian. The appellant's contention is that a far higher standard of care should be demanded of the motorist by reason of his having brought upon the public roads a lethal instrument of great mobility and power. If, says Mr. Haddock, the respondent were to walk on a crowded pavement carrying a loaded gun and with his finger on the trigger, a pedestrian who was wounded by the accidental discharge of that gun would not be held guilty of contributory negligence by reason only that he had failed to keep out of the way or had omitted to proceed upon his hands and knees.

But Mr. Haddock goes further. He has argued that this Court is bound by the celebrated case of *Rylands* v. *Fletcher* (L. R. 3 H. L. 330). In that case the plaintiff's property was damaged by water which, without any fault of his, escaped from his neighbour's, the defendant's, reservoir. The House of Lords concurred with Mr. Justice Blackburn's memorable pronouncement, which has been set to music[1]:

'We think that the true rule of law is that the person who for his own purposes brings on his land and collects and keeps there anything likely to do mischief if it escapes, must keep it in *at his peril*; and if he does not do so is *prima facie* answerable for all the damage which is the natural consequence of its escape. . . . The person whose grass or corn is eaten down by the escaping cattle of his neighbour, or whose mine is flooded by the water from his neighbour's reservoir, or whose habitation is made unhealthy by the fumes and noisome vapours of his neighbour's alkali works, is damnified without any fault of his own, and it seems but reasonable and just that the neighbour who has brought something on to his own property (*which was not naturally there*), *harmless to others so long as it is confined*

[1] *Law Students' Glee Book* (Webster and Stow, 2*s.* 6*d.*), and see *Inner Temple Idylls* (arranged by H. Strauss), 6*d.*

to his own property, but which he knows will be mischievous if it gets on his neighbour's, should be obliged to make good the damage which ensues if he does not succeed in confining it to his own property. *But for his act in bringing it there no mischief could have accrued;* and it seems but just that he should at his peril keep it there, so that no mischief may accrue, or answer for the natural and anticipated consequence. And upon authority this we think is established to be the law, whether the things so brought be beasts or water, or filth or stenches.'

'Or motor-cars,' Mr. Haddock adds. And we think he is right. Mr. Thwale's motor-car should in law be regarded as a wild beast; and the boast of its makers that it contains the concentrated power of forty-five horses makes the comparison just. If a man were to bring upon the public street forty-five horses tethered together, and were to gallop them at their full speed past a frequented crossroads, no lack of agility, judgment, or presence of mind in the pedestrian would be counted such negligence as to excuse his injury. And the fact that the forty-five horses of Mr. Thwale are enclosed in a steel case and can approach without sound or warning does not diminish, but augment, their power to do injury. The ordinary walking citizen cannot be expected to calculate to a nicety the speed, direction and future conduct of such monsters, for not even their own drivers can do that. In the face of a procession of them the wise may well blunder, the brave falter, the resolute waver, and the swift be too slow. Mr. Haddock himself is of an athletic habit, a cool thinker, accustomed to danger, a good runner and jumper; but still his equipment was not enough to save him from a mauling. What precautions then can avail the aged and infirm, the deaf, the halt, the nursemaid, and the child? If Mr. Haddock had been manifestly lame no jury would have excused Mr. Thwale for knocking him down; but the motorist is no more entitled to murder a man with two legs than a man with one. We all have a right to expect that people will not deliberately let loose mad dogs in the streets, expose us to the assaults of tigers, or go about with dangerous explosives which they are unable to control; and if they do these things they do them at their peril. Mr. Thwale has brought on to his own property and allowed to escape from it on to the public highway, which in a sense is the property of Mr. Haddock, as of all the King's subjects, a dangerous instrument 'which was not naturally there, harmless to others so long as it was confined to his own property, but which he knew would be mischievous if it got out. *But for his act in bringing it there no mischief could have accrued, and it seems but just that he should at his peril keep it there.*'

It has been argued before us that his act is one sanctified by long popular usage; but we are concerned, not with popular usage, but with the law. The fact that this point of law has never before been brought to the notice of this Court does not deprive it of substance. Lord Mildew said, in *Staggers* v. *The Metropolitan Water Board*: 'There can be no prescriptive right to murder or maim the King's subjects.' We sometimes laugh at our ancestors, who insisted that a red flag must be carried in front of every motor-car; but we begin to see that there was something in it. At any rate that precaution throws some light upon the juridical character of the motor-car at its birth, and nothing, so far as we know, has happened to alter it.

An act of wanton defiance or wilful carelessness in

the injured party might be a circumstance which would justify a reduction or even denial of damages; but *prima facie* the owner of the wild beast, as we hold this motor-car to be, is liable for the consequences of his rash act. In any case we find nothing of the sort here. Mr. Haddock, while lawfully crossing the road, was injured by a dangerous and uncontrollable monster, which had been released by the act of the respondent; and he must receive damages of five thousand pounds. We order that the motor-car be destroyed.[1]

Lord Justice Batter: I agree—but upon other grounds. I do not think that it is necessary to drag in *Rylands* v. *Fletcher*, and draw fanciful comparisons between reservoirs and vehicles. But I think that Mr. Haddock should succeed upon principles analogous to those which govern the movements of ships at sea. There seems to be present in the minds of the respondent and his advisers the notion that he has rights on the highroad prior or superior to those of Mr. Haddock.[2] The notion, of course, is contrary to history, to social justice and to well-accepted principles of Common Law.[3] But the fact remains that whenever the question arises on the highroad: 'Shall A, the walker, or B, the motor-driver, pause in his progress or deviate from his course in order to avoid a collision?', the assumption

[1] A pleasing reversion to the old law of 'deodand', under which a personal chattel which had been the immediate occasion of the death of any reasonable creature was forfeited to the Crown, to be applied to pious uses, as e.g. where an adult (but not an infant) fell from a cart or horse and was killed. See *Maltravers' Case* (1 Bole—1731) in which a homicidal bull was *held* not liable for forfeit, the deceased being a woman.

[2] It is sometimes backed by the impudent plea that the motorist pays a petrol duty which is not borne by the pedestrian. Which is like saying that he who pays duties on liquor has a better right to enter a hotel than a teetotaller: or that he who pays tobacco-duty is entitled to blow smoke in the face of a non-smoker.

[3] *Qui prior est tempore potior est jure.*

is invariably made by B[1] that it must, or will, be A who
pauses, deviates, or stops. And the defendant under
cross-examination admitted that this assumption was
operative in his mind when he saw Mr. Haddock
hovering anxiously in the gutter; which is tantamount
to saying that he has a better right to occupy the road
than Mr. Haddock. For what reason? Because he is
in control of a vehicle possessing great mobility and
Mr. Haddock is not. But what is the proper conclusion from that? That he is better able to keep out
of the way, and therefore, so far from having greater
rights, he has greater responsibilities.

The rule of the road at sea provides a striking and
instructive parallel. It is the rule at sea that a steam-
vessel shall, at her peril, keep out of the way of weaker
vessels—that is to say, of sailing-ships or oared boats.
The principle of that is the principle already adumbrated: that the steamer, having the greater power
and capacity for manœuvre, able to proceed easily at
will in any desired direction, is the better equipped for
the avoidance of collisions. The greater the power the
greater the duty; not, as the respondent seems to say,
the greater the power the greater the rights. The
steam-vessel is not too proud to alter her course or
reduce her speed in order to avoid a sailing-vessel.
Nor are those sailing-vessels which are run down by
steamers described as 'jay-sailors' or recorded contemptuously as having been sunk through 'carelessly
crossing the ocean'. The sailing-vessel, like the walker,
may be almost obsolete, but she retains her rights; she
ventures confidently across the seas and is not compelled to cower in port because of the increasing speed
and power of the steamer. On the other hand, in a

[1] This was in 1930—pre-Hore-Belisha days.

narrow or dangerous channel, where the steam-vessel no longer has freedom of manœuvre, the sailorman must not and does not foolishly insist upon his rights, a point which should be noted by the pedestrian.

These just principles and values, consistently maintained, would diminish the risk of collisions on land as they do by water.[1] And though they are not yet embodied in Statute Law they should guide the Courts in the distribution of responsibility for what we euphemistically call motor-'accidents'.

Mr. Haddock has as good a right to go about the town without undue impediment as the respondent; his appointments, and his peace of mind, are as important as Mr. Thwale's—in the present instance more so; for Mr. Haddock was on his way to work and the defendant was on his way to pleasure. So that, if there were any question of priority, Mr. Haddock would have the advantage. But there is no such question. The appellant relies solely upon the common rights of reasonable mobility upon the King's highway. A row of motor-cars is no more entitled to obstruct the pedestrian than a row of pedestrians to obstruct the motorist. A man does not, when he acquires a pistol or a gun, acquire the right to menace or retard the movements of his fellow-citizens: neither does he acquire that right when he acquires a powerful motor-car. Yet, so far as I can understand the defendant's

[1] Cf. Bracton: '*In via non velocitas sed vita valet.*' And see Wool, J., in *Archdeacon Rogers* v. *Lightning Motor Coach Co.*: 'What is the *point* of all this *speed*? Is any one a penny the better? Are we wiser, more efficient—are we even more *punctual*? Gosh, no! We start later and we arrive later. A-tishoo! When I see these young fools dashing about—A-tishoo! *Drunk* with speed, Sir Ethelred! A boy of seventeen may not buy a glass of beer; but he may drive a motor-car at seventy miles an hour. Nothing said till he kills somebody, and not much then. *What* a country! Usher, stand by—I am going to sneeze again.' (*Gresham Law Reports*, 1929, page 341)

case, he maintains that he does, and that the plaintiff has no just cause of complaint against a motor-car until it kills him.[1]

He advanced, during cross-examination, the singular defence that if Mr. Haddock had run very fast he could have crossed the road in safety sooner. But there is no law requiring the pedestrian to *run* across the King's highway. Indeed, there are many citizens who through age or infirmity are unable to run. They, too, have a right not merely to life but to convenience, dignity, and peace of mind; and the defendant has a duty not only not to kill them but not to chivvy them across the road as if they were heads of cattle or poultry. The dignity of the human race must not be made subordinate to any machine. The time may come when pedestrians will be compelled by law to tunnel under the roads, build bridges over the roads, or be fired across by means of rockets. But so long as they share the roads in common with the defendant, the defendant must so conduct himself that the careful citizen is able to walk across the common highway at a reasonable pace, without alarm, inconvenience, or injury. He has not done so. He must pay damages.

Poppitt, L.J., concurred.

NOTE—These judgments, without doubt, had a profound effect, though, at that date, many years ahead of the brutal and machine-ridden times. Lord Danesfort introduced in the House of Lords a Bill which, for the purposes of compensation, accepted the principle of *Rylands* v. *Fletcher*. Mr. Oliver Stanley, as Minister of Transport, restored the speed-limit to the Statute Book and Mr. Leslie Hore-Belisha (among his other fine reforms) put it into practice. Both owe much of the deserved credit for their efforts to the persistent toil of the Pedestrians' Association and other bodies, and to such pioneers in unpopular thought as Mr. Haddock and the two great judges reported above. Mr. Hore-Belisha's celebrated and beneficent 'Beacons' are the concrete expression of the principles enunciated by Lord Justice Batter.

[1] Cf. Hale's Maxims: '*Viventi non fit injuria.*'

(21) REX *v.* BLOGGS

WHAT IS EDUCATION?

THE Court of Criminal Appeal gave judgment in this case to-day, which arose out of the conviction of a canal boatman for failing to send his children to school.

The Lord Chief Justice: This case is simple but important. The appellant, Samuel Bloggs, is a boatman owning and navigating a pair of monkey-boats (erroneously described by Sir Ethelred Rutt as barges) on the Grand Union Canal. Mr. Bloggs is a married man and has three children, who reside with their father and mother on the two boats, which are loyally entitled *George* and *Mary*. Mr. Bloggs was summoned by the Education Authority of the County of Middlesex for failing to send his children to a school for the purpose of receiving elementary education, and he was committed.

It has to be remembered that, if the prosecution is successful, the defendant's children will be educated free of charge. The prosecutors, therefore, are wantonly seeking to increase the public expenditure. It is difficult to see why, in the present state of the national finances, the children of a class already too prolific should be educated for nothing. If a man can afford beer, tobacco, and entertainment, and a weekly contribution to a trade union, he can afford to contribute some small sum weekly towards the education of his children. The State at one time could well afford to educate them without the assistance of the parents, but it can well afford it no longer, and therefore we must look with particular suspicion on any attempt to increase the burdens of the State in this respect.

In the course of his trade or occupation as a carrier of goods or raw materials, Mr. Bloggs travels continuously up and down the canal between Birmingham and London; and he put forward the reasonable defence that it was difficult for him to send children who were constantly in motion to a school which remained stationary. He also questioned the right of a Middlesex authority to intervene in the private affairs of a family which spent more than half the week in Warwickshire and other counties. But a defence founded on nothing more than reason and practicability was easily brushed aside by a public authority, and Mr. Bloggs was driven to that second line of defence which has perplexed and divided the Courts below.

'What is Education?' says Mr. Bloggs. But it is not necessary for this Court to add one more to the many answers which learned men have made to that question. The question for us is, What is meant by Elementary Education in the Education Acts of this country? We find, after careful research, that the expression 'elementary education' is nowhere defined in that long series of statutes. The omission is wise, for the notion of what constitutes elementary education must obviously vary in every age, country, and class. But, though Parliament has been discreetly vague, the Court in this case is compelled to be definite. The respondents ask us to say that by elementary education is meant education in those elementary subjects which are ordinarily taught to our defenceless children, as reading, writing, and arithmetic. But it has been argued for Mr. Bloggs that the words mean education in the elements or first parts to be learned of any subject which may be useful or

necessary to the good citizen in that state of life for which
he is destined by Providence, heredity, or inclination.

Now, the children of Mr. Bloggs, though they have
not attended a school, have already acquired the rudi-
ments of their father's and grandfather's trade, that is
to say, the handling of boats and the navigation of
canals; they are able in an emergency to steer a boat
into a lock, to open or close a lock-gate, to make bow-
lines and reef-knots, clove hitches and fisherman's
bends, and to do many other useful and difficult things
which the members of this Court, we admit, are unable
to do. Further, it is common ground that the children
are healthy, sufficiently fed, well-behaved, and attached
to the life of the water, as their forbears for three
generations have been. Mr. and Mrs. Bloggs are
instructing them slowly in reading and writing, and
even, with reluctance, it seems, in arithmetic. It is
not contended that in these subjects they are so far
advanced as children of the same age who attend
the public elementary schools; on the other hand, the
evidence is that those children are quite unable to
make a bowline-on-a-bight, to distinguish between the
port and starboard sides[1] of a vessel, or to steer the
smallest boat into the largest lock without disaster,
while in health, discipline, manners, and practical
intelligence they are inferior to the little Bloggs.
Standardized themselves according to a single pattern,
they conceive it their right and duty to take offensive
notice of any person who seems to them to be unusual,
a man with long hair or a woman with a short skirt.
The Bloggs children do not shout 'Oy!' at passing
strangers, as do increasingly the 'educated' children of
the shore; they are more courteous to persons and more

[1] Cf. *A King by Night*: 'Her green port light.' (Edgar Wallace)

respectful of property. They do not commit what are called, it appears, 'runaway-rings', steal flowers from window-boxes or apples from trees. They would scorn to spit from bridges or throw stones at the mariner passing below. They exhibit the same good manners and gentle bearing as their parents; and since they are not in constant attendance at the cinema their speech is uncorrupted by the slang or accent of Chicago.

Now, Mr. Herbert Spencer said that if we give our pupils the knowledge which 'is of most worth'—that is, the knowledge which has indispensable practical value in regulating the affairs of life—we shall at the same time give them the best possible mental training. And Mr. Bloggs (who, by the way, can read but not write) is an unconscious follower of Mr. Spencer. It may well be that our education authorities exaggerate the value of reading, writing, and arithmetic as aids to citizenship. In these days a person unable to read would be spared the experience of much that is vulgar, depressing, or injurious; a person unable to write will commit neither forgery nor free verse; and a person not well grounded in arithmetic will not engage in betting, speculation, the defalcation of accounts, or avaricious dreams of material wealth. At any rate it will not be denied that the spread of these three studies has had many evil and dubious consequences. But the practice of navigation is at the bottom of our national prosperity and safety, and has played no small part in the formation of the British character. The charge against Mr. Bloggs is that he has given his children an elementary training in the arts of this noble profession to the neglect of certain formal studies which are not essential to a virtuous, God-fearing, and useful life in the calling of their forefathers. They are unable, it is true, to read fluently the accounts of murder trials in the Sunday newspapers; they cannot write their names upon the walls of lavatories and public monuments; they do not understand the calculation of odds or the fluctuations of stocks and shares. But these acquirements may come in time. Meanwhile, as day by day they travel through the country, the skies and fields of England are their books, their excellent parents are their newspapers, and the practical problems of navigation are their arithmetic. As for writing, there is too much writing in our country as it is; and it is a satisfaction to contemplate three children who in all probability will never become novelists nor write for the papers.

It cannot have been the intention of Nature, which fashions the flowers and fishes in such variety, that Men, the noblest works of Nature, should be all exactly alike, shaped in the same mould and fitted to the same ends. But that, it appears, is the principle which has prompted this prosecution. What is in the mind of the Education Authority, however, is no great matter. The short point in this case is that Parliament does not support them. Parliament has nowhere said that the first essentials of an elementary education are reading, writing, and arithmetic. I hold therefore that Mr. Bloggs, who is carefully, lovingly, and without cost to the State equipping his children for a useful career, is providing for them an 'elementary education' within the meaning of the Acts. He was wrongfully convicted, and the appeal must be allowed. Costs to Mr. Bloggs, and a lump sum of one hundred pounds by way of compensation for his time and trouble.

Wool, J., and *Batter, J.*, concurred.

NOTE—A Bill to compel the canal boatmen to send their children to school, though this would mean separation during term-time, was introduced into the House of Commons, and thrown out.

(22) REX *v.* 'THE COLONEL', 'SEER', 'PATH-FINDER', 'OLD JOE', 'AJAX', GILBEY, WALLACE, AND THE RACING CORRE-SPONDENT OF *THE TIMES* NEWSPAPER

THE FORTUNE-TELLERS

(*Before Mr. Justice Wool*)

AT the Old Bailey to-day the Attorney-General, Sir Antony Dewlap, opened the case for the prosecution in the Fortune-Telling case. He said:

Milord, the prisoners in the dock are charged under section 4 of the Vagrancy Act, 1824, with pretending or professing to tell fortunes. Under that Act, milord, any persons using any subtle craft, means, or device, by palmistry, or otherwise, to deceive the people are rogues and vagabonds and punishable with imprisonment and hard labour. In a previous case to-day a woman named Sibylla was tried and convicted for pretending to tell fortunes by means of palmistry; yesterday a gipsy woman was sent to prison for professing to tell fortunes by means of playing-cards. The prisoners in the dock are charged under the same section of the same statute; and, though in appearance they are more respectable than the individuals I have referred to, they are equally obliged to obey the law, and the essence of the offence with which they are charged is the same.

Milord, the essence of that offence is the deception of the people by a person pretending to have the power to predict the future. The laws of England have for many centuries regarded with jealous suspicion any claim of that kind. Our judges and legislators, knowing by long experience how difficult it is for mortal man to give a correct and accurate account of what took place only a few weeks ago, will not believe that mortal man can give correct accounts of that which has not yet taken place at all.[1] By a statute of Queen Elizabeth's reign, repealed in 1863, false prophecies were punishable as misdemeanours, as raising enthusiastic jealousies among the people and terrifying them with imaginary fears. If the prophet Isaiah were to appear in London to-day he would be at once arrested. Foresight, milord, is a quality which wins applause for the citizen, provided that he looks forward to his own future only and does not pretend to see into other people's. The distinction is perhaps a fine one——

The Judge: Not at all, Mr. Attorney. It is very simple. I may look into my own bedroom, but I must not look into a lady's. (*Laughter*)

The Attorney-General: Ha! Very good, milord. A matter of property.

The Judge: No, no—propriety. (*Laughter*)

The Attorney-General: Your Lordship is exceedingly witty and well-informed. But, with great respect, milord, that is not exactly the basis of the offence; otherwise it would be equally dangerous to give an account of other people's pasts——

The Judge: It very often is. (*Laughter*)

The Attorney-General: Milord, the prisoners in that dock have for many years been earning a livelihood by pretending to tell the fortunes or predict the futures,

[1] See *Simon's Case* (1731), in which the prisoner travelled about the country crying 'Your food will cost you more'. He was whipped at Pennyfields and stood in the pillory at Chancery Lane three days.

not of men and women, but of horses. They vary in method, in prose style, in confidence, and in popularity; but they have this in common, that they do hold out to the people who read their newspapers that they are able, by some special gift or power or information, to predict with something approaching to certainty the future conduct and fortunes of race-horses. It will be proved in evidence, milord, that for these predictions, which are issued daily—even, I regret to say, milord, on the Sabbath Day—they receive money; and that numbers of the people are deceived by their pretensions, act upon their predictions, and suffer damage. Some of the prisoners, milord, to take an example, have already predicted that a horse named Diolite will win the Derby.

The Judge: What is the Derby?

The Attorney-General: Milord, the Derby is one of the most popular horse competitions, in which colts of—— (*The Attorney-General here conferred with the Solicitor to the Treasury and continued*): Milord, I am instructed that both colts *and* fillies of the age of three years take part in this race, and that considerable sums of money are wagered upon the event.

The Judge: Is it one of these trotting-races?

The Attorney-General: No, milord, it is a galloping-race. Now, milord, in the eyes of the law there is no distinction between a man and a horse——

The Judge: Have you any authority for that, Sir Antony?

The Attorney-General: I mean, milord, for fortune-telling purposes. The woman Sibylla was sent to prison for telling a police-officer that he would have good fortune and travel abroad, that a large sum of money was coming to him, that he would go a long journey and meet a dark lady in a foreign capital. Can it be said that that man is less deceitful and dangerous who tells the people that such-and-such a horse will start from a given place at a given time, travel a given journey, and arrive at a given destination in advance of thirty other horses selected from a large number for their swiftness and staying power? The jury may well think that the latter set of prognostications is the more difficult to justify. For the conduct and career of the average man obey certain laws of probability and reason——

The Judge: Did you say 'man' or 'woman'? (*Laughter*)

The Attorney-General: 'Man', milord. (*Laughter*) Most of us, for example, have, in fact, gone a long journey and met a dark lady in a foreign capital. But the behaviour of horses, as the expert witnesses will presently testify, appears to conform to no known laws, whether of reason, psychology, or mathematical probability. Their actions are impulsive, capricious, and incalculable; their health is delicate, their nervous system easily disturbed, and their moral sense negligible. The merest straw is sufficient to upset their temperaments and the hopes which human beings have formed concerning them. And this is especially true of those highly bred and sensitive animals who compete professionally in the public horse-races. We shall hear in the course of this case, milord, of certain horses called 'favourites'—horses, milord, which because of their parentage, their past performances and the known ability of the jockeys who are to ride them, are confidently expected by a majority of the persons interested to defeat all the competitors in this race or that. But we shall also hear that it is a comparatively rare event for the so-called 'favourite' to finish first; and in fact, milord, he (or she) has been known to finish among the last, so many are the chances and accidents which in a race between horses may disappoint even the unanimous expectations of a people. Yet these are the animals, milord, whose fortunes the individuals in that dock have pretended to tell.

The Judge: Do you say, Mr. Attorney, that the prisoners have never made a prediction which proved be be correct?

The Attorney-General: No, milord; there have been cases——

The Judge: Then, if the essence of the offence is the deceit, these cases must be placed to their credit.

The Attorney-General: No, milord; with great respect, milord, they are an aggravation of the offence. For the rare occasions on which the prisoners are right tend to persuade the people that they have special powers and will be right again; and, in fact, milord, these occasions are carefully recorded and advertised for the purpose of encouraging that belief. Boastful placards, milord, such as 'Who gave you that Nap?'——

The Judge: What is a 'Nap'?

(The Attorney-General conferred with the Treasury Solicitor.)

The Attorney-General: A 'Nap', I am instructed, milord, is a prediction made with such exceptional confidence that the person addressed is advised to go 'Nap' upon the indicated horse; that is, milord, to put his shirt on it——

The Judge: Is that what is meant by a horse carrying weights?

The Attorney-General: No, milord.

The Judge (impatiently): It is all Greek to me. Go on, Sir Antony. Please don't waste time.

The Attorney-General: Milord, at a later stage I shall ask you to find different degrees of guilt among the prisoners. The prisoner from *The Times* newspaper, for example,[1] has never, I believe, gone so far as to offer his readers a 'Nap'. His method is, milord, to discuss the history and idiosyncrasies of the various horses in prose of a thoughtful and delicate style; and in conclusion he will write, after a hint of diffidence, some such phrase as, 'I must therefore take Beetroot to win'. A more modest formula, milord, than the 'Nap'; but in essence, according to the prosecution, it is the same, that is to say, a prediction that Beetroot will be successful, a pretended telling of Beetroot's fortune. Indeed, milord, there is some evidence that the restraint and quietness of this man's prophetic utterances have induced in the public a greater confidence than the boastful purveyors of 'Naps' and 'Doubles' have been able to do; that is to say, the section of the public which he addresses are made ready to bet, and therefore, in the end, to suffer damage. Nevertheless, milord, you may be prepared to consider, in mitigation of sentence, the care and beauty of this man's prose.

The Judge: What exactly is a bet? What is the procedure?

The Attorney-General had not concluded his address when the Court adjourned.

---

[1] Mr. R. C. Lyle

(23) TYKE *v.* TYKE

The Magic Hour

This unusual action was concluded in the Probate, Divorce, and Admiralty Division to-day.

The President (giving judgment): This distressing case is a suit for restitution of conjugal rights by Charlotte Tyke, *née* Charlotte Watts. Mr. Edwin Tyke, the respondent, has already been tried and convicted at the Old Bailey for that he did bigamously contract a marriage with Eliza Perkins, he being already married to Charlotte Watts. Mr. Tyke has never denied that on the 15th April, 1914, he went through the form of marriage with Miss Watts, or that, on the 1st December, 1925, he married Miss Perkins. But he maintains that the former marriage is null and void according to law. The Assize judge and jury, however, did not take that view, and Mr. Tyke has only recently emerged from prison. Not even his meditations in prison have inclined him to return to the unfortunate Charlotte; and she, with that feminine tenacity in the pursuit of an undesirable object which must always be a source of wonder to the wiser sex, has called upon the law to restore him to her.

The evidence is that these two persons were married at St. Margaret's, Fish Street, by the Venerable Archdeacon Wagshott. It is not everybody who is married by an archdeacon, and it is a circumstance which might be expected to confirm rather than detract from the validity of a wedding. The church was prettily decorated with flowers; the choir (engaged by Mr.

Tyke without thought of the cost) sang two or three appropriate hymns, and one, less appropriate perhaps, concerning the somewhat irregular alliance for which the Garden of Eden is famous. The Archdeacon delivered a brief homily to the happy pair, a great number of well-dressed and well-known people were present, and the reception took place at Susan, Lady Shapwit's, house in Park Lane. Everything that ceremony, goodwill, champagne, or money could do to bless and speed the nuptials of the happy pair appeared to have been done. But there was one little flaw.

The marriage, through some accident, was solemnized at ten minutes past three in the afternoon; and it is the law of England that a marriage shall not be solemnized after three p.m.[1] This quaint, unnecessary restriction is not found in any other civilized country; it does not apply in this country to the marriages of Jews, and it cannot be said to have any deep religious or moral significance. Any one who did say that would be making a great ass of himself. For the fact is, as any one may learn who cares to study the second-reading debate on the Marriage (Hours of Solemnization) Act, 1886, the thing is an historical accident, or rather a jumble of historical accidents, such as have often been responsible for insane but enduring contributions to our laws. Some trifle impels some law-making busybody to action; the busybody perishes, the trifle is forgotten, but the law remains: and later generations magnanimously invent a moral principle to account for it.

The old direction of the Canon Law that a marriage should take place before noon was intelligible; for it

[1] It is no longer (see page 152).

was the desire of the Church that the parties should receive the Holy Communion at the time of their marriage, and it followed that they must be married within the canonical hours for the celebration of the Eucharist, that is, between sunrise and noon. But, the rule of the Canon Law having been abandoned by Parliament in 1886, the hour of three has no more religious significance than the hour of six or seven. The reason for that abandonment is interesting. In those days it was necessary for registrars to be present at the marriages of Nonconformists, who were in many ways regarded as a sort of wild beast. In some districts these monstrous alliances were so numerous that it was found impossible for the registrars to attend them all before noon. The spectacle of the weary registrar panting across the countryside on a bicycle from one Nonconformist union to another; the spectacle, on the other hand, of the Nonconformist bride waiting radiant at the chapel door for the arrival of the registrar only to be disappointed by the arrival of noon, excited the compassion of a member of Parliament. He introduced to Parliament a measure to extend the lawful hours of marriage to *four* p.m. The Home Secretary of the day appeared to be under the erroneous impression that the limitation of hours was a part of the legislation of the eighteenth century against clandestine marriages, and that its only purpose was to avoid fraud or coercion by securing the healthy publicity of daylight. He was duly informed that the authority for the limitation was the Canon Law and the reason for it that which I have already stated. Nevertheless, he insisted that it was desirable that weddings should take place in the hours of daylight, and he observed that in the north of

England, in the winter-time, it was often dark before four p.m. He therefore, on behalf of the Government, offered to give facilities to the Bill, provided that the mover would accept as an amendment the hour of three instead of the hour of four. To this the mover, somewhat reluctantly, agreed. It does not seem to have occurred to him or to the Home Secretary that if daylight and darkness were the governing considerations the hours of marriage might well be permitted to vary according to the season of the year, as the hours of lighting-up time do to-day, and the hours of burial did then.[1]

Such is the history of our present law. It is founded neither on religion nor reason, but on the dictum of a Home Secretary that 'in the north of England in the winter months it is often dark before four p.m.' From which assertion the conclusion was drawn that all members of the Church of England, in all parts of England and Wales, at all seasons of the year, ought to be married before three o'clock in the afternoon.

It is impossible at the present date to imagine a sensible defence for this unique piece of legislation. We are not living in the turbulent society of the eighteenth century. The danger of a forced wedding, conducted at pistol-point in the dead of night, is not likely to disturb the repose of our innocent girls, whatever the hours permitted by the law. *'Cessante ratione legis cessat ipsa lex,'* says an old legal maxim, or, 'When the reason for a law perishes the law itself perishes'; but this, unhappily, is seldom or never true. Further, the hours of daylight between one p.m. and four p.m.,

---

[1] Ten a.m. to six p.m. between April 1st and October 1st, and ten a.m. to three p.m. between October 1st and April 1st. (Burial Laws Amendment Act, 1880)

during which the majority of marriages are solemnized and celebrated, are those in which by common consent the vital spark is dimmest among men. They are, in short, the hours of the day least suitable to the celebration of the most vital of all ceremonies. Lord Mildew said in *Baxter* v. *The Grand Junction Canal Co.*: 'It is impossible to be really merry at half-past three in the afternoon.' And the psychologist or cynic may well connect this law with the atmosphere of depression and disillusionment which often surrounds our English weddings, and indeed with our declining marriage-rate. Moreover, the law must be the cause of no small economic waste, by reason of the millions of citizens who are taken from their toil or duty in the middle of the day in order to attend the nuptials of their friends. Lastly, it must seem odd to any reverent mind that an ordained clergyman should be forbidden by law to give his blessing except between certain specified hours, as if he were a public-house. But of such are the laws of England, and, however lunatic, this is the law.

The question is: What is its effect in the present case? After the reception the couple departed on what I understand is called a 'honeymoon' to the Continent. The difficulties and irritations of foreign travel, the fatigue and loss of temper which are attendant upon a hurried inspection of Italian picture-galleries and churches, had a not uncommon result: Mr. Tyke, in spite of the Archdeacon's address, formed a strong dislike for his unfortunate wife. On their return to England they were waited upon by an emissary from the Bishop of the diocese, who, having heard of the irregularity of their union, was greatly distressed and desired them to be married again at the proper time of day.

Mrs. Tyke was willing enough, but Mr. Tyke—than whom, surely, there can be no more unfeeling monster alive—Mr. Tyke refused. He regretted, he said, that through an error of judgment he had taken Charlotte to be the partner of his life, and since it appeared that he had done no such thing it would be an act of gratuitous folly to do it again. Providence had come to his aid, and to refuse the gifts of Providence was proverbially foolish. A personal entreaty by the Bishop had no better result. To him Mr. Tyke impudently quoted the old legal maxim *'Ignorantia facti excusat'*, or 'A mistake of fact may excuse an innocent party to a contract'.[1] He said that he had been mistaken (perhaps deceived) on a question of fact, namely, the charm and temper of Charlotte, and that though his contract were validly made he should be excused from carrying it out.

Now by the Provisional Order (Marriages) Act, 1905, a Secretary of State may make a Provisional Order to remove invalidity or doubt in the case of marriages solemnized in England which appear to him to be invalid or of doubtful validity. And such an order was obtained by the Bishop from the Home Secretary. But that order must be confirmed by an Act of Parliament. Mr. Tyke, who had friends in Parliament, announced that he would oppose the confirming Bill. Mrs. Tyke shrank from the humiliating publicity which must result, and, still hoping to win back her husband by weeping and protestation, implored the Home Office to let the matter drop, which they did. They are naturally reluctant to resume it

---

[1] *Ignorantia facti*: see *Mouldy* v. *Mitchell* (1929) 2 H.L., where a member of the Athenaeum was found asleep in a tree and sent to the Zoo. It was *held* that the Curator of the Zoo was not liable, having accepted and detained the plaintiff under an honest mistake of fact.

after this long interval and in the present press of public business. Charlotte, in despair, has turned to the courts of law, and I have to say whether her Edwin should be ordered to return to her.

I cannot discover that the question has ever been raised in a court of law. Counsel for Charlotte Tyke quoted the dictum of a Bishop that, while the officiating clergyman in such a case is subject to pains and penalties, the marriage itself is valid, on the ground, presumably, that the Divine grace cannot be subject to the control of Greenwich Time (as adjusted by the Summer Time Act). But bishops, unfortunately, are not judges. And, on the other hand, we cannot ignore the action of the Bishop mentioned in the present case, who clearly was of opinion that the marriage was invalid; for, if it were valid, there was no point in the parties being married again. All that was necessary was to punish the Archdeacon. Nobody, it appears, has done this, nobody attaching sufficient importance to the nonsensical statute. Then there is the conviction for bigamy, which seems to imply that the first marriage was valid. But this, again, does not assist me much; for it is conceivable that the Assize judge and jury, having no special knowledge of the problems of matrimonial law, were wrong.

What, in the simplest terms, is the position? A contract has been made unlawfully and I am asked to enforce it—and to enforce it by ordering what is called specific performance. Now there is no department of affairs in which our Courts are prepared to do that. A contract unlawfully made may have certain consequences; for example, the Court will punish an act of fraud which went to the making of it. But a court of law must obviously refuse to assist either party to carry out an unlawful contract. Lord Mildew, in the case of *Wagg* v. *The Chief Constable of Ely*, has ably pointed to certain similarities between a gaming contract and a contract of marriage; and the same parallel is of assistance here. The Court will not enforce a gaming contract (lawful or not), whatever it may think of the party which repudiates it. It is a debt of honour. And Mr. Tyke has contracted a debt of honour which he refuses to pay. We can record our loathing of the man, but we can do no more.

Further, it is assumed by the Court that the reasonable man foresees and contemplates the natural and probable consequences of his own acts of folly; and the same assumption must charitably be made in considering the Acts of Parliament. It cannot be supposed that Parliament, when it says that such-and-such a contract shall not be made, intended to say that if that contract were made it should be valid and enforceable. It does not, for example, say that bank-note forgery is unlawful but that a forged bank-note shall be as good as a genuine one. *Jus ex injuria non oritur.* Evidently it meant that if a man is not married before three he is not married at all. Eliza Perkins, therefore, is Mr. Tyke's lawful wife and he was wrongfully convicted of bigamy. The woman Charlotte has suffered, but I cannot help that.[1] I shall recommend that he receive a free pardon for an offence which he never committed; and to those young persons who are anxious to marry but are uncertain of the durability of their affections I recommend that they arrange for the ceremony to take place at three-fifteen. They will thus enjoy all the romance and respectability of marriage and be able to escape from it without the scandal of

[1] Cf. Bracton: '*De feminis non curat lex.*'

divorce. The petition is dismissed. Costs to Charlotte Watts.

NOTE—In 1934 a Bill, introduced by Mr. C. E. R. Brocklebank (*Fairfield*), passed quickly through both Houses of Parliament and extended the hours of marriage to six p.m. When I first recommended this reform I was told by anxious churchmen that evening weddings would be the prelude to drunken orgies. But no such scandalous affairs have come to my notice. Indeed, the true presumption must be the other way. The later the ceremony the later the champagne. EDITOR

(24) SPARROW *v.* PIPP

The Lords Rebel

JUDGMENTS of a startling nature were delivered by the House of Lords to-day in this appeal, which was the sequel to a political libel action.

The Lord Chancellor: My Lords, in this appeal we are called upon to make decisions whose consequences may reach out far beyond the lives and fortunes of the particular parties in the case.

The appellant, Mr. Sparrow, was a candidate at a Parliamentary election, and his opponent was Mr. Pipp. In the course of a controversy between them concerning the fiscal policy of these islands Mr. Pipp saw fit to say, or suggest, that Mr. Sparrow was a crook, a divorced person, and in general unfitted morally to be the Parliamentary representative of Bogton Parva. Mr. Sparrow was defeated at the polls and brought an action for defamation.

The statements complained of were made at a public meeting by word of mouth and not committed to writing. I have had occasion before to comment on some of the strange, illogical, and antiquated features of our law of libel. One of the strangest is that distinction between slander and libel by which the spoken word, however offensive, is not actionable unless the victim can prove that he has suffered special or actual damage. There are exceptions to this rule, as, for example, where imputations are made against a woman's honour. But the honour of a man is held by the law to be of less importance. If Mr. Pipp had

written on a postcard, 'Mr. Sparrow is a crook', Mr.
Sparrow would have had a clear cause of action, but
since it was shouted at a public meeting he has to show
not only that the words are defamatory but that they
have caused him actual damage. That is undoubtedly
the law as it stands to-day.[1]

At the trial of the action before our learned brother
Mr. Justice Wool, Mr. Sparrow was unable to produce
any evidence of special damage, for it appears that
accusations of the kind complained of are such common
currency in political life that few of the electors give
much attention to them, and in any case it was impossible to prove that but for those accusations Mr.
Sparrow would have been elected. Counsel for Mr.
Pipp therefore very properly submitted to the judge
that there was no case to go to the jury. There then
followed an event without precedent in the judicial
history of our land. Mr. Justice Wool defied the
law.

We learn from counsel who were present that the
day was hot and sultry. There had been a thunder-
storm and there was the threat of further atmospheric
disturbances in the air. Our learned brother throughout the hearing had shown marked sympathy with Mr.
Sparrow and had once or twice expressed his loathing
of the offensive and, it appears, inaccurate Mr. Pipp.
Further, our learned brother was suffering from hay-
fever and had given signs of a nervous irritability which
is rarely found on the Benches of our land. And in
response to the learned counsel's submission he used

---

[1] See *The Bishop of London* v. *Beckett* (1921) 2 H.L., where the
defendant, in the course of a wireless 'Talk', said: 'My Bishop is nearly
always sozzled.' It was *held* that no action would lie, because the words
had not been included in the typescript of the 'Talk' and were not
actionable *per se*.

the following words, which I read with some reluctance from the shorthand report:

'Stuff and nonsense, Sir Ethelred! Yes, I know all about *Shrike* v. *The Glassware Union*, and I know all about *Thurtle* v. *The Dean of Lichfield*—Usher, open that window, blast you!—I know what you say is the law, but it isn't *sense*. My hat, I'm going to sneeze again!' (The learned judge here sneezed seven times.) 'Do you really think I'm going to sit here and administer a damn silly law like this? Put it to yourself, Ethelred, old boy. Do you really think at my time of life I'm going to let this absolute toad, tyke, thug, Mr. Pipp, get away with it just because of some footling decision in 1834? A-tishoo! He's insulted Sparrow and he's got to answer for it. The case must go on. Usher, another handkerchief. A-tishoo! Oh, hell!'

The case proceeded. The jury found for Mr. Sparrow and awarded him heavy damages. Mr. Pipp appealed upon the point of law, and the Court of Appeal, fortified by many decisions of your Lordships' House, were easily persuaded to allow the appeal, holding that the learned judge had done wrong in allowing the case to go to the jury.

Mr. Sparrow appealed; and it is now for your Lordships' House to say whether we are for common sense or for the Common Law. That is the naked issue, unwelcome though it must be to any member of our honourable profession. Now, what is the Common Law? It is a body of principles, customs, doctrines, rules, and decisions not made by Parliament but handed down from Court to Court, from judge to judge, through many generations. In theory we have no such thing as judge-made law. Whenever a question arises to which precedent can provide no definite answer the Court must make what is in effect a new decision; but that decision is supposed to follow necessarily from some established principle or doctrine, and the agreeable fiction is that that decision was there already, though hidden till that day in the inexhaustible womb of the Common Law.

My Lords, as you know, this is nonsense. The judges of our land are constantly making law, and have always done so. The pity is that there is not more judge-made law.[1] For most of His Majesty's judges are much better fitted for the making of laws than the queer and cowardly rabble who are elected to Parliament for that purpose by the fantastic machinery of universal suffrage. To say that is not to say that the judges of a hundred years ago are necessarily the persons best fitted to legislate for the circumstances of the present day. But that is the queer position to which our attachment to precedent has led us.

An English judge, confronted with the decision of a superior Court that the earth was flat in law, would be bound by that decision, and in a similar case must give a similar judgment, though the members of that Court may have been defunct for fifty years and the circumstances which led them to that conclusion may have disappeared. In the present case your Lordships are bound by a fatuous decision of your Lordships' House in the case of *Thurtle* v. *The Dean of Lichfield* (2 A.C. 1834). My Lords, I confess that I incline to the same opinion as our learned brother Wool, much as I deplore the inelegance of his expressions. It is manifestly childish to say that a person who shouts a

[1] Cf. Bracton: '*Judicis est jus dicere non dare, hinc illae lacrimae.*'

slander to a crowd of citizens should go free, while he who writes an insult in a private letter may be brought to book. This is but one of the many follies and anomalies, founded for the most part on nothing but historical accident, in our law of libel.[1] Parliament might amend that law, but Parliament at the present time cannot be trusted to amend the laws which matter, for the sole concern of Parliament is to take away the citizen's money and prevent him from enjoying himself.

It is not for puisne judges such as our learned brother Wool to amend the law—and, making due allowance for the effect of thunder and hay-fever, I feel bound to associate myself with the lengthy rebukes already administered by the Court of Appeal. But your Lordships have the power to amend the Common Law, provided that you are willing to abandon in some degree the devoted and mechanical adhesion to precedent which has been for centuries the foundation of our judicial practice. For my part I am willing to take the risk; and I am not willing to be bound hand and foot by the observations of Lord Mildew made in 1834—a year, my Lords, in which the world was a very different place. Since Parliament has surrendered or forgotten its proper function, which is to keep the laws abreast of the times, your Lordships' House must, in my judgment, discharge that duty. So long as I sit upon the Woolsack, whenever an appeal discloses a divergence between the Common Law and common sense it will be my practice to be guided by the latter.

[1] In *Bede's Case* (1498) K.B., 12 Hen. VII, fo. 22, defendant was owner of a 'Talking Horse' which continually asserted at the public fairs that plaintiff's wife was unfaithful. The King's Bench declined to hear him on the ground that the jurisdiction in slander belonged to the spiritual courts. (And see Wedderburn on *Witches*.)

We may as well begin with the law of libel. I hold therefore that our learned brother Wool, though inelegant and insubordinate, was right, and the appeal must be allowed.

One word more, my Lords. The question must soon arise: If we are prepared to amend the ancient Common Law, most of which is still sensible, what is to be our attitude to modern Statute Law, most of which is not? Nearly all the laws recently enacted by Parliament are vexatious and foolish, yet we are expected to enforce them as jealously as if they were necessary and good. My Lords, we are venerable, dignified, and wise, superior in almost every respect to the elected legislators of the House of Commons; yet, like the rest of His Majesty's judges, we find ourselves in the position of hired dispensers, compelled continually to dispense the prescriptions of a crazy doctor, which they know to be ineffective and even poisonous. My Lords, is it good enough? My Lords, it is not. My Lords, I give notice that from this day forth it is my intention to decide such disputes as come before me in accordance with my own good sense and judgment, ignoring both precedent and Parliament where they are opposed to me. As for the House of Commons, my Lords, the House of Commons be blowed!

Lord Lick, *Lord Arrowroot*, *Lord Pullover*, and *Lord Laburnum* (with some hesitation) concurred.

(25) REX v. PUDDLE

Blackmail

THE Hammersmith Blackmail case was concluded at the Old Bailey to-day.

Mr. Justice Trout (addressing the jury): Gentlemen, this is a very grave case. The prisoner in the dock, a Collector of Taxes for the district of South Hammersmith, stands charged with the odious crime which is commonly described as blackmail. That expression dates from very early times, when it was the custom to pay tribute to men of influence who were allied with certain robbers and brigands for protection from the devastations of the latter. The practice was made illegal by a statute of Queen Elizabeth's time, and ever since it has been classed by our Courts among the most contemptible and dangerous offences. A person, who, knowing the contents, sends or delivers a letter or writing *demanding with menaces and without reasonable cause* any chattel, money, or other property, commits felony, and is liable to penal servitude for life. The menace, the 'putting in fear', as our ancestors expressed it, is of the essence of the crime. The spectacle of one man demanding money from another must always be painful to the civilized mind; but when in addition that other is made to fear for his safety, liberty, or reputation the law steps in to protect and punish.

Now, Mr. Haddock, the prosecutor in this case, received a letter from the prisoner demanding money. The letter was printed in ink of a bright red colour, and that is a circumstance which you may well take

159

into account when you come to consider the intention of the letter and the effect which it may have had upon the mind of the recipient. For red is notoriously the colour of menace, of strife, of bloodshed and danger; and it is worthy of note that the prisoner's previous communications to Mr. Haddock had been printed in a quiet and pacific blue. The letter was as follows:

> *'Previous applications for payment of the taxes due from you on the 1st day of January, 1930, for the year 1929–1930, having been made to you without effect, DEMAND is now made for payment, and I HEREBY GIVE YOU FINAL NOTICE that if the amount be not paid or remitted to me at the above address within SEVEN DAYS from this date steps will be taken for recovery by DISTRAINT, with costs.*
>
> 'E. PUDDLE, *Collector*'

'Collector', I may observe in passing, was in other centuries a word commonly used to denote a highway-man.[1] But you will not allow that point to influence you unduly.

Now the 'demand' is clear; indeed the word, as you will notice, is printed in block capitals. And you have to say, first of all, whether or not that 'demand' is accompanied by menaces. You will take everything into consideration, the terseness, I almost said the

---

[1] In *Rex* v. *Strauss* (1928) 9 Cr. App., R. 91, a bailiff acting for the Inland Revenue was struck and killed with a book of sermons while removing a wireless set belonging to the accused, and two rabbits, the property of a favourite daughter. The defence was that distress for income-tax was a gross provocation comparable to the discovery of a wife in the arms of another (see *Rex* v. *Maddy*, 1 Ventris, 158), and such as to produce an uncontrollable impulse depriving a man of the ordinary powers of self-control. The jury, without leaving the box, returned a verdict of 'Justifiable Homicide', but the following day was Derby Day, and the decision is not regarded as settled law.

brutality, of the language, the intimidating red ink, the picking out in formidable capitals of the words 'DEMAND', 'SEVEN DAYS', and 'DISTRAINT', and any other circumstance which may seem to you calculated to cause alarm in the mind of the recipient. You will observe in particular the concluding words, 'Steps will be taken for recovery by DISTRAINT, with costs.'

'DISTRAINT.' What is the exact meaning of that? It means the forcible seizure of a person's goods; it means the invasion of his home by strangers; it amounts to licensed burglary; it means the loss not only of favourite possessions but of reputation; it means distress to wife and family, and it is significant that the correct and common term for the process is 'Distress'. Evidence has been given that a threat 'to put the bailiffs in' brings terror to any home. The prosecutor has sworn that at the sight of that one red word he suffered alarm; that he understood from the letter that, without opportunity to state his case in a court of law, his goods would be seized and his wife and family put in fear by the prisoner. The prisoner says that that was not his intention; that the words 'steps will be taken for recovery' indicated a preliminary summons to the Court. You may think that in that case he would have done better to print those words in the same large type as the word 'DISTRAINT'; and you may think, as I do, looking at all the circumstances, that the letter was deliberately planned and worded with the intention of creating alarm, and, through that alarm, extracting money from Mr. Haddock, who is a sensitive man.

You will then have to ask yourselves, Was this menacing demand for money made with reasonable

cause? You will bear in mind that Mr. Haddock is
not a debtor nor a criminal; he has not taken another's
property nor done any disgraceful thing. His only
offence is that by hard work he has earned a little
money; and the suggestion is now made that he shall
give away a fourth part of that money to other people.
That being his position, you might well expect that
he would be approached not with brusquerie but
with signal honours, not with printed threats but with
illuminated addresses. But the whole tenor of the
prisoner's communications suggests that in his opinion
Mr. Haddock is a guilty person. Observe the strange
use of the word 'recovery'—as if Mr. Haddock had
taken money from the prisoner. Mr. Haddock has
made repeated protests to the Collector and to his con-
federate, the Inspector, urging that even under the
strange customs of our land the sum demanded of him
was excessive, that due allowance had not been made
for the particular hardships and expenses of his professional calling, and that in his judgment the prisoner
and his principals have taken from him during the past
years money which they ought in conscience to restore.
While this dispute was still proceeding the prisoner sent
this letter. Mr. Haddock, a public-spirited man, conveyed the letter to the police, and it is for you to say
whether he was right. An official from the Inland
Revenue Department has drawn your attention to the
difficulties of a Mr. Snowden, the prisoner's principal,
it appears, who is in need of money. You will pay no
attention to that. We are all in need of money; and
if Mr. Snowden has an insufficient supply of money he
must spend less money, as the rest of us have to do.
Neither his avarice nor his extravagance can excuse a
breach of the law.

The jury eagerly found the prisoner guilty of black-mail, and he was sentenced to penal servitude for life, and solitary confinement for ten years, the sentences to run consecutively. The Court congratulated Mr. Haddock.

(26) REX *v.* THE HEAD MASTER OF ETON

LORD CAMPBELL'S ACT

AT Windsor to-day, before a full Bench of magistrates, a serious charge was made against the Head Master of Eton, a clergyman, who appeared to feel his position acutely. Police-Constable Boot gave evidence in support of the charge, which was preferred under the Obscene Publications Act, 1857, commonly known as Lord Campbell's Act.

Constable Boot: On the fifth of this month, acting under instructions, I proceeded with a special warrant to the premises known as Eton College and made a thorough search of the same. I found and seized there a number of books which in my opinion were of an obscene character. Defendant admitted that the said books were kept on the premises to be 'sold, distributed, lent, or otherwise published' within the meaning of the Act, to the students under his charge, who are from thirteen to nineteen years of age, your worship.

The Attorney-General: Have you carefully perused the said books?

Constable Boot: I have.

Sir Ethelred Rutt (for the defence): Your worship, I have here a hundred and forty-nine professors and schoolmasters who are prepared to go into that box and swear that the volumes in question have not the character suggested.

The Chairman: What is the use of that? The defendant himself is a schoolmaster. In a charge of burglary the evidence of a hundred and forty-nine burglars would not persuade the Court that the prisoner was incapable of house-breaking.

Sir Ethelred: But, your worship——

The Chairman: We cannot admit this evidence. The question of obscenity is for the Court to decide.

Sir Ethelred: But, your worship, you have admitted the evidence of the constable.

The Chairman: That is different.

Sir Ethelred: How?

The Chairman: Do not be impertinent, Sir Ethelred. The constable is not a schoolmaster.

Sir Ethelred: Your worship, it is a principle of English law that an accused person is assumed to be innocent until he is proved to be guilty. In this case it appears that the defendant is assumed to be guilty, since he is summoned to show cause why the books in question should not be destroyed; yet he is not permitted to prove himself innocent, for the evidence of ignorant persons is admitted against him and the evidence of educated persons is not admitted in his defence. I protest.

The Bench: Sir Ethelred, you may protest.

Counsel then addressed the Bench.

The magistrates withdrew and did not return for several hours.

On their return *The Chairman* said: This is a very painful case. During our absence we have perused, with growing interest and disgust, a number of passages in the books complained of, and in particular a book called *The Classical Dictionary*, which is written in English. Many of the books are written in a foreign language with which we are not acquainted; some of these are accompanied by English translations, and some are not; but from the character of the former we are entitled to form certain conclusions as to the character of those volumes which no one has yet been bold enough to put into English.

The Classical Dictionary is a book of six hundred and forty pages and contains a very large number of legends or stories concerning so-called classical or mythological figures. I am glad to say that no one on this Bench has had a classical education, and we were therefore able to approach these volumes with an open mind. The magistrates on my right and left include a baker, a brewer, a farmer, and a distinguished banker, and, though none of us are professors or schoolmasters, Sir Ethelred, you will admit, I think, that we are as well able as other men to say what is fit and proper to be read by young persons.

Sir Ethelred: Certainly, your worship.

The Chairman: Now we are informed that the definition of obscenity laid down by Lord Cockburn in the case of *R.* v. *Hicklin* was as follows: 'I think the test . . . is whether the tendency of the matter charged as obscenity is to deprave and corrupt those whose minds are open to such immoral influences and into whose hands a publication of this sort may fall.' The last words are important. Not only the nature of the work but the circumstances of its publication, including its price, must be taken into account. A treatise on the passion of love, philanthropically intended and decently expressed, might be most unsuitable to be read by young persons, and if it were hawked in the streets for twopence might properly be condemned under the Act, but not if it were sold at a high price by reputable booksellers, in which case it would be most unlikely to fall into the hands of young persons.[1] But in the

[1] See *Chief Constable of Burbleton* v. *Woolworth* (1929), in which defendants published a sixpenny edition of the Plays of Shakespeare. The magistrates ordered it to be destroyed.

present case the publications complained of have been deliberately purchased and kept for the consumption of young persons, and young persons drawn exclusively from the aristocracy and the governing classes, whose duty it will be in future years to set an example to their less fortunate countrymen, to mould their minds and dictate their actions. Any conduct therefore which tends to corrupt and deprave those young persons must be held especially culpable.

We find unanimously that these volumes have such a tendency. The legends in *The Classical Dictionary* have a pagan origin and are largely concerned with pagan gods; and their amorous adventures and barbaric standards of behaviour form strange subjects of study for the pupils of a Royal College situated under the walls of a Royal Castle whose august occupant is head of the Established Church. We have read with particular repugnance the record of the alleged god, Zeus, whose habit it was to assume the shape of swans, bulls, and other animals, and, thus disguised, to force his unwelcome attentions upon defenceless females of good character. The case of the woman Leda, if it were published in the newspapers to-day, would arouse the indignation of every right-thinking Englishman; and we have no doubt that our leaders of thought would mobilize the conscience of the nation to prevent the repetition of such offences. But in these books we learn that, although the unfortunate woman became the mother of two eggs, the celestial profligate was permitted to proceed without public protest to the odious case of the woman Europa, in which the abductor took the shape of a bull. No moral reproof is founded on these stories, no improving lesson is drawn from them; on the contrary, they are related with a callous indifference which, coupled with the fact that the delinquent is of a divine or pseudo-divine character, must tend to suggest to the susceptible imagination of the young that such behaviour is defensible or even desirable. The boys of Eton must not be encouraged to dress themselves as swans or wild beasts for the purpose of idle and illicit flirtation; but that can be the only effect of these deplorable anecdotes. Indeed, we learn without surprise that the Captain of the Boats was recently expelled for entering the Matron's bedroom disguised as a brown owl.

I could mention many other passages, only less disgraceful in that they relate the moral lapses of mortal men and not of gods—the case, for example, of the man Oedipus, who killed his own father and married his own mother. Then there is the revolting story of the woman Medea, who committed or was accessory to a number of atrocious murders. This woman, by false representations, induced the daughters of Pelias to cut their father in pieces and boil him; she sent to a female rival a poisoned garment which burned the unfortunate woman to death; she murdered her own brother and herself cut him into fragments; she killed and (according to one account) devoured her own children; but, so far from paying the due penalty of her crimes, she was then conveniently conveyed to safety in a chariot drawn by winged dragons. Strange food, this, for the tender minds of our growing aristocracy. It must not be forgotten that the mind can be 'corrupted and depraved' in more than one direction; tales of parricide, fratricide, and infanticide are 'obscene' in the truest sense of the word; and all through these legends there runs a strain of violence and cruelty and bloodthirsty vengeance which is as harmful to the reader as the strain of irregular passion. It is idle for us to urge upon the newspapers and the makers of films the duty of reticence in their treatment of crimes and offences if our places of education are permitted to discuss them without restraint; and it may well be that the prevalent appetite of the poor for tales of murder and wrongdoing has its real origin in the schools and colleges of the rich.

We have been asked by counsel to take into account the innocent motives of the defendant, the artistic merits of the works in question and the long tradition which has admitted them as proper reading for the young. It was decided in the year 1868 that innocence of motive is no defence to a charge under the Act; and neither art nor custom can, in this Court at least, excuse an offence against morals. We find that these books are corrupting and we order them to be destroyed. Fortunately we have only been called upon to consider a fraction of the so-called 'classics'; but after what we have seen we shall recommend to the proper authorities that a thorough survey be made of the whole body of classical literature in order that our schools and colleges may be made safe for aristocracy. The defendant is severely censured and will pay the costs of the prosecution.[1]

NOTE—The Obscene Publications Act was, very properly, designed to punish and prevent the distribution of intentionally and obviously corrupting matter—such literature and pictures as are thrust upon the traveller's attention in many Continental cities and most foreign ports. Without claiming any special licence for pornography masquerading as 'literature', it may be said that books which have not the same obvious intention and sole justification ought not to be judged and condemned (as in practice they now are) by the same standards and procedure as

[1] In a later case, *Rex* v. *Squire*, the defendant, a street bookmaker, attributed his downfall to a volume of Catullus which he had picked up in the streets of Windsor.

'feelthy pictures' or 'smutty French books'. 'Intention' should be the test (at least, in inflicting punishment): and it should not be more difficult here for the Courts to establish the presence or absence of a guilty 'intent' than it is in other crimes. In a recent prosecution under this Act a book had been published without protest or comment for four years: it was found in a public library by a sensitive inhabitant of Lancashire and reported to the police. Savage fines, amounting to £400, were inflicted. Certain passages in the book were 'frank' and might easily shock the squeamish, though no one, man or boy, was likely to be 'corrupted' by it—which is the point that matters. Nor had the book, it was clear, a pornographic or corrupting *intention*. Yet, as the law and practice are to-day, it is an accident whether the author becomes a best-seller or a criminal: and many years after a publication applauded by decent literary critics he may be condemned as a beast on the evidence of a constable, provoked by a muck-hound. EDITOR

(27) COWFAT *v.* WHEEDLE

WHAT ARE SNAILS?

(Before Mr. Justice Wool)

THE hearing of this case, which raises a legal point of far-reaching importance to gardeners and horti-culturists, was concluded to-day.

Mrs. Cowfat, who appears *in forma pauperis*, is suing her neighbour, Mrs. Wheedle, for alleged trespass and damage to property. Plaintiff and defendant live in adjoining houses in the suburb of West Munsey. Both are keen gardeners, and plaintiff alleges that defendant has made a practice of throwing snails and slugs over the dividing wall, thus damaging Mrs. Cowfat's plants and injuring her chances of gaining prizes at the West Munsey flower-show.

Mrs. Cowfat's cross-examination was continued this morning. The contrast between this witness's down-right diction and counsel's polished phrases caused much comment.

Mrs. Cowfat: I seen 'er done it—see?

Mr. Swoot (counsel for the defence): You say you saw the defendant transferring snails from her garden to yours?

Witness: I tell you I seen 'er done it. Can't speak plainer than that, can I?

Counsel: I put it to you that your story is a tissue of fabrications?

Witness: I seen 'er done it. And my clean 'olly-'ocks nothin' but 'oles from that day to this. More like a sponge, they was.

Counsel: Will you tell my Lord what time of day it was that you saw the defendant engaged in this manner?

Witness: Ask 'er 'oo it was won first prize for 'olly-'ocks, Mister.

Counsel: Answer the question, please, Mrs. Cowfat. What time of day was this?

Witness: Night-time, of course. Think she'd have the face to do it in the daylight? Nasty, creeping thing——

Counsel: Then it would be dark, Mrs. Cowfat?

Witness: Dark? I should say so. Gone half-past ten, because I'd 'eard Wheedle come back from the pub, singing somethink awful——

Counsel: Very dark?

Witness: You're right, Mister. And she's a dark one. If I was to tell you all I know——

The Judge: You are here to tell all you know, Mrs. Cowfat, provided it is relevant.

Witness: Well, then, ask 'er what Wheedle said to the lodger the night he put 'im outside. Ask 'er 'oo it was fed 'er two cats, night and morning, when she went off Whitsun——

Counsel: One moment, Mrs. Cowfat. You have told my Lord that it was very dark. And yet it was not so dark that you were unable to see the defendant throwing snails over the wall?

Witness: I seen 'er done it.

Counsel: On the 18th May did you reprove defendant for putting salt on the snails in her garden?

Witness: That's right. Nasty cruel thing! Standing watching 'em shrivel. That's what put 'er against me.

Counsel: You disapprove of that method of immo-bilizing a garden pest, Mrs. Cowfat?

Witness: I seen 'er done it.

Counsel: Will you tell my Lord how you dispose of the snails in your own garden?

Witness: Never were no snails in my garden, Mister, not before Flo Wheedle began 'er dirty games.

Counsel: Oh! So there were no snails in your garden, Mrs. Cowfat, prior to the 14th of June?

Witness: You 'eard what I said.

Counsel: A very remarkable garden, Mrs. Cowfat, in its complete freedom from destructive gasteropods?

Witness: Remarkable? You oughter seen it last summer—first prize 'olly-'ocks, sea-kale, and lettuce. *And* a second for geraniums.

Counsel: To what, Mrs. Cowfat, do you attribute your immunity from snails?

Witness: Patent fertilizers, Mister. Turns their stummicks and they don't come a second time.

Counsel: I put it to you, Mrs. Cowfat, that your immunity is susceptible of a more sinister explanation?

Witness: Pardon?

Counsel: I suggest to you that for many years past it has been your habit to transfer your snails to your neighbours' gardens?

A woman in the body of the Court: That's right.

Witness: Oh, you wicked man! Oh, how dare you! Say that again, Liz Roberts, and I'll tear your eyes out! (*Witness here became highly excited.*)

The Judge: Please control yourself.

Witness: All right, guv'nor. Only you wait till I get at 'er—see?

Counsel: Would you say, Mrs. Cowfat, that the snail was an animal *ferae naturae*?

Mr. Bottle (*Counsel for the plaintiff*): Milord, I object!

Mr. Swoot: If me learned friend will have a little patience——

Mr. Bottle: The witness cannot be expected——

The Judge: I don't *quite* see where this is leading us, Mr. Swoot.

Mr. Swoot: Milord, it is the defendant's case that she did not in fact throw snails into the plaintiff's garden, and in the alternative that, if she did, they were snails which, so far as there can be property in snails, were the property of the plaintiff, and, thirdly, that they were animals *ferae naturae* which the defendant had not brought on to her own property and therefore was under no obligation to keep upon her own property. Milord, in the case of *Rylands* v. *Fletcher*——

The Judge: Dear, dear! *Must* we have *Rylands* v. *Fletcher*?

Mr. Bottle: Milord, at the proper time I shall have a good deal to say about that case, which, in my submission, milord, is on all fours, milord, with the present——

Mr. Swoot: Milord, in that case it was held that a person who keeps a wild beast or dangerous thing upon his property is answerable for the consequences if that animal or thing escapes and does damage to the property of his neighbour; but, milord——

Witness: 'Ere, Mister——

The Judge: Do you distinguish, Mr. Swoot, between a destructive mammal and a destructive gasteropod?

Mr. Swoot: No, milord. But I distinguish between the cases. Milord, if my client had kept a tiger on her property she would be answerable for the consequences of its escape. But if a wandering tiger, milord, over which she had no control, were to come upon her property, I submit, milord, she would be entitled, milord, to take any steps which suggested themselves in order to induce it to leave her property, even, I submit,

milord, if she were to open the gate dividing her property from her neighbour's and persuade the animal by
gestures to depart through that gate——

The Judge: An interesting point, Mr. Swoot, but
does it arise?

Witness: Oy!

The Judge: Be quiet.

Witness: 'Ere, guv'nor, am I giving evidence or 'im?
I seen 'er done it—wish I may die!

Mr. Swoot: Milord, I rely upon *Swabe* v. *The Ecclesiastical Commissioners.* Milord, the snails in defendant's
garden were not brought there by her and are not
under her control, being at liberty at any time to cross
the wall into the plaintiff's garden. Milord, I ask you
to rule that the snail is an animal *ferae naturae*——

The Judge: What has Mr. Bottle to say to that?

Witness: I seen 'er done it.

After further legal argument, his *Lordship* said: Mr.
Swoot, you have conducted your argument with marked
ability. The legal points involved are of considerable
importance and complexity. The evidence discloses a
long-standing feud between two neighbours, who, as
horticulturists, are naturally anxious to rid their proper-
ties of the destructive snail, which I hold to be an animal *ferae naturae.* It appears that the plaintiff, whose
evidence was almost wholly unsatisfactory, has for long
made a practice of transferring or urging her snails into
defendant's garden, since she has a feminine shrinking
from the taking of life herself. The defendant, less
sensitive, has destroyed them with salt, admittedly
a painful and humiliating end. The plaintiff made
adverse comments upon this practice, whereupon the
defendant, according to the plaintiff, transferred them
to her neighbour's property, from which, we may

suspect, they were again ejected. We have a picture, therefore, of a state of affairs in which the snails of this neighbourhood have been changing their location with a rapidity to which they are quite unaccustomed. It is not too much to say that in West Munsey Villas it rains snails. If the evidence is to be believed, the snail war has spread beyond the original parties. The plaintiff suggests that many of her neighbours, taking the defendant's side, have conspired to collect their snails and deposit them in quite unreasonable numbers upon her hollyhocks. There are concerted operations, there are night expeditions, there are watchers at windows. The question for me is, Does this deplorable state of affairs disclose a cause of action at law? I find that it does not. A person may lawfully frighten the birds from his orchard, though he knows that as soon as they leave his own property they must enter upon his neighbour's: and similarly he is entitled to urge the wild snail with threats, entreaties, or loud noises into his neighbour's garden. Mr. Bottle asked me to draw a distinction between the persuasion or intimidation of a snail and the deliberate throwing of a snail; but that distinction is too fine for me. I must not be understood to say that defendant is entitled to pelt the plaintiff with snails; but trespass to property and trespass to the person are two different things, and in the absence of the latter I hold that the property-owner may dispose of his snails in what way he pleases. The action therefore must be dismissed. I am told that this decision will cause grave suspicion, unrest, and enmity in our towns and suburbs, but I cannot help that. It is the law.

(28) REX *v.* BALDWIN, CHURCHILL, BRIDGEMAN, AND OTHERS

The Ward-Room's Wife

THIS strange case, in which the accused are the principal members of the late Conservative Government, was concluded at the Old Bailey yesterday.

Mr. Justice Trout (*addressing the jury*)*:* This painful but important case has revealed a singular story. The prisoners in the dock are indicted at the instance of a naval officer, Commander Paravane, upon two counts —first, that they did obtain a considerable sum of money by false pretences, and second, that they did, severally and collectively, libel the Commander.

Now, a number of the officers in His Majesty's Navy are married and have children; and, as you have heard, it is the principle of the State to look with especial favour upon those who have taken upon themselves the responsibilities of matrimony and parenthood, since, for reasons not wholly clear to all of us, it is still considered desirable that the population of these already overcrowded islands should continually increase. Therefore the taxes exacted from a bachelor are greater than those required of a married man; and the income-tax of a father is reduced, though not extensively, in exact proportion to his fertility. Pensions are granted to widows, but not to spinsters equally needing support. In addition, the officers and men of His Majesty's fighting forces receive higher pay (or allowances) from the day that they lead some happy girl to the altar—that is to say, the officers and men of the Army, the officers and men of the Royal Air Force, and the men (*but not officers*) of the Royal Navy. The exception is startling. We should have been surprised to hear that a sailor of any degree had been debarred from this particular privilege, for it has been proved in evidence in this case that every nice girl forms an affection for a sailor, and, on the other hand, that seafaring men are unusually susceptible to the attractions of the opposite sex; while the common assertion that they have a wife in every port, economically considered, would seem to suggest that in this respect they are entitled to an even greater measure of consideration than others.

However that may be, we should certainly not have expected the single exception to so wide a rule to fall upon those gallant and highly trained gentlemen who command and inspire the Senior Service.

The distinction made between the officers and men of that service would increase our astonishment, if that were possible. It does credit, no doubt, to the heart of the nation, that we deny to the officer what we are willing to grant to the simple seaman, but it will not, I think, enhance our reputation for common sense. Is it to be understood that it is correct and desirable for an ordinary or able seaman to take a wife, but not for the captain of his ship? Are the children of the stoker satisfactory additions to the race, but not the offspring of an admiral? Surely we are agreed that the blood and spirit of Nelson and Drake are not confined to the forecastle? 'Hearts', if I may be permitted to imitate a celebrated poem,

> Hearts just as hard to check
> Beat on the quarter-deck,

and the arguments which support the endowment of

marriage in the one place cannot miraculously lose their substance in the other.

One of the naval witnesses, a bachelor, ventured to attack the principle itself; but it is too late, or perhaps too early, to do that. If it were accepted as a matter of policy that a reduction of the population is the first essential for a reduction of our difficulties, then we should be right, not merely to refuse assistance to those who contract matrimony, but to impose a tax or fine upon the producers of every child, increasing in severity with the size of the family. There is much in theory to be said for this; but what is material is that we do not say it. On the contrary, we publicly bewail the smallest decline in our national birth-rate, which is already lower than that of France, long derided by us as a decadent nation antagonistic to the birth of babies. We cling to the strange belief that it is possible and proper to squeeze into a suit-case of limited dimensions an unlimited number of objects; and hence, in our limited territory, we applaud and support the multiplication of infants. So long as that is our general line of thought any particular departure from it will be difficult to justify; and none perhaps could be more dubious than the one under discussion. Quality as well as quantity must be our aim; and if that be admitted it is clear that the breed of the naval officer is one of the first which an eugenical expert would be careful to include in any scientific plan for the improvement of the race.

These general observations have very little to do with the merits of this case; but when they are understood they make it more difficult to understand the conduct of the defendants. Besides, I like the sound of my own voice, and have no doubt that you enjoy it as much as I do.

Now, as might have been expected, the Silent Service have suffered almost in silence what appears to them to be an injustice to themselves and a danger to their country. But faint indications of unrest have from time to time reached the ears of our legislators; and in 1925 the defendants, impressed, no doubt, by the arguments which you have just heard, asked Parliament to vote, that is, to supply and sanction the use of, a large sum of money—four hundred and thirty thousand pounds—for the express purpose of providing what are called marriage allowances for the officers of the Navy. The House of Commons, believing in the representations of the accused and eager to correct a wrong, nobly voted the money. We can imagine the quiet thankfulness, the sober celebrations with which that news was received in the far-flung ward-rooms of the Fleet. You have heard in evidence how those already married held up their heads and sent off little presents to their wives, as if the burden were already lightened; while those not married turned their fancy for the first time to thoughts of love, or dared at last to welcome into their hearts affections which they had feared to encourage before. We do not know how many hesitating lovers were emboldened by the defendants' promise to make the fatal promise themselves; how many have wives and families to-day who but for the defendants' act would still be single. But we know that they are numerous; and heavy must be the responsibility of him who by false undertakings entraps even one man into that lifelong entanglement which we call marriage.

Sailors are notoriously trustful; and we can picture the incredulous dismay which swept across the seas and stalked through the Royal ports when, five months later, it was announced by the prisoner Baldwin that the golden dream was not to be fulfilled. Commander Paravane has told you that at the moment when he received the shocking information he was in the act of making an offer of marriage in writing. That marriage never took place. It may be that the Commander is more fortunate than some of the other victims, but he does not take that view.

Be that as it may, it is clear that the defendants did obtain a large sum of money on the strength of representations which they have not fulfilled. The somewhat feeble defence has been raised that the money was asked for, and obtained, 'provisionally' only; but this would have more force if there were any evidence that the money had been returned. On the other hand, you have heard that not long before the prisoner Baldwin's announcement a much larger sum of money was granted to persons interested in the coal-mines. That may well have been a worthy purpose; but a person who takes money intended for his mother and spends it upon his aunt will not be excused by the excellence of his aunt. The question is, Have the prisoners by their behaviour done injury to individuals? And I think that they have.

Further, the Commander asks you to say that in some of the speeches, at first sight inoffensive, there is contained an innuendo to the effect that he (and his colleagues) are not fit persons to marry and have children,[1] and in particular that they are inferior in this respect to the officers of the Army and the Air Force, and to the men under their own command. There is

---

[1] In Fox v. Commander Stanley (2 K.B., 1904) it was held that to call a man a 'son-of-a-gun' was defamatory, and the father recovered damages, the implication being that modern tubular weapons were incapable of generation and therefore the plaintiff's son must be a bastard. But see Dean Furley v. The Bishop of Winchester (1910), where the accusation was made at a Diocesan Conference.

some evidence that this suggestion may be gaining ground; for, as you have heard, on the last occasion that this topic was discussed in the House of Commons it excited the interest of less than forty of the six hundred and fifteen members, so that the House was 'counted out', and the debate ignominiously concluded. This suggests that in the opinion of the Legislature it matters little whether a naval officer is able to marry and beget children or not; and it may be that the speeches of the prisoners, when coupled with their conduct, have encouraged that opinion. But all these questions, and many others, it is for you and not for me to answer.

The jury found all the prisoners guilty on the first count, and three of them on the second.

The Judge said he would take time to consider the sentences.

NOTE—I hoped to be able to omit this report from this Work: but to-day (1935) the position is the same, and I feel it my duty to put it on record. EDITOR

(29) *IN RE* JOHN WALKER·

Prohibition and Barbarism

The House of Lords to-day delivered judgment in the Rum Row appeal.

The Lord Chancellor: My Lords, this appeal raises issues of profound gravity. In effect it is an action between the United States of America and His Majesty the King; and your decision must take account not only of municipal but international law and custom.

John Walker, a British citizen, was arrested at the instance of the United States representatives in this country, who demanded that he be extradited on a charge of murdering an American citizen. Mr. Walker is a mariner and trader; and he has long been engaged in the export trade, which is by all authorities acknowledged as the foundation of the prosperity of these islands. On the night of January 15th last he was proceeding peacefully towards the coast of America in a small craft which carried a cargo of whisky, the produce of Scotland. Without warning or provocation the occupants of an American vessel opened fire on Mr. Walker; and he, judging that he had to do with pirates or sea-rovers, returned their fire. An American citizen was killed. Mr. Walker returned safely to his country; and we are now asked to surrender his body for his trial and punishment by the American Courts.

It is a matter of dispute between the parties whether the conflict took place within the territorial waters of the United States or not. But, if my view of the case be correct, an affirmative answer to that question would not necessarily be decisive. It is true that we have agreed by a treaty of long standing to extradite, or deliver up—to use a more pleasing expression—all persons who, being charged with murder in American territory, shall seek asylum in our own. But it is necessary to consider the nature of the practice of extradition. It is in essence a courtesy, an act done in derogation of sovereignty for the mutual convenience of civilized nations. Now, we say in our Courts that he who asks for equitable treatment must himself do equity.[1] In the same way, among nations, a privilege founded on the usages of civilization cannot properly be demanded by a barbarous nation nor for any purpose which runs counter to those usages. Slavery, for example, is an institution repellent to the consciences of all civilized nations, and if we were asked to deliver up to a foreign country a person claimed by that country as a slave we should without difficulty formulate a refusal, no matter what treaties appeared to bind us. Again, the country of Russia has adopted certain stringent laws against the practice of religion and the persons of its ministers, laws which in the judgment of civilized nations are barbarous and insupportable. I can imagine, my Lords, a Russian bishop in flight from the operation of those laws. I can imagine a British seaman, true to the traditions of his race, harbouring the reverend fugitive in his vessel and conveying him to the sanctuary of these islands; but I am unable, my Lords, to imagine the arguments which would prevail upon this honourable House to deliver up that mariner or that divine to the inhuman treatment of a Russian tribunal. If we were confronted with some old treaty we should reply that when that treaty was signed we did not contemplate that the other party to it was likely

[1] And see Bracton: '*Nemo nudus curiam appropinquare debet.*'

to sink into a condition of savagery, and that by that unfortunate relapse our obligations were extinguished.

Such is the nature of extradition. And now let us examine the grounds upon which we are invited to extradite our fellow-citizen.

The deceased American, it appears, was an officer of the Preventive or Revenue Department, and his particular function was to prevent and punish the importation of spirituous liquor into the territory of the United States. The authority under which he was acting at the time of his death was an enactment entitled the Eighteenth Amendment to the American Constitution, amplified and explained by the Volstead Act; and these laws are the embodiment of a policy called 'Prohibition', that is to say, the absolute prohibition of the importation, manufacture, sale, or consumption of what is strangely known as 'alcoholic liquor'.

My Lords, in my judgment that policy and those decrees are contrary to the concerted usage of civilized nations. There are certain rights, customs, liberties, and practices which have been accepted by the enlightened peoples of the world as necessary to the life of civilized men. There is the right to personal freedom—the negation of which is slavery. There is the right to freedom of worship according to the conscience and belief of the individual—the negation of which is religious persecution. There is the right of all men to the peaceful use of the seas—the negation of which is piracy. And there is the right of free choice in such matters of personal behaviour, dress, and diet as do not affect the safety of the realm or the rights of other individuals—the negation of which is Prohibition.

My Lords, those who are guilty of slavery, piracy, or religious persecution are regarded rightly as *hostes humani generis*, outlaws of the world, persons who have violated the common laws of mankind. Such persons or peoples forfeit the rights which are commonly attached to nationality or sovereignty and may be apprehended or punished by the first-comer; and in that shameful category I include without hesitation those who are guilty of the policy or practice called Prohibition. My Lords, the use of wine is as old as the use of religion; freedom of behaviour is now as highly prized as freedom of the person, and, though I would not positively give the same value to all these rights, from a negative aspect there is nothing which justifies the violation of one more than the violation of another. It is intolerable that at the present stage of civilization peaceful traders should be assailed with fire-arms on the high seas for no offence other than the conveying from place to place of the wine of their own country. And (though this consideration has no juridical significance) such conduct must be particularly offensive to the people of these islands, whose fortunes for many centuries have been bound up with the practice of navigation and the distribution of their merchandise along the coasts of the world. Yet it is a nation confessedly guilty of such conduct which now demands of us a privilege extended, as a rule, *ex gratia* only, and only to a trusted friend.

The learned counsel who appeared for the United States pressed upon us the ingenious argument that Prohibition was to be regarded as a 'moral experiment' and therefore deserved our practical sympathy. This argument did not impress me. The evidence is that this 'moral experiment' has been in fact productive of more death, degradation, and civil dissension than any enactment of recent times.[1] Apart from that I must

[1] 'O Temperance! O Mores!' Evidence of Mr. Albert Haddock before the Royal Commission on the Licensing Laws (1929-31)

remind your Lordships that the laws of Russia, already mentioned, are also commended by the Government of Russia as a 'moral experiment'. Yet, as I have already said, we should do nothing to support them. The question is not, How do the laws of a given country appear to the Government of that country? but, How do they appear to the eyes of the civilized world? It is conceivable, my Lords, that the Government of Italy might restore the institution of slavery; but, though they declared this act to be a 'moral experiment', we should not on that account extend our approval nor surrender our sovereign rights.

My Lords, I have no doubt that the Eighteenth Amendment is an offence against the customs of the civilized world, *jus gentium*. No other civilized nation has been guilty of this offence; and the nation guilty of it now must be considered as an international outlaw. It may take effect within the coasts of North America, but it cannot be acknowledged or condoned beyond them. It follows that individuals acting in pursuance of that enactment have, as against the nationals of other countries, no rights; they have the status of pirates, cannibals, marauding savages; and they may be shot down or apprehended by the decent citizens of any civilized nation. *A fortiori*, no application based upon a supposed injury done to them can be entertained by our Courts. The appeal must be allowed and Mr. Walker must be set at liberty. This, my Lords, with some reluctance, presiding over the highest tribunal of our land, I declare to be the law.

Lord Mulberry: I agree. But I arrive at the same conclusion by a simpler route. The evidence is clear that the deceased man was pursuing Mr. Walker, *animo furandi*, in order to take his cargo from him by force;

14,

I am satisfied that with that intention he opened fire on
Mr. Walker outside the territorial waters of the United
States, that is, on the high seas, and that he had frequently acted in this manner before. Now, all authorities agree that robbery, or forcible depredation upon
the sea, *animo furandi*, is piracy. The deceased, therefore, was in fact, and in law, a pirate; and the somewhat fanciful analogies of the Lord Chancellor are not
required in order to bring him within that detestable
category. Mr. Justice Lushington, in *The Magellan
Pirates*, 1853 (1 Spinks's Eccl. and Adm. Rep., 81) said:
' . . . all persons are held to be pirates who are found
guilty of piratical acts, and piratical acts are robbery
and murder on the high seas. I do not believe that,
even where human life was at stake, our courts of
Common Law ever thought it necessary to extend their
inquiry further if it was clearly proved against the
accused that they had committed robbery and murder
on the high seas. In that case they were adjudged to
be pirates and suffered accordingly.' The Common
Law is clear, and I know of no treaty or statute which
can be held to have superseded it. Mr. Walker did
what he did in self-defence against the assaults of a
pirate, and he must be released.

Lord Lick, Lord Arrowroot, and *Lord Sheep* concurred.

NOTE—The opinions expressed by the Lord Chancellor prevailed at
last in North America, and in 1933 the Eighteenth Amendment was
repealed. Relations between Great Britain and the United States at
once improved, and lawlessness in the latter country began to abate.
See Philip Snowden's *Essays on Wine*: 'By what right do we call
ourselves Free Traders if the goodliest of all commodities may not freely
circulate?'; and Senator Honk: 'America's history began when we
threw the tea into the water: it ended when we threw the wine.' See
also A. Capone's *Handbook for Bootleggers*; and Mrs. Q. Fester: 'A
generation is growing up which does not know what alcohol *is*' (*White
Wings*).

(30) REX *v.* SKELTON AND DEW

WHAT ARE STOCKBROKERS?

THE trial of this case was concluded at the Guildhall to-day before Alderman Moody.

The Attorney-General (in his speech for the prosecution): This case, your worship, though it comes up for decision in a Court of Summary Jurisdiction only, raises issues of grave national importance. Otherwise, I need not say, I should not be appearing in person before a mere magistrate.

The Bench: Who are you?

Sir Antony Dewlap: I am the Attorney-General.

The Bench: Ah, yes, we have heard of you. Proceed.

Sir Antony: The prisoners in the dock, your worship, are charged with an offence against the Street Betting Act, 1906, by which 'any person frequenting or loitering in streets or public places on behalf either of himself or any other person, for the purpose of bookmaking or betting or wagering, or agreeing to bet or wager, will in the case of the first offence be liable on summary conviction to a fine not exceeding ten pounds and for a second offence a fine not exceeding twenty pounds.'

The prisoners are both members of the London Stock Exchange, Mr. Skelton being a broker and Mr. Dew a jobber. A jobber is one who deals in a particular 'market' or class of securities; and Mr. Dew deals particularly in the American market. Now, the members of the London Stock Exchange have a large roofed building in which to transact their business; but such is their energy and zest that after that building is closed in the afternoon many of them continue to do business outside, in Throgmorton Street and the adjoining courts. It appears, your worship, that by long habit they have come almost to regard this thoroughfare as their corporate property; and I am told that, if a member of the general public ventures to loiter, as the stockbrokers loiter, on the pavement, remarks of an increasingly unfriendly nature are addressed to him, such as 'Where did you get that hat?' For these reasons, I understand, it will be argued by counsel for the defence that Throgmorton Street is not a 'street or public place' within the meaning of the Act. But as to that, your worship, I shall call evidence to show that the public have uninterrupted physical access to the street at either end, and that they do in fact make use of it. Indeed, it would be a strange thing if the long-continued arrogance of a few citizens could deprive the King's highway of its public character.

The Bench: Be brief, Sir Antony. We are not accustomed to orations here.

Sir Antony: Your worship, the definition of a 'street or public place'——

The Bench: Do not go on about that. We are with you.

Sir Antony: I am obliged to your worship. Your worship, I need not say——

The Bench: Then do not say it.

Sir Antony: Your worship is very good.

The Bench: I am not very good. I am very dyspeptic.

Sir Antony: Perhaps your worship would care to try one of these infallible tablets? One or two, taken in a glass of water, your worship——

The Bench: Thank you. Usher, the tablets.

(His worship then took two tablets, and appeared to experience considerable relief.)

The Attorney-General (continuing): The facts, your worship, are as follows. On the 4th of this month, at about four-thirty in the afternoon, the prisoner Skelton approached the prisoner Dew in Throgmorton Street and invited him to quote a price for *Anglo-American Hot-water-bottles Deferred.* Dew replied $15\frac{1}{8}$–$16\frac{1}{2}$; and Skelton then agreed to buy from him a parcel of five thousand *Hot-water-bottles Deferred* at $16\frac{1}{2}$ in ten days' time. Your worship, that sounds a perfectly innocent transaction——

The Bench: Where do you get these tablets?

The Attorney-General: Spink's, your worship—Spink and Holiday, in Coventry Street. Now, it appears that in recent weeks there has been a considerable decline in the market value of many American securities. Prices had fallen so low that on the date in question many people in this country supposed that their next movement must be upward. It will not be denied that Mr. Skelton was agreeing to buy *Hot-water-bottles Deferred* at $16\frac{1}{2}$ on the 14th in the hope and belief that in the interval the price would rise to 30, shall we say, and that he would then be able to sell them again at the higher figure, thus making a handsome profit. Mr. Dew, on the other hand, believed and hoped that prices would continue to fall, so that on the 14th he would be able to buy at 5 and sell to Mr. Skelton, as agreed, at $16\frac{1}{2}$. Mr. Dew had in fact on the 4th no *Hot-water-bottles Deferred*, and Mr. Skelton did not in fact desire to possess any. Each party was speculating on the movements of the market; each was, as it were, 'backing his fancy', Mr. Skelton betting on a rise and Mr. Dew on a fall. In other words, it was a gambling transaction, a wagering contract, a——

The Bench: We see what you mean, Sir Antony.

Sir Antony: Your worship, there are many thousands of respectable and God-fearing citizens in this and other countries who devote every working day of their lives to transactions of this kind. In the United States, your worship, a very moral country, which has thrust out the use of alcohol from the national life, the operations of such persons have recently caused widespread ruin, distress, and suicide, have shaken the financial and industrial fabric, and have even had disagreeable repercussions abroad. *Naturam expellas*, your worship——

The Bench: Who is he?

Sir Antony: Man will have his indulgences, your worship; and it may well be that the time and treasure and energy which were previously expended on the habit of alcohol have been transferred to the habit of speculation, in which case the extent of the net national gain is dubious.[1] None of our public moralists, however, has yet upon these events made any of those severe pronouncements which the spectacle of our other indulgences so often extracts from them.

The Bench: What has all this to do with me?

Sir Antony: Your worship, the present Government has set its face against all manifestations of that vice which may be simply described as desiring something for nothing. For this reason the police are instructed energetically to enforce the laws against street-betting, a practice which above all forms of gambling is held to demoralize the poor. Any person suspected of loitering in public with intent to enable the people to back their fancies on the racecourse may be arrested without warrant[2]; and in fact such persons have been reduced to the condition of pariah dogs, slinking guiltily from

[1] Later, many thoughtful American citizens supported this hypothesis.

[2] See Wedderburn on *Wagers* (pages 1049–1162).

corner to corner. But, your worship, between their proceedings and the proceedings of the prisoners there is no distinction in logic or morals, except that one is assisting the citizens to bet on racehorses with money which they possess and the other is assisting them to bet with money which they do not possess (in many cases) upon the prosperity and health of the nation's industries. The share-capital of industry is the life-blood of a country, the fount of employment, the guarantee of progress, the foster-mother of invention. No man should be able to gamble with the life-blood of his country and to endanger by speculation the stability of manufactures and the employment of the people. Yet, as I have said, many thousands of citizens are occupied in doing this and very little else, and, so far as I know, no bishop has ever lifted up his voice against them. The confused and wavering mind of the Legislature, your worship——

The Bench: I beg your pardon?

Sir Antony: The confused and wavering mind of the Legislature——

The Bench: What about it?

Sir Antony: I was saying, your worship, when your attention wandered, that the confused and wavering mind of the Legislature had left many gaps in the laws against gambling. And so long as the prisoners conduct their operations under a roof they would seem to be lawful; though there is some support for the view that an indictment would lie against the Stock Exchange for keeping a common betting-house. But it is without doubt unlawful for a man to back his fancy in the public street, whether that fancy be a racehorse or a hot-water-bottle deferred; and I ask for a conviction.

The Bench: Anything *you* say, Sir Antony. They are convicted.

Sir Antony: Your worship, that was in the nature of a test case. In the next case five hundred and seventy-three stockbrokers are charged with loitering with intent to commit the same offence.

The Bench: Can they all be convicted before lunch?

Sir Antony: I think not, your worship.

The Bench: Then we had better have lunch. Can you spare another tablet?

The Court adjourned.

(31) REX *v.* LEATHER

Is Fox-Hunting Fun?

MR. JUSTICE PLUSH gave judgment to-day in the Harkaway Hunt case.

His Lordship: These proceedings have been instituted by the Crown against the Master of the Harkaway Foxhounds to secure a declaration that he is liable for Entertainments Duty. This tax is a singular product of our own times. Our fathers regarded the entertainment of the citizen as a lawful and desirable business, and the Roman emperors went so far as to provide free entertainment for the people, ranking this in importance next to the provision of bread. But the King-Emperor of our realm has in his wisdom seen fit not only to withhold all assistance from the purveyors of public entertainment, but to levy a heavy duty upon them. This tax is so heavy as to partake almost of the nature of a fine, only exceeded in severity by the duties on the sale of spirituous liquors; and there is reason to suppose that in the mind of the Crown the two things are coupled together as harmful practices deserving of discouragement.

The tax is not a tax upon profits but upon gross receipts; and it has been proved in evidence before me that a theatre which is not attracting the public for the reason that it is presenting one of the plays of the national poet, Shakespeare, and is therefore making a weekly loss, will still be required to render a weekly payment to the Exchequer amounting, roughly, to twenty per cent of its takings. It is within the knowledge

195

of the Court that the bookmakers of our land were recently required to pay a duty of only two per cent on their receipts; but so energetic was the objection of these valuable citizens to a tax which had no relation to profits that it was removed. The Entertainment Tax ranges from sixteen to nearly twenty per cent, varying with the prices charged for the entertainment. The impost is a strange one in an age which announces as its chief objective a general increase of leisure and recreation, and in so far as entertainment is founded upon literature and the arts the tax may be said to be a tax upon education and the mind.[1]

These considerations have a relevance, which may not immediately appear, to the question which the Court is called upon to answer: *Is fox-hunting an entertainment?*

The defendant, Lord Leather, is Master of the Harkaway Foxhounds, and he has in the box given us a clear and straightforward account of his proceedings, which I am prepared to accept as the truth. As I understand him, the country district in which he resides is subject to the ravages of a cruel and voracious quadruped of the genus *Vulpes alopex*, commonly known as fox. This creature is of a carnivorous habit and preys upon the poultry of the peasants and farmers, causing much distress of mind and monetary loss; it is cunning, swift, difficult to catch, and a prolific breeder. The defendant, therefore, a public-spirited man, has taken certain measures to rid the district of this pest and so to secure the livelihood of the poultry-keeper and the food-supply of the country. He has purchased a number of specially selected dogs and has trained them to pursue the fox across country, guided only by their sense of

[1] And see page 247 for a full examination of the tax, *per* Wool, J.

smell, which is exceptional. He has also organized a band of ladies and gentlemen who, like himself, have the interests of British agriculture at heart and are willing to assist him at whatever personal risk. These helpers, loosely called the 'Hunt', are mounted on horses, and by their mobility and knowledge of wood-craft render invaluable aid in the intimidation, apprehension, and destruction of the fox. Many of them, the defendant has told us, are willing to give up a day's work in the metropolis and make a special journey to the country in order to play a small part in one of his concerted operations against the common enemy. These operations are conducted three or four times in a week with tireless vigour all through the winter months; but even so it has been found impossible to exterminate the pest. It was not made quite clear to me why the defendant relaxes his efforts in the summer-time, but I understand that once again he has been guided by his solicitude for the farmer, whose standing crops might suffer damage from the exertions of the defendant's dogs. The fact remains that during those months the fox is unmolested, as free to multiply his own species as he is to diminish that of the hen. Indeed, the witness Turmut, a farmer, some of whose irrelevant and noisy evidence I ought not perhaps to have admitted, maintained with some heat and no little ingratitude that the defendant and his helpers would do better to conduct their campaign against the fox with rifles and shot-guns both in winter and in summer. But I was assured by the defendant that for technical reasons this is wholly impracticable.

The procedure of a hunt, as I understand it, is as follows: The fox is alarmed and dislodged from its lair by the loud barking of the dogs and the playing of musical instruments. Should the quarry escape into the open country, as, to the chagrin of the hunt, it often does, the dogs at once give chase, and the horsemen follow the dogs; other helpers follow in motor-cars along the nearest road, and many of the poor follow on foot. Now, it is the case for the Crown that all these persons, although as practical men and women they genuinely desire to rid the neighbourhood of a destructive animal, find a keen enjoyment in the process of destruction for its own sake. No one has ventured to question the single-minded purpose of the defendant, but it is argued that what for him was a crusade has become for his helpers an enjoyable spectacle, excitement, gratification—in a word, an entertainment. The witness Turmut strongly supported this view; and he remarked with some force that the number of the defendant's helpers is in fact far in excess of what is practically necessary or useful, and that it is still increasing. He went so far as to say that many of the helpers did more harm than good, but that portion of his evidence did not favourably impress me.

If the contention of the Crown be correct, there is here a development not without parallel in other departments of the national life. The Englishman never enjoys himself except for a noble purpose.[1] He does not play cricket because it is a good game, but because it creates good citizens. He does not love motor-races for their own sake, but for the advantages they bring to the engineering firms of his country. And it is common knowledge that the devoted persons who conduct and

---

[1] The same thought has been well expressed by the poet Herbert:

'No Englishman—'tis one of Nature's laws—
Enjoys himself except for some good cause.'

(*Derby Day*)

regularly attend horse-races do not do so because they like it, but for the benefit of the breed of the English horse. But their operations have attracted many thousands of citizens who do not conceal that they visit horse-races for their own selfish pleasure. Accordingly the State imposes an Entertainment Tax upon their tickets of admission; and a member of the Jockey Club would not be excused on the ground that his purpose at Epsom was to watch and foster the English thorough-bred.

The relevance of my observations on theatres will now begin to appear. The defendant has admitted in evidence that he collects an annual tribute from his helpers, from farmers, and others, who habitually attend his operations and enjoy the spectacle of his dogs and horses at their pious labours. These contributions are necessary for the maintenance of the dogs and their keepers and for other purposes; and they are willingly given by the ladies and gentlemen of the Hunt in return for the pleasure or entertainment which the defendant has provided. The Crown say therefore that he is liable to pay Entertainment Duty on the sums so received, at the statutory rates, that is to say, two shillings on the first fifteen shillings and sixpence for every five shillings or part of five shillings over fifteen shillings.

The defendant's answer is that the fox may be said to enjoy the hunt for its own sake—and even the dogs and horses—but that his human followers are governed only by philanthropic motives, and that his takings are devoted to a philanthropic purpose, the destruction of vermin and the preservation of poultry, and should therefore be exempt under the Act. Unfortunately for him this plea is disposed of by the precedents of the racecourse and the theatre. There is a school of thought which still holds that the plays of Shakespeare have an educative and uplifting character; but even if that could be established it would not exempt the rash man who presented them from handing over nearly a fifth of his takings to the Exchequer. In my judgment the contention of the Crown has substance. I hold that fox-hunting is an entertainment; that the moneys received by the defendant from the hunters and farmers are by way of payment for that entertainment, and that it must, like other entertainments, make its proper contribution to the public revenues according to law. Lord Leather is, as it were, the manager of a theatre: the Hunt are his audience and the dogs his actors. If, after remunerating his actors and paying the duty, he is out of pocket, it cannot be helped. It is a dangerous thing to give pleasure to the people. He has been Master for sixteen years, and he must pay duty not only in respect of the current year but for every preceding year since the institution of the duty by the Act of 1916. It has been urged before me that this will be a hardship; but, as Lord Mildew said in *Mope* v. *The Llandudno Sewage Commissioners*, '*Nullum tempus occurrit regi*'—or 'Time is no object to a Government Department.' Costs to the Crown, *pari passu*.

(32) BOARD OF INLAND REVENUE *v.* HADDOCK; REX *v.* HADDOCK

The Negotiable Cow

'Was the cow crossed?'

'No, your worship, it was an open cow.'

These and similar passages provoked laughter at Bow Street to-day when the Negotiable Cow case was concluded.

Sir Joshua Hoot, K.C. (appearing for the Public Prosecutor): Sir Basil, these summonses, by leave of the Court, are being heard together, an unusual but convenient arrangement.

The defendant, Mr. Albert Haddock, has for many months, in spite of earnest endeavours on both sides, been unable to establish harmonious relations between himself and the Collector of Taxes. The Collector maintains that Mr. Haddock should make over a large part of his earnings to the Government. Mr. Haddock replies that the proportion demanded is excessive, in view of the inadequate services or consideration which he himself has received from that Government. After an exchange of endearing letters, telephone calls, and even cheques, the sum demanded was reduced to fifty-seven pounds; and about this sum the exchange of opinions continued.

On the 31st of May the Collector was diverted from his respectable labours by the apparition of a noisy crowd outside his windows. The crowd, Sir Basil, had been attracted by Mr. Haddock, who was leading a large white cow of malevolent aspect. On the back and sides of the cow were clearly stencilled in red ink the following words:

'*To the London and Literary Bank, Ltd.*

'Pay the Collector of Taxes, who is no gentleman, or Order, the sum of fifty-seven pounds (and may he rot!).

'£57/0/0   'ALBERT HADDOCK'

Mr. Haddock conducted the cow into the Collector's office, tendered it to the Collector in payment of income-tax and demanded a receipt.

Sir Basil String: Did the cow bear the statutory stamp?

Sir Joshua: Yes, a twopenny stamp was affixed to the dexter horn. The Collector declined to accept the cow, objecting that it would be difficult or even impossible to pay the cow into the bank. Mr. Haddock, throughout the interview, maintained the friendliest demeanour[1]; and he now remarked that the Collector could endorse the cow to any third party to whom he owed money, adding that there must be many persons in that position. The Collector then endeavoured to endorse the cheque——

Sir Basil String: Where?

Sir Joshua: On the back of the cheque, Sir Basil, that is to say, on the abdomen of the cow. The cow, however, appeared to resent endorsement and adopted a menacing posture. The Collector, abandoning the attempt, declined finally to take the cheque. Mr. Haddock led the cow away and was arrested in Trafalgar Square for causing an obstruction. He has also been summoned by the Board of Inland Revenue for non-payment of income-tax.

[1] '*Mars est celare martem.*' (Selden, *Mare Clausum*, lib. 1, c. 21)

Mr. Haddock, in the witness-box, said that he had tendered a cheque in payment of income-tax, and if the Commissioners did not like his cheque they could do the other thing. A cheque was only an order to a bank to pay money to the person in possession of the cheque or a person named on the cheque. There was nothing in statute or customary law to say that that order must be written on a piece of paper of specified dimensions. A cheque, it was well known, could be written on a piece of notepaper. He himself had drawn cheques on the backs of menus, on napkins, on handkerchiefs, on the labels of wine-bottles; all these cheques had been duly honoured by his bank and passed through the Bankers' Clearing House. He could see no distinction in law between a cheque written on a napkin and a cheque written on a cow. The essence of each document was a written order to pay money, made in the customary form and in accordance with statutory requirements as to stamps, etc. A cheque was admittedly not legal tender in the sense that it could not lawfully be refused; but it was accepted by custom as a legitimate form of payment. There were funds in his bank sufficient to meet the cow; the Commissioners might not like the cow, but, the cow having been tendered, they were estopped from charging him with failure to pay. (Mr. Haddock here cited *Spowers* v. *The Strand Magazine*, *Lucas* v. *Finck*, and *Wadsworth* v. *The Metropolitan Water Board*.)

As to the action of the police, Mr. Haddock said it was a nice thing if in the heart of the commercial capital of the world a man could not convey a negotiable instrument down the street without being arrested. He had instituted proceedings against Constable Boot for false imprisonment.

Cross-examined as to motive, witness said that he had no cheque-forms available and, being anxious to meet his obligations promptly, had made use of the only material to hand. Later he admitted that there might have been present in his mind a desire to make the Collector of Taxes ridiculous. But why not? There was no law against deriding the income-tax[1].

Sir Basil String (after the hearing of further evidence): This case has at least brought to the notice of the Court a citizen who is unusual both in his clarity of mind and integrity of behaviour. No thinking man can regard those parts of the Finance Acts which govern the income-tax with anything but contempt. There may be something to be said—not much—for taking from those who have inherited wealth a certain proportion of that wealth for the service of the State and the benefit of the poor and needy; and those who by their own ability, brains, industry, and exertion have earned money may reasonably be invited to surrender a small portion of it towards the maintenance of those public services by which they benefit, to wit, the Police, the Navy, the Army, the public sewers, and so forth. But to compel such individuals to bestow a large part of their earnings upon other individuals, whether by way of pensions, unemployment grants, or education allowances, is manifestly barbarous and indefensible. Yet this is the law. The original and only official basis of taxation was that individual citizens, in return for their money, received collectively some services from the State, the defence of their property and persons, the care of their health or the education of their children. All that has now gone. Citizen A, who has earned money, is commanded simply to give it to Citizens B, C,

---

[1] Cf. Magna Carta: *'Jus ridendi nulli negabimus.'*

and D, who have not, and by force of habit this has
come to be regarded as a normal and proper proceeding, whatever the comparative industry or merits of
Citizens A, B, C, and D. To be alive has become a
virtue, and the mere capacity to inflate the lungs
entitles Citizen B to a substantial share in the laborious
earnings of Citizen A. The defendant, Mr. Haddock,
repels and resents this doctrine, but, since it has received the sanction of Parliament, he dutifully complies
with it. Hampered by practical difficulties, he took
the first steps he could to discharge his legal obligations
to the State. Paper was not available, so he employed
instead a favourite cow. Now, there can be nothing
obscene, offensive, or derogatory in the presentation
of a cow by one man to another. Indeed, in certain
parts of our Empire the cow is venerated as a sacred
animal. Payment in kind is the oldest form of payment, and payment in kind more often than not meant
payment in cattle. Indeed, during the Saxon period,
Mr. Haddock tells us, cattle were described as *viva
pecunia*, or 'living money', from their being received as
payment on most occasions, at certain regulated prices.[1]
So that, whether the cheque was valid or not, it was
impossible to doubt the validity of the cow; and whatever the Collector's distrust of the former it was at
least his duty to accept the latter and credit Mr.
Haddock's account with its value. But, as Mr. Haddock protested in his able argument, an order to pay is
an order to pay, whether it is made on the back of an
envelope or on the back of a cow. The evidence of
the bank is that Mr. Haddock's account was in funds.
From every point of view, therefore, the Collector of
Taxes did wrong, by custom if not by law, in refusing

[1] Mandeville uses *Catele* for 'price'. (Wharton's Law Lexicon)

to take the proffered animal, and the summons issued at his instance will be discharged.

As for the second charge, I hold again that Constable Boot did wrong. It cannot be unlawful to conduct a cow through the London streets. The horse, at the present time a much less useful animal, constantly appears in those streets without protest, and the motor-car, more unnatural and unattractive still, is more numerous than either animal. Much less can the cow be regarded as an improper or unlawful companion when it is invested (as I have shown) with all the dignity of a bill of exchange.

If people choose to congregate in one place upon the apparition of Mr. Haddock with a promissory cow, then Constable Boot should arrest the people, not Mr. Haddock. Possibly, if Mr. Haddock had paraded Cockspur Street with a paper cheque for one million pounds made payable to bearer, the crowd would have been as great, but that is not to say that Mr. Haddock would have broken the law. In my judgment Mr. Haddock has behaved throughout in the manner of a perfect knight, citizen, and taxpayer. The charge brought by the Crown is dismissed; and I hope with all my heart that in his action against Constable Boot Mr. Haddock will be successful. What is the next case, please?

(33) REX *v.* LOW

WHAT ARE POLITICIANS?

(*Before Mr. Justice Wool*)

AT the Old Bailey to-day the well-known cartoonist, Low, surrendered to his bail on a charge of criminal libel.

Certain comments of Mr. Justice Wool increased the anxiety which is felt for the health of this venerable and popular judge.

Sir Ethelred Rutt, K.C. (for the prosecution): The prisoner in the dock is indicted for libel, for that he did compose and publish in the *Evening Standard* certain defamatory libels concerning certain well-known statemen and politicians——

The Judge: What is the difference?

Sir Ethelred: Milord, by statesmen I mean the leaders of my political party, and by politicians I mean the leaders of yours.[1] (*Laughter*)

Milord, members of the jury, the story is distressing. If there is one rule of conduct on which all creeds and classes are agreed it is that we should all in this mortal sphere make the best use we can of those gifts with which we have been endowed by Nature, by Providence, by the Public Schools and Universities, or by places of education. The prisoner has been endowed with a certain aptitude for draughtsmanship; and the jury will agree with me that that is a gift which all might envy

---

[1] This distinction was used, inaccurately, by Mr. D. Lloyd George in his 'Council of Faction' speech in July, 1935. I hope that if the biographers include it among the statesman's *mots* they will give the correct version. EDITOR

—the gift of representing or recording in permanent form the beauty which we see about us—beauty, alas, which is so often fugitive and evanescent, the flowers which fade, the butterfly which to-morrow will be no more, and the sunset which will never be quite the same again. Though we were unable to rise to these heights we should all be glad if we could represent on paper the dignity and beauty of the human form and that nobility of mind which is often visible in the outward countenance of a man.

The prisoner in the dock has not thought fit to utilize his undeniable gifts in that way. He has chosen rather to hold up his fellow-men to ridicule and contempt; he has represented not the dignity and beauty of the human form but its incongruous and awkward aspects; he has picked out for illustration not the noble actions of men, the self-sacrifices, the renunciations, the splendid successes, but their weaknesses and their vanities; not the distinguished aspirations of the soul but the unimportant peculiarities of the body.

But that is not all. You may think that such a course of conduct, such a lifetime of depreciation, would be pitiful enough if the objects of this man's attacks were private citizens on whose reputations no great matter depended. But what will you think when you hear, as you will hear in evidence, that through all his working life this man has taken as the particular targets of his art the highest statesmen in the land, men who are charged, or have been charged, or hope to be charged with the government of our country and the care of her destinies?

Let me take one or two deplorable examples. Some of the jury may be familiar with the name of Viscount Brentford.

The Judge: Who is he?

Sir Ethelred: Better known, milord, as Sir William Joynson-Hicks, he was for many years Home Secretary in the late Conservative administration. There was then a General Election, which the Conservatives lost. Sir William was rewarded for his services with a peerage, and——

The Judge: When I was at the Bar there was a solicitor called Hicks—— .

Sir Ethelred: The same, I believe, milord——

The Judge: Do you mean to say they made him a peer?

Sir Ethelred: Yes, milord.

The Judge: Good God! Go on, Sir Ethelred.

Sir Ethelred: Milord, you know what is said about a man who raises his hand to strike a woman; and personally I place in the same category of shame the man who would raise a laugh at the expense of Viscount Brentford. That pious statesman will be remembered as long as he is remembered for his efforts to make the people good, to preserve them from the perils of dancing, mixed bathing, late hours, and naughty books. Yet how has the prisoner habitually represented him? He has represented him in the likeness of a chimpanzee —I beg your Lordship's pardon?

The Judge (chuckling): I was only thinking. Go on.

Sir Ethelred: And he has given to that chimpanzee the soul of a man who revels in interference and is anxious to cut down the simple pleasures of the people. Further, in at least one notorious cartoon not only is the Viscount represented as a chimpanzee, but his wife and family appear as chimpanzees as well. Exhibit A, Milord: 'The Jix Family Go Into Committee!' You will observe, milord, that the older the members of the alleged family the more like chimpanzees they become; the innuendo being, milord, that Viscount Brentford will eventually resemble the aged figure on the left of the picture. Milord, I am instructed that there is no foundation for these suggestions. Never, milord, in any shape or form, has there been anything of that sort in the Hicks family.

Then let me pass to the three living statesmen who have filled the honourable office of Prime Minister of Great Britain. In the prisoner's drawings the face of the Right Hon. Stanley Baldwin wears an expression, I think invariably, of bovine—I might almost say ovine —stupidity, an expression which suggests to any fair-minded man a constitutional reluctance for vigorous action and a congenital incapacity for continuous or ordered thought; Mr. Lloyd George wears the expression of a mischievous rodent, and Mr. Ramsay Mac-Donald an expression of sanctimonious self-satisfaction, for which again, I am instructed, milord, there is no foundation in fact.

The Judge: Where did he get the Joynson?

Sir Ethelred: I beg your Lordship's pardon?

The Judge: Never mind.

Sir Ethelred: The Lord Privy Seal, the Right Hon. J. H. Thomas, one of the leaders of a great trade union, the Minister who has particular charge of the Unemployment problem, is represented consistently in the costume of a Cambridge undergraduate on Boat-race Night; he appears to be intoxicated; his top-hat is crushed, his evening dress is ill-fitting and disordered. And the jury will have to ask themselves: What impression is likely to be made upon the mind of an unemployed labourer when he sees the Minister responsible for finding him employment portrayed in such a guise and such a condition?

It may be urged in the prisoner's defence that he has done no more than to select some salient feature of each of his victims and give it an exaggerated emphasis for the purpose of identification. But in that case, the jury may ask: Why does he not emphasize the English virtues for which Mr. Baldwin is famous, the unselfish patriotism of Mr. Lloyd George, the courage of Mr. Thomas, and that strong strain of idealism and self-effacement which has made Mr. MacDonald what he is?

He has not chosen to do that. Milord, what are in fact the features of our statesmen on which this man lays emphasis? They are, in the first place, those physical peculiarities which not even statesmen can avoid; and in the second, those human foibles and weaknesses which most of us would prefer to keep secret. If a man has long hair, a long face, or a long nose, those features become longer in every cartoon in which the victim figures. If he is known to have a fondness for pipes, for cigars, for evening dress, he is represented as indulging those appetites on every occasion, suitable or unsuitable.

The Judge: Usher, bring me a *Who's Who.*

Sir Ethelred: Now, milord, as you may be aware, there is a base sort of person who are called, or call themselves, humorists, satirists, wits, and so forth, who make it their practice, not by drawing but by writing, to hold up their fellow-men to mockery and contempt, for the purpose of causing laughter. But even these low fellows acknowledge the limitations of good taste and decorum. What would be said, milord, if a humorous writer were to write, week after week, 'Mr. Maxton wants a hair-cut,' 'Mr. Baldwin has a stupid face,' 'Viscount Brentford looks like a chimpanzee,' or 'Lord Birkenhead is addicted to cigars'? It would be said first of all that that writer was singularly lacking in invention, and, secondly, that he had offended the canons of good taste, and, thirdly, that he was exposing himself to proceedings for libel.

The Judge: 'First viscount.' Extraordinary!

Sir Ethelred: But the man in that dock, members of the jury, has been so conducting himself for many years, so far with impunity. Even a politician will turn, and that rare manœuvre has at last occurred. The prisoner has taken away the reputations of our statesmen, and it is the law that no man shall wrongfully take away the reputation of another. It is also, of course, the law that you cannot be held guilty of taking away a man's reputation if he has no reputation; and one of the questions for you to answer will be: Have the politicians any reputations to take away? Or, rather, had they before the prisoner began to work upon them?

His Lordship, no doubt, at a later stage will explain the law to you in greater detail, but for the present I may be permitted briefly to tell you that in these criminal proceedings, if the prisoner is to be acquitted, he will have to satisfy you not only that the accusations which he has made are true, but that it is in the public interest that they should be published. That raises a difficult question.

The Judge: 'Home Secretary.' Amazing!

Sir Ethelred: Is it desirable, members of the jury, that we should know the truth about our politicians and statesmen? Once a man becomes a statesman it seems that nothing can remove him from that position—no effort of ours and no error of his. You and I, in our humble walks of life, are aware that if we make too many mistakes our business will suffer, and we may even lose our employment. But a statesman may make mistakes, sometimes the same mistakes, for twenty years and still retain his office and our affections; and if we are to have them with us for ever you may think that it would be better for us to remain in blissful ignorance of their real characters. Suppose that many of them are greedy for power, avaricious or insincere; suppose, for example, that it were the case that Mr. Baldwin had an unusually stupid and unimaginative face, that the main political purpose of Mr. Lloyd George was mischief, and that the Lord Privy Seal had an incongruous appearance in evening dress, would it be in the public interest that these facts (if they were facts) should be blazoned abroad week after week in the public Press? Must not this constant depreciation of those who have the conduct of the nation's affairs tend to undermine public confidence not only in the integrity and capacity of individual statesmen, but in the electoral system by which they were elevated to office, and hence in our Parliamentary institutions and the whole principle of Democracy itself? I ask the jury to say that this man is a menace to the British Constitution.

In conclusion I will ask you to remember that our statesmen and politicians have wives and families, little children and mothers. They have hearts and feelings and nerves like other men. Figure to yourselves the anxiety, the pain that would be caused in your own households if every time you opened a certain newspaper you might expect to see the breadwinner held up as a public butt, the beloved features distorted, the little mannerisms exaggerated into vices. Ask yourselves, members of the jury, how would you like to see *your* daddy represented in the newspaper in the likeness of a chimpanzee?

Lord Brentford was then sworn.

The Judge: Hullo, Hicks! So you're a viscount now?

Lord Brentford: Yes, my Lord. Your Lordship is amused?

The Judge (laughing heartily): No, no. I was only thinking. I beg your pardon.

Lord Brentford, giving evidence, said that he was not a chimpanzee. The principal note of his character was goodness. He did not think that this had been fairly brought out by prisoner. But in these days it was better to be insulted than ignored.

Mr. Baldwin said that he was not a very stupid man On the contrary, he was as cunning as a bag of monkeys. But in British politics it was fatal to confess to the possession of brains. He therefore lay low and said nothing until every one supposed that he was in a stupor. He then rose and walloped the lot of them, after which he relapsed into reticence. This he did at intervals of about six months, and it worked very well.

Mr. J. H. Thomas said that he seldom wore full evening dress, but that when he did he looked nice.

Lord Birkenhead said that it was a new constitutional doctrine to him that a statesman who from time to time enjoyed the solace of a cigar after the exacting labours of the day was thereby disqualified from holding high office under the Crown and disentitled to the common reticence enjoyed by the private citizen in relation to his own affairs.

The prisoner, in his defence, said that he emphasized physical features, not for the purposes of mockery or malice, but as symbols to express outstanding qualities of the soul. Lord Brentford's nose, for example, represented moral integrity and devotion to duty; the Lord

Privy Seal's dishevelled dress-suit represented a dislike for out-of-date ceremony and a strong sense of realism in politics; Lord Birkenhead's cigar represented a profound interest in Oriental problems: Mr. Baldwin's pipe and expression denoted loyalty, generosity, fairness, humility, forgiveness, and patriotism, combined with charity, literary taste, and freedom from material ambition.

The hearing was adjourned.

(34) URBAN DISTRICT COUNCIL OF BURBLETON v. HADDOCK

The Freedom of the Shores

THE House of Lords delivered considered judgments in this appeal to-day.

The Lord Chancellor: Not long ago I gave notice, as the head of the judiciary, that I was not satisfied with the state of the Common Law.[1] I announced that I was not prepared in every case to follow obsequiously the decisions of the past, however impressive their authority, and that I proposed increasingly to prefer the common sense of the twentieth century to the Common Law of the nineteenth. The present appeal is a welcome opportunity to put that promise into effect.

The appellant, Mr. Albert Haddock, was prosecuted by the Town Council of Burbleton for various offences against the by-laws of that smug and unlovely township. There were four charges against him: (1) that he did swim in the sea on Sunday within the hours prohibited by the Council; (2) That he did 'macintosh-bathe', as the strange phrase is—a practice forbidden by the Council[2]; (3) That he failed or refused to pay to the Council's servants the sum of eightpence for the privilege of swimming in the sea; and (4) That he failed

[1] See *Sparrow* v. *Pipp* (page 157).
[2] It is not clear what this means. Was the appellant *swimming* in a macintosh? And, if so, what was the objection of the Council on the score of decency? A later observation by the Lord Chancellor suggests that the practice was to wear a macintosh over a swimming-suit and to deposit the former on the foreshore before entering the water. But, again, at this date it is difficult to see in what category of crimes or offences the practice was included. EDITOR

to wear a swimming costume of the type, colour, and size approved and prescribed by the Council.

Mr. Haddock was convicted on all these charges at the Petty Sessions. He appealed. He appealed again. And, at length, after legal vicissitudes too numerous to recount, he has arrived, a suppliant, at your Lordships' honourable House.

It is not contended that Mr. Haddock has annoyed or injured any individual, nor has he offended against decency. His offence may be best described, perhaps, as *lèse-municipalité*: he has entered the ocean at the time and in a manner convenient to himself, and in so doing he has wounded the dignity of a local authority persuaded erroneously that it has absolute power over the lives and conduct of all persons who venture within its jurisdiction.

Now, the Council relies upon the powers given to local authorities by the Public Health Acts Amendment Act, 1907, to make rules and regulations for the conduct of sea-bathing. It is very desirable and proper that the Council should be able to supply or regulate the supply of bathing-huts, tents, life-belts and diving-boards, indicate the presence of dangerous currents or aquatic monsters, and do all such things for the convenience and safety of the bather as private enterprise has failed to do or is doing upon extortionate terms. And that, no doubt, was the intention of Parliament. The local authority is the servant of the citizen, and such powers are given to it in order to increase its capacity for service; but too many authorities appear to regard themselves too little as servants and too much as masters. It is one thing for the Council to say to Mr. Haddock, 'You wish to swim in the sea—we will provide you with facilities, as we are empowered to do.' It is quite another thing to say to him, 'You wish to swim in the sea—we forbid you to swim in the sea except at such times and places as we prescribe, upon certain moral or religious principles with which you may or may not agree, but this is what in fact the Council have said. Let us see by what authority they say it.

No one will deny that their jurisdiction extends at least as far as high-water mark, where the land proper comes to an end. But the alleged offences were committed at low water on the foreshore, that is, in the area between high-water mark and low-water mark. And what authority has the Council there? The foreshore is vested in the Crown, and, except by special grant from the Crown, cannot be vested in any one else. There is no special grant here.

And now let us examine the reverse aspect—the positive rights, if any, of the citizen. Over a hundred years ago, in the case of *Blundell* v. *Catterall*,[1] the question arose, 'Is there or is there not a Common Law right to cross the foreshore for the purpose of bathing in the sea?' The King's Bench, by a majority (Mr. Justice Best admirably dissenting), held that there was not, though it was conceded generously that 'bathing in the waters of the sea is, generally speaking, a lawful purpose'. 'It will not be disputed,' said Mr. Justice Best, 'that the sea is common to all. Bathing in the sea, if done with decency, is not only lawful, but proper, and often necessary for many of the inhabitants of this country. There must be the right to cross the shore in order to bathe as for any lawful purpose. The universal practice of England shows the right of way over the sea-shore to be a Common Law right. All sorts of persons who resort to the sea, either for business

[1] (1821) 5 B. and Ald. 268

or pleasure, have always been accustomed to pass over
the unoccupied parts of the shore with such carriages as
were suitable to their respective purposes, and no lord
of a manor has ever attempted to interrupt such persons.
. . . Men have from the earliest times bathed in the
sea; and unless in places or at seasons when they could
not, consistently with decency, be permitted to be
naked, no one ever attempted to prevent them.'

But the majority of the Court drew a somewhat
fanciful distinction between crossing the foreshore for
the purpose of fishing or putting to sea in a boat to
fish and crossing the foreshore for the purpose of bathing,
on the ground that fishing was an ancient practice
necessary for the nation's food-supply. That argument
may have had a plausible claim at that date. The total
immersion of the body in seas or rivers was then a
rare and audacious proceeding, only attempted after
elaborate arrangements for the preservation of life and
modesty. Our grandfathers entered the sea secretly
under large umbrellas, secured with strong ropes, and
almost fully clothed. It was but natural, perhaps, that
the Court should be reluctant to find any Common
Law right to do something which was so exceptional.
But to-day all is changed. The numbers of our fishermen have not increased—indeed, I think, they have
dwindled; but we have become a nation of swimmers.
Nearly all our citizens can swim; and even those who
cannot swim enter the water without fear eagerly
and often. How great is the change is shown by an
obiter dictum of the learned judge I have named: 'I
believe the use of machines is essential to the practice
of bathing. Decency must prevent all females and infirmity many men from bathing except from a machine.'
Nor is this exercise to be dismissed as a mere enjoyment

16

or contribution to health. He who can swim may in an emergency preserve not his own life only but those of others. 'By bathing,' says the same authority, 'those who live near the sea are taught their first duty, namely, to assist mariners in distress. They acquire, by bathing, confidence amidst the waves, and learn how to seize the proper moment for giving their assistance.' And since fish, like other food, is only one means of preserving human life, it may be said truly that swimming is as important, from the national point of view, as fishing.

But it is not necessary to measure mathematically the merits of these two practices. The point is not that the subject is entitled to such-and-such a use of the sea; he is entitled to *every* use of it. 'Is it to be supposed,' said Mr. Justice Best, 'that in a country the prosperity and independence of which depend on navigation, that which is so necessary to navigation as a road for all lawful purposes to the sea should not have been secured to the public, particularly when it might be done without injury to the interests of any individual?' 'What is the ocean?' said Lord Mildew in *Pratt* v. *The Ancient Society of Fishmongers* (1872, 2 Q.B.). 'It is not too much to say that the ocean is a part of the British Constitution. For generations, for centuries, the island race have lived beside, upon, by, with, and from the sea. The sea is in their veins; and hence, as we proudly say of some of them, their very blood is blue. An England without free access to the sea is as inconceivable as a Switzerland without mountains. The bird to the air, the Arab to the desert, the Frenchman to the café, the Briton to the ocean——' But I have quoted enough. To every word of that celebrated judgment I lend my support. These are without doubt the natural and juridical relations of every inhabitant of these islands to the element which surrounds them; and once that is apprehended our task in this case becomes much easier. It becomes fantastic, for example, to think of a small body of shopkeepers forbidding a British subject to enter the sea; and the apex of absurdity is revealed when we hear that the same shopkeepers *have exacted a fee* from the subject for *their* permission to enter the sea. They have as much right or reason to charge a fee for walking along the King's highway. Indeed, many of us were brought up to regard the ocean as the King's highway[1]; and, though that concept may have had its day in relation to other countries, as between Mr. Haddock and an over-zealous body of Councillors it has a very real existence.

I find therefore that the majority of the Court of King's Bench was wrong; that there is and always has been a right at Common Law to use the foreshore for any lawful purpose, as there is to use the highway or a piece of common land. Over the area above high-water mark the Council have the powers unwisely entrusted to them by Parliament, but in the area below high-water mark they are not entitled to make regulations or to order prosecutions unless the law of the land is broken or a legal nuisance is complained of (as, for instance, the excessive noise and water-displacement of fast motor-boats), or some recognized legal injury is done to a citizen or citizens. It is lawful to swim in the sea; it is lawful to swim on Sunday (whatever the Council may say); it is lawful to dress or undress on the foreshore with due regard to decency; it is lawful to wear a costume generally considered

[1] 'The shore of the sea was holden by the King, like the sea and his highways, for all his subjects.' (Best, J.)

decent and sufficient by the reasonable majority.[1] The
Councillors were not elected as arbiters of morals or
decency; they were elected to manage the finances and
the drains, which they do not do very well. Nor by
their election were they given possession of the shore
or the sea; and the exaction of any payment from a
bather, in the absence of some consideration or service,
such as the use of a bathing-hut, is *ultra vires* and illegal.
Mr. Haddock, who in the present case, refusing to
employ the insanitary bathing-huts provided by the
Council, merely deposited his macintosh on the foreshore, was right not to pay. The conclusion is that
below high-water mark the citizen who behaves himself before the Common Law may snap his fingers at
the Council. The appeal must be allowed. I am glad
indeed to have had the opportunity to rescue from
oblivion and commend to his fellow-countrymen our
defunct but learned and sagacious brother, Mr. Justice
Best.

Lord Arrowroot: I agree. I am aware that it is the
purpose of the Council by these regulations to encourage
foreign travel among their countrymen. This decision
will hamper them in that purpose, but it cannot be
helped.

Lord Sheep: I agree. If it were not so we should have
the absurd conclusion that a local authority might
order all bathers to enter the sea in woollen stockings,
at the end of long chains.

Lord Lick and *Lord Laburnum* concurred.

---

[1] But see *Rogers* v. *The Corporation of Eastbourne* (1929) 2 K.B., in
which a large whiting, the property of the plaintiff, was arrested for
indecency.

Note—See Wedderburn on *Wharfage*: 'Probably the Lord Chancellor could have expressed himself more forcibly still. An examination of the Town Police Clauses Act, 1847, and the Public Health Acts Amendment Act shows that local authorities have power to make regulations to prevent "the indecent exposure of the person" but not to act as dress-designers or censors of beach-wear. Indecent exposure is a simple question of fact.' See Mr. Justice Wool in *Sieveking* v. *Wattle*: 'Stuff and nonsense, constable! The male torso is not indecent. If it is hairy it may be unattractive: but so is the male foot. So is your face; but the Council cannot compel you to drape it. A lady's back is not indecent: it may be attractive, but so are a lady's eyes. The Act says "indecency", not "allure". My father wore nothing but drawers. So did I. What fudge!' See also *Fashions and Ramps*, by 'A Hosier', for the secret history of the 'University' costume.

(35) BACON *v.* EGG; KIDNEY *v.* EGG

THE LAW OF CRITICISM

THE hearing of this case was concluded in the High Court to-day before Mr. Justice Trout.

His Lordship (in his summing-up to the jury): This action is one of the most entertaining in my recollection.

The defendant, Mr. Egg, is, as you have heard, renowned for the vigour of his views and the frank manner in which he expresses them as the dramatic critic of *The Moon.* Such is this renown that the managers of several theatres have ostentatiously withheld from him the customary invitation to the first performance of their plays. Among these managers is Mr. Horace Kidney, who recently presented a play by Mr. Bacon entitled *Between Ourselves.* Mr. Egg was not invited, as the other authorized critics were invited, to view without payment the first performance of *Between Ourselves*; but, being anxious to see Mr. Bacon's new work as early as possible, he purchased, or hired the use of, a seat in the pit in the usual way. The circumstance that on this occasion for the first time he wore blue spectacles and a bright red wig in order to escape the notice of Mr. Kidney is for our purposes irrelevant and may be dismissed from your minds.

Mr. Egg then wrote, and published in *The Moon,* a very unfavourable account of the play and of the manner in which it was performed. 'Dialogue, deplorable; plot, puerile; characterization, childish'—this is one of the comments particularly complained of; and he concluded by remarking that '*The fact is, Mr. Bacon does not begin to know his business; and after this production we begin to doubt whether Mr. Kidney knows his'.*

You have been told in evidence that these expressions of opinion, strong and even hostile though they may appear, are not more severe than what is commonly said about those who attempt to give pleasure and amusement to their fellow-men. But both Mr. Bacon and Mr. Kidney resented them and have brought actions for defamation against Mr. Egg.

They have based their complaints, not only on the strength and the character of the words employed by Mr. Egg (which, they admit, are not exceptional), but on the strange ground that Mr. Egg was not invited to express an opinion at all. There is here a misconception of the law which I must at once expose to you. We have been informed in this case that it is the common belief among theatrical managers that only those are entitled to criticize their productions who are invited to do so. That belief, if it exists, has no foundation in law. It has been clearly laid down that every man who publishes a book or presents a play submits himself to the judgment of the public; and any one may comment upon his work within the limits of what may be fairly called criticism. Lord Justice Bowen, in the celebrated case of *Merivale* v. *Carson*, with which you are no doubt familiar, spoke of the '*common right of public criticism which every subject of the realm equally enjoys —the right of publishing a written criticism upon a literary work which is offered to public criticism*'. And I am not permitted to find fault with what was said by Lord Justice Bowen in the year 1887. It is a favourite saying in the bars of this free country that any man is entitled to his own opinion; but, what is more, he is entitled to express it, provided it is not defamatory.

The right of criticism, then, is not confined to the professional critic; and it would be lawful for every member of an audience to write to the papers about a play which they disliked. It is fortunate, perhaps, that they do not exercise this right; on the other hand, if it did not exist, it would follow that no man would be able to write in a letter to his aunt (as we frequently do), 'I have just read *Dandelion*—it is bilge', without exposing himself to an action for defamation.

Much less can the right be conceded to one class of professional critic and withheld from another. The critic who is invited and the critic who is not, the critic in evening dress and the critic who chooses to disguise himself with blue spectacles and a red wig—all these are equally entitled to express their opinion of a drama publicly performed, not as critics but as citizens. 'Any one can criticize,' said Lord Mildew in *Twopenny* v. *The Bank of England*, and, whether or not that is true in fact, it is true in law. For the right of criticism is a public right and not a favour to be bestowed upon individuals at the pleasure of managers and authors. We have been informed that the managers of certain theatres make arrangements for the exclusion and ejection of Mr. Egg by force, if he insists upon attending their performance uninvited. In such a case I conceive that Mr. Egg might successfully bring an action for trespass, or even breach of contract, against the manager responsible for his ejection. For he who invites the public to a public entertainment may only exclude an individual on the ground that he is offensive to the public by his being noisy, quarrelsome, drunk, or diseased; and, much as he, or we, may detest the personality of Mr. Egg, there is no particular reason to suppose that he, or any dramatic critic, as such, is more likely to give that kind of offence than any other person. However, in the present case, owing to the ingenious device of the red wig, no such situation arose; and I only throw out the suggestion for the titillation of law students and legal debating societies.

Again, where legal malice is alleged, such as will remove the expressions of a critic from the region of fair comment into the domain of defamation, it might be held to be evidence of malice that a critic who knew himself to be unwelcome had insisted upon thrusting himself in and had thereafter adversely criticized the entertainment. But here no charge of special malice is made, for the plaintiffs have admitted that Mr. Egg is accustomed to express himself with the same violence whether he is invited or not. In short, ladies and gentlemen, what with one thing and another, in so far as the plaintiffs rely upon the fact that the defendant was not invited, it is my direction to you that they have no case.

This is not to say that they may not succeed upon other grounds. Now, the law of libel is almost incomprehensible, except to those who have studied it from their cradles, and even for them it is a labyrinth of uncertainties, of false clues, blind alleys, and unexplored passages. Counsel for the defence has elaborately explained it to you, and probably some part of what he told you was correct. He has claimed that Mr. Egg, in the expressions complained of, has done no more than to exercise the right of every citizen to utter a fair and honest opinion on a matter of public interest, that is, a literary work exhibited in public for the judgment of the public. Mr. Swoot, however, who appeared for the plaintiffs, has reminded us that an honest opinion, fairly expressed, upon a matter of public interest, may still be defamatory. For example, it is defamatory to use expressions reflecting upon a man in the way of his trade, profession, or calling. The law of this businesslike land is jealous to protect our professional reputations; and spoken words reflecting upon them (by a special exception to the general law of slander) are actionable *per se*, without proof of special damage. To say of a doctor that he had no knowledge of medicine, of a solicitor that he knew nothing of the law, or of a banker that he did not know his business would without doubt be defamatory, however honestly the opinion was held and however moderately that opinion was expressed. Nothing but the strongest proof that the assertions were true in substance and in fact would be sufficient excuse for them in an action for defamation; yet it is undeniably a matter of public interest that our doctors, our solicitors, and our bankers should know their business.

'Now what,' says Mr. Swoot, 'is the distinction in law between the doctor and the dramatist?' I hold that there is none. There cannot be one law of libel for the author and another for the financier. An imputation of professional incapacity or unfitness is as damaging to the one as it is to the other; and each must be entitled to the same remedy at law, unless we are prepared to say that the author is a kind of outlaw, having a lower status than the solicitor or business man and entitled to a lower standard of justice. Unfortunately this view is very commonly held, and it has been encouraged by the feeble acquiescence or noble disdain of the writing profession; but in this Court it will receive no encouragement. I hold that the author, however loathsome to the ordinary citizen, is in the eyes of the law a professional man; and the newspapers must be as careful what they say about his professional fitness as they would be in the case of a surgeon. That is to say, any comments they may make upon his work must be both honest and fair; and if they go beyond that to the statement of facts, which, if they were true, would disqualify the author from practising his profession, then they must be prepared to prove that those statements are true. In this case Mr. Egg has made no attempt to prove that Mr. Bacon and Mr. Kidney are not fitted to practise the business of entertaining the public by the writing and presentation of stage-plays. All he has shown is that this particular effort has failed to please him. That opinion he has expressed intemperately, relying upon a supposed right to say what he likes. The evidence is that by what he has said he has deterred many thousands of citizens from visiting the Joy Theatre, and at least two managers from purchasing Mr. Bacon's new play *Daffodils*. He has damaged the plaintiffs in their business and he must pay for it.

The jury found for the plaintiffs. Damages £10,000.

NOTE—'It is hoped that before the present century is ended some occupant of the Woolsack may possess sufficient virility and legal knowledge to prepare a measure for the amendment and consolidation of the law of defamation. Among other reforms: (1) the grotesque distinctions between libel and slander should be swept away (in the Age of Radio it is a little late to maintain that writing is more dangerous than speech); (2) the liability of the printer for defamatory matter printed to order in the course of his business should be abolished, since the apprehensions of printers operate frequently as an unofficial censorship; (3) an authoritative definition of "fair" comment is needed (see *Blowhard* v. *Simpkins* (1928), in which the single word "Tripe!" was *held* to be a "fair" criticism of a sculptor's life-work, because honestly believed in); (4) the rights of authors and the limitations of criticism should be clearly laid down—e.g. in *Bacon* v. *Egg* there was no appeal and the House of Lords have never considered Mr. Justice Trout's novel argument that the same care should be used in discussing publicly the competence of an author as would be required from one who criticized the professional fitness of a surgeon or business man. Under the law as at present administered no man dares to breathe a public word against a grocer; but any one may say what he likes about a painter; yet both depend for their livelihood on selling their goods. Nor is it clear why one who writes a book is held to "submit himself to public criticism", while one who exhibits a motor-car at the Motor Show is not.' (Albert Haddock, Valerian Lectures, 1930)

(36) HADDOCK AND OTHERS *v.* BOARD OF INLAND REVENUE

Wear and Tear

This was an appeal from a decision of the Income-Tax Commissioners to the High Court.

Mr. Justice Radish: The appellant in this case is a Mr. Albert Haddock, a pertinacious litigant whom we are always glad to see. And let me say that it gives me pleasure to see the Commissioners, so often and for such poor cause the initiators of litigation, for once upon their defence.

Mr. Haddock asks for a declaration that he is, and has been for some years, entitled to certain allowances or deductions for income-tax purposes under the heading of (a) Expenses and (*b*) Wear and Tear of Machinery and Plant; and on the assumption that he is right he claims that a considerable sum is owing to him in respect of past years in which the Commissioners have refused to grant him such allowances.

Mr. Haddock appears on behalf of the whole body of authors, artists, and composers, and the position of a large number of creative brain-workers will be affected by our decision.

Now the theory of Income-Tax (under Schedule D) is that it is a tax upon the *profits* of occupations, professions, or businesses. The manufacturer of soap, who makes and sells soap to the value of ten thousand pounds, at a cost to himself of eight thousand pounds, is taxed upon two thousand pounds. If there is no profit there is (in theory) no tax. He is not taxed on what comes into the till, but upon what goes into the savings bank. Further, it is recognized by the State that his soap-manufacturing machinery and plant must in the nature of things suffer wear and tear with the passage of time, and on account of that depreciation he is allowed to deduct certain sums from his income, apart from the day-to-day expenses of his business.

The position of the author, artist, or composer is very different. But it is Mr. Haddock's first complaint that the Commissioners treat him as if he were in the same position as the soap-manufacturer, except where it would benefit him to be treated so. In the vulgar phrase, he says, they have it both ways. The author is taxed, practically speaking, not on profits but on *receipts*, on almost everything that comes into the till. For the small deductions allowed to him on account of professional expenses are meagre and in no way comparable to the expenses side of the soap-manufacturer's profit-and-loss accounts.

An author, says Mr. Haddock, cannot write about nothing (though one or two come very near to it). The whole of life is his raw material, and, like other raw material, it has to be paid for. His friendships, love-affairs, marriages, journeys, sports, reading, recreation, and social relations cannot be had for nothing. Mr. Haddock argues very plausibly that his expenditure on these items, without which he would be unable to carry on his profession at all, should be entered on the 'loss' side of his profit-and-loss account. The Commissioners, however, have obstinately refused to allow him anything by way of expenses, except for such obvious and trivial items as stationery, typewriting, use of secretary, pens, pencils, indiarubber, and so forth; they have allowed him nothing for hospitality, entertainment, or travel, and they have invariably deleted from his list of professional expenses such items as champagne, Monte Carlo, night-club subscriptions, 'first-nights', Deauville, and hire of yacht at Cowes. 'But how,' says Mr. Haddock, 'can a man write about Monte Carlo or Cowes unless he goes to Monte Carlo or Cowes? How is he to study and depict the gilded life of Society without constant visits to the Saveloy Grill Room, to Covent Garden, to the Riviera, and other places where Society is to be found?' These questions seem to me to be unanswerable; and they received no satisfactory answer from the representative of the defendants in the box. Further, it is not denied that if a soap-manufacturer were compelled for business reasons to visit Cowes or Monte Carlo he would be permitted to deduct the necessary expenses of the expedition when calculating his taxable income. I see no reason why Mr. Haddock should not do the same.

Next, as to wear and tear. One of the constant disadvantages of the author's trade is that he is a one-man business, at once his own employer, designer, technician, machine-minder, and machine. Once the soap-manufacturer has equipped and organized his factory he may relax; a week's holiday, a month's illness will not suspend the output of his soap or the growth of his income. But when the author stops the machine stops and the output stops. He is unable, on holiday, in sickness, or in age, to depute his functions to any other person. Here is one more reason why a hundred pounds earned by the author should not be treated and taxed on the same terms as a hundred pounds accruing as profit to the soap-manufacturer. 'Yet,' says Mr. Haddock, 'since this is done, let it be done thoroughly and logically.

The author's machinery and plant are his brain and his physique, his fund of inventiveness, his creative powers. These are not inexhaustible; they are seldom rested (for the reasons given above); the strain upon them increases as the years go by, and in some cases, I understand, is aggravated by late hours and dissipation. If it is proper for the soap-manufacturer to be relieved in respect of the wear and tear of his machinery and the renewal thereof (which money can easily buy), how much more consideration is owing to the delicate and irreplaceable mechanism of the writer!'

Under this head Mr. Haddock has repeatedly appealed for relief in respect of sums expended on doctor's accounts, on sunlight treatment, on nourishing foods and champagne, and upon necessary holidays at Monte Carlo and Cowes. The Commissioners have refused, and I find that they were wrong.

Under both heads, therefore, Mr. Haddock's appeal succeeds. He estimates that if his expenses be properly calculated on the basis already explained he has never yet made a taxable profit; for at the end of every year of his literary operations he has been a little more in debt than the year before. In every year, therefore, he has been wrongly assessed and unlawfully taxed; and I order the Commissioners to reopen the accounts for the past seven years and repay to Mr. Haddock the very large sums owing to him.

I may add a few words for the general guidance of Inland Revenue officials in this class of case. There seems to be a notion abroad (especially in Parliament, where every erroneous notion is carefully incubated) that the author deserves less generous treatment than the soap-manufacturer, on the ground that the latter is an employer of labour. Mr. Haddock in his evidence,

some of which I read with reluctance, has ably exposed
the fallacy herein contained, though his observations
on the Derating Act were perhaps tinged with irrelevance. 'It is difficult,' he said, 'to discuss this notion
with patience. What a poop Parliament is, milord!
The authors, writers, and composers are in a sense the
biggest employers in the country, for they are the only
original creators of employment. Their books, their
articles, their music must be typed and printed and
bound and distributed, performed upon the stage, the
wireless, the gramophone, and the screen. The publishers, printers, compositors, bookbinders, and booksellers, the actors, musicians, singers, and stage-hands—
nay, the very newspaper proprietors and their enormous
staffs, owe their employment, their earnings, and their
profits to the creative mind and technical skill of the
writer, since without him their occupation would be
nothing and their machines be silent. He is the producer and they an army of middlemen; he is the true
creator of wealth, and they, if I may employ the genial
language of a certain political party, are but parasites
upon his brains and labour. Yet Parliament, in its
recent Derating Act, designed to encourage and increase employment, extends the privileges of that Act
to the printer and not to the author who finds employment for that printer, 'derates' the 'factory' section of a
newspaper office, but not the editorial side, without
which that factory would be idle and valueless. My
Lord, how characteristically crass of Parliament! How
utterly soggy! How——' But perhaps Mr. Haddock's
point is now clear enough. The question whether
the premises of authors ought to be classed as 'fac-
tories' under the Derating Act must be decided by
some other tribunal than this. But the principles and

values laid down by Mr. Haddock for the proper estimation of authors and writers are sound, and should govern the Commissioners and their officials in all their dealings with this deserving and valuable class of men. The appeal is allowed.

(37) RUMPELHEIMER *v.* HADDOCK

PORT TO PORT

THIS case, involving some difficult points of Marine and Traffic Law, was brought to a conclusion to-day.

The President of the Probate, Divorce, and Admiralty Division (who had the assistance of an assessor) giving judgment: This action was originally instituted in the King's Bench; but, Mr. Justice Juice holding that the issues disclosed pertained to the Law of Admiralty, although the ground of the claim was damage to a motor-car, the case was withdrawn from the King's Bench List and referred to this Court.

Mr. Rumpelheimer is suing Mr. Haddock for negligent behaviour on the highroad, as a result of which his motor-car, a costly Botellini-Nine, was damaged. The dispute, as is usual at the present time, is only nominally between the parties named, the real litigants being two insurance companies. If it were not for the insurance companies there would be very little litigation of any kind to-day, and members of the legal profession owe to them a debt which we can only repay by careful labour and clear decisions.

On the 21st March last Mr. Rumpelheimer was driving his motor-car along the thoroughfare known as Chiswick Mall, which runs beside the north bank of the River Thames. Now, it appears that during the high spring tides, particularly those of the equinoctial seasons, the waters of the Thames overflow the banks and cover the highway to a depth of from two feet on the river side of the road to a few inches on the landward side. Such was the condition of affairs a little before high water on the date in question, when Mr. Rumpelheimer, who had an important business appointment in the City, began his voyage along the Mall. His evidence is that he was keeping carefully to the left or landward side of the road, where it was still possible to drive through the shallow water without fear of damage. While thus engaged he was startled, he says, to see ahead of him, and coming towards him on the same side of the road, the defendant, Mr. Haddock, who was navigating with a paddle a small boat of shallow draught. The plaintiff blew his horn vigorously, but the defendant held his course. Mr. Rumpelheimer shouted courteously, 'Out of the road, you fool!' and Mr. Haddock replied, as he admitted under cross-examination, 'Port to port, you foxy beetle! Are you not acquainted with the Regulations for Prevention of Collision at Sea? I am going to starboard.'

The plaintiff judged from this speech that he had to do with a maniac, and, obeying an instinct of humanity which in the circumstances deserves all praise, he swerved to the right rather than collide with the defendant's flimsy craft. But this manœuvre brought him into the deeper water, which penetrated to the delicate mechanism of his motor and caused it to stop.

It would not be profitable or seemly to dwell upon the exchange of views which followed. Although clearly expressed they reflect small credit on the breeding and education of either party. Mr. Rumpelheimer was compelled to remain where he was until the tide fell. (Mr. Haddock, by the way, in gross breach of the customs of the sea, declined to convey him to the shore or pavement in his boat, on the ground that he feared a breach of the peace.) On the waters subsiding it was found that the car had been seriously damaged, and it had to be towed to the nearest garage. Mr. Rumpelheimer was unable to keep his appointment, and as a result, he tells us, suffered pecuniary loss.

The evidence of Mr. Haddock was most unsatisfactory, and if he thought that by singing snatches of sea-chanties he would commend himself to the Admiralty Court he was mistaken. Further, he has imported into the case a deplorable element of personal prejudice. He made certain comments on the personal appearance of the plaintiff which he must have known can have no juridical significance. He said that he had once or twice with resentment observed the defendant going about the neighbourhood in an opulent motor-car of foreign make, driving to the public danger, in excess of the statutory speed-limit, and to his (Mr. Haddock's) inconvenience and alarm. He said that plaintiff seemed to think that he might be a law unto himself on the highroads, but that he (Mr. Haddock) was blowed if he (Mr. Rumpelheimer) was going to get away with it on the high seas as well. He had therefore acted as he did, willing to discomfit Mr. Rumpelheimer, but believing that the law was on his side, that is to say, the regulations for the prevention of collisions at sea or in tidal waters.

The defendant is clearly one who insufficiently appreciates the value of the motor-car to the human race. But we must not allow our natural detestation for such an individual to cloud our judgment. The meanest citizen, impelled by the meanest motives, is entitled to insist upon the enforcement of the law. The question is, 'What is the law?'—a question which frequently arises in our Courts and sometimes receives a satisfactory answer.

Now, the law or custom of the road is that when two vehicles meet each shall keep to the left. But the law or custom of the sea is that when two vessels meet they shall go to starboard and pass port to port, that is to say, each shall keep to the right. It is the contention of Mr. Haddock that when the tide covers the road that road becomes a part of the tideway, that traffic upon it is thenceforth governed by the regulations and customs of the sea, and that he did right, therefore, to steer so as to pass Mr. Rumpelheimer on his port hand. Further, it is the duty of a steam-vessel to keep out of the way of a rowing-boat; and Mr. Haddock argues that the plaintiff's motor-car when navigating the tideway has the status of a steam-vessel, and that plaintiff has nobody but himself to blame.

With considerable reluctance we find that there is some substance in these contentions. The law of the land says one thing; the law of the water says the contrary; and it seems elementary that (upon navigable waters) the law of the water must prevail. It is idle to say that Chiswick Mall was not at the time of the accident navigable water. Mr. Haddock was, in fact, navigating it, and if Mr. Rumpelheimer chooses to navigate it at the same time he must be bound by the appropriate regulations and should make himself familiar with them. Mr. Rumpelheimer makes the rather childish objection that his motor-car is not a vessel and ought not to be treated as such. I find no difficulty there. Recent developments of the internal-combustion engine, and in particular the outboard motor, have produced a type of water-conveyance which in aspect and dignity is little more than a floating automobile; and though Mr. Rumpelheimer's motor-car appears to be unseaworthy it is otherwise as much

a boat as many motor-boats. The point is that, boat
or not, it was navigating the tideway.

Again, it was argued for the plaintiff that, since the
highroad was only covered with water by an exceptional inundation of short duration, it cannot be held to
have lost the character of a highroad. But to accept
this view would be to admit a very dangerous and confusing precedent. Suppose that large sections of our
southern counties were covered for a long period
by exceptional floods, so that the inhabitants were
compelled to cross them regularly in steam- or motor-
vessels, can it be doubted that the regulations of
the water, as to the avoidance of collisions, the carrying of lights, sound signals in case of fog, and so forth,
would be observed and enforced in that area? Yet
in principle the two cases are the same; and differences of degree cannot be allowed to derogate from
principle. The fact that a certain area of water was
once dry land and is expected to be dry land again is
unimportant. Much of what we now know as land
was once covered by the ocean, and *vice versa*; but a
motorist would not be allowed to appeal to the customs
of the sea because he was crossing the Romney Marshes,
on the ground that that land used to be sea. In the
same way it is idle for the plaintiff to urge that Chiswick Mall used to be dry land. The question in every
case must be a question of fact—Was this area at the
material dates water or dry land? And neither geographical size nor extent of time is a relevant consideration. We find in this case that the scene of the mishap
was water, and tidal water. Now, tidal waters lead to
the ocean and are navigated by the vessels of every
maritime country. The regulations upon which Mr.
Haddock relies are not of British origin or sanction

only; they govern the movements and secure the safety of the ships of the world. The nations rely upon each other to observe them faithfully and defend them jealously. It will be easily seen what international complications might ensue if it were to go forth that the Admiralty Court of Great Britain was prepared to play fast and loose with them for the benefit of a motorist, however small the issues at stake. The defendant is no gentleman, but that is neither here nor there. We find for the defendant, much as we dislike him.

NOTE—See Bracton: '*Lex non risu deletur*' or 'Ridicule will not repeal', or (Lord Mildew in *The Dukeries Case*): 'A man may laugh at the law, but the law will laugh last.' See *Rex* v. *Flanagan* (1919) 2 A.C., in which the wife of a plumber died intestate leaving issue three children and net personalty £31,482. A charge of murder was preferred against the plumber, who raised the defence that, man and wife being at Common Law one person, it could not be murder to kill his wife. The plea was allowed, and a verdict of 'Suicide while of unsound mind' was returned; but it was *held* (Mould, L.J., dissenting) that, being insane, the man was ineligible for unemployment relief. See also *Earl of Erne* v. *Maltravers and Gareth* (1893, 2 H.L.), where the Yaffle hounds hunted an aged peer for four miles over the property of the plaintiff, who had forbidden the Hunt to cross his boundaries. In an action for trespass it was *held* (Fruit, L.J., dissenting) that though the Master had been guilty of negligence in employing short-sighted foxhounds their pursuit of Lord Gareth was an Act of God which he could not have foreseen or prevented. On appeal, however, the House of Lords decided that, though not responsible for damage done by the dogs, he must make good that which was due to the passage of himself and his horse, and the case was referred to assessors for apportionment *quantum pertinet*. Later, on a writ of *quo corpore* (*Rex* v. *Maltravers*), the Master was found guilty of constructive assault in venery, and went bankrupt. (And see Wedderburn on *Water-courses*.)

(38) REX *v.* COCHRAN

The Education Tax

(Before Mr. Justice Wool)

SUMMING up to the jury in this case to-day, Mr. Justice Wool made an important pronouncement on the constitutional aspect of the Entertainments Duty. Mr. Charles B. Cochran, the famous showman and theatrical producer, asks for a declaration that persons attending his three current productions should not be required to pay Entertainment Tax, on the ground that they are 'wholly educational' in character. In order to obtain a decision on the point of principle he has refused to collect and hand over the tax, but he has paid a large sum into Court.[1] The plays in question are a religious mime called *The Miracle*, an historical tragedy by the poet Shakespeare, and a comic opera written by Mr. Albert Haddock.

His Lordship, after a brief reference to the facts, said:

The public memory is short, and the historical knowledge of many of us is defective; yet it is surprising that the newspapers of our land do not give more attention to the Entertainments Duty and more support to those who agitate for its remission or reduction. For in essence it is dangerously similar to those Taxes on Knowledge which were remitted after a protracted struggle

---

[1] One of the many odd features of this tax is that, by arrangement, the theatrical managers have all the trouble and bear most of the expense of collecting it for the State. Another is that, since, by custom, the amount of tax paid is deducted from the 'gross receipts' on which the dramatist's royalties are calculated, it is, for him too, an extra income-tax.

only eighty years ago: taxes on the communication of minds, taxes on the distribution of information and ideas, taxes inimical to freedom of expression, and taxes levied with especial harshness upon the Newspaper Press. I refer to the Newspaper Stamp Act, repealed in 1855, the Advertisements Duty, remitted in 1853, the Paper Duty, repealed in 1861, and the Security System for newspapers, not abolished till 1869.[1]

The newspapers have enjoyed their liberties so long that they loosely suppose them to be part of the scheme of nature, and ungratefully forget those champions of freedom who had to fight so hard for them in the much-admired Victorian age. But there is no powerful reason, except that of recent habit and practice, why all these burdens should not be reimposed by any government which is anxious to obtain revenue or discipline opinion and has the necessary Parliamentary majority behind it.

We cannot find, even now, any guarantee of the Freedom of the Press in any written enactment, though laymen often speak as if we could. Not even the authors of the Bill of Rights, the charter of so many liberties, demanded the right of Free Speech, the repeal of the Licensing Act, or the abolition of the Press Censorship. For even those bold patriots thought that the line must be drawn somewhere, and freedom of expression was one of the last benefits which the aspiring Briton dared to ask for or his governors to grant.

So late, then, as the year 1850 all papers and pamphlets that published news had to carry a stamp; both paper, their raw material, and advertisements, their main source of revenue, had to pay duty; and no

[1] See *History of the Taxes on Knowledge*. (C. D. Collet. *Thinker's Library*)

newspaper might be printed or published 'without first executing a bond to His Majesty, together with two or three sufficient sureties . . .'—a kind of licence system and censorship combined. Their situation, in short, was very similar to that of a theatrical manager to-day —suspected, licensed, controlled, and taxed.

Even now we enjoy the rights of free expression in a negative sense only; that is to say, we are entitled to say what we like, provided that we do not offend against the laws of blasphemy, sedition, libel, slander, and obscene publications, upset the Lord Chamberlain, use threatening or abusive words or language calculated to cause a breach of the peace. There are many to-day who regard with jealousy and fear the liberties and powers of the Press, who would be glad to see its wealth diminished by taxes upon advertisements and paper, and think that no man should be able to wield the power of two or three popular papers without first giving some security for good behaviour in the form of a deposit or bond.[1] Even now the newspapers have to be registered, and it would be easy to amend the Act of 1881 so that they could only be registered upon the execution of a bond.

If such measures are ever proposed to Parliament the startled owners of the newspapers will not be able to make the usual eloquent appeals to Magna Carta or other cardinal statutes (excepting one, which I shall mention later) nor to any principle of the Constitution that has the same unassailable character as the rights, for example, of personal freedom and fair trial and the control of taxation by the House of Commons.[2] The

[1] 'There is something to be said for the view that the ownership or control of two or more newspapers should be scheduled as a Dangerous Occupation under the Factory Acts, since, as a rule, it seems to lead to mania' (*per* Wool, J., in *Barry* v. *The Co-ordinated Press*).
[2] See Magna Carta.

Acts directed against the papers have been repealed; a few specific but unimportant privileges have been granted to them by statute, and there has grown up in the last seventy years a usage by which they are left alone; but that is all.

Therefore they should ever be on their guard against any encroachments upon liberty of expression; and therefore, I repeat, it is strange if they do not show an active and fraternal interest in the struggles of the theatre. For, though they may be surprised and even indignant to hear it, there is, in the account of principle, no real distinction between the two institutions. Both are channels for the communication of minds, for the distribution and exchange of thought, ideas, and information. A tax upon either is a tax upon knowledge and literature.

Few newspapers exist to-day solely for the dissemination of news. More and more they stretch out their hands towards literature on the one hand and mere amusement on the other. It is impossible, without an abuse of language, to say that they are wholly educational in character or that they are not instruments of entertainment, and in many cases luxuries.

Any argument which is used to justify the taxation of the theatre is applicable equally to the taxation of nearly every periodical. Some papers, it may be said, are more elevated in character than others; but so are many plays. Some theatrical entertainments are purely frivolous; but so are many papers. That is the mischief of taxation of this kind. The affairs of the mind are not uniform and measurable, like boots or bicycles. It is impossible in practice to draw a line above or below which the tax shall not be levied. Yet without such a line injustice must be done and enlightenment and education suffer; and therefore as nations advance in wisdom such taxes are cut down and finally swept away. It is disturbing that England, the leader of thought and enlightenment, should have retained such a tax for nineteen years.

The Entertainments Duty was first imposed by section 1 of the Finance (New Duties) Act of 1916, when the Great War was raging, revenue was needed, and it was deemed an unseemly luxury to be publicly amused. The tax was one of those burdens which the trustful citizens patiently accepted in the stress of war, persuaded that at the close of hostilities they would be removed. It has not; nor have the rates been reduced since the end of the war, but increased.[1]

These rates vary with the amount charged for the tickets of admission to the entertainment; but after one and threepence the rate is a penny for every fivepence paid—or twenty per cent. 'Entertainment' includes any exhibition, performance, amusement, game, or sport to which persons are admitted for payment; so that in the same wide category are included a performance of *Hamlet* and the racing of dogs, a religious drama and a travelling circus, the fiddling of a Kreisler and the roaring of a caged lion, a game of cricket or a tragedy of Ibsen. So careless a classification, ignoring wholly the elements of mind and culture, may be forgiven to harassed statesmen in time of war, when the energies of all must be centred on securing victory. But to continue it unaltered in character or incidence for seventeen years of peace is indefensible.

The tax is levied not upon profits but upon receipts, and in that respect is almost unique. It is levied not upon gamblers, bookmakers, usurers, racecourse

[1] Excepting a very small 'gesture' in the Budget of 1935.

touts, idlers, thieves, vagabonds, card-players, misers, or moneylenders, not upon those who sit in their homes and hoard their money to the prejudice of trade and employment, not upon those who devote their time and energy to the suppression of the people's pleasures, but upon respectable, good-hearted citizens who spread happiness, instruction, and culture among their fellows and maintain many thousands in employment, either by providing or attending (and thus supporting) what are loosely called places of public entertainment.

When I consider this tax I am forced to the conclusion that in the opinion of the Legislature the business of entertainment has a criminal character, or at least is so offensive that public policy demands its discouragement and gradual suppression. Among all the varied activities of our citizens only the sale of wines, spirits, and beer is pursued by the tax-collector with similar ferocity. I can think of no other respectable industry (I do not of course include the sale of wine in that category) of which Parliament would dare to demand that those engaged in it should hand over to the Exchequer a fifth part, not of what goes into the savings bank but of what comes into the till. Not even the miscreants who manage our mines and railways are required to pay (in addition to income-tax) a pound for every five pounds that pass through their hands.

Yet in this country, so proud of the language of Shakespeare, if a man is incautious enough to present to the public one of the plays of Shakespeare at a cost, shall we say, of a thousand pounds a week, he will be fortunate, as I have been assured in evidence, if he receives six hundred pounds from the public; that is to say, he will lose four hundred pounds; but he will still be required to hand over to the State a tax—I would prefer to call it a fine—of more than a hundred pounds. There are those, maybe, who will say that a man who presents a play of Shakespeare at this date deserves to be fined a hundred pounds. But this would come ill from members of the House of Commons, who have recently, in regard to moving pictures, taken upon themselves to declare that public entertainments shall or should, in certain circumstances, be of a 'cultural' character only, and have strongly distinguished between such works as the plays of Shakespeare and the works of certain American scenario-writers. I use the vague and repellent word 'cultural' with reluctance; but, whatever our legislators may mean by it, it is certain that they attach a higher 'cultural' value to the plays of Shakespeare, Sir James Barrie, and others than to the American dramas already mentioned. One would expect, therefore, to find that this punitive tax was levied on the former class of work at a lower rate, just as the more powerfully intoxicating liquors are taxed more heavily than others.[1] The same authority which decides that such-and-such a film is not fit to be seen by children and young persons could easily be empowered to declare that those who produce or witness it

[1] On any ground of reasoning, 'cultural' or economic, it is absurd to impose with equal ferocity a tax on *turnover* (not *profits*) upon the presentation of Grand Opera and the hiring of a kitchen chair to view the Boat Race. The bookmakers of the land, asked to pay a tax of 5 and, later, only 2 per cent on turnover, protested that their business would be ruined. I remember a solemn announcement that the Derby would never be run again! Mr. Winston Churchill, with unusual discretion, yielded: and the tax was remitted. Yet the Entertainments Duty, a precisely similar impost, ranges *from 16 to 20 per cent*. The defenders of the tax say that in principle it is no worse than the whisky or tobacco duty. But, at this stage of our civilization, are we really to say that for the purposes of indirect taxation we perceive no distinction between a bottle of whisky and a play of Shakespeare—between attending a Beethoven concert and buying a packet of fags? EDITOR

shall pay twopence in every fivepence, while the producers of *Alice in Wonderland* are fined only a halfpenny.

We find, in fact, no such provision, for the simple reason that the tax is entirely deficient in logic and equity. It is not even imposed on every class of entertainment. Those who choose to entertain the people in their own homes by means of books, newspapers, gramophones, and broadcasting are exempt; only those entertainers who suffer the expense of providing a special place or building (and a special staff) must suffer this cruel impost as well. A publisher may sell a hundred thousand copies of a novel, but it is not regarded as a public entertainment until it is turned into a play.

There are certain exemptions and exceptions. But these only fortify the adverse comments I have already made; for they reveal that the authorities are aware of the correct principle which should govern these matters and know that the tax is a bad one. For example, the duty is not charged where the 'entertainment' is 'of a wholly educational character' or is provided by a school not conducted for profit; nor where the entertainment is provided for educational or scientific purposes by a society not seeking to make a profit, or *with the object of reviving national pastimes*; nor is it charged in respect of entertainments consisting solely of the products of an industry, a display of skill by workers in an industry, or works of graphic art, sculpture, and arts craftsmanship, executed and exhibited by persons who practise graphic art, sculpture, or 'arts craftsmanship' *for profit* and as their main occupation; or of displays of skill by such persons in such arts or crafts.

These exemptions (and others with which I will not

trouble you), although a sort of stumbling effort towards right thinking, dismally reveal the foggy condition of the mind of Parliament. Two principles are dimly discernible: (1) that what is 'educational' ought not to be taxed; and (2) that what is done for profit ought to be taxed. But then we have the queer cross-principle, as it were, that the exhibitions of those who paint, draw, model in clay or stone, or practise 'arts craftsmanship' need pay no tax, although the purpose of them is to make a profit. The explanation of which, presumably, is that these arts are recognized as things of the mind, almost 'educational' in character, and therefore ought not, *eo nomine*, to suffer a tax in an enlightened community. But why, then, if these arts are not to be taxed in a picture-gallery, should they be taxed upon the stage? Why is the man who exhibits in Bond Street an artist's 'Sketches for *Hamlet*' to go free, but the man who uses those sketches in a stage-production of *Hamlet* to pay duty? There is no good answer to these questions, except that Parliament has failed to think clearly, and now, after nineteen years, refuses obstinately to think again.

I could detain you for a day or two with similar questions. What special value do His Majesty's Ministers attach to the art of sculpture that they exempt sculpture but make music pay? Why is the piano-player subject to duty but not the good Mr. Epstein? Why, if Mr. Cochran exhibited Mr. Epstein's works upon the stage would he then be subject to tax? And why are performances of actors not exempted either as (1) 'displays of skill by workers in the industry', or (2) 'displays of skill by persons who practise arts craftsmanship for profit and as their main occupation'? Why is a dull lecture about Shakespeare exempt but

18

not a lively production of one of Shakespeare's plays? I cannot tell.

The truth is, I suspect, that the legislators still retain in their minds, though not upon their tongues, the ancient notion that the playhouse is wicked and dangerous and ought by any means to be discouraged and put down. This is in essence the same notion that fought against printing, against literature, and against the Press; which has opposed in turn each novel form of free expression; which rages now against the moving picture, and will soon be mobilized against television in the home. For various reasons, but especially the personal attraction of female actors, it has survived with particular obstinacy against the theatre. But it has only to be defied to be defeated.

I am surprised that, before Mr. Cochran, no manager has made this wholesome challenge to the taxing power; though, according to the evidence, he is, above all, fitted to strike the first blow in a battle for enlightenment and the freedom of the arts. I think myself that he ought to succeed for more reasons than he has himself put forward. His productions are a tournament of all the arts; his actors, musicians, designers, and painters are all workers and craftsmen exhibiting their skill. It is true that he exhibits their works for profit. Why not? So do the exhibitors of graphic art and sculpture; but they are not required to pay twenty per cent upon their turnover; nor is the man who makes female underwear and exhibits it in his shop-window. He might also, I think, have said that his productions 'had the object of reviving a national pastime', to wit the theatre, which, I was assured by the expert witnesses, is dead.

Mr. Cochran, however, has chosen to found his claim

upon the single plea that his entertainments are 'wholly educational' in character. Now, who is to say what is educational and what is not? The only answer we have so far comes from a man of no great education, Mr. Spink of the Board of Customs and Excise. He said bluntly that the plays of Shakespeare are not educational, although they are the subject of prolonged study in our schools and universities. But he is a professional tax-collector, and I direct you that upon this point in this connexion his evidence is not worthy to be considered.

I might impress upon you my own opinion, but I do not propose to do so. For I think that this is a question for the jury, and a great opportunity for the jury. One of the few written landmarks in the history of the struggle for freedom of expression is Mr. Fox's Libel Act, 1792. That Act, after hot dispute, finally laid down that in a prosecution for libel it was for the jury, not for the judge, to say whether the words complained of were libellous or not. Which seems a simple thing to you, but is of large importance, giving to the jury—that is, to the people—the real custody of free expression; because in a political trial, whatever the judge or His Majesty's Ministers may say about the prisoner, it is within the powers of the jury to find that what he said was permissible, and acquit him.

I suggest to you that you have in this case an opportunity not only to defend the right but to make constitutional history. I charge you to say whether these productions are educational or not, thinking of education not as the narrow field of school-books and examinations but as the whole wide world of mental enrichment; dismissing from your minds all transitory objections to the morals of this play or the intellectual value of that, but bearing in mind the general observations I have made concerning taxes on knowledge and the free communication of minds. The jury as an institution is falling into disfavour; you have a chance to show that it may still be useful and ought to be preserved.

The jury, without retiring, found that two of the entertainments were wholly educational in character, that the third was an effort to revive a national pastime, and that all should be exempt from tax.

His Lordship: Well done!

(39) BOARD OF INLAND REVENUE *v.* HADDOCK

WHY IS THE HOUSE OF LORDS?

WE are able to-day to give some account of a startling judgment in the Court of Appeal delivered a few days before the end of term and, for reasons unknown but suspected, not hitherto reported in the Press.

The Master of the Rolls, having expressed a desire to hear no more argument from the learned counsel for the Crown, said:

This is an appeal from a judgment of a Divisional Court reversing an order by Quarter Sessions, allowing an appeal on a case stated from a decision of the magistrates granting an order to eject against an official of the Board of Inland Revenue upon a summons to show cause why the respondent should not have vacant possession of his own premises under an instruction of the Commissioners for Income Tax, afterwards reversed by the Board.

The point at issue is whether the appellants are entitled under the Land Tax Clauses of the Finance Act, 1931, to enter upon the window-box of the respondent, Mr. Albert Haddock, and there remain for the purposes of measurement and assessment on the neglect or default of the respondent to supply particulars of his window-box upon the Land (Expropriation) Tax Form Q1/73198.

The point appears to be short and simple, but this Court does not intend to consider it. It will be observed from the history of the case as already recounted that a number of intelligent dispensers of justice have already addressed their minds to it with varying results. We are asked to say that the learned High Court judges who last considered the case were in error, and that the lay magistrates whose order they reversed were right. Whatever our decision, it is certain that an indignant appeal against it will be directed to the supreme tribunal, the House of Lords, since the resources of the Crown are as inexhaustible as its impudence, and the blood of Mr. Haddock is evidently up.

In these circumstances, at the end of a long and fatiguing term of appeals, we do not feel called upon to consider this particular appeal with our customary care. But a few general observations upon our appellate system may not be out of place, and will at least satisfy the public that they are receiving full value from this distinguished Court.

The human mind is admittedly fallible, and in most professions the possibility of occasional error is admitted and even guarded against. But the legal profession is the only one in which the chances of error are admitted to be so high that an elaborate machinery has been provided for the correction of error—and not a single error, but a succession of errors. In other trades to be wrong is regarded as a matter for regret; in the law alone is it regarded as a matter of course. The House of Lords, as an appellate tribunal, is composed of eminent and experienced lawyers; but, if I may say so with respect, they are only by a small margin more eminent and experienced than the lawyers who compose this Court; indeed, it is frequently a matter of accident whether a judge selected for promotion is sent to this Court or reinforces the House of Lords. The difference in capacity is one of degree; indeed, the only real difference is that the House of Lords has the last word. But the difference in estimation is substantial, and in practice great issues and the destination of enormous sums of money are allowed to be determined by it.

Now, this is strange. The institution of one Court of Appeal may be considered a reasonable precaution; but two suggest panic. To take a fair parallel, our great doctors, I think, would not claim to be more respected or more advanced in their own science than our greatest jurists. But our surprise would be great if, after the removal of our appendix by a distinguished surgeon, we were taken before three other distinguished surgeons, who ordered our appendix to be replaced; and our surprise would give place to stupefaction if we were then referred to a tribunal of seven distinguished surgeons, who directed that our appendix should be extracted again. Yet such operations, or successions of operations, are an everyday experience in the practice of the law.

The moral, I think, is clear. A doctor may be wrong and he will admit it; but he does not assume that he will be wrong. In difficult or doubtful cases he will accept, and may even seek, the opinion of a colleague more experienced or expensive; but if he had to pronounce every opinion with the knowledge that in all probability it would be appealed against and publicly condemned as erroneous, there would be little confidence in the consulting-room on one side or the other, and few medical men would consent to continue in practice. Indeed, it says much for the patience and public spirit of our inferior judges that they devote such thought and labour to their work in these discouraging conditions, and show no resentment towards junior counsel who, at the close of a ten days' inquiry and a protracted judgment, inform the learned judge responsible for both that they will appeal against his decision.

In short, the existence side by side of the Court of Appeal and the appellate House of Lords appears to me to be indefensible in logic and unnecessary and even vicious in practice. If it be assumed that the House of Lords is in fact possessed of exceptional acuteness and knowledge of the law, it may well be said that every case of exceptional difficulty should have the benefit of these exceptional powers. But it follows from this that every such case should be certified at an early stage as one that can be usefully considered only by the House of Lords, and to that House it should be at once referred; just as a general practitioner in medicine, confronted with an obscure disease or unusual conditions outside the range of his experience and knowledge, will at once refer the sufferer to a specialist. But the litigant whose case is exceptionally complex cannot now avail himself of the supreme wisdom of the House of Lords until he has trailed his coat through a number of inferior Courts, which are *ex hypothesi* incompetent to secure his rights or remove his doubts. Which is evidently a waste of time and money.

But it is perhaps a generous assumption that the litigant thinks of the House of Lords as the possessors of exceptional wisdom. The very similar composition and capacity of that House and this Court, to which a respectful allusion has already been made, are well known to him; and that similarity must suggest to him that when the House of Lords thinks differently from us it is not so much evidence of their superior wisdom as a matter of luck. At the end of certain hotly contested cases, decided only by a majority in both the Court of

Appeal and the House of Lords, the weary and impoverished litigant, adding up the number of judges who have voted for and against him in the various Courts, has found that, *per capita*, His Majesty's judges were equally divided on the point in dispute. It is not surprising, then, if many appellants present themselves to that House in a reckless or at least a speculative mood, as a gambler who has backed a succession of losers still hopes to recover all by a wild wager on the final race. The Court of Appeal, to one in this mood, must represent a minor handicap taking place at 3.30. It is not desirable that our great tribunals be regarded in this light; but at present it is inevitable. The people may be taught to believe in one Court of Appeal; but where there are two they cannot be blamed if they believe in neither. When a man keeps two clocks which tell the time differently, his fellows will receive with suspicion his weightiest pronouncements upon the hour of the day, even if one of them happens to be right. Moreover, the expense of successive appeals must make the acquisition of justice difficult for the rich and impossible for the poor. The unsuccessful litigant who cannot afford to go beyond the Court of Appeal must always be haunted by the thought that in the House of Lords he might have won; while the Inland Revenue, relying on the public purse, can pursue their unjust claims to the end and, if they lose, can send the bill to the taxpayer.

For all these reasons we recommend that either this Court or the House of Lords (as a Court of Appeal) be abolished; or, in the alternative, that the House of Lords retain its appellate functions as a specialist body for the settlement of questions of exceptional difficulty, such cases to be referred to them upon the order of a High Court judge. As for the present case, we decline to discuss it. It will go to the House of Lords in any event, so let it go at once. The appeal is formally allowed, and good luck to Mr. Haddock!

Lord Justice Ratchet and Apple, J. concurred.

NOTE—See *In re Macdonald* (page 352), where certain oddities of House of Lords procedure are discussed. For an appeal to the Lords the case for each side has to be presented in printed form, with a printed report of the proceedings in the inferior Courts. This does not reduce the cost of an appeal.

(40) TRISTRAM *v.* THE MOON LIFE ASSURANCE COMPANY

WHY IS THE CORONER?

(Before Mr. Justice Oat)

STRONG comments on the conduct of a coroner were made by the learned judge in his summing-up to the jury in this case to-day.

His Lordship: Lord Mildew remarked in a famous case, the name of which I forget: 'It is the duty of coroners to investigate the death of the deceased and not, as some of them seem to think, the lives of the living. Even an inquest can be too inquisitive.' It is a pity that that dictum has never been brought to the attention of Dr. Busy, the Bathbourne Coroner. The office of coroner is ancient, odd, anomalous, and perhaps unnecessary.[1] It is of interest to note that as far back as the thirteenth century the coroner had gained a reputation for interfering in matters which did not properly concern him. In Magna Carta it was thought worth while to include a chapter restraining his activities, and this was later re-enacted in the Coroners' Act of 1887.

It is a commonplace that the majority of men seem to have more importance at the time of death than they have ever had before; the whole nation may become agitated about the tragic death of some unfortunate fellow to whom nobody gave a thought so long as he was alive. And some of this factitious importance

---

[1] He is not found necessary, for example, in Scotland.

appears to attach itself to the coroner, who, having to deal with the dead from time to time, makes more stir in the world than those officers of the law who have to deal with the living six days in the week.

By the strange provisions of the Coroners' Amendment Act, 1926, a coroner must be either a solicitor, a barrister, or a legally qualified medical practitioner of five years' standing in his profession. And legally qualified, by the way, does not mean, as many suppose, a doctor who has made some study of the law. It means no more than a medical practitioner lawfully qualified to be a medical practitioner, that is, a medical practitioner registered under section 34 of the Medical Act, 1858, that is, an ordinary doctor. I have never understood why, if it was necessary or desirable to go outside the ranks of the legal profession for coroners, a medical man was considered to be the only possible alternative. The doctor, so far as I know, is no better qualified to exercise judicial functions than the banker, the business man, the civil servant, landowner, soldier, sailor, or schoolmaster. Indeed, *a priori*, much as I admire the medical profession, there are good reasons for thinking the contrary.

The doctor is accustomed by training and habit to found strong theories upon circumstantial evidence, and is often compelled by the necessity for immediate action to frame a firm diagnosis at a stage when the evidence is necessarily incomplete. And once he has adopted a certain hypothesis it is extremely difficult to persuade him to abandon it. Once my dear doctor has pronounced that I have mumps or whooping-cough I have mumps or whooping-cough. A 'second opinion' may ultimately show that I have, in fact, some glandular affection or tropical disease. But the taking of a 'second opinion', as you know, is a rare proceeding, only consented to in cases of exceptional doubt or difficulty. This apparent self-confidence is without doubt a valuable part of the technique of the medical world, where the patient's belief in the infallibility of his adviser is often an essential contributor to his recovery.

But in the legal profession we do not pretend to be quite so clever. The splendid pyramid of our appeal tribunals has been erected upon the generous assumption that the judge and the lawyer are as liable to error as those whom they advise or condemn. We are always taking 'second opinions', and scarcely any of us can make a move without one. Before the writ is issued the solicitor consults a barrister, and after it is issued the barrister consults the solicitor. The judge consults the clerk of the Court, the Bar, the precedents, the jury, and even the Acts of Parliament; and when with all these aids he has arrived at a decision he is cheerfully prepared for the litigant to take a second opinion from the Court of Appeal. Of all the numerous tribunals in the land, only the House of Lords and the Judicial Committee of the Privy Council are deemed so likely to be right that no appeal can go beyond them; and even then it cannot be said that any one man has the last word, since the decision is made by the majority of three judges or more, each of whom has the opportunity to take a second opinion from each of the others.

The only one-man judicial tribunal whose pronouncements are never, in practice, subjected to a 'second opinion' is the coroner. The High Court has power, both at Common Law and by statute, to quash a coroner's inquisition and order a new one.[1] But these powers are rarely used and do not cover the whole mischief.

[1] There was such a case in 1930.

There are three dangers: (1) that by reason of the coroner's queer proceedings a person may wrongly be accused of crime; (2) that a person properly accused and tried may be unjustly hampered and endangered by a cloud of inquest-generated prejudice; and (3) that, without being tried, wholly innocent persons, witnesses or relatives, may be blackened with coroner's mud. The High Court's powers may avail in an extreme case of (1) but rarely in (2), and never in (3), for the mischief is done. Moreover, the coroner may do much damage without doing anything of which the High Court could properly take notice.

A judge may err; may even be tempted, from time to time, into irrelevant and unjust censure. But he is bound by rules and traditions, and is always aware of the possibility that his proceedings may be reviewed and reversed by a superior Court. The coroner is not.

In short, the doctor, as such, has been selected for the one judicial post where an autocratic habit of mind is likely to be most dangerous, because it is in effect an autocratic office.

To come to the present case, Mr. Reginald Tristram was found dead in his pyjamas underneath his bedroom window. He was a sleep-walker, as you have heard. But the coroner's jury, strongly directed by Dr. Ambrose Busy, brought in a verdict of *felo de se*. The effect of this was not only to cause pain and grief to his relatives and to deny to the deceased the rites of Christian burial. A clause in the policy of insurance on the life of the deceased made the policy void in the event of suicide: the insurance company have denied liability, and this action is the result.

Now, a finding of fact by a coroner's inquisition is

not in law binding on any one, although in practice, as I have said, it may have permanent effects. 'Mud sticks', as Lord Mildew said in *Boot* v. *The Ecclesiastical Commissioners*. Nor is it even *prima facie* evidence of the cause of death (see *Bird* v. *Keep* (1918) A.C., 2 K.B.) in an action which turns upon the cause of death. This Court has to consider the question whether the deceased committed suicide or not, as if it had never been considered by the coroner at all. (Which, by the way, is an interesting commentary on the airs which Dr. Busy gives himself.)

I therefore, as you heard, directed both sides that the coroner's proceedings were not even to be mentioned. I have gone out of my way to mention them myself—first, because I desired to express my detestation of Dr. Busy, and secondly, because, if he had conducted the inquiry properly, this action, in my view, need never have been brought, and it is the duty of the Courts to discourage unnecessary litigation. *Interest reipublicae ut sit finis litium.*

Acting upon this principle, I am now going to read to you an extract from the report of the proceedings at Dr. Busy's inquiry. There is one habit common among medical men which I have not mentioned: the habit of asking a great many questions not immediately concerned with the matter in hand. While our dear doctor is making up his mind whether we are suffering from mumps or meningitis, typhoid fever or incipient pneumonia, he will put to us all manner of inquiries about our recent behaviour, our diet, our bowels, our dreams, drinks, recreations, and professional cares. Unexpected clues may from time to time be stumbled upon in this way. On the other hand, the process enables the questioner to appear most knowing when he is in fact in the most profound perplexity. An innocent and even helpful practice in the examination of the patient; and we can understand the inclination of a doctor to use the same technique for the investigation of truth in court. But what is proper for the private consulting-room may be most improper at a public inquest. Dr. Busy seems to treat his witnesses as if they were panel-patients endeavouring to conceal from him the origins of some discreditable disease. British justice assumes that all those who come into court are innocent until the contrary is shown. Dr. Busy, by professional habit, assumes that all those who come before him have something wrong with them, and that it is his business to put them right.

The Coroner: What time was it when you say you found the body of your father?

George Tristram (22): As I approached the house I heard the clock strike two.

Coroner: Why were you returning home at two o'clock in the morning?

Witness: What has that got to do with it?

Coroner (*sternly*): Answer the question, sir. It is my duty to elicit the truth.

Witness: About my father's death, yes, sir, but not about my evening out.

Coroner: So you had had an 'evening out'? Were you sober?

Witness: Yes. I'd been out to supper. Dancing. You can't dance drunk.

Coroner: You had been out to supper. With a woman?

Witness: Of course. Do you suppose I should dance with a leopard?

Coroner: No impertinence, please. What is the woman's name?

Witness: Mind your own business.

Coroner: At this moment, sir, it is my duty to mind yours. I must ask you for the woman's name.

Witness: Pratt.

Coroner: Miss or Mrs.?

Witness: Mrs.

(The Coroner here ordered Mrs. Pratt to be sent for.)

Coroner: So you were having an evening out with a married woman? Was her husband aware of this?

Witness: Really, sir, what has all this got to do with——

Coroner: Answer the question.

Witness: Probably not.

Coroner: Probably not. You mean that you and this woman are deceiving the husband?

Witness: No, I don't. I mean they don't live together any more.

Coroner: Divorced?

Witness: Practically.

Coroner: Practically divorced. Then the husband has obtained a decree *nisi*?

Witness: No, you fool! *She* has.

Coroner: Oh! So you returned home at two a.m. after dancing with a successful petitioner for divorce whose decree has not been made absolute?

(The Coroner here ordered his officer to communicate with the King's Proctor.)

Coroner: Is this the Mr. Pratt who went bankrupt not long ago?

And so on. There was in this case no question of

19.

murder or manslaughter. The simple question was: 'Did the deceased fall out of the window by accident or on purpose?' But in his blundering search for an answer Dr. Busy succeeded in blackening the character of every member of the bereaved family and four of their friends. He probed the secrets of their private lives as if he were searching their intestines for a needle. Their resentment of his impertinence inflamed his suspicions; he formed the fantastic theory that they were a family of rakes who by their loose behaviour had driven the deceased to self-destruction; and this theory he impressed upon the jury.

In my judgment the medical profession in general and Dr. Busy in particular are not well qualified for the discharge of judicial functions. I may add that I think the office of coroner should be abolished, and the civilized practice of Scotland adopted in this country.

In Scotland, as I understand the matter, the preliminary inquiries into the cause of a violent or suspicious death are conducted *in private* by the police and the Procurator Fiscal (the local Public Prosecutor), who consults, if necessary, the Law Officers or their trained assistants. If they decide that there ought to be a public trial there is *one* public trial, not two: and a man suspected of murder will not come to that trial in the cloud of prejudice with which the crude procedure and publicity of our inquest system surrounds him. If the coroner's office must be retained it should be entrusted only to trained lawyers observing a strict and uniform code of procedure. We will now consider the case before us.

(41) HADDOCK v. MOGUL HOTELS, LTD.

The Last Glass

(Before Mr. Justice Plush)

This action, in which the plaintiff claims damages for assault and the return of eleven shillings and sixpence, the value of certain goods alleged to have been converted by the defendant company to their own use, was to-day concluded.

The plaintiff, towards the close of a public banquet at the Hotel Edward, ordered and paid for a bottle of German wine, in order, as he said, to honour in a proper manner the toast of the British Empire, which was the penultimate toast of the evening. Shortly before the toast was proposed a waiter named Paravicini approached and removed the bottle of wine. An altercation followed. The waiter demanded the glass of wine which plaintiff held in his hands and refused to give up. Paravicini then laid hands upon the glass, which, plaintiff claims, constitutes an assault.

In the box, asked why he refused to surrender the glass, Mr. Haddock said that he thought Paravicini was a bandit.

Sir Humphrey Codd, K.C. (for the plaintiff): A bandit? What made you think that, Mr. Haddock?

Witness: Partly his appearance; partly his actions. He had already taken property of mine without warning and demanded more without offering any reason or excuse. Such uncivilized behaviour seemed to me to be capable of only one explanation. Bandits are everywhere nowadays; you find them in post offices, banks, and jewellers' shops. What more likely than that a determined gang should have penetrated into a big hotel frequented by the wealthy class?

Sir Humphrey: Believing him to be a bandit, Mr. Haddock, did you take any steps to cause his apprehension?

Witness: Yes, sir. I thought the best thing was to hold him in conversation till the manager and police could be informed. I therefore sipped my wine and with the other hand endeavoured to attract surreptitiously the attention of the lady on my right.

Sir Humphrey: In what manner?

Witness: By pinching her knee.

Sir Humphrey: Can you recall what form the conversation with Paravicini took?

Witness: I asked him what he thought he was doing. He replied, 'It is the law.' That confirmed my suspicions——

The Judge: What do you mean by that?

Witness: My Lord, as an Englishman I knew that the laws of this free country could not possibly provide for such a violation of the liberties of the subject. (*The witness here referred to Magna Carta, the Bill of Rights, King Charles II, and the speeches of certain statesmen at the last election.*) However, to test the bandit and gain time I asked him to name the particular law to which he referred. He hesitated and said again, 'It is the law.' I said sharply, 'What law? What statute, Act of Parliament, Order in Council, Departmental Order, police regulation, or by-law have you in mind?' He made no reply. Convinced now of his dangerous character, I said, 'Very well; I shall send for the manager.' Apparently alarmed by this threat, he then laid his hand upon mine and committed the assault complained of.

Cross-examined, witness admitted that during the conversation described he had finished his glass of wine, in order to appear at his ease and thus conceal his suspicions from the Wop.

Sir Ethelred Rutt (for the defendant): I beg your pardon?

Witness: The Wop. The Dago. The Italian.

Sir Ethelred: Do you now know that Paravicini is a waiter employed at the Hotel Edward?

Witness: Yes, sir; but that is not the point.

The Judge: You must not tell counsel what is the point of the case. It is a legal presumption that he knows.

Sir Ethelred: Have you ever heard of the Licensing Act, 1921?

Witness: No, sir.

Sir Ethelred: I put it to you that, in fact, you have made a close study of the Licensing Acts.

Witness: You are not entitled to put a statement to me. You are only entitled to ask a question.

The Judge: Mr. Haddock, you are not to instruct counsel in their duties. Nevertheless, Sir Ethelred, the witness is right. If he says that he has never heard of the Licensing Act you must accept his answer, and it is a waste of time to tell him that he has. The practice of 'putting it' is increasing and must be discouraged. In any case, the question appears to me to be irrelevant.

Sir Ethelred: With great respect, milord, the witness referred to Magna Carta.

The Judge: A man may well have heard of Magna Carta, Sir Ethelred, and be wholly unfamiliar with the Licensing Act. The former is part of every schoolboy's historical studies; the latter, rightly, is not.

Sir Ethelred: Ha!

His Lordship (summing up to the jury): The plaintiff's story is one which you may find it easy to receive with credence; and the frankness and generous feeling with which it was told have secured at least the confidence of the Court. He is invited by a well-known and worthy society to a banquet, the object of which is to celebrate the past glories of the British Empire and inspire the company with enthusiasm for its future. High in the list of those glories, I need hardly say, is the liberty of the subject, so hardly won by our forefathers, so dearly prized by their posterity in all the free and democratic countries which compose the British Commonwealth. The speeches are long—the Empire is a spacious theme—and the evening draws on. The climax approaches—the speech of Lord Gaythorpe, once Governor-General of the Dominion of Australia, to the noble toast of 'The Empire'. The plaintiff is present as an invited guest; he has been already requested by his hosts to drink to the health of a number of specified persons and causes, an ancient and civilized custom which is believed to have not only a symbolical but a certain spiritual value, uniting the company in hope and aspiration. In this manner he has already honoured the health of His Majesty the King, the Queen, the Prince of Wales, and all the Royal Family, and he proposes to do the same for the Empire. For any ceremonial purposes the otherwise excellent liquid, water, is unsuitable in colour and other respects.[1] He therefore acquires for lawful consideration an expensive bottle of wine; but just as he prepares to dedicate it to the Imperial toast, an individual of foreign, swarthy, and, as you have seen, somewhat alarming appearance

[1] See Wedderburn on *Wine.*

approaches the plaintiff from behind and, without a word of explanation or excuse, removes his property.

His astonishment is understandable, and a man having himself in less perfect control might well have been provoked to some retaliatory act of violence. He has told us that he had never heard of the Licensing Act, 1921; but even if he had he is not to be blamed if in all the circumstances the thought did not enter his mind that his hosts could contemplate or the law permit an act so lacking in fitness and in dignity.

He was therefore right to ask his assailant by what authority he acted; and I regard it as the gravest feature in the case that the man Paravicini was unable to give any precise or reassuring reply. For those who claim to interfere by law with the property, persons, or proceedings of others should be able, on demand, to give a clear account of the source, text, and scope of their authority. Otherwise the citizen can never be sure that they are not exceeding or misinterpreting their powers. Every waiter should have by heart the whole of the Licensing Acts (both 1910 and 1921) and the orders made thereunder by magistrates, chiefs of police, and others; and I wish the proprietors of catering establishments to note that such is the view of the Court.

We know, and the plaintiff now knows, that he was in fact violating the law in consuming even his one glass of wine at the time he did. But you are not to suppose that that is a consideration relevant to this case; for he is not charged here with illegal consumption. If he were, his ignorance of the law would not excuse him. But neither does that of the defendants or their servants. Even if the plaintiff was knowingly guilty of illegal consumption the defendants were not entitled to assault him, or, in my judgment, to take from him his property lawfully acquired. If they apprehend the commission of an offence on their premises it is their right and duty to warn the individual, for otherwise they may be charged with permitting the offence; and if an offence is committed it is their right and duty to summon and inform the officers of the law. But they are not themselves policemen, and they are not entitled to touch his property or person unless he himself is guilty of violence or of such conduct as will make him a trespasser upon their premises, or a person so undesirable, by reason of oaths, obscenity, or drunkenness, that he may lawfully be ejected. It is impossible to bring into any of these categories a sober subject who is about to listen to a long speech concerning the future of the British Empire; and it would be intolerable if it were. It is my direction to you that you should find for the plaintiff; and I hope that, for the sake of public example, you will award him heavy damages. I hope that this case will be widely noted. The plaintiff referred to Magna Carta; but in the pre-Carta days of King John the subject was seldom compelled to suffer such indignities as you have heard described to-day.

The jury found for the plaintiff. Damages, £5,000.

NOTE—It is to be hoped that caterers and purveyors of refreshment will take careful note of the decision, as requested by his Lordship. The effect of it is that, having issued a warning to the customers that they ought by law to desist from consuming, the proprietor has discharged his duty, and is not entitled immediately to do more. If, after a reasonable interval for compliance, it appears to him that they are still consuming unlawfully, he may, and should, send for the police and inform the officers that an offence is being committed. But if every proprietor behaves in this manner there will not be enough police to go round, and by degrees a little liberty may be restored, in fact, though not in law. EDITOR

(42) REX *v.* GEORGE, MACDONALD, MAXTON, AND OTHERS

CORRUPT PRACTICES

THE Political Bribery case was concluded at the Old Bailey to-day, when nearly four hundred Members of Parliament crowded the dock.

Mr. Justice Trout (in his summing-up to the jury): You have heard the lengthy and well-paid addresses of counsel, and you will now, if you can, divert your gaze from the distinguished figures in that dock and pay some attention to me.

The prisoners include the whole of the Parliamentary Labour and Liberal Parties, His Majesty's Ministers (with three exceptions) and the man George. They are charged under a section of the Corrupt Practices Act, 1854 (incorporated in the Corrupt Practices Act, 1883), which says that any person shall be guilty of bribery who

> '*shall directly or indirectly, by himself or by any other person on his behalf, give or procure, or agree to give or procure, or offer, promise, or promise to procure, or to endeavour to procure any office or employment to or for any voter, or to or for any person on behalf of any voter, or to or for any other person in order to induce such votes or refrain from voting.*'

Now, you have heard in evidence that at the last General Parliamentary Election all the accused persons presented themselves as candidates to their respective constituencies, and the evidence is clear also in every case that they did promise to procure employment for certain voters, as a result of which promises they did induce the exercise of millions of votes in their own interest. The promises varied in extent and confidence. Some of the prisoners contented themselves with promising to procure employment for particular sections of the people in particular trades, such as coal-mining, or the cotton industry; others promised to find 'Work for All', and among these must be numbered the prisoner George, whose generous belief in his own capacity to find remunerative employment for all our citizens made a special impression on some of the witnesses.

There is very little evidence that their promises have in fact been carried out; but that is not a relevant consideration. The charge is one of bribery, not of deceit or false pretences (though that aspect of the matter may call for inquiry on some other occasion). It is sufficient for the prosecution in this case to prove that the undertakings were made and that votes were given in return for them.

It may occur to you, gentlemen, members of a later generation than my own, to inquire why these facts, if proved, should constitute an offence. The answer is that in the year 1854 a very different view of the nature and responsibilities of the vote was held from that which is common to-day. In the much-abused nineteenth century the exercise of the suffrage was valued more as a public duty than as a private right. Men voted, or were expected to vote, after long internal debate, for reasons directed to the general welfare; to remove an incompetent Ministry, to uphold the honour or save the soul of their country, to defend religion or succour the oppressed, but not to advance their personal fortunes. And Parliament, in the statutes already cited, took special steps to secure that the vote should never be bartered for private material gain, whether in the shape of money, place, or employment.

All this, as some of the prisoners confessed, almost with pride, has changed. It is now a commonplace for Parliamentary candidates to invite the support of the voter by the simple assurance that, if they are elected, the voter will receive more money, more food, and more material pleasure. It is odd, perhaps, that this increase of materialism in politics should coincide with the advent to power of certain political parties which claim a monopoly of ideals; but it is the fact. The result is that the vote is generally regarded not as a precious instrument by which each man may do his country good, but as a weapon of offence or cajolery by which his country may be influenced to satisfy his material desires.

If this is the state of the public mind (and that is not, I think, in dispute), it follows that those laws which govern the conduct of elections must be enforced with especial severity and watchfulness. Our conditions, in some cases our consciences, may have changed, but the law remains the same. It is an offence to persuade the citizen to vote for this man or for that by holding out promises to provide him with employment; for this is to corrupt the character not only of the candidate but of the voter. It is also to bring into the arena of political warfare matters of trade and industry which are much better left out of it; but that is by the way. There is no doubt in my mind, and there can be little in yours, that this offence—the offence of bribery—has been committed by all the prisoners. The penalties provided by the Act are heavy, but you must not be deterred by that consideration from bringing in a true verdict. The penalties are: twelve months' imprisonment, with or without hard labour (or a fine of two hundred pounds), deprivation of the suffrage for seven years, and removal from and disqualification for any public office; and if the offender be a candidate, he also loses his seat (if elected) and is disqualified for ever from representing the constituency. Gentlemen, you will now consider your verdict.

The jury, without leaving the box, found all the prisoners guilty, and in imposing the maximum sentences the judge said:

I have decided to inflict imprisonment rather than a fine in order to ensure that none of these persons shall be free to take part in the approaching General Election. It has been urged before me that the sudden incarceration of the whole Cabinet may cause some trouble, but I am satisfied that the inconvenience will be both trifling and temporary. Two hundred Members of the House of Commons will still remain at large, and these should without difficulty be able to provide a Government. I may add that these proceedings were taken at the instance of a Mr. Albert Haddock, and the nation has to thank him, not for the first time, for his enterprise and public spirit.

NOTE—This case, decided in January, 1931, had a profound influence upon the technique of politics. In the election which followed the 'crisis' of the autumn, 1931, His Majesty's Ministers vied with each other in promising the electors not benefits but blows. 'We have reduced,' they said, 'your wages and your allowances and increased your taxes; and if we are elected there may be worse to come.' The more they threatened and bullied the people the more the people cheered. The Government was returned to power by an unparalleled majority, while those who promised the people more work and higher wages and allowances were almost obliterated.

(43) WILLOW *v.* CAPITAL PICTURES CORPORATION

What is a Judge?

(Before Mr. Justice Wool)

MUCH comment was provoked in legal circles yesterday by what was described as an 'unconventional outburst' of the learned judge during the hearing of this action.

Miss Gene Willow, it will be remembered, is claiming damages from the defendant corporation for breach of an agreement under which she was to receive one thousand pounds a week during the making of the film *Mermaids*. Because of the alleged reluctance or refusal of the plaintiff to enter the water at certain temperatures, the making of the film took fifteen weeks instead of five, as anticipated.

At the moment of his Lordship's intervention Sir Humphrey Codd was giving the jury a vivid picture of the plaintiff's sufferings. 'Imagine,' he said, 'the position of my unfortunate client——'

The Judge: Stuff and nonsense!

Sir Humphrey: I beg your Lordship's pardon?

The Judge: I said 'Stuff and nonsense!' Sir Humphrey, and I say it again, with a satisfaction that I am unable to conceal. This case wearies me——

Sir Humphrey: May it please your Lordship——

The Judge: It does *not* please my Lordship. Do you know how much I am paid for sitting up here and listening to all this bilge?

Sir Humphrey: 'Bilge', milord?

The Judge: Bilge, Sir Humphrey. Drivel, drivel, bilge and drivel. Dregs. Ullage. Cabbage-water——

Sir Humphrey: With profound submission, milord——

The Judge: A pittance, Sir Humphrey—a pittance, less twenty per cent.[1] A calculated affront—less twenty per cent. I sit here all day attending to the tedious affairs of other people. The time has come, Sir Humphrey, to call attention to my own. This blonde cow of yours——

Sir Humphrey: Milord, the plaintiff's case——

The Judge: Fritter the plaintiff's case! I say, this blonde cow of yours comes here complaining because she has only got five thousand pounds for five weeks' work. Wants another ten thousand pounds. I get five thousand pounds for working *all the year*—less twenty per cent cut; less twenty-five per cent income-tax; less super-tax at the Lord knows what rate! Employ that rather egg-shaped dome of yours, Sir Humphrey, and you will perceive that the answer to that sum is a figure quite insufficient to keep one of His Majesty's judges reasonably supplied with good clean underlinen, to say nothing of his abundant progeny. For that grotesque figure, Sir Humphrey, I doubt if you could persuade this golden-haired hen of yours to sing one silly song——

Sir Humphrey: Really, milord——

The Judge: Don't splutter, Sir Humphrey. And, by the way, sit down. I'm off. I'm enjoying myself. This may go on for some time.

Sir Humphrey resumed his seat.

Continuing in a more normal manner, his Lordship said:

[1] Presumably a reference to the 'cuts' in salaries and wages imposed upon judges and other public servants in 1931.

I pass now to the constitutional aspect of the matter. The wisdom of our ancestors has devised many ingenious safeguards to secure that His Majesty's judges shall be independent of all corrupting or intimidating influences, whether proceeding from the Throne, from Parliament, or the Executive. We are His Majesty's judges—not Parliament's judges, Sir Humphrey, not the Cabinet's judges, not the People's judges, not even, in the accepted constitutional sense, the 'Crown's' judges, but His Majesty's. And not even His Majesty has the same unfettered control over his judges as he has over others of his servants. His Majesty's civil servants, His Majesty's soldiers and sailors hold office during His Majesty's pleasure, and can in law be dismissed at a moment's notice. So, Sir Humphrey, before the Act of Settlement (12 & 13 Wm. III, c. 2) could we. But by that Act, and by section 5 of the Judicature Act, 1875, it was sagaciously provided that the judges hold their office during good behaviour; and from that office they can only be removed by His Majesty upon receipt of an address from both Houses of Parliament. *Both* Houses, Sir Humphrey—mark that. Thus neither the Monarch in person, nor his Ministers by the exercise of their powers of advice to him, nor the dominant political party by a vote of the House of Commons, nor even the great Electorate by an unmistakable expression of opinion at the polls can diminish by a single hour the tenure of office of one of His Majesty's judges. Secure alike from the intrigues of courtiers, the malice of Ministers, the spleen of parties and the windy passions of the mob, nothing but our own demise or misbehaviour can threaten us. And that misbehaviour must be so notorious that not only the volatile and jealous Commons but the sagacious

Lords themselves can be persuaded to present to the Throne a reluctant petition that we be dismissed.

It is not for nothing, Sir Humphrey, that those who have to hold the scales of justice evenly have been provided with a firm, unshakable base on which to perform that delicate operation. Thus only can we discharge our duties without fear or favour, affection or ill-will. Yet in the year 1931 all these constitutional thingummies, Sir Humphrey——

Sir Humphrey: I beg your Lordship's pardon?

The Judge: Thingummies—were recklessly thrown aside. In that year it was decided by the Executive that all the Crown's servants—that is, all those who draw salaries or wages from the public funds—should have those payments reduced by certain percentages. That may have been a wise decision or not. What was clearly erroneous, unconstitutional, and too absolutely fish-brained for words was the assumption that His Majesty's judges could rightly be included in the general category of Crown servants. For that is to say that our conditions of service are the same as those of policemen, private soldiers, or third-class clerks in a Government Department; which, as I have shown, is not so.

Now, the salaries paid by the Crown to its servants are matters which may be debated, and ultimately determined, by the House of Commons, and, since the House of Lords may not interfere with a money Bill, it may not question a decision of the Commons concerning the salary of a Crown servant. If, then, the proceedings of 1931 were admitted to have validity, we should have to say that a judge's office can only be taken away by the action of both Houses of Parliament, but his salary may be taken away by one House acting alone. Which is absurd. For if the Commons can reduce his salary by twenty per cent they can reduce it by a hundred per cent, which is tantamount to dismissal. And if they can reduce it because they apprehend a national emergency they can reduce it because they dislike him. Moreover, they can influence, or attempt to influence, his judgment by a mere threat to reduce his salary. In short, the House of Commons is in control of His Majesty's judges; and the same Constitution which with one hand gives them complete independence with the other hand snatches it away. But the Constitution cannot be thought to contain any part which is in gross contradiction to another part of it. I hold, therefore, that the reduction of our salaries, though loyally submitted to in the dangerous stress of the time, was an act having an unconstitutional flavour and should be rescinded. I am told that it would be impossible to restore our salaries without restoring the full pay of policemen. One answer to that is that judges are not policemen; another answer is that policemen should be properly treated too.

The same argument of course applies to the deduction of income-tax, super-tax, and all the tax family. For what is to prevent the Commons from levying a tax of twenty shillings in the pound on the salaries of judges? Since the Parliament Act, nothing. But what then becomes of the independence of the judiciary? Our salaries were fixed in the year 1825 or thereabouts at five thousand pounds (which then was wealth), and they were free of income-tax until the seventies. Today, Sir Humphrey, we receive, after deductions, about three thousand pounds, the earnings of a rising junior. It is not enough. The State cannot expect to secure a permanent supply of good and incorruptible judges for the price of a rising junior. *Justice should be cheap but judges expensive.* We used to speak of a man rising to the Bench; the day is not far distant when no really competent lawyer will consent to descend so low. You yourself, Sir Humphrey, would cackle in my face if I suggested that you and I should change places. What a situation! In short, old bubbler, the affairs of your little platinum pal do not interest me. The Court will now rise in protest.

Sir Humphrey: But, milord, it is only half-past two!

The Judge: The Court will rise.

The Court rose.

NOTE—This case was reported on February 22nd, 1933; and it is a pity that the Government did not act quietly at once. In July certain 'popular' daily papers, never very far behind the weeklies, got wind of the matter and began to press the judges' claim. Mr. Baldwin, answering a question in the House of Commons, said: 'I do not see why the judges should be excused their "cuts", any more than I am.' A somewhat unseemly public controversy followed, which might easily have been avoided. See Gladstone's advice to John Morley: 'Read *Punch.*' EDITOR

(44) REX *v.* JACKSON

ARE SUICIDES INSANE?

(Before Mr. Justice Mole)

A SEQUEL to a death pact, the trial at the Old Bailey of Oliver Jackson, 22, was continued to-day, when Sir Ethelred Rutt, K.C., made an impassioned plea for acquittal to the jury.

Jackson and a young woman, Emily Jones, 20, took poison together, as a result of which Jones died; but Jackson, after a long illness, survived.

This young man (said Sir Ethelred) stands before you charged with murder and attempted suicide. He looks a normal and healthy young man; he gave his evidence clearly and well; he appears to be responsible for his actions. He has admitted that he helped to administer to the dead woman the poison by which she died, and afterwards took some himself. Yet I ask you to acquit him on both charges on the ground that he is, or was, of unsound mind and not responsible for his actions.

The Judge: This is not a very promising line of defence, Sir Ethelred.

Sir Ethelred: You wait, milord. Members of the jury, at the inquest on Emily Jones, the coroner's jury brought in a verdict that she took her own life while of unsound mind. At that date the prisoner was grievously ill in in a prison hospital and was not expected to live. If he had died at the same time as Jones there is no doubt that the same coroner's court would have found that he had committed suicide while of unsound mind.

The Judge: Why?

Sir Ethelred: Milord, I shall come to that presently. But, gentlemen, he was carefully nursed back to life at the State's expense and by the servants of the State, and he is now charged by the State with a crime the penalty of which is death. Now, the State cannot have it both ways——

The Judge: It generally does.

Sir Ethelred: I cannot compete with your Lordship in worldly wisdom. It is the genial habit of the State, for one reason or another, to assume that a citizen who takes his own life was out of his mind when he did so. This is partly due to the antiquated provisions concerning the burial of suicides, and in part is a form of conceit in the State, which likes to think that it so well disposes the lives of the citizens that any one who wishes to leave it must be mad. But, whatever the reason, it is beyond all reason to say that he who does a thing successfully is of unsound mind, but that he who fails to do the same thing is of sound mind. For this——

The Judge: Steady, Sir Ethelred! What was that?

Sir Ethelred: Milord, the sounder the mind the more likely it is to direct the actions of the body with efficiency. Therefore, if a successful suicide be invariably mad, a would-be suicide who fails must be raving——

The Judge: Does the jury follow that?

The Foreman: We are not quite clear.

Sir Ethelred: That will come. Now, what was the particular evidence at this inquiry which led the jury to the conclusion that this unfortunate young woman,

Emily Jones, was of unsound mind? It was evidence applicable not to the woman only but to the prisoner Jackson as well, and applicable in precisely equal proportions. For it was, as you have heard, a letter found near the scene of the tragedy and signed by both parties. An extraordinary letter: criticizing the Government; questioning the capacity of statesmen and bankers; decrying the Gold Standard, Herr Hitler, ex-President Hoover, the Trade Unions, the Means Test, the Licensing Laws, the very House of Lords; suggesting changes in the laws and customs of the country which could only proceed from a disordered mind; attributing the joint misfortunes of the writers to persons and institutions which any British jury is bound to respect; and condemning with especial vigour the mother of Jones and the father of the prisoner.

Now, the coroner, Dr. Busy, following the admirable custom of our excellent coroners——

(At this point cheers broke out in the public galleries and the judge ordered a man to be removed. This was done.)

Sir Ethelred (continuing): The coroner, I say, was not content to establish the cause of death, but conducted a minute inquiry into the habits, social life, and moral outlook of all the relations of the deceased woman and as many of her friends as could be identified and brought to the court; also he made a long speech about greyhound-racing. The inquest lasted three days, but was much enjoyed by nearly every one. In particular, the coroner made some strong and severe comments upon the way of life of the dead woman's mother and the prisoner's father, the former of whom, it appears, keeps bees in her bedroom, while the latter bets on

greyhounds and listens to secular music in the Bud-
well Recreation Ground on Sunday afternoons. The
coroner founded these adverse comments, as you have
heard, upon certain observations in the letter I have
mentioned; though this did not prevent him from
directing the jury that that letter was written by one
person of unsound mind and another who, though still
alive, had probably been in the same condition at the
time of writing——

The Judge: Are you not wandering a trifle, Sir
Ethelred?

Sir Ethelred: It may be so, milord. No, not exactly.
The point is, milord: May it please your Lordship,
gentlemen of the jury, the coroner's investigations disclosed that the misfortunes of the prisoner Jackson
were even more acute than those of the dead woman,
Jones. Both were passionately, as the phrase is, 'in
love', and, owing to their economic circumstances, were
unable to marry; but in addition the prisoner has been
unemployed almost continuously since the age of sixteen; and his father, as I have already mentioned, is
a man of Bohemian tendencies and has been a source
of disquiet to his son. That is what I meant, milord,
when I said that the coroner's court would certainly
have found that the prisoner was of unsound mind if he
had died, which he has not. *A fortiori*, milord, if the
dead woman, Jones——

The Judge: I see what you mean, Sir Ethelred.

Sir Ethelred: I should like, if I may, milord, to dwell
for a moment upon your Lordship's sagacity, insight,
and knowledge of the world.

The Judge: Proceed, Sir Ethelred. It is not necessary.

Sir Ethelred: To proceed, milord?

The Judge: To dwell.

Sir Ethelred: Your Lordship is as modest as he is handsome. Milord——

The Judge: Does the jury see what you mean?

The Foreman of the Jury: Counsel means, milord, that the prisoner must be more mad than what the deceased was on account of more troubles and that.

Sir Ethelred: Exactly. Gentlemen, to all intents and purposes you may consider that Jones and Jackson are one person, for they were united in misfortune, love, and political opinions, in mind, body, and soul. A British jury has found that one half of this person was of unsound mind when it took poison. You, another British jury, are asked by the Crown to say that the other half of the same person was of perfectly sound mind when doing the same action at the same moment, though this half had even greater cause for desperation and loss of control. In other words, one British jury is being asked to go in flat contradiction of another. But this is impossible. For every British jury is the same—that is, it is the highest—with great respect to his Lordship—it is the highest and only infallible repository of wisdom and justice. Every British jury is always right[1]; it follows then that upon the same subject two British juries cannot come to a different decision; for that would mean that one of them was wrong—which is out of the question. Therefore the decision already arrived at is correct: the prisoner was of unsound mind at the time of the tragedy; and you will acquit him.

The Judge (summing up to the jury): I confess to a condition of faint cerebral nebulosity; but on the whole I do believe Sir Ethelred is right.

[1] But see the same counsel's remarks upon juries in *British Phosphates and Beef-Extract, Ltd.* v. *The United Alkali and Guano Simplex Association* (page 346).

The jury, without leaving the box, acquitted the accused on both charges.

The Judge: But, Sir Ethelred, if he is of unsound mind, he ought to be sent to a place.

Sir Ethelred: No, milord. With great respect, milord, he has become sane again—the shock.

The Judge: Oh, I see. Very well, he may go.

(45) BOLD *v.* THE ATTORNEY-GENERAL

WHAT IS THE CROWN?

THE House of Lords to-day dismissed this appeal.

The Lord Chancellor said:

We are compelled reluctantly to dismiss this appeal without considering the merits of the appellant's claim. The appellant, General Bold, is persuaded that a wrong has been done to him by the Crown in relation to his conditions of service in His Majesty's Army, of which he is, or was, a distinguished member. *Prima facie,* I am inclined to think that his contention has substance; but it would be improper for me even to discuss it, for the reason that, whether it be valid in equity or not, the action at law is wrongly conceived and will not lie.

This is not the common case of an inexperienced litigant impatiently seeking justice through an inappropriate channel. The General has already appealed to the War Office by letter, in person and in vain; he has, under section 42 of the Army Act, presented a petition to His Majesty the King (though it is not clear whether His Majesty ever received it); he has applied to the Secretary of State for an inquiry; he has brought an action against the Secretary of State for War; he has, under section 42 of the Army Act, presented a Council, and has instituted other legal measures, all of which were found by the High Court to be erroneous in form. In despair, and again in error, he began this action against the Attorney-General. So, by way of a monotonous succession of unfavourable decisions, his appeal for justice has reached at last the ears of your

Lordships; and we are compelled to send him away, though we are not satisfied that justice has been done.

This conclusion must be so repugnant to your Lordships' House, which is the final fount, the loftiest pinnacle of British justice, that I cannot record it without a word or two of comment and protestation.

One of the first actions of a loyal young Englishman who begins to study the law of the land is to read carefully the pages which are concerned with the King; and he learns with some surprise the ancient constitutional and legal principle that the King can do no wrong. He is surprised for this reason; that the whole course of his historical studies at school has led him to believe that at the material dates of English history the King was always doing wrong. Leaving out of account the past hundred years or more, in which our country has been blessed with monarchs of blameless character and reputation, the kings whose names are most firmly fixed in the national memory are those who continually did wrong, whether in a constitutional, political, social, moral, or religious sense; and I am quite sure that the familiar names of John, Charles, James, and Henry are at this moment present in your Lordships' minds. It is not too much to say that the whole Constitution has been erected upon the assumption that the King not only is capable of doing wrong but is more likely to do wrong than other men if he is given the chance. To this hypothesis we owe the Great Charter, the Petition of Right, the Bill of Rights, the Act of Settlement, the Habeas Corpus Act, the doctrine of Ministerial responsibility, the independence of the judiciary, the very existence of the two Houses of Parliament, and indeed, all the essential pillars in the noble fabric of the Constitution.

It is odd, then, that this maxim should survive in a political system which was invented to contradict it, and that our forefathers, who were compelled to rebel against the practice, should have reverently retained the principle. For in origin, I suspect, these words were not so much a testimony to royal infallibility as a convenient excuse for royal misfeasance. King John, I believe, was the first monarch to announce to his people that the King could do no wrong. But times have changed; and at the present time, if the maxim were no more than a loyal expression of confidence in the wisdom and integrity of the present occupant of the throne and his family, few subjects, I think, would be found to quarrel with it.

Unhappily, as the appellant has discovered, it has important legal and practical corollaries, which are in no way relevant to the character of the Monarch; and these are widely open to question. One of those fogs of ambiguity so dear to the laws of England surrounds our usage of the words 'King' and 'Crown'. The 'Crown' in this country is the symbol not only of loyalty but of the State, and distinguishes not only the palace but the village post office and police station. When we speak of the 'Crown' we sometimes mean the Monarch himself; but more often we mean the Government or some Department of it, or some department of some Department, and sometimes in practice, it is to be feared, some subordinate clerk in some department of some Department. All these Departments, nominally controlled by one who is nominally the King's Minister, enjoy in practice the benefit of the doctrine that the King can do no wrong. So that if a subject be injured through the negligent or dangerous driving of a Post Office van he has at law no remedy

against the Crown or Post Office; whereas in like cas
he could recover damages from a private compan`
which employed the driver. For the Crown is incap
able of negligence; neither can it be charged with libe
or fraud or any other tortious act; nor is it responsible
like the rest of us, for the tortious acts of its servant
done within the general scope of their employment.[1]

My Lords, this cannot be justified except by loos
or arrogant thinking. It is well that the King's auth
ority in the constitutional exercise of his prerogativ
should be beyond question; and it is very well tha
in his own person he should be spared from the vexa
tious pursuit of litigants, for he can be trusted to d
justice and right in his own affairs. But beyond tha
the ancient maxim should no longer have effect. Ther
is no good reason, except in time of war or civil emer
gency, why a Government Department should not b
amenable to the ordinary law of tort in its relations wit
the subject or its own servants; nor can I perceive wh`
a contract of service in the Army or Navy should not b
as sacred and as strictly enforceable as a contract o
service in a restaurant or drug-store. This is no trivia
or academic matter; for the Crown or State is con
stantly enlarging the scope of its activities and th
number of its servants; and there is a powerfu
political party which proposes to increase them in
definitely. If their dream be ever realized the whol
machinery of industry and trade will be controlled b
the State or Crown; almost every citizen will be in th
King's employ; almost every motor-van will be drive
by a servant of the Crown; and at every turn of life th
maxim that the King can do no wrong will, if it sti

[1] *Tort*: a civil injury or wrong. But a tort may also be a crim
e.g. assault, fraud, and libel.

survives, be operative. The laundry-woman who spoils our shirts, the grocer who gives us false measure, the journalist who defames us will all be servants of the Crown; and it will be impossible to pursue their employers in the Courts. It will be idle too for the ordinary citizen (if any remain) to found a claim for justice on the splendid promises of Magna Carta or the Bill of Rights.[1]

He will still, however, be able to proceed against the individual servant of the Crown who has injured him, though not against his Department nor the Minister at the head of it. I am happy to tell the appellant in this case that, if he is indeed the victim of a tortious act, it has been done by some one at the War Office; and if he can find that individual he can proceed against him (provided it is not the Secretary of State); and if the tortfeasor (when found) be a man of substance, the appellant may recover damages. I wish him luck. The appeal must be dismissed.

Lord Lick: I concur. What bilge it all is!

Lord Arrowroot: I concur. The principle in this case means 'The Soldier Has No Rights'. Why should he?

Lord Sheep: I do not agree. The King is one thing; an Office in Whitehall is another. The maxim says 'The King'. A writ of *mandamus* should issue to the Army Council.

The appeal was dismissed, Lord Sheep dissenting.

NOTE—The political party presumably referred to by his Lordship is that party which has for many years announced that it intends 'to nationalize the means of production, distribution, and exchange'—that is, every important industry in the land. The majority of that party

[1] See *Red Rags for John Bull* (Jim Thorne): 'We shall keep the King —to dish the Tories. The King can do no wrong; and we shall be King—see?'

still graciously concede that the Monarchy will be permitted to survive, and therefore a real dilemma will confront them. Either, by Act of Parliament, the doctrine that the King can do no wrong will have to be abolished or modified or the citizen will have no effective remedy in tort or contract against any industry. Have the 'Planners' ever considered this point? EDITOR

(46) TRIPP v. THE MILKO CORPORATION, LTD.

The Echoing Horn

Mr. Justice Wool to-day gave a startling judgment in the Motor-horn case. He said:

In this case the plaintiff seeks an injunction from the Court to prevent the continuance of an alleged nuisance. His house is situated in the residential district of Kensington, at a corner where four roads meet. Although near to the Cromwell Road, it is remote from the main lines of traffic, and when the plaintiff purchased his house the neighbourhood was reckoned 'quiet', if that word can still be said to have any meaning. But the drivers of taxi-cabs, private motor-cars, and other vehicles discovered that by passing down the 'quiet' street of the plaintiff it was possible to escape from the congestion of the main Kensington Road into the wide and comparatively empty spaces of the Cromwell Road, where they are able to proceed with that haste which is now deemed fashionable and necessary. Two of the roads at the plaintiff's corner converge at an acute angle, the two roads most in use are completely hidden from each other, and the passage of the corner is admittedly dangerous—that is, if due care be not employed; so much so that during some of the hours of daylight a constable is posted there on point-duty. Most drivers, however, according to the evidence, do not reduce speed as they approach, but diligently sound their 'horns', whether, it appears, the constable is there or not. And the plaintiff tells us that all day and for a great part of the night[1] the ears and nerves of himself and his family are harassed by loud bronchial and guttural noises in the street.

Since on a strict analysis the purpose of each of these noises is only to make the unimportant announcement that another motor-car is approaching,[2] the plaintiff contends with some reason that when set against the peace and quiet of himself, his household, and his neighbours, these noises are out of proportion and excessive.

Now Lord Justice James said in the right-of-way case of *Thorpe* v. *Brumfitt* (1873) L.R., 6 Ch. 650: 'Suppose one person leaves a wheelbarrow standing on a way; that may cause no appreciable inconvenience. But if a hundred do so, that may cause a serious inconvenience which a person entitled to the use of the way has a right to prevent. And it is no defence to any one person among the hundred to say that what he does causes of itself no damage to the complainant.' And Mr. Justice Chitty in *Lambton* v. *Mellish*, embracing nuisance under the same principle, said: 'If the acts of two persons, each being aware of what the other is doing, amount in the aggregate to what is an actionable wrong, each is amenable to the remedy against the aggregate cause of complaint.'

Accordingly, assuming that the plaintiff is right in his contention that the continual making of loud, guttural, or bronchial noises outside his house is an actionable nuisance, it would have been open to him to go into the street and name as defendant in the present action the first driver who hooted at his gates, even though the latter could prove that he had only made one small guttural or bronchial noise out of the multitude and had never passed that way before.

[1] This was in March, 1932.   [2] See page 342, note.

No doubt, however, the plaintiff saw certain difficulties in selecting a merely casual defendant, and he has wisely chosen to proceed against one whose offence, if any, can be proved, as it has been proved, to be frequently repeated, though the distinction, it must be emphasized, is only one of degree.

The defendant company are the owners of a large motor-lorry which carries milk into the metropolis in an enormous cylindrical tank resembling a monstrous gun. The plaintiff's evidence is that four or five times a week he is awakened by the passing of this vehicle at about four o'clock in the morning. Such is its weight that the house vibrates and trembles, and the plaintiff, starting suddenly from sleep, has often apprehended an earthquake. The engine appears to be old and ill-tended, and 'It sounds,' says the plaintiff, 'as if the lorry were always in low gear.' Moreover, as it approaches the corner, the driver invariably sounds a prolonged, raucous, and metallic blast. The driver, in the box, did not dispute the facts. He gave the simple but interesting defence that 'it is a dangerous corner'.[1]

Now why is it a dangerous corner? Who made it dangerous? It was not dangerous when the plaintiff bought his house. It was not dangerous in the days when the hansom-cab and horse-carriage used the street, or, if it was, the drivers did not think it necessary to make loud bronchial, guttural, and sleep-destroying noises as they approached it. They reined in their horses and made the corner a safe one. It would not be dangerous to-day if two processions or two

[1] 'Certain motorists, like certain savage tribes, suppose that by making a loud noise they can make a dangerous place less dangerous. Civilized persons know that they only make it noisier.' (Strauss on *Savage Ways*)

regiments of soldiers, moving in opposite directions, were to meet at this corner. The only thing that has made it dangerous is the passage of motor-cars driven in such a manner and at such a speed that if they do not warn the world of their approach they may cause damage to life and property. In order to avoid doing damage to those on the roads the defendants say that they are entitled to do damage to those in the adjoining houses —damage to nerves and health and mental efficiency —by making loud bronchial or guttural noises.

Was there ever so queer, selfish, and anti-social a proposition? The notion that there is some virtue in the sounding of motor-horns as a prelude to collisions has in the past, I am aware, received the thoughtless blessing of magistrates and policemen; but it cannot survive juridical analysis and will receive no encouragement in this Court. What the defendants say in effect is: 'I am a public danger. I am so dangerous that I am entitled to wake up the neighbourhood by shouting "Look out! I am coming!"; but once I have shouted I am not to be blamed for what happens.' Which is as if one man were to say to another, 'I am going to hit you,' and after the blow excuse himself by saying, 'I told you so.'

If a man fired off a revolver in the public street he would not be forgiven because he fired a warning rocket first; and if he let loose a man-eating tiger on the highway it would be no defence that the tiger was accustomed to give a very loud roar before pouncing on its prey.

As was observed by the Master of the Rolls in *Haddock* v. *Thwale*,[1] there is no juridical distinction between fire-arms, wild beasts, and motor-cars where the safety

[1] See page 127.

and peace of the King's subjects on the King's highway
are concerned. It is the duty of those who choose to
possess dangerous things, instruments, or beasts, so to
control them that they will do no damage. It is the
duty of the defendant's driver so to direct his dangerous
vehicle that no warning of his approach is necessary,
and if a deaf cripple be crossing the road round the
next corner he will still be able to avoid him. The continual making of offensive noises does not excuse but
is an aggravation of uncivilized behaviour. We do
not say that a dog which bites savagely is harmless
provided it barks loudly as well; on the contrary,
a continually barking dog would be condemned as a
nuisance though it never bit at all.

In the present case I am satisfied that the defendants
have brought a nuisance to the plaintiff's door, and it
must be stopped. There is in the Traffic Act a feeble
provision against the unnecessary sounding of horns by
stationary motor-cars. In my view their use should
be prohibited upon motor-cars in motion; and in my
judgment the Common Law of nuisance does in effect
prohibit their use wherever that law is appropriate
—wherever, that is, the Courts are satisfied that a
substantial offence is being done to ears, minds, and
feelings, to the quiet and comfort of peaceable homes,
and to the value of property. A man who took a flat
in Piccadilly to-day with his ears open, so to speak,
might not receive much sympathy in such an action
(though it is no defence in law that the plaintiff came
to a nuisance); but Mr. Tripp purchased his house
on a tacit understanding with the community that he
might live there in quiet. His quiet has been destroyed
and law and sympathy are both on his side. He shall
have an injunction; and if he cares to proceed against

the next man who sounds a horn at his door he will succeed again. 'The echoing horn', as the poet Gray remarked, 'no more shall wake him from his lowly bed.' As Lord Mildew said in *Rosemary Dye Works* v. *The B.B.C.*, 'There is too much noise. Let us reduce it.'

NOTE—Two years later, in 1934, Mr. Leslie Hore-Belisha, M.P., Minister of Transport, boldly accepted the principle of this judgment by prohibiting the use of motor-horns after eleven-thirty p.m. in London. Mention should be made here, too, of the good work done by the Anti-Noise League, led by Lord Horder, Mr. H. G. Strauss, and others. EDITOR

(47) HADDOCK *v.* JONES

Law of Libel Reformed

The House of Lords to-day allowed this important appeal.

The Lord Chancellor said:

I have had occasion to observe before that this House will not, if I have any influence, invariably consider itself bound by its own past decisions where these do not appear to be well adjusted to the needs and conditions of the present time; and I wish the fact to be as widely known as possible, for the knowledge must act as a wholesome spur to litigation. There are many celebrated decisions of this House which are to my mind erroneous and yet have the force and authority of a statute. The would-be litigant whose case is clearly covered by one of these decisions is compelled as a rule to suffer his wrongs or grievances in silence. He is advised by counsel that in 1873 the House of Lords by a majority decided that two and two make five—and there is an end of the matter; which is bad for business, to say nothing of the law. For the citizen is rare who has the tenacity of the admirable Mr. Haddock and will press his claim through one discouraging appeal after another in the distant hope that the House of Lords may change its mind for his particular benefit. But once it be known that this House is as capable of changing its mind as the House of Commons, and as likely to do so, then the bold and speculative genius of the race will without doubt bring more and more suppliants for justice before us, to the joint advantage of themselves, the legal profession, and the law of the land.

In the present case the appellant, Mr. Albert Haddock, is a writer of fiction; and in a book called *Tea for Three* he presented a fictitious character called Hilary Jones, who was a poet and lived at Bloomsbury. The name of the respondent is Hilary Jones, and he brought an action for defamation against Mr. Haddock. Mr. Haddock had never heard of this gentleman's existence, and proved to the satisfaction of the Court that he had had no intention of defaming him.

The real Mr. Jones does not live at Bloomsbury, but in Scotland; he is not, as the Jones of the book is described, 'short, sallow, and rat-like', but robust and rubicund; nor is ne, like the character in the book, a bachelor of 'Bohemian' tendencies, but a married man and a churchwarden. Indeed, the differences between the real and the imaginary Hilary Jones are so numerous and important that it would seem at first impossible to connect the two. Unfortunately the real Hilary Jones does from time to time contribute verse on nature subjects to *The Dunoon Gazette*. A number of the simple people of Dunoon therefore supposed that the author had had their fellow-citizen in mind, and concluded that the latter, on his visits to the metropolis, was guilty of the Bohemian behaviour attributed to the character in the book—or so they swore in the box.

It must be manifest to any reasonable mind that the first precaution of an author who proposed to write a malicious defamation of another person in a work of fiction would be to give him a fictitious name. So that of all the numerous individuals upon this planet the plaintiff was perhaps the one least likely to have been intended. But this did not occur to the simple people of Dunoon; and if it occurred to the jury it was put out of their minds by counsel for the plaintiff and by the learned judge, who very properly informed them of the decision of this House in the case of *Hulton* v. *Jones*. In that case the plaintiff was also named Jones—Artemus Jones (the tribe of Jones appears to be sensitive). He complained that he had been defamed by an article concerning a fictitious character named Artemus Jones, and he was awarded £1,750 in damages, though neither the writer of the article nor the editor of the paper had been aware of the plaintiff's existence.

In the present case Mr. Haddock has been ordered to pay £2,000 in damages to Mr. Hilary Jones. He appealed in vain to the Court of Appeal, who rightly assumed that your Lordships' House knew best; and here the splendid fellow is.

My Lords, I think he is not only splendid but right. Libel is a tortious or wrongful act. And one of the conditions generally required by the law to establish liability in an action for tort is the existence of either wrongful intention or culpable negligence. I forget whether any of your Lordships know Latin, but the appropriate and well-accepted maxim is: '*Actus non facit reum nisi mens sit rea*' ('It is not the deed which makes the wrongdoer, but the wrongful intention'). For the purpose of all penalties, civil or criminal, is deterrent, to prevent the commission or repetition of offences.[1] But no man can be deterred by a threat of punishment from doing something which he does not intend to do and does his best to avoid.[2] Thus, a man who kills

---

[1] See Salmond's *Law of Torts*, pages 12–13; but see also pages 14–17 for exceptions.

[2] 'In *criminal* cases *mens rea* is used in a narrower sense to include wrongful intention only. . . . In the law of torts, however, the term must be taken to include negligence also.' (Salmond)

another with a motor-car will, in the absence of wrong-ful intent and reckless or negligent behaviour, suffer no penalty and pay no damages; and it is a queer thing if he who takes away life is to be more easily treated than he who takes away a shred of reputation.

Now, in this case Mr. Haddock can be charged neither with offensive intention nor with punishable negligence. Indeed, to choose so common a name as Jones for the villain of a piece appears to me to be a wise precaution, and a writer cannot be expected to examine the history and character of every person called Jones before he does so. For all I know, and for all Mr. Haddock knows, there may be in these islands not one Hilary Jones but a thousand; and five hundred of these may from time to time be guilty of verse, may be churchwardens or in some other detail resemble the character in the book. If one of them can recover damages against Mr. Haddock I do not see why they should not all do so, which would mean that a man could be punished five hundred times for a single action, though it was done with innocent intention.

My Lords, this is absurd; and therefore it cannot be the law. Lord Chancellor Loreburn, in the case of Artemus Jones, defended the decision by reasoning which, with all respect, appears to me to be erroneous and batty.

'A man in good faith,' he said, 'may publish a libel believing it to be true, and it may be found by the jury that he acted in good faith believing it to be true; but that in fact the statement was false. Under those circumstances he has no defence to the action, however excellent his intention. *If the intention of the writer is immaterial in considering whether the matter*

*written is defamatory I do not see why it need be relevant
in considering whether it be defamatory of the plaintiff. . . .*
Just as the defendant could not excuse himself from
malice by showing that he wrote it in the most
benevolent spirit, so he cannot show that the libel
was not of and concerning the plaintiff by proving
that he never heard of the plaintiff. His intention
in both respects equally is inferred from what he did.
His remedy is to abstain from defamatory words.'

My Lords, the answer to all that is easy. In one
case the man has chosen to say things about a specific
individual, and if they turn out to be untrue he takes
the consequences. He has pointed a gun, so to speak,
not thinking it to be loaded, and it has gone off. In the
other case he has not pointed a gun at any one; he has
not said anything about any one; and for the harm done,
if any, he is not responsible. Nor is any one responsible,
except perhaps the plaintiff's friends. It is as if two
motor-cars had collided in a genuine 'accident'; neither
side being to blame, the damage must lie where it falls,
for no good purpose is to be served by shifting it. Two
Joneses have here collided; but no award of damages
in this case will prevent the next novelist from depicting
a character with the name of Jones.

And how, if he uses words at all, is Mr. Haddock
to be sure that he 'abstains from defamatory words'?
For the most innocent words may be made defamatory
by circumstances or by other people. Suppose that he
has an Amelia Jones in his book—a noble character
who is a mother. An Amelia Jones, who is not married,
comes to the Court accompanied by friends and neighbours who swear that they thought their Amelia was
intended. The words, if applied to the virtuous

spinster, are defamatory. Is Mr. Haddock to pay damages? If the leading decision is to stand—Yes. But my answer is—No. For otherwise I do not see how the admirable practice of fiction is to continue. Unscrupulous persons will have only to search the pages of every new novel until they find their own names, summon a few friends, proceed to the High Court, and draw their damages. It will be open to any one-armed gentleman named Hook, to proceed against the author of *Peter Pan*. The only alternative is that the characters of fiction should be represented solely by algebraical signs—'X then kissed Y on the lips', and so forth; which is to me a deplorable alternative. The appeal must be allowed.

Their Lordships concurred.

NOTE—In a High Court action decided three weeks later, Mr. Blennerhassett, a stockbroker, claimed damages from the publishers of an advertisement in which his name was innocently used. Evidence was given that he had been mocked on the Stock Exchange as a result of the advertisement, but the judge withheld the case from the jury and found for the defendants, evidently holding that he was bound by the judgment reported above. It may be taken, then, that *Hulton* v. *Jones* is no longer law. Some later cases confirm this view, though no inferior Court can express it openly. EDITOR

(48) REX *v.* THE MINISTER FOR DRAINS

THE EMPLOYMENT TAX

THE Lord Chief Justice to-day delivered his considered judgment in this important action. He said:

It appears that the Inland Revenue authorities are conducting a deliberate campaign against Ministers of the Crown; for this is the second claim of this character against a member of the Cabinet that I have had to consider within a fortnight. In the present case I am asked to say that the defendant has broken the law for the past seven years by employing a male servant, a Mr. Samuel Poppet, without a licence. The annual fee or tax chargeable upon such a licence is fifteen shillings, so that the total sum claimed by the Crown is only £5 5s. 0d. But much more is at stake in these proceedings than that.

At the present difficult time, when millions of able-bodied men are out of employment and those who provide employment are considered to be doing a public service, it may seem odd that any man should be taxed for giving employment to another in whatever capacity. This tax dates from the reign of Queen Victoria,[1] but the logical basis of its survival is not clear to me. In the official and voluminous categories of taxes it appears in company with the taxes on dogs, horse-carriages, gun-licences, and armorial bearings; and I note that the same fee will entitle the citizen either to a male servant or a horse-carriage with fewer than four wheels.[2]

In Victorian times the possession of a manservant

[1] An Act of 1869.   [2] See Wedderburn on *Wheeled Traffic.*

was an indication of wealth; but few private citizens retain to-day a house-steward, master of the horse, groom of the chambers, clerk of the kitchen, confectioner, postilion, or page. Certain of His Majesty's judges struggle through their domestic life with the assistance of a single valet; but it will not be suggested that this is a surer proof of affluence than the employment of three or four maidservants. Possibly we have here a relic of the excellent but now, alas! almost extinct tradition that man is a superior being to woman, so that a male servant, as such, is accounted a luxury.

Nor can the tax be any longer defended as diverting the rugged males of our land from the soft attractions of domestic service into the rougher pursuits of seamanship, soldiering, or exploration. It is now a good and patriotic thing to give employment to any man in any capacity, however domestic. There are in our midst many disabled soldiers and sailors who, though unhappily useless in the factory or the mine, may find honourable and contented occupation as personal servants in the office or the home. I believe that employers who make the proud announcement that their names are on the King's Roll by reason of their employing a certain proportion of ex-service men would not be struck off that Roll if it were found that a number of these men were employed as male personal servants. And yet for every one of them they must pay a tax of fifteen shillings *per annum*.

The definition in the Act (32 & 33 Vic., c. 14) is wide, and embraces all classes of both indoor and outdoor servants, but with some exemptions. To qualify for the tax the man must be employed in a personal, domestic, or menial capacity. That is the law, and I am here to see that it is obeyed.

I come now to the circumstances of the present case.
Mr. Samuel Poppet is employed by the Minister for
Drains as his 'personal private secretary'. Note the
word 'personal'. For it is contended for the defence
that his services are purely of an intellectual character
and cannot be described as personal, domestic, or
menial; that he prepares the material for, and sometimes himself composes, his master's speeches; looks up
the figures of exports and imports; collects damaging
quotations from the speeches of the Opposition, and
cuts out leading articles from *The Times* newspaper
concerning subjects which the Minister imperfectly
understands. I am not at all persuaded that these
services might not fairly be described as 'personal'.
Few things surely are so 'personal' as a man's speech;
and it has been powerfully argued before me that
between preparing the words which are to come out
of his mouth and preparing the food which is to
go into it there is, in law, small difference, if any.
Mr. Poppet, under cross-examination, admitted that it
has even been his duty to devise new jokes or exhume
old ones, for the decoration of the Minister's speeches;
and he who decorates a man's speech does a service
which seems not much less 'personal' than the decorat-
ing of a lady's face.

But upon this point I think it will not be necessary
for me to make a definite decision. Mr. Poppet has
other duties; and from the very frank account he gave to
the Court of the manner in which he had occupied the
previous day it is clear that they are many and various.
He attended at the Minister's residence at an early hour,
when the defendant, though awake and alert, was still
in bed. They discussed together a speech which the
Minister was to deliver at the inauguration of a new

sewer in South London. He dictated and the secretary took down in shorthand a number of letters to constituents, three to personal friends, and two to relatives. That done, the secretary was asked to 'turn on the bath, like a good fellow', and he has told us that in fact he *did* turn on the bath. While the Minister was bathing Mr. Poppet interviewed the Minister's cook about the Minister's evening meal, to which guests were invited, rang up a garage about the repair of his motor-car, and ordered by telephone some flowers for the dinner-table. While the Minister was dressing they discussed the Gold Standard, the new sewer, the Minister's car, his constituency, his income-tax assessment, international debts, the question of a new pair of braces, and the arrival of an aunt in London whom Mr. Poppet was to meet and, if possible, send back to the country.

When the defendant left the house Mr. Poppet remained. He put the finishing touches to the speech, wrote out with his own hand four menu cards for the dinner-table, telephoned to the Minister's sister about her allowance, and began to type the letters dictated in the bedroom.

While he was thus engaged he was requested by telephone to proceed to the Ministry with a pair of trousers, as the Minister had fallen in the muddy street and soiled those which he wore to an extent which would make them impossible for wear at the opening of the new sewer. Mr. Poppet went at once to the Ministry with a pair of trousers, the notes for the speech, and a new pair of braces which he thoughtfully purchased on the way in case the old pair should have been broken by the shock of the fall.

But we need not follow Mr. Poppet through all the diverse activities of his long and interesting day. Enough has been said to satisfy any reasonable man that a

reat part of Mr. Poppet's time is spent in services of
. 'personal' and even a 'domestic' character. He is a
male servant within the meaning of the Act, and the
Crown must succeed.

The duties of personal private secretaries do not, I
imagine, vary very greatly, and this decision may be
taken to cover all cases where males are similarly employed. The exemption of female secretaries may seem
illogical, but this Court is not responsible for that. Sir
Ethelred Rutt, for the defence, has argued, a little
petulantly, that it can never have been the intention of
Parliament to levy such a tax on the personal attend-
ants of Ministers, Statesmen, and Members of the House
of Commons. But, as Lord Mildew said in *Bluff* v.
Father Gray, 'If Parliament does not mean what it
says it must say so.'[1] Things have come to a pretty
pass if it is to be said that Ministers are to receive from
the Courts more favourable treatment than others. The
way to remove a fantastic measure from the Statute
Book is *not to evade or ignore but to enforce it*; and it
is no bad thing that Ministers should be brought
in this way to recognize the true nature of exactions
with which they thoughtlessly afflict their fellows. It
is idle to say that this is a small tax falling only on a few.
Injustice is a great evil, however small its scope. The
collection of a lunatic and inequitable tax, however
few the victims, must tend to breed an un-English
dislike of taxation in general and a dangerous distrust
of the House of Commons, whose sole excuse for existence is the defence of the common people from unjust
exactions by the executive. I find this to be a grave
case of evasion, and I shall send the papers in the case
to the Public Prosecutor.

[1] Cf. Bracton: '*Lex semper stultitia praesumitur.*'

(49) DAHLIA, LTD. *v.* YVONNE

ACT OF GOD

AN interesting point was argued yesterday in the House of Lords. The House, by a majority (Lords Sheep and Bottle dissenting), allowed the appeal of Dahlia, Ltd., against a decision of the Court of Appeal, reversing a judgment of Mr. Justice Tooth. The Lord Chancellor had read a learned judgment to this effect, awarding damages of five thousand pounds with costs against the respondent, Madame Yvonne; and the House was in the act of rising when Mr. David, for the respondent, a young barrister making his first appearance before the House, asked that costs in the appeal should be borne by the Crown on the ground that the judgment was in the nature of an Act of God.

The Lord Chancellor (resuming a sitting position): I beg your pardon?

Mr. David: An Act of God, milord.

Lord Flake: What is an Act of God?

Mr. David: The decision of this House, milord. Milord, in the case of *Rumble* v. *Spatt* (1893) 2 H.L., at page 147——

The Lord Chancellor: Mr. David, the authority of this House is without doubt very great, and I do not like to discourage junior counsel from making proper expressions of their respect, but it is never wise to exaggerate. Would you kindly explain yourself?

Mr. David: May it please your Lordships, it is well settled that, in the absence of any express provision to the contrary, a defendant cannot be held liable to make good any damage caused not by his own default but by the Act of God. An earthquake, milord, which destroys a theatre will relieve the manager from his promise to produce an author's play in that theatre before a given date; an insurance company will not be held liable to replace furniture destroyed by a sudden and unprecedented flood in London unless the risks specified in the policy include damage arising out of the Act of God; a conflagration, milord, which swept——

Lord Mew: Earthquakes, floods, conflagrations? What has all this to do with us?

Mr. David: Milords, in *Rump* v. *The Stepney Guardians*——

Lord Flake: There is no question of a conflagration here. The jury found that the bun was in fact composed of salicylic acid, and we have found for the appellants on the point of law.

Mr. David: Milord, with great respect, in *Rump* v. *The Stepney Guardians*—milord, in all these cases the principle is that a man can only be held responsible for damage which he might reasonably be expected to anticipate and so to avert or control. Milord, in the case of a volcanic eruption——

Lord Mew (*sharply*): Yes, but there is no volcanic eruption here.

Mr. David: Milord, with great respect, milord, the point is a little delicate——

Lord Flake: So delicate, Mr. David, as to be, so far, invisible.

Mr. David: If your Lordships will bear with me for a very few moments, I hope to show—— Milord, the definition of an Act of God laid down by Lord Mildew in *Turbot* v. *The Mayor of Swindon*——

Lord Bottle: Was that the Violin case?

Mr. David: No, milord, the Bicycle case. Milord, in that case an Act of God was defined as '*something which no reasonable man could have expected*'.

Lord Sheep: But the respondent had a *duty* not to supply buns which were composed, or mainly composed, of salicylic acid.

Mr. David: Milord, I was not referring to the bun.

The Lord Chancellor: Then what in the world are you talking about?

Mr. David (who appeared to be suffering some embarrassment): Milord, in my submission—milord, if your Lordships will forgive me—milord, with great respect, milord, the contention is that a decision of your Lordships' House is something which no reasonable man could have expected——

Lord Flake: What did you say?

Mr. David: Something which no reasonable man could have expected, milord—a decision of your Lordships' House, milord—an Act of God, milord. And therefore, milord, no man can be made responsible in costs or damages as a result of it.

(For a few moments, our correspondent informs us, there was complete silence in the House of Lords.)

The Lord Chancellor: Are you quite well, Mr. David?

Mr. David: Yes, milord.

The Lord Chancellor: I should be reluctant to send your name to the Bar Council, Mr. David. Perhaps we did not hear you correctly.

Mr. David: Milord, it must be evident *a priori* that no reasonable man can foresee a decision of the House of Lords, for otherwise no reasonable man would appeal to the House of Lords, only to lose his case. In the present appeal, milords, three of your Lordships have found for the appellants and two for the respondent; and by the definition already cited, milords, the working of your Lordships' minds——

Lord Bottle: We accept the definition, Mr. David, but must not the event, to fall within the rule, be some large and cataclysmic operation of nature—an earthquake, flood, hurricane, or conflagration?

Mr. David: In my submission, not necessarily, milord. I can conceive that a widespread epidemic of plague or infectious fever might be held to be an Act of God, though caused by a single minute and invisible bacillus——

The Lord Chancellor: Are you now comparing their Lordships' minds with an infectious fever?

Mr. David: Not exactly, milord. Milord, to take another example, it might be held that the going off the Gold Standard——

Lord Mew: That was due to the King's enemies, not the Act of God.

Mr. David: I am obliged to your Lordship for the interruption, which greatly assists my argument. The principle is the same in both cases, milords, that is, the incalculable nature of the event. No man can foresee an Act of God or the conduct of the King's enemies, and therefore no man is mulcted in money by the Courts for anything that follows from these proceedings, since it would be inequitable to hold a man responsible in law for that for which he cannot *ex hypothesi* be responsible in fact. A decision of your Lordships' House on a difficult point of law, with great respect, milord, is as incalculable as the onset of a flood, fever, or fire, and by the same reasoning it would be inequitable for either side to be compelled to pay for it.

Lord Bottle: But would not your reasoning apply

with equal force to the costs of the hearing in the High Court or the Court of Appeal?

Mr. David: In the Court of Appeal, perhaps, milord, but not in the High Court, for there the proceedings consist mainly in a finding of fact by the jury, and a reasonable man may be expected to foresee that a British jury will discover the true facts. But the appellate Courts are concerned with discovering the state of the law, and here the element of uncertainty is so great as to make the event incalculable. Moreover, in this tribunal there are five judges, not one judge, so that the chances to be calculated are much more various and numerous. Where there is one judge he is either dyspeptic or he is not; but where there are five, three may be dyspeptic and two not; one may be irritable, one deaf, and three dyspeptic; or there may be one dyspeptic, two——

The Lord Chancellor: I do not think you need work out all the permutations, Mr. David. We see what you mean.

Mr. David: I am much obliged to your Lordship. It follows, therefore, that he whose fortunes depend upon a decision of your Lordships' House is involved, as it were, in a speculation or gamble; and where, as in the case of my client, he is dragged into the speculation by the act of another, it is against equity and the rule of law that he should be called upon to pay for the result. In the case of *Rump* v. *The Stepney Guardians*, milords——

The Lord Chancellor: Mr. David, you will have an opportunity to conclude or withdraw your argument to-morrow. And we advise you in the meantime to consult a doctor.

The House then rose. In legal circles the decision of the House is awaited with much interest. It was observed by legal spectators that Lords Bottle and Sheep appeared to be considerably impressed by counsel's argument.

NOTE—In the event, the costs were paid by Madame Yvonne, Mr. David's client. A little later Mr. David was offered a legal appointment in the Home Office, and he has not been heard of again. EDITOR

(50) ALEY *v.* FISH

JUSTICE FOR MEN

JUDGMENT was delivered by the House of Lords to-day in the Slander of Men case.

The Lord Chancellor said:

This is one of those cases where, in my judgment, your Lordships' House should be ready to act not only as interpreters but renovators of the Common Law. The appellant, Mr. Aley, brought an unsuccessful suit for slander in the High Court (which held that there was no case to go to the jury), and he appealed in vain to the Court of Appeal; but, following the example of the good Mr. Haddock, he has refused to accept as final the precedents and authorities which were, very properly, considered binding by the Courts below, and has now come to the ultimate fount of justice for refreshment.

The facts are these. In the course of a verbal controversy concerning the Origins of Music, the respondent, who is a musical critic, said to Mr. Aley, who is a composer, 'You are a ——'; and he employed a word which is generally considered to impute immoral conduct, though its etymological origin has never been clear to me. Mr. Fish has made no attempt to show that the accusation was founded on fact; indeed in his pleadings he put forward the queer defence that the word was used in an affectionate manner and might almost be regarded as a term of endearment. Mr. Aley, on the other hand, does not claim that he has suffered any particular damage; he has not, for example, been requested to resign from his clubs. The music which he writes is still classed as 'good' music and therefore is not much performed; but this was the position before. Nevertheless the accusation appears to have rankled, and Mr. Aley sued for damages.

Now, according to the fantastic law of libel and slander, though a person wounded by the written word may recover damages without proof that he has in fact suffered any material loss, in an action for slander he must establish special or actual damage—except in four cases. One of these exceptions (to which I shall return) is the case where the man is slandered as a professional or business man. Another was grafted on to the Common Law by an extraordinary statute—the Slander of Women Act, 1891. By that Act it was enacted that spoken words imputing a lack of virtue to any woman or girl shall not require special damage to render them actionable. But this Act does not apply to Scotland.

As to men, the old rule of law was left intact—that is to say, a man cannot complain of such words, if they do no damage, unless he is a beneficed clergyman.

We have, then, this somewhat surprising position. In the absence of proof of special damage:

(1) It is not dangerous, at law, to say in public to a judge, 'You are a ——.'

(2) It is dangerous to say to a beneficed clergyman, 'You are a ——' (but not, it would appear, to a retired bishop).[1]

[1] See Strauss on *Ecclesiastical Dignitaries*:
'And since a retired bishop cannot claim that any words injure him as a professional or business man, it would appear that one may say anything about a retired bishop, in the absence of writing or special damage.' But see *Rex* v. *Coventry*, where an archdeacon tried it on.

(3) It is dangerous to say to a woman, 'You are a
——', but not in Scotland, where such an assertion,
presumably, would not be resented, or, to adopt a
more pleasing alternative, is so unlikely to be made
that the protection of the Act was not considered
necessary.

My Lords, you are acquainted with the earnest
efforts of the past fifty years to secure what is called
the Equality of the Sexes and to raise the female to the
same status as the male. It would be as simple and as
sensible to provide by Act of Parliament that the moon,
from a given date, should have the same size as the sun.
But let that pass. There is here one of the numerous
instances in which during the course of this clumsy
agitation the balance has been tipped in the opposite
direction and the male transferred to an unnatural
position of subjection.[1] It was well observed by the
learned Master of the Rolls, in the celebrated case of
Fardell v. *Potts*,[2] that at Common Law there was no
such thing as a reasonable woman, though that austere
conception has suffered considerable attrition during
recent years. Just as under the old law a woman was
held to have no sense, a man under the new law, it
appears, is held to have no morals. Or, to use the fine

---

[1] See Wedderburn on *Women* (2nd edition, page 748): 'It is an offence
for a man to dress up as a woman, but not for a woman to dress as a
man. The explanation is that a man who imitates a woman must be
mad, but a woman who models herself upon a man is only making an
effort to improve herself.' See also *Tallow* v. *Foot* (1918) 2 A.C. A
husband is liable for the torts of his wife. In that case Mrs. Foot said
that Miss Tallow had misbehaved with her husband, and pleaded
justification in an action for slander. Miss Tallow was awarded
damages, the charges not being proved to the satisfaction of the jury.
And Mr. Foot had to pay the damages, that is, for an untrue and
defamatory statement made about himself, but not by himself. See
also *Walton* v. *Hardy* (1933).

[2] page 1.

old expression of our forefathers, 'honour'—a woman's
'honour' is a precious and delicate thing (except in
Scotland), but not a man's (unless he be a beneficed
clergyman).

My Lords, there are matters here for your consideration of much deeper importance than the question
whether Mr. Fish did right to say that Mr. Aley was a
——. It is the constant hope of all good citizens that
the race is continually improving upon the achieve-
ments of its fathers, and to this hope we cling even where
the evidence is least encouraging. In the sphere of
art or literature, for example, it may by some be
regarded as a forlorn and even a presumptuous hope.
But surely in the sphere of morals we do right to entertain it. It may be difficult to paint, to write, to design
great buildings as nobly as our forefathers did; but
who will take so low a view of his own generation as to
say that we cannot hope to behave as well as they did?
And I would remind your Lordships that we have enjoyed, as they did not, the advantages of fifty years of
free public elementary education, and may therefore,
without arrogance, expect to behave even better.

Very well, then. Now, one of the favourite aims of
those reformers who labour to improve the lot of the
female and the morals of the male is the extinction of
the old idea that there may be one canon of moral
behaviour for women and another for men. To these
reformers we owe a recent statute in the department of
Divorce.[1] Before that Act a single unauthorized em-
brace was sufficient foundation for the divorce of a wife;
but a husband, to render himself liable to a decree,
must not only transfer his affections to another lady
but give clear proof that he had done so by knocking

[1] The Act of 1923

his wife about or leaving her defenceless for two years or more; the notion being that for a woman to be unfaithful was a rare, shocking, and definitive event (even in Scotland), but was a normal proceeding in the life of a man and proved nothing of any importance.

This notion, no doubt, had some correspondence with the facts in the far-off century which gave it birth, when men were less domestic and women more neglected, and even members of your Lordships' House were not ashamed of a certain irresponsibility in the distribution of their affections. There may be those—but not, I hope, in this House—who will maintain that there is reason behind it still. Be that as it may, it has been deliberately renounced by the nation in the Act of Parliament already mentioned. And here in this appeal we are confronted with a forgotten fragment of it still adhering to the Common Law. What are your Lordships to do? If the authorities of the past be still respected Mr. Aley's appeal must be dismissed; and to-morrow the news will be flashed across the world that, by the laws of England, in the judgment of your Lordships' House, a man, as such, has no virtue to speak of—or not, at least, in the sense that merely to deny it is to damage him. The libertines in our midst will be rejoiced to hear that the law at least has one foot still in the eighteenth century; and the forces of morality will be correspondingly cast down. The young student, bending over his Law Reports, will be shocked to learn that there are still two standards of morality before the law, that enemies will speak at their peril against his mother's honour but may say what they like about his father's (unless his mother is a resident in Scotland or his father is expelled from his clubs). And he will be yet more horrified when he

turns to the third exception to the rule we are considering; for this suggests—nay, clearly shows—that the law
sets a higher value upon professional than upon moral
reputation. For if you say of a man, 'He is an unfaithful solicitor,' he may mulct you in damages without
proof of damage, but not if you say, 'He is an unfaithful
husband.'

The Lord Chancellor, who seemed to be deeply
moved, gulped and continued:

My Lords, this is too much. We are not competent
to pass a Slander of Men Act; but we can in this case
do what amounts to the same thing; we can abandon
precedent and amend the Common Law. The law
must march with the times. Mr. Aley's appeal must
succeed and a new trial be ordered.

Their Lordships concurred.

NOTE—While this Work was passing through the press a Bill—the
Law Reform (Married Women and Tortfeasors) Bill—was passing
through Parliament, which will, when law, put an end to the scandal
mentioned in the footnote on page 322. This Bill is only one of the
fruits of the Law Reform Committee wisely appointed by Lord Sankey,
when Lord Chancellor, and admirably presided over by the Master of
the Rolls (Lord Hanworth). There are many more points in this Work
which deserve their attention, but, without doubt, these are already on
the list. EDITOR

(51) MACINTOSH AND OTHERS *v.* HADDOCK, HADDOCK, HADDOCK, HADDOCK, AND HADDOCK, LTD. (BRITISH MASTER-PIECES, LTD., INTERVENING)

Incorporation of Haddock

(Before Mr. Justice Adam)

This is a petition for the compulsory winding up of a private company.

Sir Alister Banner, K.C.: I appear for the petitioners in these rather unusual proceedings. The respondent company, milord, Messrs. Haddock, Haddock, Haddock, Haddock, and——

The Judge: Has this anything to do with Mr. Albert Haddock?

Sir Alister: Yes, milord.

The Judge (perking up): Ah! then we are in for some jolly litigation.

Sir Alister: Milord, the petitioners include a number of writers, and two very old publishing businesses. There is no question here of default by the company in discharge of duties or liabilities, failure in business, or inability to pay debts. The business of the company is in a flourishing condition and has declared a dividend of——

The Judge: Then what is it all about?

Sir Alister: My clients ask you to say, milord, that it is 'just and equitable' that the company be wound up, as you have power to do under section 129 of the Companies Act.

The Judge: In these sad days, Sir Alister, we have quite enough to do winding up firms which have failed. Do you really ask me to spend a fine day dissolving a prosperous one?

Sir Alister: If your Lordship will have patience. . . . Milord, Mr. Albert Haddock is a writer——

Sir Ethelred Rutt (for the respondents): Was a writer. That is the whole point of the case.

Sir Alister: Very well. *Was* a writer. And, milord, following the example of other and more prosperous writers, he turned himself into a limited company, in which all the shares are held by himself, his family, and one or two friends. The original purpose of this manœuvre was the evasion of certain taxes——

Sir Ethelred: Milord, I protest. Me learned friend has no right—such a thing would not be said if a bootmaker turned himself into a company——

The Judge: Peace, peace, Sir Ethelred! What Sir Alister means, I think, is that Mr. Haddock took legitimate advantage of the laws of the land in order to ease the burden of taxation at certain points where admittedly it bears with undue severity upon the better class of author.

Sir Alister: Yes, milord. Anyhow, milord, that is not the point of this petition.

Sir Ethelred: Then why the——

Sir Alister: The position is, milord, according to the respondents, that Mr. Albert Haddock the writer has ceased to exist. Mr. Albert Haddock the man is employed as managing director of Haddock, Haddock, etc., and Co. Among the 'objects' of the company set forth in the Memorandum of Association are included 'the composing, writing, painting, publishing, and sale of literary and journalistic works in the English language, whether in verse or prose, and upon any subject

whatsoever', and Mr. Haddock is employed to assis
and direct the business of the company. Since it wa
formed, milord, no writings have appeared over the
old signature of Albert Haddock, but many have appeared signed 'Haddock, Haddock and Co.', or 'Alber
Haddock (for Haddock and Co.)'; and it is represented
that these works are not the works of Mr. Haddock
but the works of the firm, the company, the corporation——

The Judge: Well, well, there is nothing strange in
that. If a man is employed to make new shoes by a
company the shoes are made by the company, not him;
and if the shoes pinch, the company will bear the
blame, not he. So, if the company's books offend
against the law of libel——

Sir Alister: But, milord——

The Judge: I suppose you are going to try to puzzle
me with the question, 'Can a corporation write?' I
do not know why it should not. A corporation has
the same powers of contracting as a natural person,
and if it can write a good contract why not a good poem
or book? It can be sued for libel and summoned before
the magistrates to answer for an obscene or blasphemous
publication; so there is no danger there. It was held
by the Court of Appeal in *Wilmott* v. *London Road Car
Company, Ltd.* (1910) 2 Ch. 525, that a limited company
was capable of being 'a respectable and responsible
person', so there can be no great difficulty about its
being a modern novelist.

Sir Ethelred: Ha!

The Judge: Probably—I am not sure—its novels,
like its contracts, should be made under seal. Does
the corporation's seal accompany the signature of its
novels?

Sir Ethelred: Yes, milord. Invariably.

The Judge: Then it all seems plain sailing, Sir Alister.

Sir Alister: Your Lordship's interventions are always xtraordinarily satisfying and helpful. But, milord, here is the question of copyright.

The Judge: Copyright?

Sir Alister: Copyright. Milord, by the Act of 1911 he copyright in the literary works endures only for he author's lifetime and fifty years after his death[1]; after which it becomes the property of the world.

The Judge: I know. A damned shame.

Sir Alister: That is as it may be, milord. But, milord, a corporation *never dies*——

The Judge: True. I begin to see.

Sir Alister: That is, unless it is wound up by its own resolution or an order of the Court. Mr. Haddock may die to-morrow, but his company may live for another two hundred years or more.

The Judge: Ah! A nice point—a really charming point—a thoroughly lovable point. Proceed, Sir Alister.

Sir Alister: And so, milord, if the respondents' contention is permitted to prevail the literary works which they produce will be taken out of the operation of the Copyright Act so long as the corporation remains in being, and will not become public property until fifty years after the company is wound up.

The Judge: Delicious!

Sir Alister: Now, milord, it is common ground that all the works of Mr. Haddock——

Sir Ethelred: The company.

Sir Alister: The works of the company are masterpieces; and therefore they are likely to have a value

[1] Or, in effect, twenty-five years; for during the *second* twenty-five years any person may publish the work on payment of ten per cent to the owner of the copyright.

for much longer than fifty years after the death of the author——

Sir Ethelred: The managing director.

Sir Alister: And, acting upon that assumption, the company have sold to certain persons, and in particular to British Masterpieces, Ltd., a very far-seeing firm, the right to republish their works *in perpetuity* (with certain safeguards on both sides which need not concern us for the moment). That is to say, in a hundred years' time, if there should be a fashionable revival of interest in these works, the descendants of Mr. Haddock will be able to dictate the conditions upon which they shall be performed and published, and enjoy at least a share of the profits——

The Judge: Very proper. Ha!

Sir Alister: While the descendants of his contemporaries will not. Milord, it is obvious that by this arrangement those writers who are not corporations are placed at a disadvantage because they cannot secure such favourable terms; and, together with certain publishers and others who make a cheap and profitable business of the exploitation of non-copyright works, they contend that in justice and equity the company should be dissolved. Milord, I shall now call evidence——

The Judge: I don't want to hear your evidence, Sir Alister. Your opening appears to me to have disclosed no cause of action at all. You say that this is an attempt to dodge the Copyright Act. I think it is more than that—it succeeds. And what a good thing if it does! If a man builds a great house he can leave it to his son when he dies. And if his son lives for eighty years it will still be his property when he dies; and he can leave it to his children, and so on. And at last some far-off descendant can say with pride, 'This house (or business) has been in the family for three hundred years,' although by taxation and other means he will be prevented from selfishly retaining the whole profits. The great-grandchildren of a soap-manufacturer may draw not only moral but monetary encouragement from the labour and enterprise of their ancestor. But the descendants of Charles Dickens, of Offenbach and Johann Strauss can only say, 'These great works were once in our family, but now they are public property, and Tom, Dick, or Harry may do what they will with them and draw what profit they can. They may mutilate our tunes, re-write our stories, present our tragedies as farces.' I observe that a modern author has recently taken upon himself to re-write a book called *David Copperfield*, and that nine shillings per volume is the price demanded for this odd and unsolicited tinkering. If Charles Dickens had been able to take the sensible precautions of Mr. Haddock, no man would be able to re-write him with impunity or make money from his work without some reasonable tribute to his descendants. As for the petitioner authors, their remedy is to take the same course as Mr. Haddock. The petition is dismissed. But the case has delighted me.

NOTE—The provisions of copyright law with regard to gramophone records would excite astonishment if any one were interested in the poverty of artists. An author or composer who gives consent for his work to be reproduced by a gramophone company can only claim a statutory royalty fixed by the Board of Trade; and thereafter any one else can reproduce the work on the same terms; that is to say, he is compelled to sell but is forbidden to bargain, and can make no stipulation as to the method in which the work is reproduced, e.g. he cannot prevent a musical composition from being performed by a bad singer or player. Moreover, his rate of remuneration does not increase as the sales increase, but remains the same whether the gramophone company sells one record or a million. No other class of 'worker' would be expected to accept a statutory *maximum* wage, or be deprived by Parliament of his freedom of contract. Even the singer can make his own terms, but not the writers of the song. The present royalty is six and a quarter per cent on the sale price, or nearly twopence on a half-crown record, divisible between author and composer, and, sometimes, publisher—not to mention the theatrical manager. EDITOR

(52) THE POSTMASTER-GENERAL *v.* SLOT

THE BOOKMAKER'S TELEPHONE

(Before Mr. Justice Plush)

A CONSIDERED judgment was delivered in the Bookmaker's Telephone case to-day. His Lordship said:

In this difficult case the Post Office claims certain sums, being the amount of a quarter's arrears of fees for the hire and use of one of His Majesty's telephones. It is clear that the defendant *did* make the usual agreement to pay the usual charges for the use of the telephone; and the charges are above the average, for he seems to have passed most of the day in sending messages about the land by telephone and telegram. But the evidence is that he has gone out of business and refuses to pay; he has not made an appearance nor entered any defence, and in the ordinary course judgment would be entered for the Crown, with costs.

But the position is complicated by the nature of the defendant's business. Mr. Slot is, or was at the date of the contract and during the period in which the charges were incurred, a 'credit' bookmaker, or, as he prefers to describe himself, a 'Turf Accountant'. The character of this business was known to the Post Office when the contract was made: he is described in their own *Telephone Directory* as a 'Turf Accountant', and it is not contended that the Post Office were so innocent as to suppose that by 'Turf Accountant' was meant a man who dealt with accounts concerning

333

some innocent traffic in the raw material of tennis lawns or cricket grounds. The Post Office knew he was a bookmaker; not, it is true, a 'cash' bookmaker, who bets unlawfully (except upon a racecourse), but a 'credit' bookmaker, who bets in his own house and is winked at by the law.

He is winked at, that is to say, he is not chivvied about and from time to time arrested by the police, as is his brother who bets in cash, in his own house or in the public street.

Why is he winked at? It is quite wrong to suppose, as many people do, that the law perceives some mystical virtue in betting on credit which places it on a higher moral plane than betting on a 'cash down' basis. Indeed, as the good Mr. Haddock has often observed, the contrary might well be asserted, for he who bets in cash bets with money which he actually possesses, while he who bets on credit bets with money which he may not possess, and, if he loses, will have to acquire by fair means or foul. As Lord Mildew said in *Fox* v. *The Sporting Life* (1917) 2 A.C.: 'Few men steal in order to bet in cash; but many have stolen because they betted on credit.'

Then what is the reason of the wink? The defendant owned and occupied the premises in question purely for the purpose of a betting business; and in them he betted for and with the public all day and every day. Yet this house is not a 'betting-house' under the Betting Act of 1853, for that Act was passed before the telephone was thought of, and it described a betting-house as a place to which persons were induced to 'resort' for the purpose of betting. And forty-one years later (in the case of *The Queen* v. *Brown*) some learned judges of the High Court held that the word 'resorting' must be construed in the ordinary sense of physically resorting, so that a house kept for the purpose of betting by telephone, telegram, and letter was not a betting-house. But for the fact that credit-betting was an indulgence of the rich and not of the poor, Parliament no doubt would have quickly blocked this loophole in the law; but, as it was, nothing was done. And so, through the evasions of judges, the indolence of the Legislature, and the ignorance of the people, what began as an historical accident has gradually acquired the status of a moral principle. The student of the laws of England may rub his eyes in pained astonishment, but it is not the first time that such a thing has happened, and I do not suppose that it will be the last.

The wink, then, is only a wink, and, like other winks, should not be thought to have any serious or moral significance. The general attitude of the law to the transactions of the bookmaker, whether 'cash' or 'credit', is the same—that is to say, unfriendly and even, in certain cases, forbidding. The Court will not lift a finger to enforce the betting agreements of him or his clients, or, as a rule, assist them in any matter which springs from the same source.

Now this attitude is founded on a principle much wider than the law's disfavour towards gaming, wagering, and betting. *Ex turpi causa non oritur actio*, or, as it was ably expressed by Lord Lick in *Stopes* v. *The Ealing Guardians*, 'A good cause of action cannot be founded on a moral swamp'; or, less elegantly, by Lord Mildew in *French Plays, Ltd.* v. *The Mayor of Hackney* (1910) 2 K.B., 'A dirty dog will get no dinner from the Courts.'

One clear consequence which flows from this principle is that the Court will not assist a person to recover the price of an article which he knows, when he is selling it, is being purchased for an illegal or immoral purpose. Far off in 1866 (*Pearce* v. *Brooks*, L.R. 1 Ex. 213), it was held that a coachbuilder who knows that a woman is a woman of a certain character cannot recover for the price of a miniature brougham which he lets her have on credit, being well aware that she is going to use the dazzling equipage to attract the gentlemen of the town. '*I have always considered it to be settled law*,' said Chief Baron Pollock, '*that any person who contributes to the performance of an illegal act by supplying a thing with knowledge that it is going to be used for that purpose, cannot recover the price of the thing so supplied. . . . Nor can any distinction be made between an illegal and an immoral purpose. . . .*'

Thus, a man who unlawfully supplies drugs to a known drug-fiend will not be permitted to sue him or her for the price.

The present case appears to me to be exactly similar in character. The Crown regards the business of the defendant as an immoral one, and one that ought to be discouraged. If the defendant comes whining to the Crown Courts for justice he will be shooed away with righteous cries of horror. The Postmaster-General, a Minister of the Crown, knows perfectly well what his business is, for, with a surprising lack of principle, the Crown prints a description of it in the Crown's own telephone-book. The Crown knows perfectly well that without postal, telegraph, and telephone facilities the defendant would be unable to carry on his immoral business at all, for his clients would then be compelled to visit him in person, which would render him liable to prosecution as the keeper of a betting-house. The Crown knows further that of all the facilities which it supplies to the defendant the telephone is the most vital, that it is indeed the principal tool of his trade; yet it supplies the telephone, the instrument of immorality. And now it comes to the Court to recover the price of it.

There appears to be no limit to the hypocrisies of His Majesty's Ministers in the matter of wagering and betting (it is worth while to observe that at the very time of the making of this contract the Postmaster-General and his staff were busily opening the letters of the public in order to intercept and arrest any letters containing sweepstake tickets from Ireland); but there is a limit to the forbearance of His Majesty's judges. The Crown, like other litigants, must come to the Courts with clean hands. It cannot with one hand grab the profits of immorality and with the other beckon to the law for succour. This is a most clear case of *causa turpis*, and no legal action therefore can be permitted to arise from it.

It was urged by the Attorney-General that I should be influenced by a recent decision of the Court of Appeal, where it was held that a street bookmaker could properly be compelled to pay income-tax on the profits of his unlawful business. But there is a very clear distinction between that case and this. The maxim is not *Ex turpi causa non oritur* prosecution—but *actio*. The earning of an income in any manner is to-day almost a criminal offence; and, Parliament having expressly decreed that all incomes shall suffer certain deductions, however nobly or ignobly earned, the Crown does right not to spare the criminal's gains, if it can lay hands upon them. Moreover, in that case there was no question of contract and no question of the Crown itself having condoned or encouraged the unlawful business on which it levied the tax. If it had been proved that the Crown had knowledge of the character of the defendant's business and had deliberately refrained from arresting him in order that his profits and his income-tax might be as high as possible, I think that my learned brothers might have come to a very different decision.

But that question does not arise. The Crown is here confronted with a venerable principle of the Common Law, and it can cite no Act of Parliament in derogation thereof. The sanctity of contract is not an empty phrase; it expresses the exceptional regard for moral values with which the Courts approach any matter relating to contract. In other departments of litigation we are sometimes compelled to assist a villain and give reluctantly the legal victory to one side, the moral palm to the other. But he who founds his claim upon a contract must have not only the law but the prophets behind him; for contract is at the bottom of all business, and at the bottom of all business there must be honest dealing. It would be idle to punish men for breaking a proper contract if men were permitted to enforce improper ones. The sanctity of contract is for the righteous and not for the blasphemer. A private citizen would not be permitted to recover the hire of a revolver which he knew was to be used to commit murder; but that is the position of the Crown in this case.

The action is dismissed, with costs against the Crown.

(53) REX *v.* HADDOCK

THE HUMAN HEN

MR. ALBERT HADDOCK surrendered to his bail at Marlborough Street Police Court to-day.

Mr. Slit (for the prosecution): The police, sir, are anxious that the accused in this case shall be severely dealt with; but they are not certain what for. It is not the first time that Mr. Haddock has hampered the police by behaving in a manner obviously undesirable but difficult to classify.[1] On the fourteenth of this month he was detained by Constable Boot in Piccadilly and taken to Vine Street Station, and he is now charged with:

(*a*) Assault
(*b*) Committing or being a public nuisance
(*c*) Conduct calculated to cause a breach of the King's peace
(*d*) Causing an obstruction
(*e*) Attempt to do bodily harm
(*f*) Offensive and insulting behaviour
(*g*) Threatening words and gestures
(*h*) Causing a public mischief

and if none of these charges should succeed the Bench will be asked to make an order under the Lunacy Act.

The accused is a very fast runner; and on the afternoon of the fourteenth, at a time when both the street

---

[1] See *Rex* v. *Haddock* (page 24), where he jumped off Hammersmith Bridge.

and the pavement were crowded, he was seen running at a great pace along the pavement——

The Metropolitan Magistrate: Was there any collision with other foot-passengers?

Mr. Slit: No, sir—no actual collision or injury.

The Magistrate: Then there is no battery?

Mr. Slit: No, sir; but as you are aware, there may be an assault without battery, indeed, without actual touching. I should tell the Court that the accused was very oddly equipped. He wore running-shorts and rubber shoes, and attached to a belt round his middle was a large motor-horn having an exceptionally raucous and intimidating note. As he bounded along the pavement, darting nimbly between one pedestrian and another, he constantly sounded this horn and shouted, 'Look out, I'm coming!' and even, on one occasion, 'If you don't look out you will be hurt!' Warned or alarmed by these sounds, a great many persons did jump out of the way or change their course to let the accused go by; and one or two elderly persons, persuaded by the sound of a motor-horn behind them that a motor-car had strayed on to the pavement, ran in alarm to one side with a precipitancy by no means beneficial to tired hearts and aged nervous systems. On these facts, your worship, we ask the Bench for a conviction. Call Constable Boot.

Constable Boot (giving evidence of arrest): Accused, when taken into custody, made a statement. He said, 'What the —— h—— has it got to do with you?'

The Magistrate: Come, come, officer, don't beat about the bush. What did the accused say?

Witness: He said, 'What the blank h——'

The Magistrate: No, no, we must have the exact words. This Court is not a kindergarten.

Witness (then repeated the alleged expressions of accused, and continued): I replied, 'I want no obscene or obstroperous language from you—see?'

Accused responded, 'I am training pedestrians.'

A crowd having collected and which adopted a menacing attitude, I then took accused into custody for his own safety.

The Magistrate: For his *own* safety? You did not see him endanger the lives or limbs of others?

Witness: No, sir. He dodged in and out like.

Haddock (in the box, asked leave to make a statement. He said): Speed is the goods, your honour. Speed is nuts. Speed wins the knighthoods. Speed excites the sub-editors. Speed is a front-page story. Speed——

The Magistrate: What is all this about?

Witness: I was saying, your worship, that rapid movement from place to place was one of the blessings, triumphs, and essentials of modern civilization. There is no old-fashioned speed-limit on the roads or pavements. We may drive our motor-cars as fast as we think fit, provided that we hit nothing and nobody. I was merely behaving like a motor-car.

The Magistrate: Send for the medical officer.

Witness (continuing): All the motor-cars are going faster. But some go faster than others. And when a faster one overtakes a slow one it makes a rude and unpleasant noise to tell the other to get out of the way——

The Magistrate: To give warning of its approach.

Witness: As you will. And if a fast motor-car sees a man, woman, or child, a nursemaid with a perambulator, a dog, or a hen in its path, it makes a loud, rude, and alarming noise to tell the man, woman, child,

nursemaid, dog, or hen to get out of the way.[1] The
old woman, child, nursemaid, dog, or hen are then
expected to proceed to a place of safety as quickly as
possible. Many motorists expect them to break into a
run; and in practice most of them *do* break into a run.
Nobody thinks that this is bad manners or in any way remarkable. I was merely behaving like a motor-car——

The Magistrate: But——

Witness: The result is that men, women, and children
are becoming more and more expert in getting out of
the way, though the hen still does it best; and the
policy of the Government is not to reduce the speed of
motor-cars[2] (for that would be fantastic and fatal), but
to increase the speed of pedestrians. It is hoped to
educate the pedestrian to such a degree of alertness and
alacrity that he will at last approximate to the hen.
The hen, your worship—— Your worship, I wish to
call a small, middle-aged hen to give evidence——

The Magistrate (kindly): Very well, Mr. Haddock. The
doctor will be here soon and he will bring you a hen.

Witness: The hen, your worship, has a very mobile
and flexible neck, and an eye on each side of the head,
so that she can look right and look left at the same
time. By continual slight movements of the neck she
becomes aware of motor-cars approaching noiselessly
behind her; she has exceptional agility and a power
of instant acceleration in emergency. In short, the
perfect pedestrian. Owing to the difference in natural
advantages, it may be some time before we produce the
human hen, but we are advancing.

---

[1] Contrast the agreeable sounds made by steam-vessels which, as a
rule, convey not only warning but useful information about the steamer's
intentions—as 'I am going to starboard', 'My engines are going astern',
or 'I am about to make a circular movement turning to port'. See
Strauss on *The Law of Boating*.   [2] This was pre-Hore-Belisha.

The trouble is, your honour, that the training is not continuous. The pavements have not kept pace with the roads. On the roads the race is to the swiftest; but on the pavements there is neither swift nor slow. The man who can run fast has to plod along at the same dull pace as a crowd of people who run more slowly or cannot run at all. There is here, therefore, a vast waste of energy and potential speed; and speed, as I have said, being the goods, this must be a bad thing. Besides, the dreamy pedestrian who has just had a good shake-up crossing the road is able, when he reaches the pavement, to fall back into his former condition of reverie or stupor and amble along quietly at his own sweet will. Every step he takes on the pavement is a hold-up in his education, a step away from the human hen.

Accordingly, your worship, I was behaving like a motor-car. Though I do not possess a motor-car I have an itch for speed. I love to bound and leap along, delighting in my strength and swiftness, and anxious to show other men that I can run faster than they can. Besides, I have a great many appointments; and my appointments are more important than other men's. Why should I be held up on a crowded pavement by a lot of slow-moving old trouts who are not in a hurry and couldn't hurry if they were?

I found, your honour, that when I leaped and bounded through a crowd without giving audible warning I jostled the old trouts, and sometimes knocked them down; and the old trouts naturally resented it. But now that I sound my little horn they scuttle out of the way and are perfectly safe. Also, they are kept in good training for the roads, or would be if all the fast-moving men behaved as I do. So what all the fuss is about is frankly baffling, dear old worship, or honour, as the case may be.

The Magistrate: I shall remand the accused for examination as to his mental condition; but unless the medical report recommends his detention I do not think that there is any case here for the Court to determine.

The accused has not committed an assault; or, if he has, then every motorist who sounds his horn commits an assault. Nor has he attempted to do bodily harm; indeed he has taken special measures to avoid it. He has not caused an obstruction, except in the sense that his arrest attracted a crowd; but the constable is to blame for that, not he. So far from causing an obstruction he made the centre of the pavement clearer for the faster-moving walkers. A fast car which causes a slow one to draw in to the side of the road does not cause an obstruction; nor, in the absence of offensive words or gestures, would its driver be charged with conduct conducive to a breach of the peace.

The sounding of the horn is not a threat but a warning, benevolent and not offensive in intention and sanctioned by the law. Indeed, a man who saw that he might injure another and deliberately refrained from warning him would be a monster and doubly answerable at law if he *did* cause injury. And, though the sound be unmusical and harsh, the use of a single horn in Piccadilly at a busy hour can hardly be accounted a Common Law nuisance when three or four hundred similar horns are in full blast a few yards away.

The conduct of the accused was admittedly unusual; but novelty of behaviour is not necessarily a crime, though it may be evidence of imbecility. The progress of the first motor-car down Piccadilly was, without doubt, as startling and alarming to many as the proceedings of the accused now appear on the Piccadilly pavement.

It seemed, not very long ago, a monstrous thing that a man should bring a swiftly moving machine upon the highway—a machine that roared like a dragon at those who stood in its path, a machine that claimed a superior status to the walking citizen by virtue simply of its speed and strength. For this looked like the discredited doctrine that Might is Right. Yet this once monstrous thing is now an accepted and normal part of our lives. And if we allow extraordinary behaviour to become normal on the roads, we must expect it in the end to leap over the narrow frontier of the gutter and become normal on the pavements. As the accused has said, there is no speed-limit on the pavements, and, provided he does no damage or wrong, presumably a man may move as fast as he likes.

I have no doubt that as the delicious benefits of speed and noise become more and more appreciated we shall sweep away the old-fashioned and haphazard habits of the pedestrian population. Every walker will be required to carry lights and a horn and proceed as fast as he can upon the particular foot-track which is allotted to him, according to his capacity and speed. This cannot fail to improve the character of the nation and assist the officers of justice; for slow walking leads to sauntering, and sauntering to loitering, and from loitering the step is short to loitering with intent to commit a felony.

It is true, however, that we have not yet arrived at that degree of civilization; and meanwhile it may be that Mr. Haddock, like other pioneers, will have to be put away in a home. Remanded.

NOTE—Two years later the 30-m.p.h. speed-limit, demanded by Mr. Haddock for many years, was imposed in 'built-up areas'.

(54) BRITISH PHOSPHATES AND BEEF-EXTRACT, LTD. *v.* THE UNITED ALKALI AND GUANO SIMPLEX ASSOCIATION

WHY IS A JURY?

(Before Mr. Justice Mole)

THIS complicated action has now lasted thirteen days. Sir Ethelred Rutt, K.C., whose health has recently been causing general concern, made a startling attack upon the jury in his closing speech for the plaintiff to-day. He said:

May it please your Lordship, members of the jury, me learned friend has just completed an eloquent speech which continued for two days, and was at least one day too long. I must confess it wearied me——

Sir Humphrey Codd, K.C. (jumping up): Milord——

The Judge: Be seated, Sir Humphrey. Sir Ethelred no doubt refers to the theme and not to the manner of your remarks.

Sir Ethelred: No, milord, I referred to the whole thing. But the passages which pained me most, members of the jury, were the sickly compliments he paid to you. At fairly regular intervals in his dreary recitations from documents and Law Reports he would break off to tell you that you were intelligent men and women and therefore you would think this; that you were men of the world and so would have noticed that; that you were reasonable, attentive, honourable, and God knows what, and so would certainly conclude the other. Perhaps he thought the only way in which he could hope to keep you awake was to throw bouquets at your heads. *What* a pie-face!

Sir Humphrey: Really, milord, I do protest——

The Judge: Calm yourself, Sir Humphrey. Counsel's language is not perhaps 'Parliamentary', but it is not unusual in a court of law. I think that you yourself described his client as a blackmailer and forger.

Sir Humphrey Codd became seated, muttering.

Sir Ethelred (continuing): Now, ladies and gentlemen, I do not propose to slobber insincerities at you, though I too in my time have had occasion to wheedle a jury and drag out the *Vox Humana* stop in a closing speech. Of all the overrated contraptions in the British Constitution I rank highest—I mean lowest—the jury system. It may have been useful in the old days—and may be useful again—to protect the subject against a tyrannical Executive[1]; and any one who apprehends that he may receive injustice from a judge of the High Court sitting alone—a fantastic conception, milord— should be able to call for a jury to hear his cause. On some broad simple issues too—in libel actions, for example—a jury may help to keep the Courts in touch with modern opinion, though even there, as often as not, the verdict of twelve good men and true is false and wicked, staggering and crazy. But in a case——

The Judge: Sir Ethelred, will there be any charge for your lecture on the jury system?

Sir Ethelred: No, milord. Milord, I was just coming to the present case. Look at it! It's lasted a fortnight. The most complicated dispute in my experience. The documents were a mile high when we began; and they now measure three, for the reports of the proceedings in this Court amount to two (to which the speeches of

[1] See *Rex* v. *Cochran* (page 253).

24

me learned friend, milord, have contributed about half a mile)——

Sir Humphrey: Milord——

Sir Ethelred: All about debentures and mergers and mortgages and subsidiary companies—twenty-five subsidiary companies on one side alone! Not to mention the expert evidence about the scientific stuff—all that fandango about the magnesium alkaloid and the patent vapour-feed. The chemists on the two sides flatly contradicted each other, and so did the accountants. I don't believe there's an accountant on either side who really knows what some of the figures mean; I don't believe there's a single person in this Court——

The Judge: There is one person in this Court, Sir Ethelred, who has a firm grasp of the whole case.

Sir Ethelred: I beg your Lordship's pardon. Certainly, milord. But, milord, with great respect, that rather bears out—ah—what I was saying—ah—for that one person, milord, as this is a jury case, will not have to answer the important questions in the case. You, milord, have had the advantage at every stage of this protracted bicker of seeing the shorthand reports of the previous day's proceedings, with copies of the material documents, diagrams, maps, schedules, balance-sheets, accounts, and so forth. So, milord, have me learned friend and myself, each of whom is attended by a small cloud of solicitors and junior counsel. We are all three possessed of exceptional intelligence and are equipped by long training and practice for the rapid understanding of complex figures and affairs; and if at any moment we are in doubt we can request each other or our advisers for information and assistance. Yet you will recall, milord, how often we have found ourselves—sometimes all three of us—

in an incontestable fog about some vital point, exactly what a witness said or a correspondent wrote, the date of an interview, the amount of a cheque or bribe, the wording of a formula, the position of a building; and how many minutes we have spent each day upon excavating the forgotten facts from the desert of documents with which we are surrounded. And how, milord, can we expect these twelve poor mutts on the jury——

The Judge: What is a mutt?

Sir Ethelred: Milord, a mutt——

The Judge: Sir Ethelred, no doubt you know best the lines of advocacy most likely to advance the interests of your clients; but is it quite wise to describe the jury as 'mutts', which, though I am not familiar with it, I judge instinctively to be a term of depreciation?

Sir Ethelred: Milord, 'mutt' is a relative term. The Prime Minister, if he were requested to transpose a musical composition in A flat major into the key of E minor would readily confess himself a mutt in relation to that particular task.

The Judge: Very well, Sir Ethelred. Proceed.

Sir Ethelred (turning to the jury): How, I say, can you poor mutts be expected to get a grip of this colossal conundrum *without the assistance of any documents at all*? No shorthand notes, no maps, no accounts, except now and then when his Lordship decides it is time you were given a bone to play with, and we let you have a hasty glance at a diagram that doesn't matter. The whole thing's fantastic! There you sit on your hard seats, with scarcely room to wriggle, wondering what it is all about. Decent fellows, I dare say, some of you, but with no particular intelligence or financial training, and wildly divergent in character and opinion. And presently his Lordship will ask you to answer—and answer *unanimously*—about seventeen extremely unanswerable questions: 'Did the defendant knowingly make a false assertion?' and so forth. How the deuce do you know? You don't even know when you've made a false assertion yourselves. And *unanimous*! I look at you, twelve good men and true—or rather, ten good men and true and two women[1]—and I try to think of any simple subject about which the twelve of you would be likely to agree unanimously if you were assembled together by chance in any place outside this Court; at a dinner-party, on a committee. The simplest questions of fact, morals, ethics, history, arithmetic—and you'd be all over the shop.[2] And yet when we shut you up in a cold room with nothing to eat you can arrive at unanimous decisions about questions that baffle the wisest brains of the Bench and Bar. I find that highly suspicious. I don't believe——

The Judge: Do the jury wish Sir Ethelred to continue?

The Foreman of the Jury: Yes, milord; we find the gentleman refreshing.

The Judge: Then perhaps Sir Ethelred will make a gradual approach towards the case which is before us?

Sir Ethelred: No, milord, that is just the point. Members of the jury, for the reasons adumbrated I consider it quite idle to discuss this difficult case with you at all. Though I spoke with the tongues of men and of angels and for as long as me learned friend, it would still be a complete gamble which side you came

[1] Not, perhaps, a necessary or chivalrous distinction.
[2] See *Haddock* v. *Mansfield*, where a jury found that it was not defamatory to say that a modern novel was 'objectionable, filthy, and immoral', though they did not think that this was a reasonable description of the book in question. And see Wedderburn on *Women Jurors*.

down on. For all I know, the gentleman with the
strongest personality in that box may particularly dislike me or have a warm admiration for Sir Humphrey
Codd. One of us two is right in this case and represents
truth and honesty; the other does not; and all I propose
to tell you is that I am the one who is right. But I will
fortify that bald assertion with the reminder that I
have at least, to your knowledge, told the truth about
me learned friend, about the jury system, and about
yourselves. Which is more than Sir Humphrey can
say. And I ask you to argue that if I am demonstrably
truthful and right about so much I am probably truthful and right about the rest. Good afternoon.

The Foreman: We find for the plaintiff.

The Judge: But I haven't summed up! This will
take three days.

The Foreman: Milord, it is not necessary. We are all
sure Sir Ethelred is right. Milord, it is the wish of
the jury to give three hearty cheers for Sir Ethelred
Rutt!

The Judge: Oh, very well. Judgment for the plaintiff.
This jury must not serve again.

NOTE—The learned counsel seems to have left out of account the
point of view of the jurors. In a recent case (*Cole* v. *The Chiswick Sewage
Farm*) it was found on the third day of the hearing that one of the jury
was stone-deaf and had not understood a word of the proceedings.
When asked why he had not revealed the fact before, he said that he
had enjoyed watching the lawyers and thought he was doing no harm.
'I am sorry to go, because I liked the job,' remarked the juryman as he
left the box. 'I have not heard a word, but I liked being here. I am
sorry I forgot to say I was deaf.' To serve on a jury is to be free from
the telephone, the tax-collector, from noise and other troubles for a
much longer period than most citizens ever enjoy in ordinary life. See
the *Memoirs of a Dramatist* (Ballock & Co.), where Mr. Athol Fitch
records that he wrote two plays during the judge's summing-up in
British Fuel Oil, Ltd. v. *The University of London* (1926).

(55) *IN RE* MACDONALD—BATHBOURNE CLINIC *v.* BATHBOURNE HOSPITAL

ENTER THE LADY CHANCELLOR

GEORGINA, Lady Slate, first Lady Chancellor of England, took her seat on the Woolsack to-day and at once complained about the discomfort of the thing. She said:

What an arrangement! Why the highest judicial officer in the land cannot be given a proper seat with arms to it I cannot understand. Can any one tell me the reason of this? Is it part of the plot to keep women down?

Sir Ethelred Rutt, K.C. (in the course of a respectful Address from the Bar): With great respect, milady, the seating arrangements of your great office have been the same for three centuries. In the reign of Queen Elizabeth, milady, an Act of Parliament was passed to prevent the exportation of wool; and to keep in mind this source of our national wealth woolsacks were placed in the House of Lords whenever the judges sat.

The Lady Chancellor: How like men! In America at the present time there is an embargo on the exportation of gold. Does the Chief Justice have to sit on a bag of bullion?

Sir Ethelred Rutt, K.C.: Ha!

The Lady Chancellor: The wool trade, I believe, is not a principal source of the wealth of England to-day?

Sir Ethelred: Milady, this is one of those ancient customs which survive long after the circumstances which gave them birth. Provided they have no harmful effect, they are a charming ornament to the Constitution; they remind us gratefully of the past; they link the generations and the centuries; they are like an old-fashioned lantern which is fitted with the electric light; they——

The Lady Chancellor: They are ridiculous, and ridicule is harmful. I feel a fool.

Sir Ethelred (after a brief consultation): Milady, with great respect, I am asked to say on behalf of my learned friends and their advisers that in our judgment you do not look a fool.

The Lady Chancellor: I will not be wooed on the Woolsack, Sir Ethelred. And why are all you distinguished barristers and solicitors cooped up in that insanitary pen, while my four noble colleagues and myself have the whole House to sprawl about in?

Sir Ethelred: It is perfectly true, milady, that my learned colleagues and myself are a little cramped for space; and on a hot day, wearing as we must the extremely long and heavy wigs which are deemed necessary for one who addresses a legal argument to your Ladyship's House, we find the conditions, I will not say insanitary, but troublesome. But this again is founded on constitutional principle. My colleagues and myself are not members of your noble House and therefore cannot be permitted to proceed beyond the Bar of the House.

The Lady Chancellor: Well, there will have to be an alteration. A tribunal in which an enormous space is given to the judges and a very small space to the lawyers in the case, who are much more numerous, is evidently grotesque. Why don't we take the Albert Hall?

Sir Ethelred: Milady, there is very little about this

tribunal or its procedure which would emerge with
credit from the test of pure reason. It is a legal tribunal which has grown out of a political assembly and
still bears traces of its origin. Nominally it represents
the entire House of Peers sitting in judicature; and
our grandfathers were present at appeals in this
House which were more debates than trials. By the
Appellate Jurisdiction Act, 1876, the unprofessional
peers were finally debarred from speaking or voting at
these proceedings; but there is still nothing to prevent
the seven hundred lay members of the House from
attending the Chamber to hear an appeal; in which
case the accommodation would not be excessive.

The Lady Chancellor: But what about the public?
They all want to see *me*.

Sir Ethelred: Milady, this is not even now a public
trial in the full sense, since persons not concerned in
the appeal can only attend by consent of the House. So
that, although the Courts of Justice are in principle
open to all, the Highest Court of Justice is not; and the
majority of the citizens pass to their graves without ever
beholding one of the most quaint and fascinating
spectacles in London—the House of Lords sitting in
judicature, a spectacle now enhanced by the addition
of your Ladyship.

The Lady Chancellor: What a country!

Sir Ethelred: Your own exalted office, milady, with
great respect, is an aggregation of miscellaneous functions and powers which the accidents of history have
assembled together, but no sensible man would think
of uniting in a single person if he had the task of
creating a new Constitution. You are at once a Judge
and a Cabinet Minister—a combination which is opposed to the fundamental constitutional doctrine of the

independence of the judiciary. You are the head of the finest judicial system in the world, and were presumably selected by His Majesty because by your judicial capacity and knowledge of the law you were the person best fitted to be the first judge in the land.

Yet your appointment depended on the success of a particular political party at the polls; and if next week a General Election were to throw that party from office you would be removed from yours. Which is difficult to distinguish from the derided American doctrine that the party in power possesses the best lawyers.

Contrary, again, to respected constitutional principles, you are both judge and patron, having the appointment of all justices of the peace throughout the kingdom, the appointment and removal of county court judges, and the power to remove coroners. Such patronage should indubitably be kept separate from all political considerations, yet you are the nominee of a political party and at the mercy of political circumstance. It is open to you as Lord Chancellor to remove from office any justices who offend you as a politician and to appoint only such as are politically congenial. You may lose your office within a week or two, and yet before you lose it you may prepare for a revolution by populating the magistrates' benches with persons of subversive tendencies.

Nor is this the sum of your powers or patronage. Since in the early days of our history the Chancellor was, as a rule, an ecclesiastic and presided over the King's Chapel, he became the Keeper of the King's Conscience and patron of the Crown livings. You are the general superintendent of all charitable uses, and are also the general guardian of all infants, idiots, and lunatics, though the necessary connexion between the head of the law and the care of the insane is not easy to perceive. You are President of the High Court, a Judge of the Court of Appeal, as well as prolocutor of the House of Lords; and I know of nothing to prevent you from attending all three Courts in the same case and coming to a different decision in each. Compared with your Ladyship, the learned and celebrated *Pooh-Bah* was a one-stringed instrument of narrow range. At once a statesman, politician, judge, administrator, ecclesiastic, patron, lawyer—half god, half Government Department——

The Lady Chancellor: This is all very learned and genial, Sir Ethelred, but the ghastly thing is that you seem to be perfectly content with these muddle-headed arrangements.

Sir Ethelred: Yes, milady. I am an Englishman and a King's counsel. It is not for me to suggest amendments to the British Constitution.

The Lady Chancellor: Well, I am a woman and the Constitution needs a dusting. Let us begin with the fantastic piece of furniture on which I sit. How do I get rid of it?

(Complete silence prevailed in the House for some moments.)

Lord Arrowroot: Did I understand my noble and learned sister to say that she desires to dispense with the Woolsack?

The Lady Chancellor: Certainly. What do I do? The Office of Works, or what?

(*Lord Ratchet* fainted.)

Lord Arrowroot: If such a breach with tradition were conceivable, I imagine that the physical transference would be executed by—ah—yes—the Office of Works.

Or possibly Black Rod or the Serjeant-at-Arms. But I take it that my learned sister is jesting?

The Lady Chancellor: Not a bit. The thing offends me. I want a dignified but comfortable mahogany arm-chair. Presumably the Lady Chancellor can sit in the kind of seat she prefers. Why not?

Lord Lick: It is very unusual.

The Lady Chancellor: What will happen if I order the Woolsack to be removed? Tell me that.

Lord Arrowroot: It is impossible to tell your Ladyship that, for such a thing has never been contemplated.

The Lady Chancellor: Is there any law against it?

Lord Lick: I can think of no statute or authority which covers the case of a Lord Chancellor transplanting the Woolsack.

Lord Arrowroot: There is no precedent for the removal of the Woolsack from the House of Lords.

The Lady Chancellor: There was no precedent for the bringing of the Woolsack into the House of Lords.

Lord Lick: For centuries it has been the ambition of every lawyer to sit on the Woolsack.

The Lady Chancellor: Men lawyers!—Let the Serjeant-at-Arms attend me.

The Lady Chancellor (continuing): While we are waiting I should like to thank your Lordships and the poor poops of lawyers who are imprisoned yonder for the expressions of good will which I have received. I hope, as you pretend to hope, that I may long continue to hold this office. But let me add a word of warning. I have climbed to this giddy height by hard work and hypocrisy, following the rutted tracks of your profession and pretending to respect your man-made customs in the administration of man-made laws. I have quoted

your musty precedents, defended your pompous principles, and plentifully imitated that masculine logic
of which you are so proud. But all the time I was
laughing up my capacious sleeve. And now that I
am at last High Priestess of the Law there is going to
be an alteration. Not man's inhuman reasoning, but
woman's wit, darting to the heart of things, leaping
over precedents, piercing the fogs of platitude, shall
determine and distribute justice. In short, my Lords
and gentlemen, I propose to make you all sit up. And
I shall begin with the Woolsack.

I take this Woolsack as a symbol, an example, and
a battle-ground. The moment I sat upon it my
woman's intuition told me that it was wrong; and not
all your historical anecdotes will persuade me that it is
right. Serjeant-at-Arms, remove the Woolsack!

Lord Arrowroot: I would respectfully remind your
Ladyship that the authority of your office is not unlimited. The decisions of this House are made by a
majority of the votes cast. I beg to move 'That the
Woolsack stand fast'.

The Lady Chancellor: Well, I'm—— Ahem! Will
those of that opinion say 'Aye'?

*Lord Arrowroot, Lord Lick, Lord Ratchet, and Lord
Mallow:* Aye.

The Lady Chancellor: How like men! So all that talk
about my powers was humbug?

Lord Arrowroot: The Constitution, my Lady, though
it has not won your Ladyship's respect, has always
been able to find measures to remedy or prevent an
abuse of power.

Lord Lick: That is the point of the Constitution.

The Lady Chancellor (excitedly): Halt! I have an idea.
Have I not heard somewhere some mumbo-jumbo

about the Woolsack being regarded as being outside the precincts of the House?

Lord Arrowroot: That is correct.

Lord Lick: There is authority for that opinion.

The Lady Chancellor: Well, if it is outside the precincts of the House you four miserable constitutional wool-gatherers have nothing to do with it. For sitting in judicature you have no original jurisdiction and are only here to determine appeals which come up from the Courts below.

Lord Lick: That is well settled.

The Lady Chancellor: You have no authority, for example, to give orders about the furniture in the Library or the Lobby?

Lord Arrowroot: True.

The Lady Chancellor: I rule, therefore, that the resolution just passed was *ultra vires*. Let the Constitution laugh that off!

Lord Arrowroot: We might commit you for contempt.

The Lady Chancellor: Oh, no. The only thing that can stop me is a resolution of the whole House at an ordinary sitting. But I shall be presiding over the House and could refuse to put the question. Anyhow, long before the House meets the Woolsack will have been ejected. All this is rather marvellous. Serjeant-at-Arms, remove this object.

The Woolsack was removed.

Lord Mallow: By the way, milady, presiding on an appeal, you should not be sitting on the Woolsack.

The Lady Chancellor: Gosh! Why didn't you say so before?

(56) REX *v.* VENABLES AND OTHERS

The Dead Pronunciation

Extraordinary confusion prevailed this morning in the Lord Chief Justice's Court when Mr. Ambrose Wick applied for a writ of *certiorari* to issue to the Petty Sessional Bench of Chimney Magna.

Mr. Wick, a young advocate appearing in the High Court for the first time, said:

My Lord, in these proceedings I ask for a rule *neessee* of *kairtiorahree*——

The Lord Chief Justice: I beg your pardon?

Mr. Wick: Kairtiorahree. I am going to submit, my Lord, that an order of the Chimney Magna justices was *ooltrah weerayze*——

The Court: I hope you will do nothing of the sort, Mr. Wick. What is all this about?

Mr. Wick: My Lord, under the Emergency Drainage Act, 1923, the magistrates have power to make an order *pro hahk weekay* as between the beneficial owner of any sewer, culvert or conndewit, and the *day yooray* tenant of the storm-water channel for the assessment, my Lord, *pahree pahssoo*——

The Court: Are you a Welshman, Mr. Wick?

Mr. Wick: No, my Lord.

The Court: Then why do you not make yourself more plain? What do you mean by '*ooltrah weerayze*' and '*day yooray*'? Are they patent medicines or foreign potentates? So far the Court has no idea to what your application is directed.

Mr. Wick: My Lord, *ooltrah weerayze*—'beyond the powers'——

The Court: Can it be that you have in mind the Latin expression *ultra vires*?

Mr. Wick: No, my Lord; I never heard that expression before. My Lord, in my submission the order of the magistrates was *ooltrah weerayze*——

The Court: Stop! Listen, Mr. Wick. The two groups of sounds last formed by you have no meaning for me, and I order you not to make use of them again. Proceed, please.

Mr. Wick: If your Lordship pleases.

Continuing, the young advocate outlined the facts which had led up to the magistrates' order: Mr. Pottle, the *day yooray* tenant of the storm-water channel, was *preemah fakiay* the beneficial——

The Court: Do you mean *prima facie*, Mr. Wick?

Mr. Wick: No, my Lord—*preemah fakiay*.

The Court (after a moment's hesitation): Go on.

Mr. Wick: And, my Lord, as the *preemah fakiay* beneficial owner, he claimed by prescription the *yooss waynahndee et piscahndee* over the upper waters of the Float River, which issued through the conndewit——

The Court: Nullum tempus occurrit regi, Mr. Wick.

Mr. Wick: I beg your Lordship's pardon?

The Court: Nullum tempus occurrit regi.

Mr. Wick: With great respect, my Lord, I don't quite understand.

The Court: Oh, my sacred aunt! Would you understand if I said: '*Noolloom tempooss okkooreet raygee*'?

Mr. Wick (with a happy smile): Perfectly, milord—perfectly. I am very grateful to your Lordship. My Lord, I was coming to that point. But, my Lord, Mr. Pottle, summoned before the magistrates upon *soob poynah*——

The Court: Soob what?

Mr. Wick: Soob poynah, my Lord.

The Court: Do you mean that he was *sub-poenaed*?

Mr. Wick: No, my Lord.

The Court: Mr. Wick, I am sorry, but this is not to be endured. I should be reluctant to think that you were treating the Court with levity——

Mr. Wick: My *Lord*—indeed, no! *Noan possoomooss.*

The Court: Do not break into Latin again, Mr. Wick. I take it that you have but recently concluded your education and that this is the first appearance in the King's Courts of what is called, or *was* called, the New Pronunciation of Latin——

Mr. Wick: My Lord, I pronounce the Latin tongue as I was taught at school.

The Lord Chief Justice: Exactly. You are not to be blamed, Mr. Wick. But I am bound to make it clear to you, to the rest of your gallant generation and to the generations that come after, that His Majesty's judges will not permit the speaking of the Latin tongue after that fashion in the King's Courts. I cannot hear you, Mr. Wick, for the very good reason that I cannot understand you. We are using different languages. It might be possible to establish communication between us by the use of an interpreter. I see no necessity for that expensive and protracted process, though I am tempted to compel the attendance of one of your pastors and masters to discharge the office of interpreter and witness the unhappy plight to which they have brought you. It is not for me at my time of life to learn a new language; it is not for the King's judges to remodel their diction according to the whims of pedagogues or the habits of the Junior Bar. The bitter conclusion is, Mr. Wick, that you must go away and learn to pronounce the Latin tongue correctly, according to the immemorial practice of your profession.

I hope that these observations will be communicated by you to the particular pedagogues responsible for your predicament and by the newspapers to the general world of education. It may have been hoped in the schools that by catching and corrupting a few generations of the young it would be possible to force this lisping, hybrid, artificial baby-talk upon the learned professions. That hope must have been moribund for many years, and it gives me pleasure now to sign its certificate of death.

In the legal profession, above all others, the Latin tongue is a living force, a priceless aid to precision of thought, to verbal economy and practical efficiency. Any knowing business man who mocks the study of the 'dead' languages has only to sit in our Courts for an hour or two to learn how very far from dead the Latin language is; and if he still regards its use as the elegant foible of a number of old fogies I hope that he will try to translate into a few brief businesslike words such common phrases as *a priori, de jure, ultra vires, ex parte, status quo* and many others. We have taken these words from Rome, as we have taken much of her law, and made them English. I do not believe that the wisest scholars can surely say how Julius Caesar pronounced his name, and I care nothing if they can. For if I had abundant proof that the general answered to Yooliooss Kayzar I should not be persuaded to say that an act of the Chimney Magna justices was *ooltrah weerayze*. It is safe to prophesy that these hateful sounds will never proceed from the lips of an English judge, however many innocent boys are instructed to make them at school.

The same may be said of all the professions in which the 'dead' languages are not merely the toys of pedagogues but the constant tools of practical men. I suffer

25

from lumbago; I grow geraniums; I go to the cinema. And when my doctor diagnoses loombahgo, my gardener cultivates gerahniooms, or my cook enjoys herself at the kyneemah I shall begin to think that the pedagogues are making headway.

As for the political world, the numerous Latin words in current political usage are sufficiently mystifying to the man-in-the-tavern without our attempting to make him pronounce them as some good don believes they might have been pronounced by Cicero or Horace. Even the mocking business man is not ashamed to draw his dividends at so much *per centum*; but not all the pedants of Arabia will induce him to draw them *pair kentoom*.

It follows, I think, that a system of teaching Latin which runs contrary to the practical use of Latin wherever Latin is practically employed is wrong and ought to be abandoned. This has been said before; but it is time for it to be said by one of His Majesty's judges. For our profession more than any other employs the naked Latin word as it was written by the Romans; and we alone are in a position to enforce our will upon this matter by guiding the speech of those who practise before us.

Mr. Wick, I am sorry for you. I look forward to seeing you before me again, cured of the horrid habits your professors taught you, and able to take that place in the ranks of your profession which your talents evidently deserve. Meanwhile, through your unhappy person, I issue, in the name of His Majesty's judges, this edict to the educationists ('What', as Mr. Haddock has so ably said, 'a word!'): The New Pronunciation is dead and must be buried.

The Court rose.

(57) FOWL *v.* MYER

The Doctrine of Enticement

THE House of Lords to-day annihilated the doctrine of 'enticement'.

The Lady Chancellor: I think I remarked, presiding for the first time over your Lordships' proceedings, that I did not intend to follow slavishly the precedents of man-made law. And this appeal appears to be an occasion which calls for a little clear feminine thinking and plain feminine speech.

In this case the appellant, Mrs. Fowl, was sued by Mrs. Myer for 'enticing' her husband Mr. Myer away from her. Mrs. Myer was awarded damages of £10,000 by a jury in the Court of our learned brother Trout. The Court of Appeal, by a majority, declined to reverse the decision or reduce the damages, and Mrs. Fowl has appealed to your Lordships' House.

Mrs. Myer's action is a logical sequel to a series of lunatic decisions by certain male judges in the Courts below. It was held, first that a husband, and then that a wife, had an action for damages against the person who enticed, lured, procured or persuaded the other spouse to leave his or her side, denying to him or her the mutual society, comfort, and assistance for which the married state is designed. The remedy, it is said, is independent of the remedies to be obtained in the Divorce Court, and such an action may succeed, although there is no evidence of misconduct such as would be required to found a successful petition for dissolution of marriage. Indeed, as I understand the argument, a man might be ordered to pay damages as an enticer in the Court to-day and as a co-respondent in another Court to-morrow. For, though the same wife be in question, the ground of action is different. She may be seduced without being persuaded to leave home, and *vice versa*. In the one case the husband is compensated for the loss of his wife's society and in the other for the loss of chastity. This distinction may satisfy the legal mind; but the ordinary citizen will think that we have here a grave exception to the ancient maxim that one bite is sufficient for a single cherry.

But if this is indeed the law—that is, if a man may be successfully sued for 'enticing' away, although he has done nothing of which the Divorce Court will take notice—it follows that the enticer need not be a lover at all. The enticer may entice with the best intentions. She may be the wife's mother, and, convinced that her son-in-law is a bad man or husband, persuade her daughter to return to her original home. Or suppose that a religious fanatic, in opposition to the expressed wishes of the husband, persuades the wife to leave his side and devote the rest of her life to missionary work in China or Tibet. Or the enticer may be a theatrical manager who, against the expressed desire of the husband, persuades the wife to follow the theatrical calling, and so to give very little of her company to the husband. If the action lies at all it must lie in such a case, for the husband has lost the society and comfort of the wife through the direct persuasion of another.

But this is absurd; and while I occupy this high office I shall never be heard to say, as inferior judges are so often compelled to say, 'It is absurd, but it is the law.' What is absurd shall not in this House be the law. The whole doctrine of enticement, as applied to wives and husbands, is antiquated nonsense. It is founded on two barbarous notions, both of which, I had thought, were recognized as obsolete: first, that a wife was the property of her husband—a chattel, a slave, classed with a man's horse, ox, and ass, as a thing not to be coveted by his neighbour, and therefore having a money-value; and second (though this is but a corollary of the first), that a woman had no mind of her own and was incapable of choosing between right and wrong. Any man who was present was able to sway her into any course of action: therefore her husband was deemed to have coerced her into any wrongful act done in his presence, and, if she went away with any other man, she must have gone by persuasion and not of her own free will and choice.

The wife, then, was a sort of slave; and in the old authorities the husband's rights were described as the right to *consortium et servitium*, though I notice that learned counsel in these days delicately omit the last two words. As a sort of slave the husband could compel her to remain in his house; and it followed from that that he had a right of action against any one who took the feeble-minded creature away. But he can no longer compel her to live with him, by judicial process or otherwise, and the reasonable opinion is that the other right of action has perished also.

I often dwell with satisfaction upon the case of *The Queen* v. *Jackson* (1891) 1 Q.B. 671, for this, in my judgment, is the true charter of the married woman, though few are the wives who ever heard of it. That was the glorious action in which the Court of Appeal decided that a husband may not seize and detain the person of his wife, though he has an order for the restitution of conjugal rights and she refuses to return home.

When the cook walks out the master has two actions for damages open to him—one against the cook for a breach of contract, and another, in tort, against the person who persuaded her to break it.

But when his wife walks out he has no real remedy. He cannot have her arrested; he cannot (since *The Queen* v. *Jackson*) hold her by force, for she is no longer a chattel. She is now a responsible person, able to call not only her property but her soul her own. He cannot bring an action for damages against her, and therefore it cannot be right that he should be allowed to extract damages from a third party who persuaded her to go. For this is a Common Law action and the Common Law principles of justice must prevail. Either the wife's going away is wrongful, in which case, as a responsible person, she should be punished too; or it is not wrongful, in which case neither ought to be punished.

It is clear that the law does not seriously regard it as a wrongful act from the lack of assistance which it gives to the husband. What can he do? He can go to the Court and ask for restitution of conjugal rights; and a most unsatisfying remedy that is. For the Court will solemnly make an order for the restitution of his conjugal rights, that is, for the return of his wife to his arms. But no power in the world can enforce that order. The wife may sit in the house opposite, decline to budge, and perhaps (though this is not established) make faces at him. The Court can no longer commit her for her contempt in disobeying the order; and if the enraged husband seizes and detains her the Court will sternly order her release, as in the glorious case of *The Queen* v. *Jackson* (1891).

The order for restitution of conjugal rights will

assist the husband to obtain a judicial separation; but there, in the absence of infidelity, his remedies end.

The wife, in short, may walk out of his house and remain out of it, so far as the law is concerned, without a care in the world. And I may add that the husband, as a rule, is obliged to pay the expenses of the litigation on both sides.

Such, baldly and briefly stated, is the position in the nine hundred and ninety-nine cases where the wife has no property of her own. In the thousandth case, where the wife has substantial earnings or property of her own, the Court, by statute, may, if it thinks fit, order a settlement of part of her property or the payment of part of her earnings for the benefit of the husband and any children of the marriage. But in practice the Court has very rarely thought fit; and the cases are so few that they do not affect the general position. In any event it is not a payment in the nature of damages.

This will appear to some to be a shocking state of affairs, but only to those who have refused to realize that the world, and woman in particular, has moved ahead in recent times. Even the law has moved, but unevenly; one foot drags a long way behind the other. And the action for enticement is a good example.

My Lords and husbands, these feeble wriggles will not prevail. I doubt, my Lords, if it still can be said that a husband has a 'right' to his wife's society. '*Ubi jus, ubi remedium*'—'Where there is a right there is a remedy.' But here, in any real sense, there is no remedy at all. The order for restitution is an empty form and is not even seriously intended by the Court. The only 'right' left to the husband is a right to insist that she remains chaste, and divorce her if she does not. He has no 'right' to insist upon her presence, and so it cannot be an actionable wrong to take her away.

And I warn the British husband that there is more to come. If he cannot effectively forbid his wife to walk out of the house for good, he cannot evidently forbid her to leave him for a shorter period; for the greater must include the less. There comes a time in the life of every wife when, however faithful and affectionate, she feels: 'This house, this man are on my nerves. I must go away for a month or two and return refreshed to the duties of the home.' But too often she is restrained from going by the angry commands of the husband, which she supposes to be backed with legal authority. I have to tell her that they are not. Nor are the blustering prohibitions, so often heard, that a wife shall not go out of the house to this place or to that. Only yesterday Lord Slate forbade me to go to the greyhound-races. I referred him to the case of *The Queen* v. *Jackson* (1891). 'If,' I said, 'I choose to go to Kamschatka for the rest of my days, you can neither prevent nor punish me. Evidently, then, I am free to go to Shepherd's Bush for a single evening.' In other words, the two emotions most odious in a spouse—unreasoning jealousy and tyrannical possessiveness—have no longer any legal excuse, for the commands which they inspire need not be obeyed and cannot be enforced.

My Lords, for my part I rejoice at the change; and I dwell with satisfaction on the case of *The Queen* v. *Jackson* (1891). The 'enticement' action is a roundabout attempt to steal from the wife what she won on that great day, the right to determine, as a responsible person, in what house she will live.

But the height of absurdity is reached when it is

sought to give the same supposed right of action to the wife, and permit her to claim damages from a woman who has 'enticed' her husband away. For this is to introduce two entirely new doctrines to the English law; first, that a husband too is a sort of chattel, having an assessable money-value; and, secondly, that he is, at law, as feeble-minded as the woman was.

My Lords, all this is bunk. A wife has never been able to recover damages from a female co-respondent or, as we lawyers describe her, 'intervener', for the reason that the husband was never her chattel. The action for enticement is a crude attempt to introduce that doctrine by the back-door, and it is astonishing that any judge should have been found to encourage it. The barbarous idea that either spouse can be valued in cash by a jury ought not at this date to be extended but abolished utterly.

What has happened here has happened often before in the history of our laws. Some medieval conception is at last swept away by statute or the Courts, but the work is not done thoroughly, and the off-shoots, the outhouses, as it were, of the main structure are allowed to remain, forgotten and neglected. Then some cunning jurist discovers one of the moss-grown outhouses and exhibits it to the Courts as a venerable structure with an independent existence which ought to be preserved. Its origin is forgotten; it is cleaned, buttressed, and painted; and before we know where we are the Courts are busily adding new stories to it.

I object to this action for another reason, that it unfairly penalises the well-to-do. It is in essence a vindictive and a greedy action, for it would never be brought against a poor man, though he persuaded fifty wives to leave their homes. Which means that there is to be one standard of behaviour for the poor and another for the well-to-do. No man with an income will dare to speak to an unhappy wife or lend a sympathetic ear to her troubles, for the next day she may leave the home and he be served with a writ for persuading her to go. Legal actions concerning the personal relationships of men and women must always be odious to a civilized community. They should as much as possible be diminished, not increased; and where they are unavoidable they should turn upon public policy and not on pounds, shillings and pence. Certainly the accidents of income should never be the deciding factors which bring such matters before the Court. If an enticer ought to be punished he ought to be punished whether he is rich or poor.

But the truth is that the whole discussion is uncivilized and crazy. This is the year A.D. 1933—not B.C.; and it staggers me to hear British judges and King's counsel debating solemnly whether blood-money is payable to the husband whose wife can no longer endure his society. They are back in the primeval woods, pursuing with bow and arrow the stranger who has dared to speak to a woman of the tribe; but we shall not go with them.

No, my Lords, the law has at last begun to realize that all talk of 'rights' and 'rights of action' is barbarous and out of date in relation to human hearts and affections; for these cannot, like heads of cattle or pieces of land, be assigned irrevocably to this person or that. Nor can they be priced and valued when they are transferred to another. The man or woman who comes to this House and says that he or she is burning with a holy love for an absconding spouse, but will take a thousand pounds by way of compensation, that man or woman will receive no encouragement from me, whatever ingenious form the action may take. My Lords and husbands, I dwell with satisfaction on the glorious case of *The Queen* v. *Jackson* (1891). The appeal must be allowed.

Their Lordships, trembling, concurred.

(58) BOARD OF INLAND REVENUE *v.* HADDOCK

The Judges' Reply

This appeal, heard[1] in the Court of Appeal on the last day of Term, and not fully reported in the daily Press owing to Cowes Week and other distractions, is expected to have far-reaching constitutional effects.

The Board of Inland Revenue appealed from a decision of the High Court that certain exactions and demands made by them upon Mr. Albert Haddock were harsh, excessive, and unlawful.

As soon as their Lordships (the Master of the Rolls, Foot, L.J., and Rowlock, L.J.) had taken their places, Sir Ethelred Rutt, K.C. (for Mr. Haddock) said:

My Lord, with great respect, my Lord, I object to your Lordships hearing this appeal.

The Master of the Rolls: To which of our Lordships?

Sir Ethelred: To all your Lordships.

The Master of the Rolls: Oh, yes? And upon what grounds?

Sir Ethelred: My Lord, I am compelled to touch upon the painful theme of your Lordships' salaries——

Lord Justice Foot: I think they have been touched enough. (*Laughter*)

Sir Ethelred: My Lord, it has been established by question and answer in the House of Commons that in the opinion of His Majesty's Ministers the reductions in your Lordships' salaries were made, and are to be continued, upon the same footing as the reductions

---

[1] Or, rather, not heard. Editor

suffered by the ordinary servants of the Crown. That is to say, they were made in the interests of economy at a time of national stress, and will be removed when the times are better, the revenue more buoyant, and the national finances more sound.

Lord Justice Rowlock: We hope so, Sir Ethelred.

Sir Ethelred: Exactly, my Lord; that is my point.

Lord Justice Rowlock: I beg your pardon?

Sir Ethelred: You hope that the revenue will increase.

The Master of the Rolls: I take it that all loyal subjects do that, Sir Ethelred.

Sir Ethelred: Yes, my Lord. But your Lordships have now a special reason for that hope, for whenever the national revenue exceeds the national expenditure by an ample margin you expect that your salaries will again be paid to you in full. You have therefore a direct and personal interest in any addition to the revenue. Now, my Lord, this is a revenue case. If you allow this appeal the revenue will be increased and you will be by a small stage nearer to the restoration of your salaries. You are in the position, that is, of a judge who finds that he has a direct financial interest, as by the possession of shares, in the financial prosperity of one of the parties to a suit which comes before him. In such a case, my Lord, it is well settled that counsel may respectfully object that it is not proper for the judge to try the case; and my Lords, with great respect, I do so object.

The Master of the Rolls: But if we are not competent to hear this appeal, Sir Ethelred, what judges are?

Sir Ethelred: I cannot tell, my Lord.

The Master of the Rolls: Suppose we find in your favour and the Crown appeals to the Lords?

Sir Ethelred: I shall make the same objection, my Lord, for the Lords are in the same position.

The Master of the Rolls: The Lady Chancellor too?

Sir Ethelred: Especially the Lady Chancellor. For the Lady Chancellor is not only personally interested in the increase of the revenue, but is a political officer and a member of the Cabinet which is responsible for balancing the Budget.

The Master of the Rolls: Then how is the point at issue to be determined?

Sir Ethelred: My Lord, I see no difficulty there. Mr. Haddock was successful in the Court below, and the matter may well be allowed to rest where it lies.

The Master of the Rolls: Sir Ethelred, the Court will retire for private consultation.

When their Lordships returned to Court the Master of the Rolls said: Sir Ethelred, we think with some reluctance that the objection you have taken is a good one. His Majesty's judges are incorruptible in fact, and it is generally assumed that they are incorruptible. But this assumption is subject to qualification. It is recognized that we are human; and therefore certain precautions are taken, not so much to prevent corruption among us (which is in fact impossible) but to prevent our being placed in situations where, corruption being in theory a possibility, the malicious and ignorant may be tempted to suggest that it is a fact.

If Mr. Haddock were a limited company in which my learned brethren and myself held substantial blocks of shares no one, I think, would seriously suggest that that fact would be likely to influence by one jot or tittle our decision upon the point at issue between the Crown and the company, though, if the sums at stake were large and our decision adverse to the company, he result might be that our dividends ceased, our shares became unmarketable, and our capital was lost. Not even Sir Ethelred, I think, would——

Sir Ethelred: Certainly not, my Lord. My Lord, I do hope——

The Master of the Rolls: Be at ease, Sir Ethelred. We understand you perfectly. Yet it would be most improper for us to try such a case, and we should certainly decline to do so. It would be improper, for one thing, because in our anxiety to do justice without regard to our own interests we might, being human, be unduly swayed by the arguments of the Crown and so in the event do injustice to the company.

The investments of their Lordships, such as they are, are so widely distributed that such a situation has never in practice arisen—until to-day.

For Sir Ethelred is clearly right. The State, as to matters of revenue, is in essence a vast trading concern the prosperity of which depends upon keeping its revenue at a figure slightly in advance of its expenditure. Before the year 1931, for more than two centuries His Majesty's judges were personally uninterested in the success or failure of this operation. Whether trade was good or bad, whether the flow of revenue was lively or sluggish, whether the Budget was balanced or not, they received the same salaries, fixed and certain. But now by the rash act of His Majesty's Ministers it has been established that the amount of our salaries must rise and fall, *pari passu*, with the rise and fall of the national fortune in a financial sense. We are, as it were, not shareholders but directors in the Crown trading concern, anxiously waiting for the Crown to show a profit that we may draw our fees in full; and therefore we cannot be judges in a case where the Crown claims money from a private citizen. In the present case there are at stake only a few thousand pounds claimed by Mr. Haddock for late suppers and other professional expenses. But it often happens that a revenue case concerns a sum amounting to millions—a sum sufficient to pay the judges' salaries ten times over. In present conditions it is putting too much of a strain not upon us but upon the public confidence in us to expect us to decide such a case. The learned judge in the Court below decided in Mr. Haddock's favour. But it may well be that, unconsciously, his mind was swayed towards Mr. Haddock by the fear that it might be said that he favoured the Crown.

The practical conclusion of all this must be that until the old conditions of our remuneration (or, as it is better described in America, 'compensation') are restored His Majesty's judges must refuse to hear revenue cases or any case in which the Crown claims money. This means that Mr. Haddock and others will be able to snap their fingers at the revenue authorities and pay nothing by way of taxation except what they consider to be just and right. This may prove to be embarrassing to the Crown, but the Crown is responsible for the mess, and the remedy is in the Crown's own hands. Meanwhile, Mr. Attorney-General, we cannot hear you. Good morning.

(59) PIPP, M. L., *v.* PIPP, K., AND FORREST

The Decree Nisi

Mr. Justice Wool, who, owing to illness, is doing duty in the Divorce Court, astonished legal circles by a characteristic judgment in this case to-day.

At the close of the learned arguments he said:

In this case there is no doubt that the Court ought to decree that the marriage of Mr. and Mrs. Pipp be dissolved on the petition of the wife; and so I do decree. But, unfamiliar as I am with this Court, I learn with some surprise that, according to statute, this decree will not take effect for six months from the present date. It is a decree *nisi*—or 'unless'. In other words, I am to say: 'The Court thinks that this marriage ought to be dissolved, *unless* within six months the Court finds that it has made a mistake.' Gosh! Sir Ethelred, what a thing for a British Court to say!

We have here surely one of the strangest provisions in the Statute Book, which is a vast jungle of strange and primitive things. In the first place, it offends my dignity and, I think, the dignity of British justice, for it is a confession of failure. I am accustomed on the Bench to make up my mind once and for all. I hear the evidence, I study the witnesses, I judge to the best of my ability whether they are speaking the truth or not; I listen to learned counsel, and then I decide. I decide that, in my judgment, for what it is worth, A's case is a good one and B's is not. I am prepared to be reversed upon appeal by judges of greater learning and ability; but I am not prepared to reverse myself a few months

379

26

later an opinion at which I have arrived with so much trouble and thought. I am not prepared to say to a plaintiff, 'Yes, you are quite right; your partner in business has done the dirty on you, and the partnership should be dissolved. But don't be surprised if in six months' time I say, "Yah! I never meant it! The partnership must be kept in being." ' For this appears to be the utterance of an imbecile or an infant; and I never was asked to say such a thing before.

What is the ground of this lunatic arrangement? It is that Mrs. Pipp may not be telling the whole truth; that there may have been collusion and so forth; and that in the interval the King's Proctor may go procking about and find that in some material particular the Court is being deceived. But if the Court is being deceived we ought to discover it here and now; and if it is necessary for the Proctor to prock about in people's private lives he should do it before the case comes into Court, not after.

I do not myself think that any such procking is either desirable or decent. This Court is equipped with all the elaborate and expensive apparatus for the discovery of truth that centuries of experience have made available, with learned judges and learned counsel, the rules of evidence, the sanctity of the Oath, and the penalties for contempt and perjury. And if that apparatus is to be relied upon elsewhere I see no reason for distrusting it here. In no other department of justice is it thought necessary to employ a sort of extra-judicial spy whose business it is to peep through the key-holes of litigants and find out that His Majesty's judges are being deceived. If it is a good thing in divorce suits it must be a good thing in libel actions, in insurance and running-down cases, or actions for fraud. In every case the parties may say one thing in Court and another in their homes and offices. But the Court in every other case relies upon its own powers to catch the liars out.

I think myself that the methods of the King's Proctor are least of all desirable in cases relating to marriage, where the private lives and affections of the citizen are the subject of investigation. But I had better not say what I think about the whole business of prockery or those prigs in the House of Commons will reduce my salary again.

So much, then, for the dignity of the Court. The thought that in six months from now the King's Proctor may come prancing into this Court and say to me, 'Ha! ha! old man, you were wrong! You thought that Mrs. Pipp was an honest woman, but she was lying all the time!' is inexpressibly repugnant to me. But I am thinking also, in humane fashion, of the sufferings of Mrs. Pipp. Consider her position. It is idle to say that six months is but a short time to wait: though for those who are more happily situated it is an easy thing to say. Time, as we know, must be measured in relative terms. Six months is not a short time to a soldier in the trenches nor to a lonely man upon a desert island. It will not be a short time to Mrs. Pipp. Three years have passed already since her husband left her, and seven months since the petition was filed. She is young, lively, and attractive, and I have no doubt that there is some young gentleman who wishes to marry her. But for the next six months she must be in effect a lonely woman on a desert island. I tell her that she is to be free, but for six months she is free upon probation only. She knows that the King's Proctor is at her heels, scrutinizing not only her past but her present behaviour.

She knows that a single foolish step may cost her freedom. She knows that any one who cares to write an
anonymous letter, though it may be malicious and
untrue, may bring more trouble upon her. She will
hardly dare to speak to any man and must shun entirely
the one man in the world for whose company she
hungers. Every time she draws a blind she will look
for a watcher outside, and every time she retires for the
night she will look, if she is wise, for the King's Proctor
under the bed. She will be advised by her solicitor, I
am told, that it is dangerous for her to return home
later than half-past ten or eleven at night. For six
months she will feel herself a marked woman, a hunted
woman, a woman who is neither wife, widow, nor
spinster, bound by particular curfews and codes of
conduct—a thing apart from the common run of
humanity.

All this might be well enough, by way of penalty, if
she were the guilty party; but she is not. And while
this innocent woman is followed from place to place by
the King's Proctor's agents and her own nervous fears,
the guilty husband and his paramour may do what
they will. Is it really to be said that in these conditions
six months is but a short time to wait?

It is not. And I do not see why Mrs. Pipp, after all
that she has suffered, should be sentenced to a further
six months of humiliating and mournful suspense
through the inability of the law to make up its mind.
Sir Ethelred Rutt has kindly explained to me the real
foundation of the whole queer business. It is that the
English law of divorce, by its insanity, encourages lying.
Every one who comes into this Court is presumed to be
lying until the contrary is shown; and therefore we have
a special officer and a special period for the detection

of any liars who may escape on the first examination. In Scotland the law encourages the parties to tell the truth, so that there is no King's Proctor and no six months' suspense. In short, the laws of Scotland are civilized and sound, but the laws of England are barbarous.

On that large subject, however, I will say no more for the present. I have heard Mrs. Pipp cross-examined; I have watched her carefully and believe her to be honest. I therefore this morning grant her a decree of dissolution *nisi*, but this is to be antedated by six months, that is, with the appropriate date in February last; and after lunch I shall make the decree absolute. (*Loud cheers in court*)

Thanks, one and all. What's the next bit of nonsense, please?

(60) REX v. SMITH

FELONY AND MISDEMEANOUR

THIS was an appeal to the High Court upon a case stated by a Metropolitan magistrate.

The Lord Chief Justice: This is one of the cases in which His Majesty's judges, through no fault of their own, are unable to do justice and can but gloomily enforce the law and respectfully condemn the Legislature. The appellant, Mr. Smith, was passing peacefully along a London street when he observed a miscreant ripping the tyres of an unattended and stationary motor-car. A man of more than usual courage and determination, Mr. Smith seized the man and succeeded in detaining him by force until a police-constable arrived. The malefactor was duly prosecuted and punished for his offence; but, having, it appears, some knowledge of the law, he issued a counter-summons against Mr. Smith for assault, upon which Mr. Smith was convicted. Against this conviction Mr. Smith has appealed.

I am sorry to have to say that the magistrate was right and that Mr. Smith was properly convicted. Mr. Smith may well be surprised, for the citizen is frequently informed that it is the duty of all able-bodied persons to assist the officers of the law to the utmost of their powers in the prevention of crime and, in certain circumstances, the apprehension of the criminal. Unfortunately the important words in the sentence last spoken are the words, 'in certain circumstances', and they are the snare into which the gallant Mr. Smith has fallen.

Mr. Smith's conviction rests upon the ancient but now, in substance, meaningless distinction between felony and misdemeanour, which ought to be abolished.

All indictable offences are either felonies or misdemeanours. A felony, at Common Law, was a crime so strongly deprecated by the State that, apart from any other punishment, it involved the forfeiture of the offender's property. Lesser crimes were known as 'Transgressions' or 'Trespasses', and later 'Misdemeanours', and these did not inevitably carry forfeiture. Statutes from time to time added new crimes to both categories. Originally all felonies (except petty larceny) were punished with death, but not misdemeanours. Forfeiture for felony, however, was abolished in 1870, and the death penalty is now practically restricted to the felony of murder (though I must warn Mr. Haddock, if he is in Court, that he may still be hanged for setting fire to a Royal Dockyard or to any ship in the Port of London). Thus the origins of the distinction have disappeared, and there appears to be no logical ground for its retention. Yet it survives.

Felonies, to particularize, include murder, suicide, manslaughter, burglary, housebreaking, embezzlement, larceny, and bigamy; while some of the better-known *misdemeanours* are perjury, conspiracy, fraud, libel, false pretences, riot, and assault.

It cannot even be said that all felonies are more repellent crimes than all misdemeanours; for it is a felony to steal a penny, but only a misdemeanour to defraud a man of a million pounds. Most of us would think that perjury, conspiracy, and criminal libel were offences at least as dangerous and detestable as a mild burglary or inadvertent act of bigamy. But the former are misdemeanours only and the latter felonies. Perjury, as the admirable Mr. Kenny has pointed out,[1] may cause the death of an innocent person, yet is only a misdemeanour; while it is a felony to keep a horse-slaughterer's yard without a licence. Embezzlement is a felony but fraud a misdemeanour. To carry off a young woman is sometimes one and sometimes the other.

If it were only an historical curiosity, like the Woolsack, which did not impede the flow of justice, I should not have much to say against this quaint old classification of offences. Unfortunately some practical consequences of importance do still proceed from it.

For example, the convicted felon loses any office or pension; he cannot vote for nor sit in Parliament, nor hold military or civil or ecclesiastical office until he has been pardoned or has worked out his sentence. 'These disqualifications' (I am again quoting the good Mr. Kenny) 'are not entailed by any misdemeanour.' So that if a Bishop, Colonel or Member of Parliament commits a burglary he will be deprived of his office; but if he is found guilty of perjury or fraud he may still, so far as the Common Law is concerned, continue to be a Bishop, Colonel, or Member of Parliament, as the case may be.

I now come to the strange but, to the appellant, vital distinction which in the present case must govern this reluctant Court. Since felonies were at one time the most heinous of offences, the immediate apprehension of the felon was of paramount importance to the State; and in an age when the officers of justice were less numerous and well-equipped than they are to-day, wide powers of arrest were granted not only to the constable but to the private citizen. Any person—

[1] *Outlines of Criminal Law*

constable or citizen—who sees a felony committed not only may but *must*, so far as his powers permit, arrest the felon at once; and he may use any violence that may be necessary to do so.   Further, if the felony has already been committed the law permits the private citizen to arrest another whom he suspects upon reasonable grounds to be guilty.

But in the case of a misdemeanour the Common Law was more cautious.   Not even an eye-witness of a misdemeanour might arrest the offender without first obtaining a warrant from a magistrate; and that is still the law, apart from certain exceptions introduced by statute—as, for example, where a private citizen finds another signalling to a smuggling vessel, committing an offence against the Coinage Offences Act, 1861, or, upon certain conditions, the Malicious Damage Act, 1861.

Now, to slash the tyres of a stationary motor-car is not a felony but a misdemeanour; nor is it covered by any of the statutory exceptions to the general rule, for private motor-cars were not imagined by the authors of the Malicious Damage Act, 1861.

At law, therefore, Mr. Smith was not entitled to seize the body of the miscreant.   His proper course was to stand at a reasonable distance and deliver a moral address upon the iniquity of malicious damage.   He might, I think, have added a warning that if the miscreant was not careful he would tell his mother; but even this might have made Mr. Smith liable to a summons for using abusive or threatening language.

I would add, for the general guidance of citizens like Mr. Smith who go about seeking to protect the lives and property of their fellow-citizens, the following rule of conduct: 'Ignorance of the law excuses no man'; and, though there are vast areas of the law with which I am not familiar, the citizen is expected to know it all.

Mr. Smith, then, and those like him, must study the text-books upon criminal law until they have mastered the differences between felony and misdemeanour. If they are unable to commit them to memory they should carry upon their persons a list—or rather two lists, in parallel columns—of the various indictable offences, the felonies on one side and the misdemeanours on the other. On perceiving another citizen engaged in what appears to be a violent and unlawful act, they should not lay hands upon him until they have consulted their lists and assured themselves that the circumstances are such as to justify them in making an arrest. If after this precaution they are still in doubt as to the precise nature of the offence, or if they have mislaid their lists, the only proper course is to invite the assistance of the miscreant, who, *ex hypothesi*, should know better than any other citizen what class of offence he is committing.

A man who is found handling documents in an office after working-hours may be guilty of housebreaking, embezzlement, or larceny (which are felonies), or only of fraud or trespass (which are misdemeanours), or perhaps of forgery (which may be either one or the other); and before Mr. Smith takes the risk of arresting him the man should be asked to make his position clear. In the present case Mr. Smith should have said, 'Pardon me, sir, but in your opinion is your conduct felonious? *Prima facie*, I should say that it was covered by the Malicious Damage Act, 1861, but in the laws of England, as you know, there is many an unsuspected hiatus, and, unhappily, I have left my copy of the Statute Book at home. If you yourself are in any doubt, sir, the simplest course would be for you, first, to strike me on the nose and then to threaten to do it again; for I am entitled to arrest a person committing a breach of the peace in my presence and while there is danger that the peace may continue to be broken.' If during this address the miscreant had made off, Mr. Smith would at least have put himself on the right side of the law. As it was, he neglected these simple precautions and he has been properly convicted of assault.

The appeal is dismissed.

(61) REX *v.* BITTER

The Agent Provocateur

The Court of Criminal Appeal to-day quashed the conviction of a publican for the sale of a sweepstake ticket upon novel grounds.

The Lord Chief Justice, in the course of his judgment, denounced in vigorous terms the improper use of the police *agent provocateur*. He said:

In this case the defendant, Mr. Bitter, a publican, was convicted by the magistrates on a charge of selling a ticket in an unlawful sweepstake. Mr. Bitter's evidence, which has not been disputed by any one, was as follows. An elderly lady of comfortable and even robust physique became a frequent visitor to the bar-parlour of his inn, 'The Red Cow'. By some means not yet disclosed this worthy female (who looked, according to Mr. Bitter, 'more like a missionary') became aware that he was the possessor of a 'book' or packet of tickets for the Irish Sweepstake, the distribution of which is unlawful in this country. On five separate occasions the lady implored Mr. Bitter to sell her such a ticket. On four occasions Mr. Bitter refused. We do not know why he refused, nor is the Court concerned to inquire. For all the Court knows Mr. Bitter found this 'book' in the street and was anxious to keep its dangerous contents from circulation among the public.

Be that as it may, on the fifth occasion Mr. Bitter yielded. The woman, he says (and his story has not been denied), besought him almost with tears in her eyes to do her this small favour. She represented herself as a lonely female who had small joy in life and little hope of material happiness. The possession of a remote chance of winning £30,000 would brighten her drab existence, she said, for five or six weeks. There was nobody else, she said, in her small and indigent circle of acquaintances from whom she could obtain a ticket. So eager was she to have one that she would give him twelve shillings and sixpence for it—two shillings and sixpence more than the official price.

Whether moved by compassion or cupidity or the fatigue and indifference which importunity produces, Mr. Bitter at last consented. The woman took and paid for the ticket, and later laid an information against him. It turned out that she was a policewoman, a cunning actress, cleverly disguised.

I cannot in this Court form phrases which would sufficiently express my disgust for these manœuvres. We were told by earnest reformers that the addition of women to the police force was necessary for the protection of women and young children, because male constables were lacking in the finer feelings. If women constables are to be employed for this sort of purpose they might as well have stayed in the home.

But the sex of the *agent provocateur* is immaterial. Male or female, there is a short and simple description of their operations: it is dirty work and is to be discouraged —except in special conditions which I shall indicate later. In this country we boast of the fairness of our judicial system. The scales are weighted, as many think, in the prisoner's favour. Upon arrest he is warned at once that anything he says may be taken down and used in evidence against him. Any confession that he may make will not be admitted as evidence against him if it appears that it was extracted from him by unfair means; that is, by any threat or inducement. If he goes into the box he is not compelled to answer any questions the answer to which may incriminate him. These guarantees of fair treatment are the wonder of the world. But what is the value of these elaborate precautions to ensure that an arrested person shall be fairly and honourably treated if the cause of his arrest has been dishonestly manufactured?

We condemn the use of the 'Third Degree' to extract a confession; but the 'Third Degree' means little more than continual badgering; and in this case Mr. Bitter was continually badgered not to confess but to commit the offence. What is the ethical distinction?

I sympathize with police-officers who find that the the strict rules of evidence prevent them from bringing a known malefactor to justice. But if there is any serious leakage of justice from this cause the remedy is to relax the rules of evidence in Court, where a judge has control of what goes on, and not to permit irregularities outside, where he has not.

There are circumstances without doubt in which such methods can be justified—I mean in case of serious crime or danger to the State. The Crown need have no conscientious scruples in the pursuit of the treason-monger, the murderer, the blackmailer, the forger, the incendiary, or the persistent thief.

But even here some sense of proportion must be preserved. If a man were suspected of habitual arson it would evidently be an excess of zeal to persuade him to burn down the House of Commons in order to secure his incarceration. A police-officer in disguise may legitimately watch and inform upon a reckless and dangerous motor-driver, but not if he himself has challenged him to a race upon the public highway. For there two dangers are created instead of one. The remedy, in short, is worse than the disease.

In that last sentence is contained the clue to the whole problem. By that criterion all the methods of punitive justice must be assessed; and by it the use of the disguised *agent provocateur* for the pursuit and punishment of petty offences must emphatically be condemned.

Sporadic splutterings from magisterial benches have from time to time recorded vaguely this opinion; but I do not think that the High Court has ever laid down the simple principles which ought to govern the matter; and therefore I will do so now.

(1) The normal costume of a police-officer should be the police-uniform. It is the symbol of authority, the guarantee of good faith, and the terror of the wrongdoer. Whenever it is taken off all three are weakened.

(2) The foundation of public order is the trustful co-operation of police and public. It is the duty of every good citizen to assist the police in the suppression of crime and the apprehension of the criminal. But this relation cannot subsist if the police are taught to behave like criminals and the public are taught to distrust the police. And how is the citizen to distinguish between police and malefactor when both are dressed and behave alike?

(3) Nevertheless it may be necessary when serious crime is in question to employ the police (*a*) as spies, in disguise, to deceive the murderer or dangerous criminal; or even (*b*) as *agents provocateurs* to obtain the evidence necessary for a conviction, e.g. in the case of blackmail. In such cases the remedy (*a*) is not worse than the

disease; though (*b*) may be, and should be employed only with reluctance and discretion.

(4) Neither (*a*) nor (*b*) should be employed in case of petty offences, for here the remedy is worse than the disease. More is lost to the State by way of damage to the mutual confidence between police and public than is gained by the apprehension of the offender. (*a*) The spy teaches the citizen to regard the policeman not as a friend but as a dishonest enemy; (*b*) the *agent provocateur* creates offences under pretence of preventing them; and the police in either case are taught to think that any manœuvre is fair and desirable which results in a conviction. Thus both the public and the police are corrupted.

I observe with regret in the public sheets that these methods are being employed increasingly throughout the land in case of the small offences with which our modern life abounds. I do not blame the police-officers, but those authorities, whoever they are, who order or permit the mischief. Indeed, once begun, it is easy to perceive the temptation to extend it. It is the hope of every young detective that he may one day go about in masterly disguises and entrap the murderer or horrid blackmailer; and unless he is checked he sees no reason why he should not try his 'prentice hand on the beer-drinker or the seller of sweepstake tickets.

Moreover, there is the fascination of fancy dress. I have noticed at the Royal Tournament how much our gallant soldiers enjoy themselves when they are permitted to discard their uniforms and appear as actors in the costume of dervishes, Red Indians, or Cossacks. No doubt it was similarly refreshing, in the first instance, for the police-constable to visit night-clubs in evening dress; and one thing leads on to another. What is right in a night-club is right in a public-house or club; what is seemly for a policeman becomes seemly for a policewoman. If the police may spy upon the 'Night-Hawks' in the evening costume of a peer they may enter the Athenaeum in the habit of a bishop or lurk upon the Labour Benches disguised as railwaymen.

I wish to say that the process has already gone too far. There are ample halls and theatres in the cities where our excellent police may indulge their taste for private theatricals; but this inoffensive hobby must not be allowed to corrupt the stream of justice. I have seen it stated that the Metropolitan police force is being 'militarized'. This kind of case suggests to me that the word is ill-chosen, for militarization must involve the teaching of the soldier's code of honour. No soldier, I am sure, would authorize or defend the mean devices by which Mr. Bitter's conviction was secured. The soldier knows very well what is done to a soldier found upon the battle-field in civilian clothes; the soldier, more than any man, detests the spy and thinks that there are certain things which even in uniform he ought not to do to an enemy.

No, this is not 'militarization'; it is some new poison which has found its way into our English life, I know not from what quarter, and it is for His Majesty's judges to cast it out.

In the present case we find that Mr. Bitter was improperly convicted. There is nothing to show that without the agency of the policewoman this ticket would have been put in circulation at all. The offence, if any, was hers, and I order that she be arrested and charged.

The conviction of Mr. Bitter is quashed. God save the King!

27

Plush, J., and Raddle, J., concurred.

NOTE—'In April, 1933, a bookseller was sentenced to three months' imprisonment and a fine of £100 and ten guineas costs for selling two obscene books on the evidence of a young police-officer who was said to have represented himself to be an army officer. The books in question were not stocked by the accused bookseller, and it was stated at the trial that it took great persuasion and pressure on the part of the policeman, extended over no fewer than six visits, to induce him to procure them.' (*Week-End Review*)

Lord Trenchard, Commissioner of the Metropolitan Police about this time, is known to have disliked these practices and did not encourage their employment in London. It was alleged that during a Hunger Marchers' demonstration in Hyde Park police-officers disguised as labourers with cloth caps and red ties had mingled with the 'demonstrators' and deliberately provoked a disturbance. This was denied, after inquiry, and Lord Trenchard said that such behaviour would be impossible and contrary to orders. But it was admitted that 'plain-clothes' officers were moving among the crowd, and, where this is known and political feeling runs fiercely, such accusations are likely to be made. If only for the sake of the police, therefore, it is desirable that the principles laid down by the learned judge should be observed on such occasions unless there is clear reason to apprehend danger and take special precautions. It is said that only the 'plain-clothes' man can catch the rough who heaves a brick through the shop window. But if the officer were in uniform would the brick be heaved? EDITOR

(62) REX *v.* PRATT AND MERRY

THE TAX ON VIRTUE

AT the Old Bailey to-day Mr. Justice Plush declined to allow this case, a prosecution by the Crown, to go to the jury. He said:

In this unusual and painful case the defendants are charged with a conspiracy to cause a public mischief by diminishing the revenue. The female defendant, May Merry, is a distinguished actress earning a considerable income of her own. The male defendant, Mr. Pratt, is, or rather was, her husband, and he is a professor of economics, equally distinguished but not so prosperous. The couple lived happily together for fourteen years, and there was issue of the marriage three children.

Among their friends and neighbours they were regarded as a model couple; and in the spring of last year much surprise and consternation were caused by the news that the wife was filing a petition for a dissolution of marriage. The news was true, as it sometimes is, and a dissolution was duly decreed, the custody of the children being granted to the wife. But two days after the decree absolute was pronounced the two defendants again took up residence together in their London house; and there they have cohabited ever since, with their family, happily, according to the evidence, but technically in sin.

The writer of an anonymous letter brought these facts to the notice of the King's Proctor, who was asked to make an inquiry upon the ground that the divorce must have been obtained collusively or in other ways have been an abuse of the processes of law. The King's Proctor held that he was *functus officio*, that is, he had no status or excuse for interference in a matter which had been finally determined by the Court. The papers in the case showed without question that the divorce had been duly obtained according to the forms and practices of that queer branch of the law; but, not being wholly satisfied by his inquiries, he referred the matter to the Public Prosecutor.

The defendants, when challenged, made no secret of their position. Mr. Pratt had caused himself to be divorced strictly according to the forms of law, in order to free himself from the excessive burden of income-tax and surtax imposed upon him by the married state. While the couple were married their incomes were added together and assessed for taxation purposes as one income, and the impecunious husband was responsible for the tax upon the whole, though he was quite unable at law to get at a penny of his wife's money if she should see fit to withhold it. Further, though his own income never came near to the exalted regions of surtax or super-tax, he was compelled by the bulking of the two incomes to pay super-tax upon most of his own modest earnings; and if at any time his wife had declined to pay he might have been sent to prison for refusing to pay surtax on an income which has never qualified for it.

Resenting this position and without consulting his wife, he provided her with evidence which would formally justify her in seeking a divorce; and formally she took advantage of it. There is no evidence of connivance or collusion; and if there had been anything of the sort we must assume that the learned President of the Divorce Court would have discovered it. The wife may have known what was in the husband's mind after he took the fatal step, but it is not suggested that she knew before. The necessary facts were proved, and the motive of the parties is not material so far as the law of divorce is concerned; nor is there any law against a divorced couple living happily ever after.

The Crown, then, was in the familiar position of one who wants to find fault but cannot say why, smelling an offence but unable to identify it; and the Crown now says that the facts disclose an unlawful conspiracy not to defraud but to diminish the revenue. There is no doubt that the revenue has been diminished. Now that the parties are single they are separately assessed; each of them enjoys a 'personal allowance' of £100 instead of an allowance of £150 between them; Mr. Pratt pays only the ordinary income-tax upon his slender income; he is not responsible for the taxes on his wife's; and the total contribution to the revenue of the two of them is substantially less.

It is, no doubt, an undesirable thing to act deliberately in such a way as to diminish the revenue; but it need not necessarily be unlawful. A successful surgeon, for example, who decides that he will retire at forty and live quietly in a tub will diminish the revenue by the amount of the tax upon his former earnings. If we all decided to sell all that we have and give it to the poor we should cause an alarming fall in the revenue and probably an economic crisis. A solemn thought. But we should not be liable to an indictment for conspiracy.

In other words, it is an offence to evade income-tax but not to avoid it. If every loving couple in the land decided that they would refrain from marriage because of the extra taxation which it involves they could not

be punished by any existing law. Yet it would be a
great mischief. For it has always been regarded as the
public policy of the land that those who love each other
should marry and have children. Accordingly the law
of the land makes it easy to enter the married state
but extremely difficult to leave it; and the children of
married persons have still certain advantages (though
these are diminishing) over the children of those who
are not. There are various provisions which reflect
the same policy—a contract or legacy, for example,
restraining a person from marriage is void.

One would expect to find, then, that the law of
income-tax, being the only law that in the modern
State has any real importance, would be framed in
conformity with the same venerable policy; that it
would say to Mr. and Mrs. Pratt, 'Since you have
taken upon yourselves the responsibility of matrimony,
the upkeep of a house and the rearing of a family, which
are institutions dear to the State, you shall pay less by
way of taxation than you would have paid if you had
remained two independent celibates or lived together
without the lawful tie.'

What we do find is the exact opposite. The State
said to Mr. Pratt, 'You are married, therefore you shall
pay more.' And Mr. Pratt replied, 'Then I will not be
married.' In other words, we have here a direct conflict between a modern Act of Parliament and the public
policy of the land as expressed in other Acts of Parliament and the principles of the Common Law. This is
no new or exceptional thing; for many Acts of Parliament in these days appear to have been made by men
walking in their sleep—by a Legislature whose right
hand is not aware what its left hand doeth. If we are
asked to enforce such statutes we have no alternative

but to obey. But the present case is different. We are asked to extend the vague and elastic law of conspiracy to cover a set of facts not hitherto contemplated—to create, in effect, a new offence. We are not ready to do so. We cannot find that at law the defendants have done anything wrong. It is as if the State had said, 'You have a motor-car. We shall tax you for it,' and the Pratts had replied, 'Then we will get rid of the motor-car.'

Counsel for the Crown seemed to suggest that the defendants had no cause for complaint, because together they were well off and could afford to pay the extra taxes. But the principle is the same whether the married persons are rich or poor. It is in effect a tax upon marriage and a tax upon virtue, and no man can be punished for evading such a tax unless Parliament expressly says so. It may be that the policy of Parliament has changed and that marriage is to be regarded in future as a taxable luxury. Without doubt much revenue could be extracted from such a popular commodity. Marriages, like intoxicating liquors, might be graded according to their strength; and the most passionate, happy, or fruitful couples could be made to pay more than the lukewarm or miserable. There are possibilities here. But until Parliament has declared its will we are bound by the Common Law.

I find that there is here no evidence of a Common Law conspiracy, and I shall direct the jury to acquit the defendants. Further, I think that they have done good service in drawing attention to a grave evil, and I recommend that £6,000 be paid to them out of public funds.

(63) REX *v.* BITTER

What is 'Publishing'?

At Bow Street yesterday the Chief Metropolitan magistrate, Sir Basil String, considered an interesting point arising under the Betting and Lotteries Act, 1924. Mr. Bitter, the licensee of 'The Red Cow', was charged with an offence under section 22 (1) (*c*) of the Act by 'publishing' a 'list of prize-winners or winning tickets in an unlawful lottery'.

Mr. Sheep (*for the Crown*): The facts are that the defendant has a wireless receiving set in the private parlour behind the public bar, and by means of a loud-speaker the sounds received by this instrument are made audible to any visitors to the house who may happen to be taking refreshment in the bar.

On the evening of April 1st Mr. Bitter's customers were surprised to hear issuing from the loud-speaker a list of winning tickets in a sweepstake or lottery, with the names of the holders and the amounts of their winnings——

The Magistrate: But I thought that all sweepstakes and lotteries had been stopped?

Mr. Sheep: Yes, sir. But it appears that a large sweepstake is still conducted in the Irish Free State for the benefit of the sick. This particular sweepstake, I am instructed, was connected in some way with the Grand National horse-race——

The Magistrate: Does that take place in Ireland?

Mr. Sheep: No, sir. My instructions are, sir, that it is run in the vicinity of Liverpool.

Some of Mr. Bitter's customers (counsel continued), being law-abiding citizens, were shocked to hear this information broadcast in the English tongue; and I am happy to include in that category the name of the good Mr. Haddock. Others who, by what means I know not, had possessed themselves of tickets in this unlawful foreign lottery or knew of friends or relatives in that position, were interested to hear the announcement. Some, indeed, returned to the inn at about the same time on the evenings of April 2nd, 3rd, 4th, 5th, and 6th, when the winning tickets in the classes DA to ET, HA to LD, LE to MZ, NA to PZ, and QA to ZW respectively were given out. And two or three persons, as you will hear in evidence, were enabled by the information thus acquired to secure substantial money-prizes for themselves or friends, with the natural result that they will be encouraged to acquire tickets in future lotteries, to say nothing of the moral and physical damage which they are bound to suffer through visiting a public-house on six evenings in succession. Now, sir——

The Magistrate: But are you telling me that the B.B.C. is making these announcements? I thought Sir John Reith——

Mr. Sheep: No, sir. There is a transmitting station at Luxemburg, in Europe, the use of which, I understand, is hired from time to time by the Irish Hospitals Trust.

The Magistrate: All this is very shocking. Can it not be stopped?

Mr. Sheep: No, Sir Basil.

The Magistrate: What is the legal position? If the announcer of prohibited news be a British subject, can he not be proceeded against?

Mr. Sheep: Sir Basil, he is on foreign soil.

The Magistrate: But his voice is heard in England, and that is his intention. It is as if he fired a gun into this country from outside the three-mile limit. The moment he landed on these shores he would be arrested.

Mr. Sheep: These speculations, sir, are full of interest. But in the present case it is Mr. Bitter whose actions are in question. Whether or not the announcer in a foreign country can be held liable for his utterance in this, it seems clear that Mr. Bitter did deliberately 'tune in' his instrument to a certain station at a certain hour with the intent that certain information should be made known to any member of the public who might be present; or, in other words, he has been guilty of publishing the information contrary to law.

Mr. Bitter pleaded 'Not Guilty'. In the box he admitted the facts as stated by the Crown, but denied that he had deliberately tuned in the sweepstake announcements.

Counsel: What were you doing then?

Mr. Bitter: I was trying to get Warsaw.

Counsel: You were trying to get Warsaw and you got Luxemburg instead?

Mr. Bitter: Yes, sir.

Counsel: And this happened for six successive evenings?

Mr. Bitter: Yes, sir.

Counsel: For how long, Mr. Bitter, have you used this set?

Mr. Bitter: Two years.

Counsel: Two years? And you expect the Court to believe your story?

Mr. Bitter: Yes, sir.

The Magistrate: I do not follow. Surely by now, Mr. Bitter, you are able to adjust the instrument to one station or another as desired?

Mr. Bitter: Your honour, the wave-lengths are terrible close. Warsaw 1339, your worship, and Luxemburg 1304.

The Magistrate: I have never listened in, but the margin seems considerable.

Mr. Bitter: No, my Lord. And Luxemburg being nearer, your worship, and stronger, your honour, it's terrible hard to get Warsaw without Luxemburg, your grace.

Mr. Blow (for the defence): I propose, Sir Basil, to call expert evidence to that effect.

The Magistrate: I see, Mr. Bitter. And why did you wish to 'get', as you say, Warsaw?

Mr. Bitter: My Lord, the Warsaw programmes are terrible popular at my house. Mr. Haddock, sir, and one or two others, always asking me to turn on Warsaw. My wife, my Lord, is going to have a baby, and she has cravings, sir, same as many women do, your honour, in that condition. Just now it's a craving for Polish music. I'm very partial to a bit of Polish myself, your worship. I don't understand it, but it gives me a comfortable feeling.

The Magistrate: Oh!

(There was silence in Court for a short time.)

Mr. Sheep: Can you recall, Mr. Bitter, any particular items which you or your customers were anxious to hear on the evenings in question?

Mr. Bitter: Yes, sir. As it happens, I have the programme with me. On the Monday, sir, at six o'clock, there was a nice programme of choral records and later on a talk for farmers. On the Tuesday, sir, there were some operetta records Mr. Haddock asked for particular, and some Polish preludes by Madame Ottaw my wife had a fair hunger for. On the Wednesday——

Mr. Sheep: That will do, Mr. Bitter.

Mr. Haddock and a radio expert gave evidence in support of Mr. Bitter.

Sir Basil String: There are two questions the Court has to answer. First, assuming a guilty intent, do the defendant's actions constitute an offence? And, secondly, had he in fact a guilty intent? As to the first I have no doubt. Although a man who turns on the wireless in a public or semi-public place does not 'publish' in the ordinary sense the announcements transmitted by his instrument, it is clear that he is by his deliberate act causing or enabling the public to receive information which they might not otherwise obtain; and that, in the present subject-matter, is precisely what Parliament has ordained that a man is not to do. My answer to the first question, then, is in the affirmative.

But a man is not to be made criminally liable for an offence which he never intended to commit nor could by reasonable care have avoided. Mr. Bitter has told the Court in a straightforward manner that for various reasons he has a particular desire to hear the programmes of Poland; and we were told that the programmes of Britain were not always of such a character as to make that assertion improbable. Further, the expert evidence has satisfied me that it is in fact difficult to seek Warsaw without receiving Luxemburg. Indeed, the only shadow of doubt in my mind about the case is caused by the apparition in Court of Mr. Haddock; and even that doubt is not substantial enough to form the basis of a conviction.

I must conclude, then, that Mr. Bitter is the victim of circumstances. In his passionate but blameless pursuit of Polish music and culture in the ether he has stumbled upon the degrading aftermath of a foreign sweepstake. But that may happen to any one.

The charge is dismissed.

(64) H.M. CUSTOMS AND EXCISE *v.* BATH-BOURNE LITERARY SOCIETY

Is Laughter Illegal?

(Before Mr. Justice Wool)

The Witness: So then I told them the one about the door-mat.

The Judge: Do you mean the Old Man of Kilmoon?

Witness: No, my Lord, the stockbroker.

The Judge: Did that make them laugh?

Witness: Not much, my Lord.

The Judge: Strange. I always make them laugh with that one.

This was one of the many sparkling passages in the cross-examination of Mr. Poker, the humorous writer, to-day. The action concerns a lecture delivered by Mr. Poker to the Bathbourne Literary Society on 'The Ethics of Fun'.

Sir Alister Banner, K.C., for the Society, explained that as a rule the lectures delivered by literary and scientific men were exempted from Entertainments Duty, because, in the words of the Act, they were

'lectures provided for partly educational purposes by a Society, Institute, or Committee, not conducted or established for profit'.

But whenever the lecturer had the reputation of a humorist or the title of the lecture had reference to humour it was the practice of the local Customs officer

to report the matter to the Custom House near Billings-
gate——

The Judge: What is all this? What in the world has
the Custom House to do with lectures?

Sir Alister: Milord, the Entertainments Duty is an
Excise Duty and is collected by the Board of Customs
and Excise——

The Judge: But I thought you said that lectures were
exempt?

Sir Alister: If they are educational—or partly
educational.

The Judge: But cannot a lecture on humour be
educational?

Sir Alister: In my submission, yes, milord. That is
the defendant's contention. And, in fact, I understand, such lectures are sometimes exempt. But while
concerning a lecture on Milton, Mount Everest, or
Pre-Raphaelite Art no questions are asked, for a lecture
by a humorous writer there is a special procedure.
The local Customs officer makes his report and the
Board of Customs and Excise requires the lecturer to
send them a short synopsis of his lecture——

The Judge: God bless my soul!

Sir Alister: The assumption being, milord, that if a
humorous writer is advertised as about to give a lecture
the people come to the hall to be entertained and not
to be instructed——

The Judge: But why not both?

Sir Alister: I cannot say, milord. Milord, I understand that in the opinion of all Government Departments all fun is *prima facie* illegal, and, if it is not illegal,
deserves to be taxed. In the present case, milord, the
Society was taxed in respect of Mr. Poker's lecture on
'The Ethics of Fun', and not only for their own sake,

but on behalf of all other literary societies, they ask for a declaration that a humorous lecture is not necessarily more worthy to be taxed than a serious lecture, and that, provided information of an instructive kind is imparted, the two categories of lectures cannot, for the purposes of Entertainments Duty, be distinguished.

The Judge: In all my experience I cannot recall so strange a case. What it comes to, Sir Alister, is this, is it not? A lecture is exempt from tax as long as it is dull enough.

Sir Alister: Yes, milord.

The Judge: And the moment a lecturer is suspected of being not only instructive but amusing it exposes those who have initiated it to a heavy tax, although they have not made the arrangement for the purposes of private profit?

Sir Alister: Yes, milord.

The Judge: As I think I said before—God bless my soul!

The Attorney-General: Milord, in the submission of the Crown the lecture was not a *bona fide* lecture at all. Mr. Poker——

The Judge: How do you mean—'not a *bona fide* lecture'? Do you mean that it was really a stage-play, a musical concert, or an exhibition of performing animals?

The Attorney-General: No, milord.

The Judge: Then what do you mean? We have been told that Mr. Poker stood on a platform in the ordinary way, in his ordinary clothes, without the assistance of grease-paint, limelight, or orchestral accompaniment, and read from a manuscript the opinions he had formed on the Ethics of Fun. If what he had to say was not worthy of the name of lecture that is a matter for the Society to deal with; and since the Society invited him and, having heard him, paid his fee without demur, we may assume that technically the lecture was worthy of the name. Certainly it is a question more likely to be answered correctly by a long established literary society than by a Customs officer, however gifted.

The Attorney-General: But, milord, Mr. Poker told funny stories. He told the one about the man with the cleft palate.

The Judge: Oh, did he? Let Mr. Poker be recalled.

Mr. Poker having entered the box, the judge said:

So you told them the one about the man with the cleft palate, did you? Tell it again.

Mr. Poker related the alleged anecdote.

The Judge: Why did you tell them that one, Mr. Poker?

Mr. Poker: Milord, in the course of my analysis of the Ethics of Fun I gave the audience, by way of illustration, some examples of fun which in my judgment are not ethically justifiable—jokes, for example, which are based upon physical deformity or sickness, and, though they may cause laughter, leave a residuum of——

The Judge: All that is very right and proper, Sir Antony; I cannot imagine anything more truly educative.

The Attorney-General: But, milord, he told the one about the door-mat.

The Judge: What do you say to that, Mr. Poker?

Mr. Poker: Milord, the story I have just told leads up to Part Seven of my lecture, which deals with the general theory that all humour is founded on misfortune.

The Judge: I see.

(Then followed the passage reported above.)

Giving judgment, his Lordship said:

In my opinion, the Crown has no case at all, and the defendant Society has done well to contest the claim. It springs from two wrongful but widely spread beliefs: first, that what is instructive cannot be amusing; and, second, that what is amusing ought not to be allowed and, if it cannot be prevented, ought to be discouraged.

The first is the common fallacy of confusing heaviness with weight, of supposing that a light touch is the same thing as levity. Statesmen who make the House of Commons laugh are almost always suspected of insincerity and shallowness. A speech which is witty we are inclined to dismiss as so much 'froth', forgetting that froth is the best sign that there is good beer below. But a dull speaker, like a plain woman, is credited with all the virtues, for we charitably suppose that a surface so unattractive must be compensated by interior blessings.

This distrust of laughter is especially strange in the English race, which prides itself so loudly upon its sense of humour; but its existence is not to be denied, and it is creeping into the administration of the laws. I have remarked before that while an amusing performance of one of Shakespeare's plays is heavily taxed a dull lecture about all of them goes free.

I have never clearly understood why the principle is not logically carried out; that is, why a comic play does not have to pay more than a gloomy one. But this refinement did not occur to the Legislature; and that is one more reason why I must reject the present claim of the Crown. Our wise Parliament distinguished between lectures and entertainments; and if I were to say that the addition of laughter may make a lecture liable to taxation which is not liable without it, I might as well say at once that laughter is illegal, which I do not propose to do. It holds, I think, the same position as betting in the eyes of the law; that is, it is an indulgence which is discouraged but not yet forbidden. And that being so, the more the people are lectured on the ethical use of it the better.

Judgment for the defendants.

(65) REX *v.* HADDOCK

(Before Mr. Justice Wool)

IN these extraordinary proceedings the accused, Mr. Albert Haddock, was indicted at the Old Bailey for an offence against the Betting and Lotteries Act, 1934, committed at the House of Commons.

While waiting in the Central Hall for an interview with his Member of Parliament Mr. Haddock, it is understood, sold a ticket in an Irish sweepstake to another Member with whom he was acquainted. A policeman on duty observed the transaction and charged Mr. Haddock, who, reserving his defence, was sent for trial by the Chief Metropolitan magistrate at Bow Street.

At the Old Bailey to-day the Attorney-General, Sir Antony Dewlap, was about to open the case for the prosecution when the prisoner said:

Pardon me, my Lord, but I submit, with great respect, that you have no jurisdiction to try me on this charge.

The Judge (whose hay-fever is no better): Why not? A-tishoo!

Mr. Haddock: Because, my Lord, the Act under which I am indicted does not apply in the House of Commons.

The Judge: Again, Mr. Haddock—if it is not impertinent—why not?

Mr. Haddock: My Lord, the Act contains elaborate provisions for the suppression of the sale and distribution of unlawful lottery tickets. If it is suspected that any premises are being used for the purpose of the commission of an offence under Part II of the Act, that is, in connexion with a lottery, a magistrate may grant a search-warrant to any constable authorizing him to enter those premises, if necessary by force, my Lord: section 27, my Lord. But obviously no magistrate would grant a warrant to enter by force and search the House of Commons for lottery tickets. In other words the Act does not apply there: and therefore I cannot be convicted of an offence committed there.

The Judge: But—a-tishoo! Usher, that Noso stuff! It seems to give some small relief. But, Mr. Haddock, because some parts of a statute are not in practice applicable to certain premises, it by no means follows that none of it is applicable. Take, for example, the Licensing Acts——

Mr. Haddock: Yes, my Lord?

The Judge: Some parts of those ridiculous statutes, perhaps, would be difficult to apply to the Houses of Parliament; but no one would suggest, I think, that upon that account intoxicating liquor could be there supplied without a justice's licence, in non-permitted hours, or without payment of the usual Liquor Excise Licence Duties.

Mr. Haddock: Yes, my Lord.

The Judge: I beg your pardon?

Mr. Haddock: My Lord, with great respect, there is a case—it is in the Law Reports——

The Judge: I never read the Law Reports. It is difficult enough to follow the movements of our numerous Foreign Secretaries. What is the case?

Mr. Haddock: My Lord, it is *Rex* v. *Sir R. F. Graham-Campbell and others. Ex parte Herbert* (1935) 1 K.B., at page 594.

The Judge: Ah, yes, I have it. A-tish-oo! Drat this hay-plague!

Mr. Haddock: My Lord, in that case an ill-disciplined author named Herbert laid an information against the members of the Kitchen Committee of the House of Commons and the Manager of the Refreshment Department. The magistrate at Bow Street declined jurisdiction, and the Divisional Court held that he was right. The Lord Chief Justice, my Lord, said that 'the bulk of the provisions of the Licensing Acts are quite inapplicable to the House of Commons'.

The Judge: Why? And which?

Mr. Haddock: My Lord, his Lordship did not say.

The Judge: Under my Court at the Royal Courts of Justice there is a bar, in respect of which there is held a publican's licence. What is good enough for the Royal Courts of Justice should be good enough for the House of Commons.

Mr. Haddock: My Lord, Mr. Justice Avory came to the same conclusion as the Lord Chief Justice, and he added this: 'It being impracticable and impossible to apply the general provisions of the Licensing (Consolidation) Act, 1910, to the House of Commons, it is equally impracticable and impossible to apply s. 65, sub.-s. 1, which forbids the sale of liquor without a licence.'

The Judge: God bless my soul!

Mr. Haddock: And he continued: 'Once it is made clear that the Licensing (Consolidation) Act, 1910, cannot be applied to the House of Commons it follows that no court of law has jurisdiction to entertain such an application as was made to the magistrate in this case.'

The Judge (reading): God bless my soul again! So he

did. Then, Mr. Attorney, it seems to me that the prisoner is right; for I see no distinction between the Betting Act and the Licensing Acts. They are both—a-tishoo! Blast! I have no jurisdiction.

Sir Antony Dewlap: My Lord, there is this distinction. In the case cited by the prisoner the Court found, as you will see in the head-note, that in the sale of liquor in the precincts of the House without a licence the House of Commons was acting, through its Kitchen Committee, in a matter which fell within the scope of the internal affairs of the House, and therefore, within the privileges of the House——

The Judge: I do not know how the Court knew that, for it appears that no evidence was heard on either side.

Sir Antony: My Lord, it was held to be manifest from the terms of the information laid by the prosecutor.

The Judge: God bless me! What next?

Sir Antony: But in this case, my Lord, the prisoner, who is not a Member of the House, made an unlawful transaction with a Member of the House who was not acting under the authority of the House——

The Judge: But how do I know all this? You are not permitted to give evidence, Sir Antony: and it is elementary that the Court should not assume that which has to be proved.

Sir Antony: My Lord, I shall call evidence——

The Judge: But you cannot call evidence if I have no jurisdiction, for then I cannot hear it. Do you see the point, Sir Antony?

The Attorney-General: Yes, my Lord.

The Judge: You see, for all I know at the moment, the Member to whom the prisoner sold the lottery ticket was purchasing it by the Speaker's orders on behalf of the whole House, or as an authorized member of the Kitchen Committee, to defray, by the winning of a prize, an annual deficit incurred in litigation or otherwise. This may seem unlikely, but it is not, to my mind, more unlikely than that the House of Commons should claim, and defend in the Courts, at the public expense, their right to defy the Licensing Acts, of which they are the authors. On the other hand, for all I know, the prisoner and his friend may have been acting in an unauthorized and disgraceful manner. We can only come at the truth by calling and hearing sworn evidence and presenting that evidence to the jury. But I may not hear sworn evidence about the behaviour of any man except where I have jurisdiction: for jurisdiction means the right to hear the evidence and determine the issue. And here, it seems to me, I am bound by the authority of *Rex* v. *Sir R. F. Graham-Campbell, ex parte Herbert*. My learned and illustrious brethren in that case did not find merely that though acts had been done contrary to the terms of the Licensing Acts, these acts could be justified or excused by the privileges of the House of Commons. They found that no Court *would even inquire* what acts had been done and whether what was done was contrary to the provisions of the Licensing Acts. At the mere words 'Licensing Acts', in relation to the House of Commons, the King's Courts surrender jurisdiction and decline inquiry. That, it seems to me, is the meaning of this decision, and I feel bound to follow it.

Now, the jurisdiction of the King's Courts does not come and go, like summer lightning. It cannot perish to-day, be electrically revived to-morrow, and the next day conveniently withdrawn again, according to the demands of political convenience. Either it is here, or it is not. If it is expelled by the magical words 'Licensing Acts' the words 'Betting Act' have not sufficient magic to bring it back. One modern Act of Parliament, directed to the control or suppression of a vice, has the same power as another. I must not, and do not, question the decision of my learned brethren. But I think that, goaded, or perhaps out-manœuvred, by the infamous Herbert and his advisers, they have committed themselves to the proposition that the Courts cannot or will not inquire into anything done in the House of Commons——

Sir Antony Dewlap: My Lord, with great respect, there is a distinction between an act done by a Member of Parliament and an act done by a member of the public.

The Judge: A-tish-oo! I do not quite follow you, Sir Antony. The alleged crime in this case, as I understand it, is an illegal transaction between the prisoner and a Member of Parliament. If the prisoner is guilty of the offence charged, the Member must be guilty of aiding and abetting. Do you say that the Member is excused for his part of the transaction on the ground of privilege, but that the prisoner is not? Surely, either all parts of the transaction are privileged as the internal proceedings of the House of Commons, or else no part of it is privileged? There can be no subtle distinction, Sir Antony, between the two halves of an umbrella— Oh, Gosh! A-tish-oo!

Sir Antony: My Lord——

The Judge: The moment, Sir Antony, I inquire into any aspect of the transaction I am accepting jurisdiction. Mr. Haddock will no doubt allege that he and his friend, the Member, did what they did with the authority and approval of the House of Commons.

I must then determine, with the assistance of a jury, whether he is speaking the truth or not. For this purpose the officers or Members of the House—if necessary, the great Speaker himself—will have to be summoned to give evidence before me, to say, for example, whether in fact the Speaker does authorize or encourage the sale of sweepstake tickets and gin. In other words, I shall be inquiring into 'the internal affairs of the House', that is——

Sir Antony: But, my Lord, if the prisoner were handed over to the police by the House of Commons——

The Judge: Need we consider that, Sir Antony, when in fact he was not? But even if he were, I should still have to inquire what went on in the House and examine its affairs and Members: that is, I should have to accept the jurisdiction from which, according to *Rex* v. *Sir R. F. Graham-Campbell*, I am shut out. In the eyes of the King's Courts one statute is as good (or bad) as another. If the Members can sell and supply intoxicating liquor, not only to other Members, but to the general public, to newspapermen, constituents, and servants, then they can do a great many other unlawful (or privileged?) acts with impunity. They can keep petroleum without a licence, or sell each other noxious drugs (for between noxious drugs and intoxicating liquor Parliament, the Courts, and the good people at Geneva perceive no distinction). They can play at roulette in the Central Hall, to the scandal of the visitors and in the presence of the police. They can organize a great sweepstake in the Library and send out tickets to the public. They can fire off rockets from the Terrace, contrary to the Regulations of the Port of London Authority. They can keep dogs on the premises without a licence and cruelly treat them without fear of

punishment. They can invite loose women to frequent
the lobbies and allow such behaviour as in any other
place would lead to a prosecution for the keeping of
a disorderly house. They can acquire fire-arms and
assemble explosives without a licence or certificate; they
can fight duels among themselves in the Smoking-room
or Crypt, and threaten with revolvers (or rubber
truncheons) the visitors whom they dislike. They can
act as pawnbrokers without a licence, as unregistered
moneylenders, as receivers of stolen goods. They can
exhibit lewd pictures or sell obscene books; they can
erect an unlicensed slaughter-house or wireless station
on their premises. Neither their births, deaths, nor
infectious diseases need be notified or registered. They
can allow their drains to become a nuisance and
injurious to public health, and defy an order from the
justices to put them right. If they can sell liquor
without regard to Licensing Acts, they can sell milk or
cream without regard to the Sale of Food and Drugs
Act; they can sell bad meat and adulterated bread;
they can sell morphine without a certificate and opium
without a licence.

All these matters might equally be said to 'fall within
the scope of the internal affairs of the House'. In all
the statutes 'in these cases made and provided' there
will be found many clauses which are 'quite inapplicable' to the House of Commons: and, according to my
learned brethren, if many of the provisions of an Act
are 'inapplicable' to that House the whole is inapplicable. (*The Attorney-General here made an inaudible inter-
jection.*) And it is idle, Sir Antony, to splutter about
'Members and non-Members', for, as I have hinted
already, if I inquire into the behaviour of non-Members
in that place I cannot ignore the behaviour of

Members: but to inquire into their behaviour is to accept jurisdiction.

I am not at all clear which clauses of the Licensing Acts were considered by the High Court to be 'quite inapplicable' to the House of Commons. The most important clauses impose limits upon the hours of drinking, since continuous drinking is believed to be injurious to the citizen's health, efficiency, and industry: but, if that is so, such limitations are more, not less, desirable for the legislator, whose work is the most vital of all, the making of our laws. Then there are the provisions devoted to the payment of taxes by those who sell or consume intoxicating liquor: and I see nothing fantastic in the notion that those who impose the taxes should also help to pay them. It may be that the provisions that the magistrates may order licensed premises to be closed in case of riot or that the name of the licensee shall be fixed or painted in a conspicuous place are not considered consonant with the dignity of the House of Commons: but that might also be said of the Royal Courts of Justice, and, as I have already said, we do not there claim to be refreshed except with the usual licence and at the statutory hours.

The vital point, as that master of jurisimprudence, Mr. Haddock, has already perceived, is that in the last resort the law—Common or Statute—must be enforced by the King's Courts sending the King's officers to attach the persons or property of individuals or to enter premises, if necessary, by force. I suspect that the Legislature would resent the apparition of a constable armed with a search-warrant under section 82 of the Licensing Act of 1910: and that was probably in their Lordships' minds. But, if they can resent the forcible pursuit of one crime, they can resent the pursuit of another: and I humbly, dutifully, but with reluctance, accept this conclusion. It seems to me that the King's Courts have made a surrender which in stouter periods of our history would have been repugnant and impossible, whether to the greatest judge or the humblest magistrate. The Courts are the great bulwark against tyranny: and tyranny need not always take the shape of a king, a dictator, a general, or a nobleman: it may easily be disguised as a democratic assembly. The pronouncements of the King's judges upon the privileges of Parliament are various and confusing: but among them all I prefer the virile observations of Mr. Justice Stephen in *Bradlaugh* v. *Gossett*: 'I know of no authority for the proposition that an ordinary crime committed in the House of Commons would be withdrawn from the ordinary course of criminal justice'; of Lord Denman, Lord Chief Justice, in *Stockdale* v. *Hansard*: 'It has not been contended that either House of Parliament can authorize any person to commit with impunity a known and undoubted breach of the law'; and of the same great judge (in the same case): 'Parliament is said to be supreme: I must fully acknowledge its supremacy. It follows then that neither branch of it is supreme when acting by itself.'

But my learned brethren of the Divisional Court have preferred to found their decision upon a more vague and anaemic saying of Lord Denman: '*The Commons of England are not invested with more of power and dignity by their legislative character than by that which they bear as the grand inquest of the nation.*' (Not perhaps a very happy phrase.) '*All the privileges that can be required for the energetic discharge of the duties inherent in that high trust are conceded without a murmur or a doubt.*' This passage, quoted with solemnity by the present Lord Chief

Justice, can only, in the context, mean that the un-licensed and unrestricted consumption of intoxicating liquor is 'required for the energetic discharge of Parliament's duties'. That may well be so; but it is not easily reconciled with the fierce denial of the same facilities to the ordinary citizen in the energetic discharge of his not unimportant duties. Nor, by the way, does it appear that these privileges are any longer conceded 'without a murmur or a doubt'.

But, as I have said, Sir Antony, I accept and follow the decision: though I fear that it may have much more serious consequences than are now apprehended. For instance—a-tish-oo! Blast! For instance—usher, the spray! Those consequences may one day have to be considered by the King's Courts. To-day—usher, bring me wine; my ears tickle. To-day it is enough to say that Mr. Haddock's plea to the jurisdiction succeeds. He ought not to be in that dock, cannot be tried by this Court, and must be immediately released.

Mr. Haddock was discharged.

(66) PALE, M. R., *v.* PALE, H. J., AND HUME (THE KING'S PROCTOR SHOWING CAUSE)

'Not a Crime'[1]

Owing to the death of the late President of the Probate, Divorce, and Admiralty Division and the continued illness of his successor and his assistant, the business of the Divorce Court has accumulated alarming arrears. Five of the High Court judges are absent from duty with influenza, and, at the request of the Lord Chief Justice, Mr. Justice Wool, who retired this year, has stepped into the breach. While his public spirit is generally applauded, one or two of his decisions have been the cause of comment and surprise among some of those accustomed to the practice of the Court. Delivering judgment in this case to-day his Lordship, in spite of his seventy years, spoke with all his familiar vigour and directness.

I thank God (he said) that in all my thirty-seven years on the Bench I never had to do with this disgusting Court. And when I say disgusting I am not thinking of the unfortunate citizens who are compelled to enter it as litigant parties; I am thinking of the law, and to some extent—with great respect to my learned brethren now coughing and sneezing in their homes —the way in which it is administered. With great respect, as aforesaid, and wishing all the best to the learned invalids, I think it is a fortunate accident that has dragged this aged person from his well-merited

[1] 'Divorce is release from misfortune, and not a crime.' Extract from *The Laws of Norway* (*Divorce Problems of To-day*. E. S. P. Haynes)

repose to blow a gale of humanity and common sense
about the dusty corners of this Division. Though,
talking of blowing, this asthma of mine is a fair cow, as
the Australians say.

After a slight pause for breath, his Lordship continued:

By the way, I hope that there are a great number of
reporters here; and whatever the Act may say I order
that a full verbatim report may be published of the
proceedings in this case. Publicity, we are told, is a
wholesome corrective and deterrent; and therefore the
state of the law and the inertia of Parliament should
be continually and brutally advertised. The recent
Act[1] has done good service in that it has spared many
unfortunate persons from exposure to barbarous publicity about their private affairs; but it also serves to
conceal from public attention the fantastic antics of
the law. It is significant that those who were most
anxious to limit by legislation the publicity of divorce
proceedings are also the persons most anxious to preserve the law as it is. As often happens, they blamed
the newspapers for recording certain things, instead
of blaming the law which made those things possible,
and even necessary. The Press and literature are, in
the main, a faithful mirror of our times; and, if the
reflection displeases us, it is but an idle and cowardly
gesture to hang a veil across the mirror. A rake whose
own face increasingly disturbs him does not, if he is a
man of sense, throw stones at his looking-glass; he takes
steps to improve his behaviour and his appearance.
The old divorce reports were considered harmful to
the public because they contained a great deal about
people committing misconduct (and when I say misconduct I do not mean misconduct, which, after all,

[1] Judicial Proceedings (Regulation of Reports) Act, 1926

might mean no more than extravagance or drunkenness; but I say misconduct because if I used the word
which is used in the Commandments the tender representatives of the Press would blush, and damage might
be done to the sensitive morals of the British race);
and the reason why the reports were full of misconduct
was that under the law no citizen can be divorced unless
it be proved in a public court of law that he or she
has committed misconduct. That uncivilized necessity,
not the naughty newspapers, is the root of the trouble; and
this particular case is a good, or rather a foul, example.

Now, marriage is a partnership. I do not think that,
even in this quarrelsome region of human affairs, many
people will be found ready to quarrel with that assertion. It is a partnership, I hasten to add, of a special
character, having a spiritual root or two, and, by the
accidents of history, a faint ecclesiastical aroma. But
it remains in essence a practical arrangement, by which
two reasonable beings agree to share certain rights and
duties. If it were not so, it would never come up for
consideration in this Court at all. For this is not a
court of religion, and Parliament would not (in 1857)
have given us the powers of life and death over marriage if Parliament had thought that marriage was
a purely mystical relation ordained by divine law.
It is possible to hold, as some do, that marriage is a
holy sacrament, and therefore cannot be terminated by
man or the courts of men; and we may, and do, respect
the holders of that opinion, provided that they are
content to govern their own lives by it and leave the
lives of others to more humane direction. It is possible,
again, to hold that marriage is a civil contract, made by
men and dissoluble by men; and this ought surely to
be the view of any court of law, which is an institution

29

designed for the practical assistance of men on the material and not the spiritual side of their lives. What is impossible, both in reason and expediency, is to combine the two views—to say that marriage is both a sacrament and a civil contract, governed at one moment by the principles of Common Law and at another by the remnants of ecclesiastical tradition— enforceable by one set of rules but not avoidable except by another. For this is to make the worst of two worlds. But this, unhappily, is the impossible compromise which we are attempting to operate in England (though not in Scotland). A man who claims his just rights under a contract of marriage is supported (up to a point) by the doctrines of the civil law; but a man who wishes to surrender his rights under a contract of marriage is impeded by obstacles which have an ecclesiastical origin wholly alien to the principles of civil law. For example, it is impossible to imagine a civil action in which, both parties having violated clauses which were essential to the real purpose of a contract, the Court would nevertheless insist that the contract should still subsist and be binding on them both. But that, as we shall presently see, is a common-place occurrence in the practice of this Court (though not in the parallel tribunals of Scotland).

I said just now that marriage was a partnership. Do not, Sir Humphrey Codd, permit those rather ruminant features of yours to assume an expression which suggests that in your judgment my remarks have an inclination towards irrelevance and repetition. Believe me, Sir Humphrey, I know what I am about. It is impossible, Sir Humphrey, to erect the humblest building without paying some attention to the foundations; and these remarks are but the outline of the foundations of a judgment which, in an hour or two from now, will, I think, extract from you at least a reluctant titter of admiration.

Sir Humphrey Codd, K.C.: I beg your Lordship's pardon. I have been suffering recently from insomnia.

The Judge: This judgment, too, I fear, will tend to keep you awake. But I accept the apology. As I fancy that I said before, marriage is a partnership. Now, the English law relating to a business partnership is sound and certain. Like all human relationships, a partnership, notwithstanding the best intentions on every hand, may break down. It is open then to any partner to come to the Court and apply for a dissolution: and a decree for dissolution of the partnership may be made in any one of the following cases, which I should like all those present to note with care:

(i) When a partner is found lunatic by inquisition, or is shown to be of permanently unsound mind.

(ii) When a partner, other than the partner suing, becomes in any way permanently incapable of performing his part of the partnership contract.

(iii) When a partner, other than the partner suing, has been guilty of such conduct as in the opinion of the Court prejudicially affects the carrying on of the business.

(iv) When a partner, other than the partner suing, wilfully or persistently commits a breach of the partnership agreement or otherwise so conducts himself in matters relating to the partnership agreement that it is not reasonably practicable for the other partner or partners to carry on the business with him.

(v) When the business can only be carried on at a loss.

(vi) When circumstances have arisen which, in the opinion of the Court, render it just and equitable that the partnership be dissolved.

Now, leaving paragraph (v) out of account, substitute the word 'marriage' for the word 'business' and you have here a sensible set of provisions which might well be the guiding principles of a court of divorce. Number (i) provides for lunacy; number (ii) would mean habitual drunkenness, cruelty, incurable disease, genuine incompatibility, prolonged imprisonment, immorality and so forth; number (iv) not only misconduct but persistent philandering or neglect, which are often of much greater and more lasting importance than misconduct; and number (vi) all those miscellaneous and unforeseen contingencies in which the discretion of an English Court can generally be trusted to do justice and right. Indeed, if I were charged to remodel the Divorce Laws, which is not likely, I might enact that, with certain modifications, section 35 of the Partnership Act, 1890, be applied to the dissolution of matrimonial partnerships.

This, I am aware, means divorce by mutual consent: but I am not much afraid of that, given the proper and obvious safeguards. Time is the great safeguard, and I should make use of it at both ends of matrimony—in defence, mark you, of that institution. While making divorce easier I should make marriage more difficult. Two young strangers may meet in a railway-train to-day 'and be man and wife in a fortnight—or less. This is absurd. And when they decide to separate or seek divorce there is no official[1] who says, 'Wait!

[1] Except—among the poor—a few rare magistrates, such as Mr. Claud Mullins. Among the 'well-to-do'—no one.

Consider! Go back and think again!' This is absurd.
The State only employs the safeguard of time—in the
decree *nisi*—when the mischief is done: discouraging
deceit but not divorce. This is most absurd of all.

Well, then, I should erect the safeguard of time at
three points. There should be a decree *nisi* for *marriage*
—no one to marry until six months after the first
official notification, except by special licence in special
circumstances, as, for example, to legitimize a child.
I should permit no couple to apply for my 'dissolution
of partnership' until, say, three years after marriage:
and when the application was made, the judge (hearing
it in private) would say, 'You may be right and wise:
I do not say that you are not. But go away for six
months and think it over. If, when you come back,
you are of the same mind, you shall have your way.'
Those six months would have real value to the State—
and Marriage. And, with such safeguards, I do not
think that any calamitous outbreak of immorality or
licence would result from my amendment of the law.
Where there are children, of course, there must be
further safeguards for their protection—and, it may be,
some longer delay. But I am not so much impressed
as are the strict opponents of divorce by the argument
of children. The children of France, Switzerland,
Belgium, Holland, Norway, Sweden, Denmark, Scotland, and other countries where the marriage laws are
more civilized, are not, so far as I know, in a worse
position than the children of England. If a marriage
is dissolved, the children must be provided for, and
this the Courts are carefully doing every day. But
what good it does to children to tie their mother to a
lunatic or drunkard, to compel two people who are
'at daggers drawn' to live in the same house with them,

or to force their father to commit adultery because
their mother can no longer endure his presence—what
benefit is thus bestowed upon the children has never
been explained to me. And the argument of children
would be the more convincing if the law made things
easier in such a case as this where there are no children.
But it does not. If the main purpose of matrimony
is, as the Marriage Service says, the procreation of
children, one would suppose that Church and State
would delight to dissolve a childless marriage, if only
on the principle of 'Second time lucky'. But it does not.
Children or no children, the obstructions are the same,
and I believe the argument to be dishonest. I am
ready, for the sake of the children, to modify my reform
in detail, but not to abandon the principle.

Let us now turn to the case before us and consider
the law and practice of divorce as we have it. Hugh
Pale (21) married Rose Ray (22) in May, 1917. It is
within the recollection of the Court that the last
European War (commonly called Great, as all wars
are called by those concerned in them) was raging at
that date. The boy was an officer in His Majesty's
forces, the girl a member of a Voluntary Aid Detach-
ment, serving at the hospital to which Mr. Pale was
sent on receipt of a gunshot wound, neither dangerous
nor glorious, in the left buttock. During the four
weeks of his recovery Hugh Pale concluded that the
affection each felt for the other was of a deep and
enduring character, and that they were designed by
Fate, compelled by passion, and fitted by nature to
be the partners of each other's lives. The petitioner
formed the same conclusion, and they were married.

They were mistaken. But I do not think that there
is any one in this Court (with the possible exception of

Sir Humphrey Codd) who is so free from error that he will blame this youthful couple for that. Certainly it is not for an elderly judge, remembering that not far off two Courts of Appeal sit waiting to review his errors of judgment, to condemn unmercifully the errors of the young. It may be that in both these two young minds the shadow of war, the near possibility of death, the certainty of an immediate separation, were present and powerful, persuading them to take a long and irrevocable step with less consideration than they would have used in time of peace. Again, it would be repugnant to blame them; for at that particular time the safety of the realm owed much to the impetuous decisions of the young, and His Majesty's armed forces could not have existed without them. Young Pale may have been wrong to marry in haste; some now think that he was wrong to join the Army in haste. It may or may be not so; the point is that, mistaken or not, he was not compelled by law to remain a soldier for ever. Not many months later Parliament gave him the suffrage—that is, he was pronounced a fit person to judge what party and what policy were best for England and the Empire. It is very probable that he gave his vote to those who said that the Kaiser should and would be hanged; if so, it is probable that he made a mistake: but, if so, he was not bound by that mistake for ever. At the next election he was free to confess his error and vote for those who said that the Kaiser ought *not* to be hanged. We are all liable to error at every turn of life; and it is the general and generous practice of the human race to recognize and to forgive that weakness; so that, as a rule, if a man be honest and ready to learn, the passage of time and the growth of wisdom can wipe out all the blunders of his past. Mr. Pale, in his thirty-seven years, may have made many important errors of judgment, in war and in peace, in battle and in business; he may have jeopardized the lives of soldiers by his orders, the safety of the State by his vote, the prosperity of employees by his arithmetic, his own welfare by his choice of a partner or a profession; but all such errors are forgotten, or can, at least, be corrected by a man of character. Only in the most difficult choice of all—the choice of a partner not for business but for life—is a man expected to be infallible, considered ungentlemanly if he confesses to error, and disgraceful if he attempts to correct it; though the mistake may have been made by a very young man in the circumstances I have described. It might be said that no man so young should be permitted to select a wife; but that cannot be said now that he is permitted to select a Government. The only thing that can be said is that he should in both cases be given reasonable freedom to revise his judgment and select again. Wake up, Sir Humphrey, I am coming back to the case.

Mr. and Mrs. Pale decided that they had been mistaken; not soon, not lightly, not without patient and genuine effort; not, in short, till seven years had passed. I regard the period as important, for much may happen in seven years, and if two people cannot learn to live together in harmony in seven years there is little purpose in prolonging the experiment (unless there are children of the marriage, which was not the case here). The two were not 'well matched'. They were very badly matched; and that was the end of it. Extreme persons of two kinds have brought into disrepute the expression 'incompatibility of temperament'; but what is employed as an excuse by one man may well be the genuine affliction of a hundred of his neighbours. Because some worn-out soldiers simulated 'shell-shock' in order to escape from battle, authentic 'shell-shock' did not cease to exist; and the authorities, being sensible men, did not ordain that all those who had 'shell-shock' should remain in the trenches. That indefatigable reformer, Mr. E. S. P. Haynes, has remarked in one of his many fine books: 'The existence of such incompatibility in a purely physical sense is as well known among human beings as it is among animals. There seems, therefore, an obvious presumption that it can be psychical as well as physical. . . . Milton vividly described such incompatibility.' Indeed, it is too much to expect of Providence that the square peg and the round hole will never be brought together; and unless we are to use the language of the romantic verse-writers and suppose that some benignant cherub flits about the world selecting for matrimony only such couples as are mental and spiritual fits we must recognize the possibility of an occasional case of faulty assortment.

But, short of such genuine and irremovable 'incompatibility', there are all kinds of hidden elements and developments which the most prudent and prolonged deliberation will not reveal to two young people who are proposing marriage. Young Mr. Pale, transferred abruptly from the school-room to the battle-field, was still unripe in character and mind, without fixed ambitions or philosophy of life. He was a healthy young animal, pleasure-loving and gay. While convalescing he accompanied Miss Ray to plays and musical comedies; they found that they had a common admiration for Mr. George Robey, though both were out of sympathy with the Scandinavian drama; they liked the same restaurants, danced well together, and had a common friend in His Majesty's Navy. The identity of tastes and interests seemed to the young lovers complete and magical.

They were married; and after three days the young man returned to the battle-field. They were not to know that at the end of the war he would be a very different young man—shaken, sobered, inspired with purpose and the ideal of service, fond of dancing and merry crowds no longer but seeking quiet always and given to brooding. He worked long and late in a publisher's office and gave many of his evenings to social service at a University Settlement in the East End of London.

Nor were they to know what manner of life was awaiting his wife. A healthy and cheerful person like her spouse, she had, nevertheless, in the execution of her hospital work shown a pleasing earnestness and attention to duty. One of the young man's earliest letters describes how soothing he found it, lying on his painful bed, to watch the small, grave face of the young assistant as she dusted the cupboards or arranged the flowers. He was not to know that all that time she was imagining herself a film and stage star. Towards the end of the war the young woman obtained employment at one of the numerous places of entertainment in the metropolis, where we are told that she danced attractively and sang a song called 'You are the One'. It soon appeared that she had a vocation for the craft of entertainment; she became, and is still, a successful and highly paid performer on the musical stage.

Now, the profession of acting is as creditable as any other, and indeed is superior to many in a moral sense, since its function is to give pleasure and even instruction to the people. But its hours of employment, of eating,

sleeping, and recreation are different from those of the
majority; and some of its customs, though innocent
enough, are calculated to startle and alarm all those
who would describe their own way of life as 'normal'.
At that same hour which saw the return of the husband
from his day's work the wife was leaving home for the
labours of the evening. Like the majority of her profession (and indeed all other professions), she found it
better, for efficiency, to take the evening meal after her
labours and not before; and so, at about midnight, when
the weary husband was ready for sleep, the wife would
be ready for a hearty repast at a restaurant. Having
retired to bed late, she slept late, very sensibly, in the
morning; and did not wake, as a rule, till long after
her husband departed for his office. On weekdays, it
seems true to say, they rarely met. It was open to the
husband, at a sacrifice of sleep, to attend his wife to
the midnight supper; or he might sit in her dressing-
room and enjoy brief glimpses of her while she changed
her costume, blacked her eyelashes, or painted her
eyes bright blue. But in both cases he felt himself
awkward and in the way, caught in an atmosphere to
which he was alien. The wife, popular and affectionate, and a public figure, had many friends, numerous
admirers. A gentleman was never lacking to escort
her to supper, and to pay for it; and it was rarely
that she supped at home. On Sundays only could the
husband hope for continuous periods of his wife's
society; and even that day, for her hard-working and
gregarious profession, is often a day of rehearsals and
friendly gatherings of actors. The habit of crowds is
one that grows on the mind; Mrs. Pale soon became
restless when alone with her husband, and visitors and
cocktail-parties disturbed the quiet of the week-ends.

Mr. Pale implored her to give up the profession which was keeping them apart; but she loved her art, enjoyed the possession of money, had no children, and kept the home capably, and she said with some reason that she might as well request Mr. Pale to abandon his own work, which was of no greater public importance and brought less money into the home.

Irritability, quarrels, jealousies, nerve-strain, damage to sleep, to health and efficiency followed. There was, it must be noted, no suggestion of infidelity at this time; the distracted husband conceived himself from time to time to be jealous of this man or that, but his real and reasonable jealousy was against his wife's profession and way of life. After seven years they agreed, informally, to separate—that is, to live apart. It is clear that a real affection still subsisted on both sides, but it is still more clear that a joint life was impossible for them.

Now, at this stage, if the wise principles of the law of partnership were applicable to marriage, a simple, civilized, and sure procedure would have been open to this not wholly undeserving couple. One, or both, might have come to the Court and said, 'We are guilty of no crime, of no dishonourable conduct; we made a mistake, we have honestly tried to make the best of it, and failed. In our considered judgment it is impossible for this partnership of marriage to succeed; moreover, the failure of the marriage relationship is adversely affecting our usefulness to the State in our respective callings; we therefore ask the Court to release us from our obligations under the contract.' The Court would have then considered the story, as I have told it, and decided that, in all the circumstances, and subject to the delay-conditions already mentioned, this was a case where a dissolution might equitably and justly be granted, without the creation of any hardship to individuals or danger to the State.

But if, at that stage, the parties had come to the Divorce Court and told their story the judge would have been compelled to answer, 'Highly interesting, I am sure. But neither of you has committed misconduct. Go away and commit misconduct, one of you, and then come back and tell us all about it.'

And if they had answered innocently, 'Very well, my Lord, we will both commit misconduct, and so make doubly sure,' the judge would have had to answer, 'Not a bit of it. If both commit misconduct the marriage will stand. Only one of you must do this thing, and you must not consult together which one of you it is to be; for that will be collusion, connivance, or conduct conducing, and hateful to the law. Good morning.'

Such is the barbarous condition of the law: and so, no doubt, the couple were instructed by their legal advisers. Neither party had any immediate desire to commit misconduct, whether for their own benefit or the satisfaction of the law, nor, if they did, to have the story published in the newspapers. If the wife had become a raving lunatic or 'taken to drink'; or if the husband had cruelly and consistently beaten her; or if either of them had been sent to prison for life, the position would have been the same. Misconduct or nothing. 'The law,' the Court would have said, 'is not concerned to make you happy, but to preserve the purity of married life. And therefore one of you must behave impurely. If not, the law will bind you till you die to a lunatic, a drunkard, a wife-beater, or a convicted felon.'

In the year 1924 the couple went into separate residences, rapidly improved in health, and resigned themselves to their odd situation.

During the two years which followed both parties formed other and happier attachments. Mrs. Pale fell in love with a Mr. Cole, who writes, or wrote then, the more serious leading articles in the —— newspaper. Mr. Cole, like Mrs. Pale, was, as a rule, a night-worker; during the daylight hours he was often at leisure to enjoy her company, and the composition and correction of his leading articles was nearly always con-cluded at an hour which made it convenient for him to call at the theatre and take Mrs. Pale out to supper. In short, the routine of their working lives was a good fit, the one to the other; and, however improbable it may appear, there was a good psychological fit as well. I may add, by the way, that the fact that two men so serious in disposition as Mr. Pale and Mr. Cole have loved the petitioner has inclined me to the opinion that, although an actress, she cannot be a worthless woman.

But respectability has its drawbacks. Mr. Cole and Mrs. Pale were anxious to be permanently united; but such is the respectability of the —— newspaper that Mr. Cole, for fear of losing his employment, was reluctant to appear publicly in the always embarrassing and sometimes fatal capacity of an official 'co-respon-dent'. And who can blame him? Gosh! what a word! In the good old days we called a lover a lover; or if we disliked him we called him a ——, or a ——, or even a ——. But now we call him a 'co-respondent'—and wonder that the Divorce Court has a squalid reputation. Lancelot was a 'co-respondent'; and Paris was a 'co-respondent'; Menelaus was a 'petitioner' and Helen of

Troy a 'respondent'. But if they had been described by those titles I do not think the world would understand their stories as well as they do. Gosh! it is like calling cricket a 'ball-game' and thinking that that is all there is to be said about it. Gosh again!

But I digress. In May, 1926, Mrs. Pale, with all due precaution, that is to say, with furtive conversations in low-class eating-houses and a generous use of the phrase 'without prejudice', intimated to Mr. Pale that she wished to be free of him, in order to marry again, and that she expected or hoped that he would behave like a gentleman—meaning by this that she wished him to commit misconduct in so ostentatious a manner that even the Divorce Court would consent to take notice of it.

Now, meanwhile, Mr. Pale had formed a strong affection for a Miss Aurelia Latimer, a social worker in high standing at the St. Hilda's Mission in Bethnal Green, E. These two also desired to marry; but Miss Latimer's position as a guide, philosopher, and friend to the poor made it quite impossible for her to confess in public to misconduct. In any case it was not in her character to commit misconduct, even in confidence, and she permitted to Mr. Pale only the most formal embraces.

Three courses, then, were open to Mr. Pale, all repugnant to a man of sensibility and scruple: he could ignore the request of his wife and condemn them both for ever to a barren or immoral existence; he could seduce the modest Aurelia and publish her shame to the world; or he could commit formal misconduct with a stranger for whom he felt no real affection.

Those who have followed this recital so far (in which category I am unable to include Sir Humphrey Codd,

K.C.) will now understand why I said that it is desirable for such cases as this to be reported in the fullest detail, to the discredit not of the parties but of the law. For this is not a fantastic nor exceptional tale; it could be often told, but it is not. And it is impossible for the majority, who are happily or, at least, contentedly, married, to imagine it.

Mr. Pale at length, and with much distaste, selected the third of the three alternatives I have named; and the unfortunate case of *Pale, M. R.*, v. *Pale, H. J., and Laurel* was the result. Miss Laurel, a lady of uncertain age and no pronounced personality, agreed, for a money consideration, to accompany Mr. Pale to a south-coast pleasure-resort and there spend a night in such circumstances as would convince the Court that the two had committed misconduct. Mr. Pale, unaccustomed to this kind of life, was perhaps a clumsy practitioner in the arts of deceit; but in this of all Courts I hope that we are not to think harshly of a man because he is innocent. After a few games of backgammon (and one of bezique) with Miss Laurel Mr. Pale passed an uncomfortable night upon a couch. In the morning he transferred himself to Miss Laurel's side, rang the bell, and assumed, so far as he could judge, the expression and posture of one who has just passed a night of carnal and illicit indulgence. A maid called Parkins entered the room and beheld the couple without apparent surprise or shock. Mr. Pale, remembering the reputation of the hotel (which is known in certain circles as the Junior Divorce Court), reflected that the situation might not be so unusual to the maid as it was to him. Thinking to impress himself upon her memory he gave her a one pound note, and said meaningly, 'You will remember me, will you not?'

The maid liked his honest face (and his donation) and said warmly, 'That I will, sir!' Mr. Pale, having paid his hotel bill, despatched it to his wife; and, after some months, her petition for divorce was heard. The suit was undefended; the hotel bill was produced, and the maid Parkins was called to tell her tale.

Now, it so happened that a few days earlier the learned President of this Division had formed the opinion that the practice of divorce was becoming too simple, frequent, and popular. In particular he determined to discourage what he called the hotel-bill class of action. It is more than an idle saying that some people 'never have the luck'; and it was entirely congruous with the rest of Mr. Pale's matrimonial career that his case should happen to come up for decision at this particular time. The learned President, to the surprise and alarm of all those in Court, laid down at an early stage of the hearing three propositions:

(1) That the fact of two people taking food and even wine together was not conclusive evidence that misconduct had been committed.

(2) That the Court would not necessarily regard a flying visit to the south coast as fatal to the marriage bond.

(3) That in future the Court would permit no man to be divorced upon the vague ground that he had passed a night beside the English Channel in the company of A Woman. The woman must be named, identified, and served with the petition.

Such, I believe, is the present practice of the Court. It is often said to be a presumption of the English Courts that a man is innocent till the contrary is shown;

30

but in the Divorce Court the presumption is that every Englishman is lying. If he swears that he never exchanged more than a handshake and a kind word with a given lady the Court will suspect the worst; and very little direct evidence may be sufficient to prove him guilty of it. But if he confesses to misconduct, the Court, as if affronted by the suggestion that an Englishman could be capable of such a thing, will insist upon an elaborate chain of unimpeachable proof. In the former case five minutes may be sufficient, in the latter a day and a night may not. Indeed, I am told that the best solicitors now advise their clients to make it a week, so strong is the confidence of the Bench in the chastity of (undefended) Englishmen.

Mrs. Pale's petition appeared to the President to be tinged with unreality. The evidence of the maid Parkins was taken: but Parkins seems to have made a faulty appreciation of the situation. She had heard with alarm, but without understanding, the stern words of the judge; she gathered that Mr. Pale, who had been kind to her, was accused of some wrongful act, and innocently supposed that that act must be misconduct. Therefore, when she was asked to say whether she recognized Mr. Pale as the gentleman who had occupied Room 41 she looked at him earnestly and said, 'No, sir, nothing like him,' fondly believing that in this way she was doing her benefactor a service. The signed proof of her evidence was put to her; but she was not to be shifted. After this the case fell to the ground; the petition was dismissed, with stern warnings to all concerned in it, and Mr. and Mrs. Pale left the Court as firmly married as before.

Let it be noted that, up to this point, so far as is known, nobody had committed misconduct or

descended to 'intimacy', to use the other strange euphe-
mism; and, if it was committed later, nothing but the
law can be held to blame. Let it be noted too that the
parties in this case are well-to-do; and if they are put
to such trouble to obtain their freedom what must
be the difficulties of poorer citizens who cannot afford
to hire the services of detectives and Laurels or to stay
at large hotels upon our southern shores?

After an interval of two years the unfortunate Mr.
Pale made another attempt to behave like a gentleman.
This time, wisely advised by his solicitors, he prepared
to make a stay of a week beside the sea (with a Miss
Millicent Hume); and, advised by his own experience,
to impress himself upon the domestic staff of the hotel
by a marked reluctance to distribute money. The
escapade, although prolonged to a fortnight, was lacking in romance, and unexpectedly expensive. For on
the first evening Miss Hume complained of a high
temperature and a rash, and went to bed with measles.
The unfortunate Mr. Pale, having brought a lady to
the hotel as his wife, could not with decency depart and
leave her on a bed of sickness. He was compelled to
send, and pay, for a doctor; and he spent most of the
fortnight filling hot-water bottles, purchasing grapes,
listening to the startling story of the fevered woman's
life, soothing the irritable humours of a convalescent,
and in general discharging the always difficult functions
of a husband in a sick-room.

Mr. Pale's discomfort was not diminished by the
letters of Miss Aurelia Latimer, which, during the
second week, became increasingly inquisitive and sad.
But he may have been consoled by the thought that no
Court could complain on this occasion that his association with the Woman Named had not been of a

genuinely intimate character. The evidence was made available to Mrs. Pale and a second petition was filed.

The usual repellent preliminaries were carried out, but, because of the previous fiasco, with more than usual thoroughness. Private detectives were employed to watch Mr. Pale; and, in order to show that the attachment was continuing, he appeared with Miss Hume at restaurants and theatres, and once invited her to spend a night at his rooms. A detective, by appointment, was at hand when she entered the building, and called at an early hour the following morning; was introduced to Miss Hume in her dressing-gown, satisfied himself that there was a bed in the room, made notes, and withdrew. Not less embarrassing, perhaps, to the sensitive Mr. Pale was what I may call the Identification Parade at the solicitor's office. I asked him particularly about that myself, having a perhaps morbid interest in the sufferings of my fellow-men. Mr. Pale and Miss Hume, it appears, were requested to sit in a special position in a special room, having their backs to a small glass peep-hole in one of the walls. Mrs. Pale (in the next room) was led to the same peep-hole in order that she might say, 'Yes, that is my husband. And is that the woman who has stolen him from me? Oh, dear!' With her was a Miss Bright, a hotel chambermaid, who had to say, 'Yes, that is the couple in Number Seventeen.' Meanwhile the other two had to carry on, as best they could, a conversation both intimate and natural, as if they did not know that they were being observed by the petitioner, and their friend Miss Bright. I call this barbarous: I call the whole thing barbarous and degrading. And all this uncivilized and filthy nonsense is forced upon our citizens by the champions of morality and purity. Oh, Gosh! Oh, Gosh!

After this expletive, a favourite with the judge, his Lordship paused a moment or two and then continued:

This episode gained in humanity what it lost in verisimilitude through the behaviour of Mrs. Pale's dog. This sagacious animal, ignoring peep-holes and the niceties of divorce procedure, guided only by affection and the sense of smell, rushed from the side of his mistress to the door of the room which contained his late master, and there barked so passionately that Mr. Pale had to admit him. Mrs. Pale anxiously pursued her hound and was confronted with her husband and the Woman Named—I beg her pardon, Miss Hume. The endearing antics of the dog (whose name, if I recollect aright, is Montagu Norman) made formal stiffness impossible; the four parties had a friendly chat and laughed heartily together over Miss Hume's measles and Mr. Pale's bedside manner.

But this was no more than a momentary gleam in the long, dark tunnel of Mr. Pale's matrimonial affairs. What with persuading Miss Latimer that there was nothing between him and Miss Hume, and persuading this Court that there was a great deal, the poor man was distracted. But at last the case came on, the Court was genial and a decree *nisi* was pronounced. Subject to the statutory six months' delay (which is not, by the way, considered necessary in Scotland), the way now seemed clear for Mrs. Pale and Mr. Cole, and Mr. Pale and Miss Latimer, respectively, to be united in law as well as in love. Miss Latimer, I imagine, apologized for her ungenerous suspicions, and Mr. Pale, maybe, looked almost happy.

But now a new character makes an entrance—the

King's Proctor. The King's Proctor is, I believe, an officer peculiar to the country of England. At any rate, he is not considered necessary in Scotland, a country which is not especially celebrated for laxity of morals. His main function in the region of divorce is to detect, report to the Court, and so discourage, collusion. In England, as I have said, the presumption is that all the parties to a divorce suit are lying; and therefore we employ a special spy to catch them out, dignify him with the name of His Majesty, and think that we are more moral than our neighbours. Ha!

But the King's Proctor is kept as short of funds by the Treasury as, in the account of ethics, he deserves: and he cannot afford to pursue every case which, if all were known, would merit his attentions. A petitioner who has passed through this Court without exciting its suspicions may think himself unlucky to find the King's Proctor after him: unlucky for this reason, that there are always many others who have done what he did but go free. This bad luck, I believe, is brought upon him, as a rule, by the malignity of another, and takes, most often, the meanest form of malignity—the anonymous letter. It is, I think, extraordinary that the anonymous letter, despised by every decent citizen, frequently the cause of a criminal charge, the supreme expression of cowardice and spleen, should be the principal agent that sets a department of State, an officer of Justice, in motion. But so it is: and so it was in this case. An anonymous letter was received, the work, it is supposed of a woman who had once admired, or loved, Mr. Cole. Those who rub righteous hands together when they read that the King's Proctor has caught out a deceitful husband or wife might feel less satisfied if they were to use their imaginations and ask themselves, first, what made these people lie? and, secondly, by what methods were they discovered? They are compelled to lie because the law is bad; and they are found out by methods which are worse. Anonymous letters, back-door espionage, the cross-examination of cooks, the bribery of maids and porters, the searching of hotel registers, the watching of windows, the tracking of taxi-cabs, the exploitation of malicious gossip and interested malignity—and all this done in the King's name to preserve the sanctity of the home. These are methods which serve well enough for the apprehension of the dangerous criminal or enemy of the State, the man who murders or sells his country, but not for the hounding down of two unfortunates in love who may have done no harm to any human being, who cannot help themselves—and get no help from the law. It is like spreading poisoned gas for the destruction of a butterfly the colour of which is considered unpleasing. More discredit is done to the State by the manner of detection than to the lovers by the thing detected; the remedy, in short, is worse than the disease. In happier times I should have said that these methods were un-English; but, alas! I cannot say that now. For this race, which once was proud of its openness and honest dealing, is lending itself increasingly to official trickery, spying, and deceit in matters affecting the personal lives of the people—to the disguised inspector, the hired informer, and the *agent provocateur*. 'Peeping Tom' may still receive the execration of the people, but he is now an honoured servant of the State; and the King's Proctor (poor man) is the king of Peeping Toms.

There might be something said for having an expensive officer attached to the Divorce Court whose

business it was to reconcile the parties and try to keep a
failing marriage genuinely in being.[1] The Canon Law
was at least consistent, for, while rejecting the possibility of divorce, it did all that it could to prevent a
separation. Our law too often promotes separation
while hindering divorce. The King's Proctor's office,
instead of being a kind of helpful Official Uncle, is
purely vindictive in relation to the parties and useless in
relation to the institution of marriage.

The King's Proctor's men, then, poked and rum-
maged about in Mrs. Pale's past, much as a preventive
officer will search for contraband in her portmanteau.
And they found something—something which she had
failed to declare. They found the very real and lasting
affection between Mrs. Pale and the faithful Mr. Cole.
At about the same time as Mr. Pale and Miss Hume
were suffering together, the patience and self-restraint
of the other couple, it appears, broke down. At all
events, the investigations showed that they spent a
night together in a small yacht, unaccompanied by any
mariner or chaperon, and another at a cottage near
Aylesbury, in circumstances which were clearly com-
patible with the commission of 'intimacy'. I have no
doubt myself that intimacy did take place; indeed,
by this time it would have been highly surprising and
unnatural if it had not.

The King's Proctor formed the same conclusion.
He intervened, by leave of the Court, to show cause why
the decree *nisi* obtained by Mrs. Pale should not be
made absolute; the cause being that Mrs. Pale had
herself been guilty of misconduct and had failed at
the trial to disclose this material fact to the Court.

[1] Mr. Claud Mullins, the magistrate, is now working on these lines.
EDITOR

The fact was material because of the extraordinary doctrine of 'Recrimination', which says that if a spouse petitions for a divorce on the ground of intimacy it is a sufficient answer to say that he or she has been guilty of intimacy too. Which, as I hinted before, is like saying that if both parties to the contract break the principal clause of it the contract is binding on both; but if only one breaks it, both may be released. If the pot successfully calls the kettle black both must remain dirty.

But this is the law, as the learned President, solemnly and even angrily, informed Mrs. Pale. In such a case it is open to the Court in its discretion to overlook the guilt of the petitioning spouse, and, if in all the circumstances it seems just and desirable, to grant a decree in spite of it. But the Court has to be very nicely treated before it will do that; the petitioner must grovel and freely confess all. There have been cases where the Court has refused to exercise its discretion because a guilty petitioner has confessed to two acts of misconduct and afterwards the King's Nose-poker has discovered that in fact there were four. Any deliberate concealment sets the Court on its dignity, and that is nearly always fatal; it is as if an alleged penitent had obtained absolution for his sins but omitted to mention a murder or two. Mrs. Pale was informed by the President that she had abused the process of the Court, and did not deserve the benevolent exercise of its discretion; that, both spouses having committed misconduct, the marriage ought to stand; that the case had been a particularly distasteful one, disclosing a class of persons entirely without principle, lacking in respect for the marriage bond, for general morals, and the machinery of justice; and he was tempted to say at once that the decree *nisi* must be rescinded; but that rather than make his decision in the state of mind which the petitioner's conduct had produced in him he would reserve judgment.

At this point the unfortunate Mr. Pale, judging that the cup of freedom was once more to be dashed from his lips, for the first time expressed himself in a forcible manner. Standing up in Court, to the astonishment of all present, he said (I have the transcript before me):

My Lord, perhaps I can help you. From all that dish-water you said just now I gather that because both of us have done the wrong thing the law refuses to do the right thing. You might as well say that if two dogs are always fighting they ought to be shut up in the same kennel. However, what I want to say is this. I never committed misconduct. I never had any intention to behave intimately. But I had to behave like a gentle-man——

The President: This Court, Mr. Pale, does not approve of gentlemen who behave like gentlemen.

The Respondent: That only shows what a bog of a Court this is! Anyhow, I didn't. You can ask the hotel people. I never met Miss Hume till the day we went there; and during the whole time we were there the poor woman had measles. I'm not, as you ought to be able to see, the intimate type; and if the Court thinks that a man like me is likely to commit intimacy with an unattractive stranger who has the measles, then the mind of the Court is more of a swamp than I thought it was. Anyhow, I didn't. And that makes the whole thing simple. My poor wife, it seems, has committed intimacy, so you can't divorce me. But I haven't, so you can divorce *her*. And that, my Lord, is what I suggest you should do. You're the President of this cesspool, and presumably you can do what you like. For my part, I do not mind telling you, I am blank well congested with the whole blank business.

(Respondent here resumed his seat.)

The President: This case, like a drifting corpse, slowly increases in gravity and horror. Mr. Pale, I shall overlook your impertinence, and even your ignorance of legal forms. But what you have just said amounts to this, that you have taken part in a criminal conspiracy to deceive the Court and pervert the process of justice. There is little more for me to do in this case; there may be much for the Public Prosecutor. The hearing will be adjourned till Wednesday of next week.

What my learned brother would have said on the following Wednesday we cannot tell, for on the Tuesday he died. He led a fine life, he leaves a great gap, and I for one feel more than common sympathy with one who had to spend so many sunny days, so many precious years, presiding over this Court. But Mr. and Mrs. Pale are still bound to each other by the legal tie of marriage, which means, in any human sense, nothing to either of them. And it falls to me, at long last, to consider what can be done for them.

I invited Mr. Pale to tell me the whole story, and he told it, as I have told it, though not, I think, in such distinguished terms. I like Mr. Pale; I am sorry for him, and for his wife. But, before the law, the situation is as the late President tersely described it. Either Mr. Pale has committed misconduct, in which case the couple cannot be divorced, or he has not committed misconduct, in which case he can be sent to prison for pretending that he has.

Let us assume, for a moment, that he has. And then let us digress for another moment or two, and consider what would happen in a like case if this couple had been married and were domiciled in the adjacent country of Scotland. Everything would be much simpler, and, in my judgment, sounder. First, and most important, in the enlightened country of Scotland the doctrine of Recrimination, as we know it, does not exist. The guilt of both spouses does not preclude a divorce, though the guilt of each may affect the monetary dispositions which accompany it. The spouse, that is to say, whose infidelity provoked the backsliding of the other, will suffer in costs, and, if I am rightly informed, in other ways. Both parties therefore can tell the whole truth without the fear that it will cost them their freedom, and one, at least, has a direct monetary incentive to tell the whole truth.

From this grand principle, that it pays to tell the truth, proceed two minor but substantial advantages. First, no King's Proctor; because, where there is no temptation to lie, no special officer is needed to detect the liar. The Court can be trusted to discover the dishonest in court, as it does in other matters; and collusion, by the way, is no more encouraged in Scotland than it is here. Second, no six months' suspense before a decree of divorce is made absolute. The decree, once made, is final. Why not? In every other class of litigation the Court makes up its mind, once and for always, and will not reconsider its decision, except by the order of a superior Court, upon appeal. It is the duty of every Court to make up its mind once and for always. To say to-day, 'Yes,' and to say to-morrow, 'Yah! I didn't mean it,' is the action of a crazy child; and when one considers how much that

'Yes' must mean to the lives and fortunes of the parties, it is seen to be worse than crazy. This, again, could only be possible in a system which penalizes truth and puts a premium on misconduct.

In this case, then, if I were a Scottish judge sitting in Edinburgh, and if I were persuaded that Mr. Pale, as well as Mrs. Pale, had committed misconduct, I should say without hesitation or difficulty that the marriage ought to be dissolved; for the roots of it are dead, and what remains is but decaying matter, checking the life of fresh young plants and a disgrace and even a danger to society. I should then have to consider whether the conduct of either party had been so culpable a contributor to the result that he or she might justly be made to suffer in a money sense. I might find, for example, that the wife had proved wantonly unfaithful within a year or two after the marriage and so provoked a desperate husband to seek consolation elsewhere; I might find, again, that the husband had by neglect or carelessness almost encouraged the wife to infidelity. In this case I find nothing of the sort. In the earlier stages of their unfortunate association I find that neither party did anything blameworthy, unless we are to blame them for a youthful error of judgment, in supposing that they were perfect partners for life. For the blameworthy proceedings of recent years the law is responsible and nothing else. It is said that they have abused the processes of the law; in my judgment the law has abused the processes of their private lives, the secrets of their hearts, the fundamentals of their human nature. There is an old and somewhat foolish saying that 'Hard cases make bad law,' and therefore the law must be left as it is. It would be equally true to say, 'Bad law makes hard cases,' and therefore the law must be amended. The real truth lies somewhere between. Mere freaks of fortune should not be made an excuse for weakening a law which is sound. But a law which is seen to multiply hard cases, not through any accident but by its necessary elements, is not worth preserving, for the law was made for man, not man for the law.

What, then, am I to do? I have no doubt. It would pain me deeply if I had to say that in Scotland the judges had so much more sense, or the people so much more virtue, that things could be done there which were impossible in England; and I refuse to say it. I propose to exercise my discretion in such a manner that all concerned in this case will be content; I propose to do justice and right; and I think that neither the community nor morality will suffer in consequence. This marriage must be dissolved upon the suit of both parties, and I decline to say that either of them is the 'guilty' party.

It may be that this is the last judgment I am to deliver in this world; but if it had been the only one I should think that I had done good service to my country; and if I thought that it would leave some enduring mark upon the laws I should die happy. I wish that I were rich enough to have it printed and distributed to every adult citizen; and I wish that I were a writer so popular that it would be studied by the millions. The mischief is that those who have the knowledge in such matters have not the ear of the people; and those who have the ear of the people are more concerned to entertain than to enlighten or arouse them. Those, as I have said, who are happily married themselves require no alteration of the law, are inclined to assume that the misfortunes of others must proceed from their faults, and fear that to relieve the unfortunate may somehow diminish the status of the virtuous. The general mass, if they consider the law at all, regard it as they regard some monster at the Zoo. It is odd, it is extraordinary; but there it is, they have known it all their lives, they suppose that there must be some good reason for it and accept it as inevitable and natural. This is no bad attitude of mind in which to contemplate the works of God, even when they take the shape of a hippopotamus or giraffe; for there is no way of altering the hippopotamus, if that should be desired. But the English law of divorce is the work of man, it is supported neither by divine sanction nor human reason, it is neither natural nor inevitable, and could very easily be altered. It is like one of those crazy pieces of architecture which here and there disfigure the countryside. They excite the derision of all who look at them with fresh eyes for the first time, yet they become by the passage of time such familiar features of the landscape that when it is proposed to pull them down there is a passionate outcry from the inhabitants who have grown up with them. It is the duty of those of us who can perceive with fresh eyes the monstrosities of the law to point at them continuously until they are pulled down. This law, as I have said, and shall say again, for it cannot be too often repeated, is defended as a shield of chastity; but in this case it has been the cause of unchaste conduct by five persons, if we include the Misses Laurel and Hume. It is supposed to uphold decency, but itself outrages every principle of decency. Those who defend it talk of sacraments; but those who have to enforce it are reminded of the sewer. It is intended, we are told, to preserve the distinction between the mating of animals and human love, which has a spiritual and intellectual splendour denied to the brute beasts; yet by insisting that the physical act of love is the one foundation of marriage it makes us one with the beasts. It is illogical. It is cruel. It is barbarous. It is disgusting. Judgment for Mr. and Mrs. Pale—with costs against the King's Proctor.

NOTE—And see *Holy Deadlock*, in which a similar case is described at greater length.

INDEX

ACTING PROFESSION:
    Devotion to toil, 118, 437
    Exhibitions of, why subject to Entertainments Duty? 251
    Irregular hours of, 437
    Membership of, not *prima facie* evidence of immorality, 118, 436
    Monastic character of, 119
    Tribute to, by Sir Nigel Playfair, 119; by Wool, J., 123, 436; by
        Lord Lavender, 117
ACT OF GOD:
    Definition, 316
ACTRESSES:
    Appearance of, inappropriate subject for reflection on the Sabbath,
      16
ADULTERATED FOOD:
    May be sold at the House of Commons, 421
AGATE, JAMES:
    Diminution of congregations by, 16
Agents Provocateurs:
    Boot, Constable, admitted prince of, 80
    Cases of, 80, 396
    Classical example of, 81 (*see* 'King's Proctor')
    Condemned, 81, 390-6
    Held—no longer un-English, 449
    Principles which ought to limit the use of, in England, explained, 393
    Suggested employment of, for prevention of murder, 80
    Trenchard, Lord, discourages employment of, 396
    Use of, increasing, 79, 394, 449
ALCOHOL:
    Comparative unimportance of, at public-houses, 31
    Encouragement of sales of, by Licensing Justices, 34
    Increase in consumption of, at 'The Red Cow', 34
ANCESTORS:
    Wisdom of our, 42, 73, 93
ANONYMOUS LETTERS:
    Strange employment of, by British Justice, 448
ARREST:
    Citizen's powers of, are not the same in felony and misdemeanour,
      387
ARSON:
    Is lawful, in the House of Commons, 419
ART:
    Plastic, queerly exempted from Entertainments Duty, 251
    Theatrical, feared extinction of, through Entertainments Duty, 248,
      252

31

MESOPOTAMIA:
    Godless discussion of, on the Sabbath, 16 (*see* 'Garvin')
MILDEW, LORD:
    Dictum on 'Act of God', 315, 316
    Dictum on 'Bees in bonnets', 112
    Dictum on 'Betting', 334
    Dictum on 'Boot', 122
    Dictum on 'Breakfast', 98
    Dictum on 'Clothes in relation to the gentleman', 22
    Dictum on 'Coroners', 261
    Dictum on 'Criticism', 226
    Dictum on 'Dead men', 59
    Dictum on 'Dirty dogs', 335
    Dictum on 'Englishman's home', 33
    Dictum on 'Government Departments', 200
    Dictum on 'Laughter', 242
    Dictum on 'Merriness', 148
    Dictum on 'Mud', 265
    Dictum on 'Murder', 128
    Dictum on 'Noise', 302
    Dictum on 'Parliament', 313
    Dictum on 'Precedents', 109
    Dictum on 'The dotting of i's', 72
    Dictum on 'The Ocean', 220
    Dictum on 'Whole and part', 57
MILK:
    Tuberculous, may be sold in the House of Commons, 421
MINISTERS, HIS MAJESTY'S:
    Break promises, 180, 247, 276
    Condone gaming and wagering, 333
    Encourage vice, 334–6
    Endanger Constitution, 282
    Hypocrisy of, 337
    Increase unemployment, 309
    Persecute genius, 235, 245, 248, 331
    Suppress knowledge, 246
    Surprising passion for plastic art, 251
MISCONDUCT:
    Week-end excursions to south coast not necessarily evidence of, 443
MONEYLENDERS:
    May operate at the House of Commons without a licence, 421
MOODY, ALDERMAN:
    Dyspepsia of, 190
    Hatred of verbiage, 190
    Imperfect acquaintance with dead languages, 192
    Unusual failure to appreciate importance of Attorney-General, 189
MORAL EXPERIMENTS:
    Do not justify uncivilized laws, 186 (*see* 'Eighteenth Amendment')
MORPHINE:
    May be manufactured and sold, without a licence, at the House of
        Commons, 421

PASSPORT SYSTEM—(*contd.*)
    Lack of enterprise in youth of race believed connected with, 115
    Nature of, examined, 114
    Pioneer spirit, diminished by, 115
    Reluctance to emigrate attributed to, 115
PEDESTRIANS:
    Comparison with sailing-ships, 130
    Haddock, chivalrous defence of, 339
    Rights of, 131, 132, 345
    And see 'Hen'
'PEEPING TOM':
    See 'King's Proctor'
PERJURY:
    Is a misdemeanour, 385 (*but see* 'Bigamy')
PERSONALITY:
    Shameful exploitation of, 78, 80 (*and see* 'Boot')
PETROLEUM:
    May be kept at the House of Commons, without a licence, 420
PHILANDERING:
    Provocation of, by Licensing Justices, 35
PIRATES:
    See 'Eighteenth Amendment'
PLAYFAIR, SIR NIGEL:
    Tribute of, to acting profession, 119
PLUSH, MR. JUSTICE:
    Rebukes caterers, 273
    Rebukes Crown, 336
    Rebukes Government, 337
    Rebukes Haddock, 271
    Rebukes Postmaster-General, 336
    Rebukes Sir Ethelred Rutt, K.C., 271
    Rebukes waiters, 273
POETRY:
    Held—a corporation is capable of, 328
POISONS:
    May be sold by unregistered persons, in the House of Commons, 420, 421
POLICE-UNIFORM:
    Held—should be the normal wear of a police-officer, 393
POLICEWOMAN:
    Duplicity of, 391
    Refining influence of, not noticeable, 391 (*see* '*Agents Provocateurs*')
POOR, THE:
    Corruption of, by Licensing Justices, 34, 35
POPULATION, REDUCTION OF:
    Difficulty found in defending selection of Naval Officers as first subjects of experiments tending towards policy of, 179
    Indecisive attitude of nation to question of, 179, 400, 432
    Meagre contribution of system of free education towards, 133

Jarrold & Sons, Limited, The Empire Press, Norwich